Mark Versus Mr. Hacker.doc

This book is Copyrighted © 2016 by Mark Manning. All rights are reserved.
ISBN number is 978-1-365-25166-5.

None of the names used within this document are meant to convey ownership of those names such as Microsoft's® Windows® or Apple's® Macintosh® systems. They simply are used as references to a given operating system's items.

Microsoft® is the registered name of Microsoft Corporation, Inc.
Windows® is the registered name of Microsoft's Operating System
Apple® is the registered name of Apple Computer, Inc.
Macintosh® is the registered name of a computer system from Apple Computer, Inc.
Windows XP® is the registered name of one version of the Windows Operating System from Microsoft Corporation, Inc.
Windows Vista® is the registered name of one version of the Windows Operating System from Microsoft Corporation, Inc.
Windows 7® is the registered name of one version of the Windows Operating System from Microsoft Corporation, Inc.
Windows 8® is the registered name of one version of the Windows Operating System from Microsoft Corporation, Inc.
Windows 8.1® is the registered name of one version of the Windows Operating System from Microsoft Corporation, Inc.
Windows 10® is the registered name of one version of the Windows Operating System from Microsoft Corporation, Inc.
IBM® is the registered name of International Business Machines, Incorporated.

Table of Contents

Table of Contents 3
MARK VERSUS MR. HACKER 4
   HOW THE BOOK IS ORGANIZED 4
   FINDING OUT ABOUT MR. HACKER 4
   HALF STEP #1: HOW TO TELL YOU HAVE A HACKER 7
   HALF STEP #2 : SETTING UP THE EVENT VIEWER 13
   HALF STEP #3 : THE TASK MANAGER 14
   HALF STEP #4 : TCPVIEW 18
   HALF STEP #5 : FOLDER OPTIONS YOU SHOULD USE 22
   HALF STEP #6 : SYSTEM RESTORE 26
   HALF STEP #7 : STOP AUTOMATIC REPAIR 27
   STEP #1 : FILE AND PRINTER SHARING 30
   STEP #2 : THE GROUP POLICY PLUG-IN 39
   STEP #3: INSTALLING THE GROUP POLICY PLUG-IN 46
   STEP #4 : USING THE GROUP POLICY PLUG-IN 50
      Security Options 61
      Audit Policy 62
      Account Policies 62
   STEP #5 : THE EVENT VIEWER LOGS 63
   STEP #6 : REMOTE DESKTOP 65
   STEP #7 : LOG IN REMOTELY TO YOUR SYSTEM 70
   STEP #8 : TEAMVIEWER 77
Windows Vista Figures 81
Windows 7 Figures 128
Windows 8/8.1 Figures 183
Windows 10 Figures 244

MARK VERSUS MR. HACKER

This write-up is for anyone who buys a new Windows Operating System computer. It makes no difference which version of Microsoft's operating system. Ever since XP these problems have been around and no one has written up anything to help people out in the manner in which I am writing.

Some time ago a hacker got on to my Windows XP system. We also have Windows Vista, Windows 7 and Windows 8.1 at our house. This hacker got on to my Windows XP system and used it as a launching pad to try to take over the rest of our systems. This is how I figured out they were doing that as well as what I found out about the Windows Operating System. So without wasting any more of your time – here is my story:

HOW THE BOOK IS ORGANIZED

Originally, I wrote this book for Windows XP because that is the operating system I use. But I realized that **everyone** needed to know all of this for every one of the current operating systems Microsoft has produced. So I revamped how I am presenting this information. How I am setting up the book is all of the information is at the front using Windows XP and then the screen captures from the other various operating systems come later. So go back to the Table Of Contents, find your operating system's screen shots, and put some kind of a bookmark there. Then as you read you just flip back to the screen captures to see what I am talking about. I realize this is a clunky way to do this but it is a whole lot better than making you buy six different books or repeating my self over and over again. If you find this a bit frustrating – I apologize in advance. This was the most compact way I could figure out to present all of this to you. Please bear with me.

The truth is though, after a while you will find yourself not even looking back there because these screens are so similar. They are either just put in a slightly different location or their layouts have changed somewhat. So once you have down pat how to find them – you won't even need to go back to your operating system's screen shots to see what they look like. But if you do – they will still be there when you need them.

FINDING OUT ABOUT MR. HACKER

I was working away on my computer (I happen to like Windows XP) when I began noticing, over a period of weeks, that my system was running slower and slower. I tried the normal things. I ran my antivirus software, then the spyware/malware program, then I defragmented the hard drive, and finally I cleaned the registry. And…..nothing. It still ran slow and I was getting a bit frustrated to say the least.

But being a computer geek (or nerd) since 1972 – I wasn't about to let this problem go so I began doing research. Then an idea occurred to me by accident. You see, I set my Power Options so that the monitor will not turn off at all. I realized that if this was some kind of a hacker attack that the hacker would get on to my system and make use of it. So if I changed my Power Options to turn off the monitor after an hour and no one was getting on to my system then the monitor would be turned off when I woke up. Now, this may not always be true but I figured –why not give it a chance and see what happens. So I set my screen saver to come on after 15 minutes and I also set my Power Options to turn off the monitor after an hour. Now – why an hour? Because it is usually less than an hour before a hacker will try to get on your system. So let's say I go to bed at midnight and I leave my system up and running. Within an hour's time a hacker will try to get on to my system. How do I know this? Well, it was just a guess. But that is what I did. I left my system up and running over night.

I just realized – I need to tell you **WHY** I did the above. Think about it. If you are using your system – the screen saver (and most importantly – the power off option for the monitor) is never invoked. So IF a hacker IS getting onto my system THEN the screen saver or power off option will not happen. The hacker doesn't know this. They only know that they can see the screen on their computer system. What they also don't know is – that by getting onto my system – MY system turns the monitor back on. It can't be helped. It just happens. And if they change the setting – that is noted in the system logs. (More about that later.) The truth is – most hackers don't even give a second's thought about the power settings on your system. After all – why? It doesn't affect them – except in this manner. ☺ Also note that IF your computer is in the same room you sleep in. then WHEN the hacker gets onto your system and the monitor turns on – it might also wake you up and then you can sit there and watch the hacker take over your system – or- the smart thing to do is to them immediately shut your system down. Now back to my story.

The next day – the monitor was still turned on. Ok. So I knew someone was getting on to my system – right? No. It was still just a maybe. One of the reasons I **always** buy the Professional version of Windows is because it comes with all of the software pre-installed. What do I mean by "ALL"? I mean that if you have the HOME version of Windows (any version) and you go to Start->Control Panel->Administrative Tools – you will only see **some** of the software that comes with the professional version. The important component you are missing is the Local Security Policy plug-in. This is one of the most important programs any Windows OS has yet Microsoft left it out of the HOME version on purpose. Thus making it impossible for you to prevent hackers from coming in to your system through back doors that are left wide open.

I went into the Local Security Policy component in the Control Panel->Administrator Tools and in that component I set things up so I could see what was going on in my system. I then left my system up a second night. The next day I checked the Event Log and found out that I had logged in to my own system twenty or so times. Only – I was sound asleep. So **NOW** I knew I had a hacker who was logging in to my system and I had to do something about it – fast.

So back to researching on the internet. I visited several really nice sites that told you just about nothing of value. It really is so weird to go to some website where you think they are going to tell you how to stop hackers and all they really want to do is to sell you some gimmick that doesn't work (I know – I've tried a lot of them). But still I persisted in going to websites and reading up on what I could do. Even the Microsoft website doesn't have anything of real value most of the time. This is because the actual information you need is obliterated by the mounds of useless information. If any company should win an award for creating thousands of web pages that say absolutely nothing except "Go look at **this** web page" which just has more useless information on it – it should be Microsoft. I thought that the old IBM manuals were bad back in the 1970s when I tried to read them. Heck – IBM could take some pointers from Microsoft on not telling anyone anything useful. This isn't to say that **all** of the web pages Microsoft has are not worth looking at. Far from it. Every now and then you do come across some web page that actually tells you something. But for the most part – Microsoft's website is not worth looking at. Still, slowly but surely I was making headway.

Without going into lots of detail – suffice it to say it took me several weeks to figure everything out. Which was - there were some gaping holes in the Windows Operating System that were put there by Microsoft and these holes can and do give hackers an easy way to get in to your system.

So now, in the next chapter, I start telling you how to close up all of these holes. I hope you are ready because this is going to be one fast paced book on how to fix your system so hackers can not get in to it. I will try to explain what I am showing you but you will also have to use your common sense, some imagination, and finding, reading, and downloading information and files on the internet to get through this book. That's because I am presenting the Windows XP version as well as the Vista, Windows 7, Windows 8, Windows 8.1, and now Windows 10 and Microsoft intentionally changed how things are accessed on each version so I now have screen captures for each of the operating systems. In fact, if Windows XP isn't your operating system – stop here and go find where your operating system is in the book. Then come back and continue on.

Before we begin let me tell you the most important thing that you can do – you can write to Microsoft and insist that they put the Local Security Policy widget back in to the HOME version. It really is the most important tool that they left out and only if everyone writes to Microsoft and complains about it will they even consider putting it back in again. Ok. Enough of that – on with the book.

HALF STEP #1: HOW TO TELL YOU HAVE A HACKER

I left this out when I first wrote this book. Now I am putting it in. So I'm naming this set of instructions as "Half Steps" because it doesn't do anything other than tell you that you might have a hacker, it gives you different ways to find out what the hacker is doing, and it tells you a few things you really ought to know about but Microsoft doesn't tell you.

What we are going to do first is to show you the steps to set up your Power Options so you can see if you have a hacker on your computer. We have to bring up the Control Panel first. We do this by selecting Start->Control Panel.

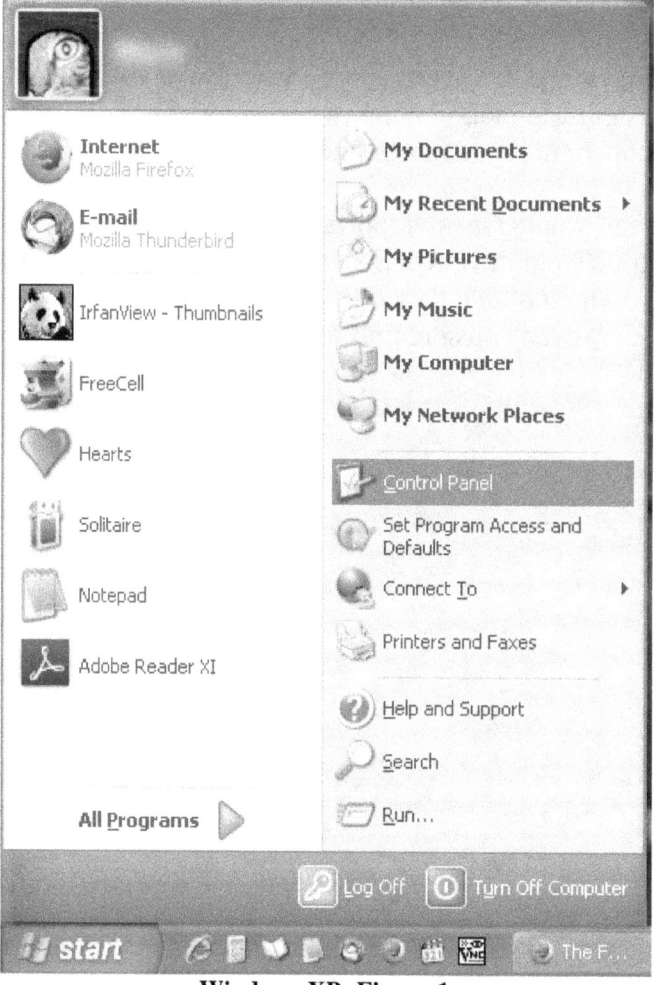

Windows XP -Figure 1

Note that although your screen might look different – it should still show the "Control Panel" on it somewhere. Also, starting with Windows 8, Microsoft made it so you have to right-single-click in order to get to the screen that lets you select the Control Panel.

So on the previous image you see I have selected the Control Panel and when it comes up it looks like this on my system:

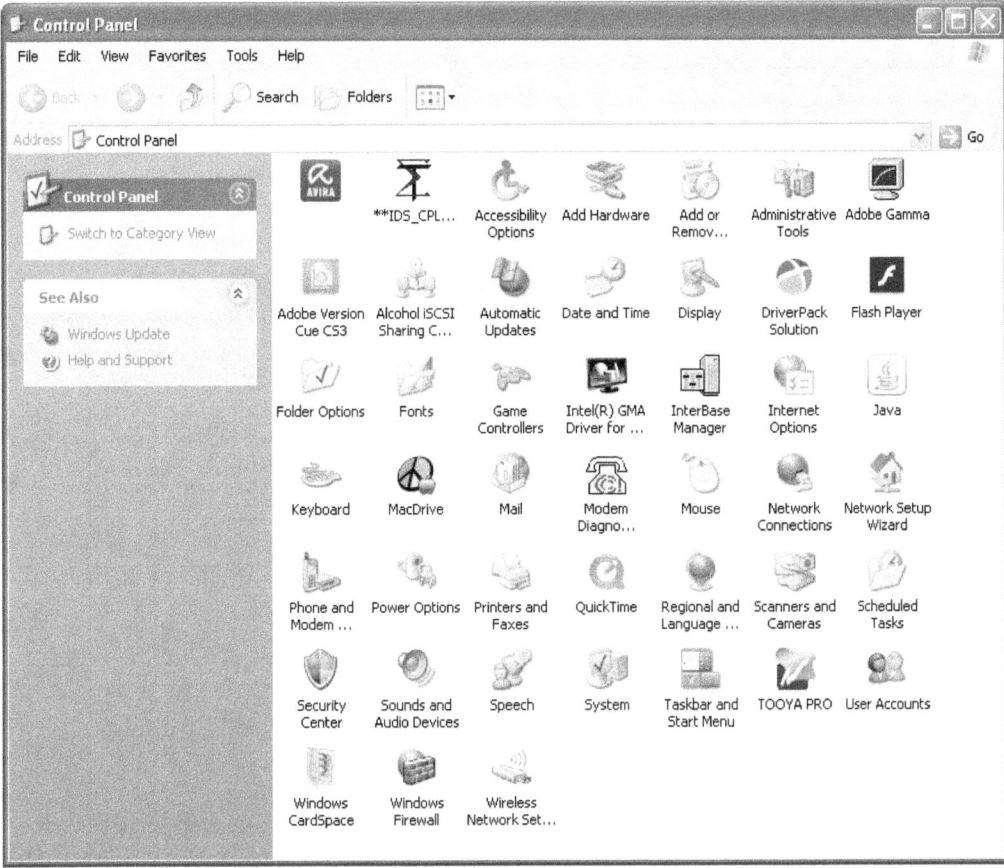

Windows XP - Figure 2

You are going to be using this a lot so you should get comfortable seeing it or looking at it. Now, I have quite a lot of things in my Control Panel including Avira (anti-virus program and first icon), "Driver Pack Solution" which keeps my drivers up to date, and several other things which you will not have. But then, I did say I was a computer geek and a computer programmer.

The first thing we want to do is to modify the Screen Saver program so it only goes in to the Screen Saver after fifteen minutes. On my Windows XP Control Panel you do this by just selecting "Display". Do you see it? It is on the second row down and the fifth icon going from left to right.

Here, I'll mark it for you.

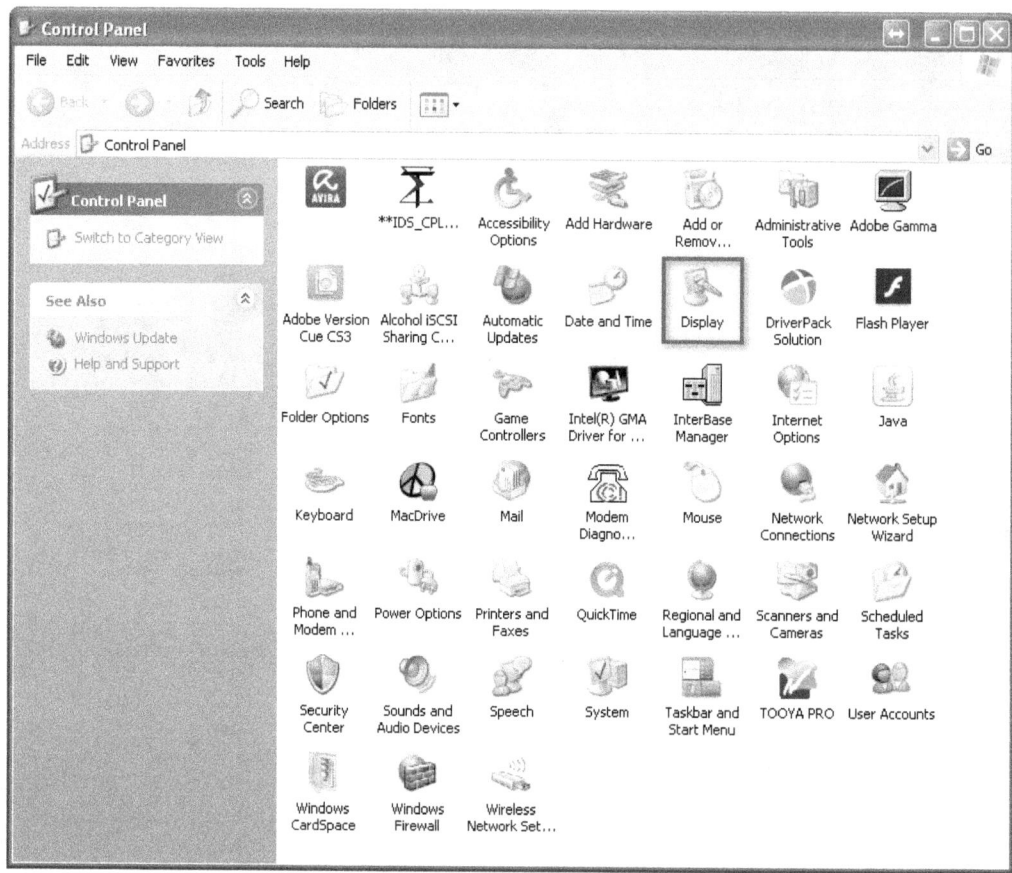

Windows XP - Figure 3

Ok. So now we have the Control Panel up and running and now we need to look at the Display dialog.

Left double-click on the Display icon and that will bring up the Display dialog.

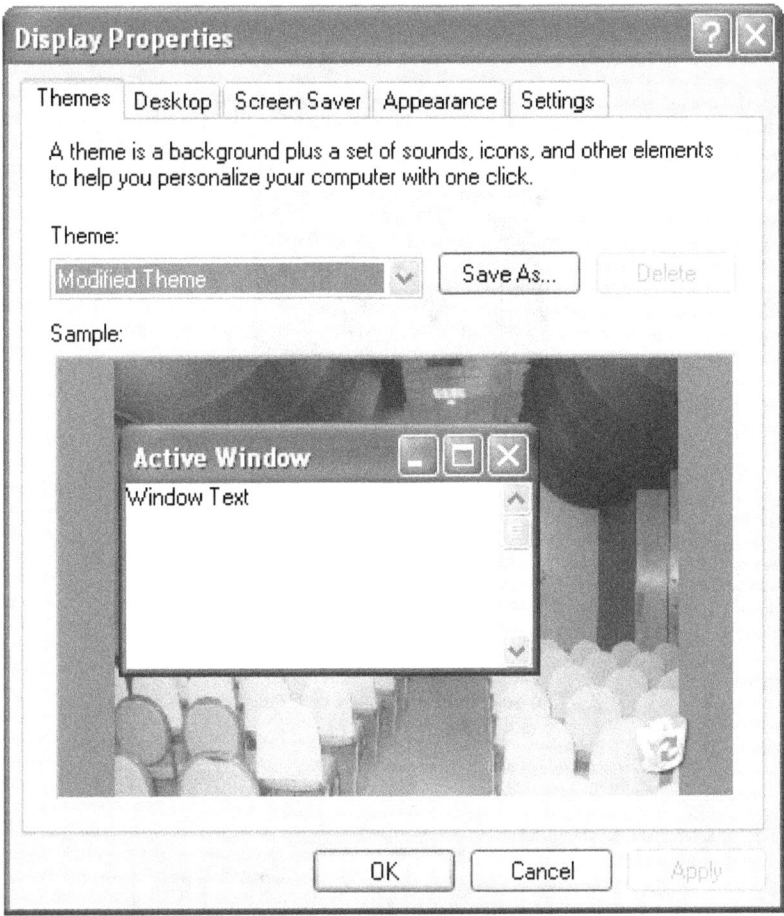

Windows XP - Figure 4

So this is what mine looks like when you first bring it up. If you look across the top of the inner area of the dialog you will see some tabs sticking up. Left single click on the "Screen Saver" tab.

The Screen Saver tab should look like this:

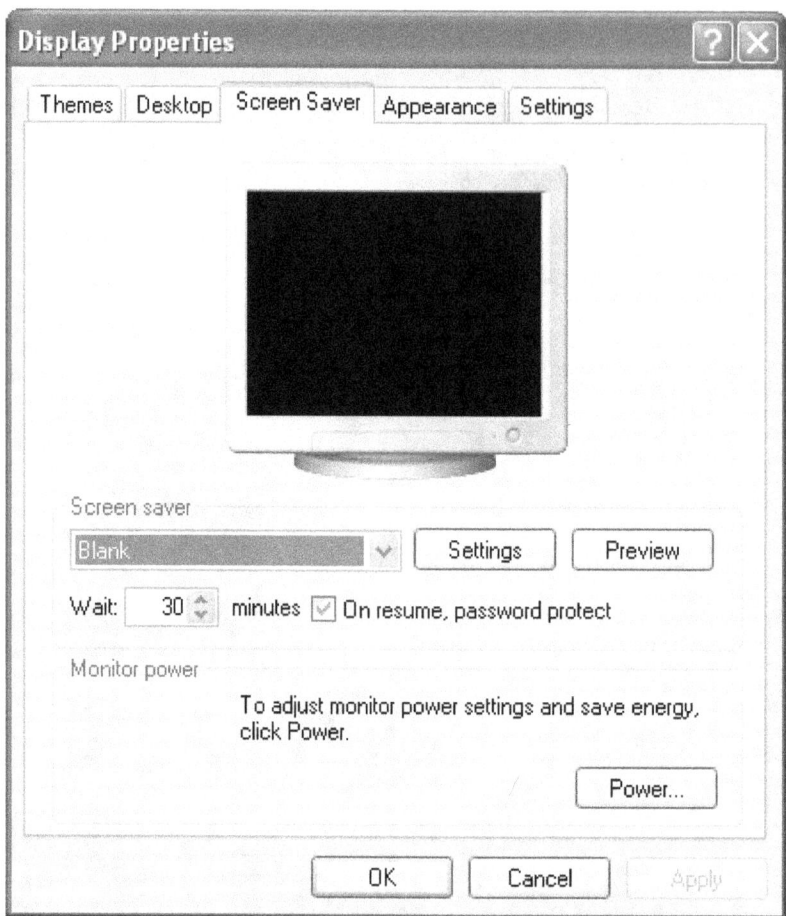

Windows XP - Figure 5

Now here you see that I have set the "Wait" period to be 30 minutes but for this experiment you should set it to be 15 minutes. If you do not have a screen saver set then you should set it to something OTHER THAN the Blank screen. This is because we don't want you to think everything is ok when it is not. So select a screen saver that will have some color to it and maybe has something that moves around. Once you have done that left single click on the "OK" button to close the Screen Saver dialog.

Now we want to bring up the Power Options dialog. This is five rows down and one icon over from the left on my Control Panel dialog.

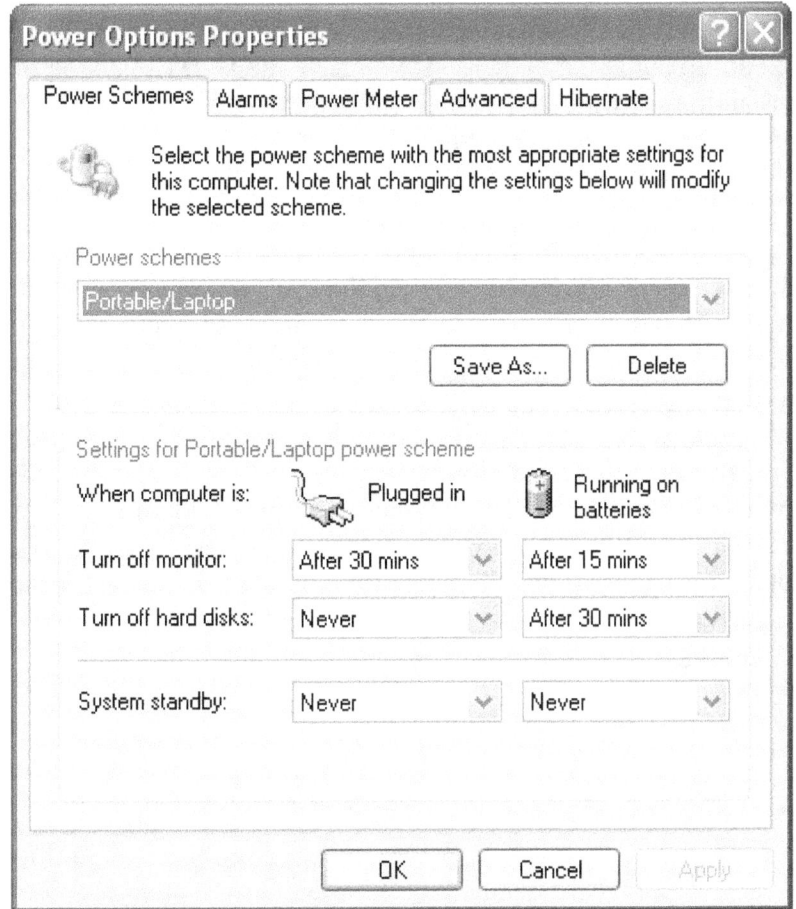

Windows XP - Figure 6

Now, I know for a fact that Windows 7's Power Options dialog looks nothing like what I'm showing here. Just use your common sense (or go look at the screen shots for Windows Vista, 7, 8/8.1, and 10) and find the Power Options where it lets you set when to turn off the monitor, hard drives, and so forth. As you can see above, I never turn my hard drives off when I am plugged in and I never let the system go in to standby mode. What we really are after here though is to only turn off your monitor after a specific period of time. Right now I have this set to 30 minutes. But we are trying to see if a hacker is getting onto our system. So set this to be 60 minutes. So an HOUR after you go to bed – your monitor should turn itself off. The thing about hackers is – if you leave your system up and running after you go to bed – they will usually be on it before an hour is up. So set this to be for 60 minutes and then click the "OK" button.

Then go enjoy the rest of your day. When you are going to go to bed, leave your computer up and running and play a game like Solitaire and then go to bed. When you wake up in the morning if the monitor is still up and running – there is a good chance that you have a hacker who is using your system while you sleep. Or, as I have said, if you monitor comes on during the night – it is most probably because a hacker just got on to your system.

HALF STEP #2 : SETTING UP THE EVENT VIEWER

Surprise! ☺ There is nothing here! What happened? Well, this is covered later on in this book already so I decided not to put anything here. If you have the HOME version of Windows you will first have to install the software I tell you about in here so you can't set it up yet anyway. Just keep going through the book and you will find how to set things up later so you can see if someone actually is logging in to your system.

Let me give you one of the secrets I found out about hackers: If they can figure out what your account name is (like "Owner", or your name) then they will log in to your computer as YOU. This makes it really hard to tell if or when someone is logged in to your computer. Because all you see is YOU on the computer when really there is someone else on your computer at the same time. At that point all you can do is to go by your gut feelings. Is your system running really slow? Does it seem to run slowly at some times but ok at other times? You probably have a hacker (or you do programming like me). In my case, the hacker was getting on to my system using the SYSTEM account and then changing over to running under my account. So even if I brought up the Task Manager all I ever saw was me, the SYSTEM account, NETWORK SERVICES, and other normal programs that were running. Ah! I know. I forgot to tell you how to start the Task Manager. Let's go!

HALF STEP #3 : THE TASK MANAGER

The task manager is very easy to bring up. Just right single click on the blue bar at the bottom of your computer screen.

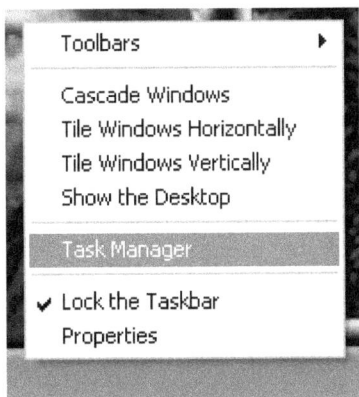

Windows XP - Figure 7

Although you can't see it clearly, the blue bar at the bottom is the one that goes completely across the computer's screen. Once selected, this will bring up the Task Manager:

It should come up and look something like this:

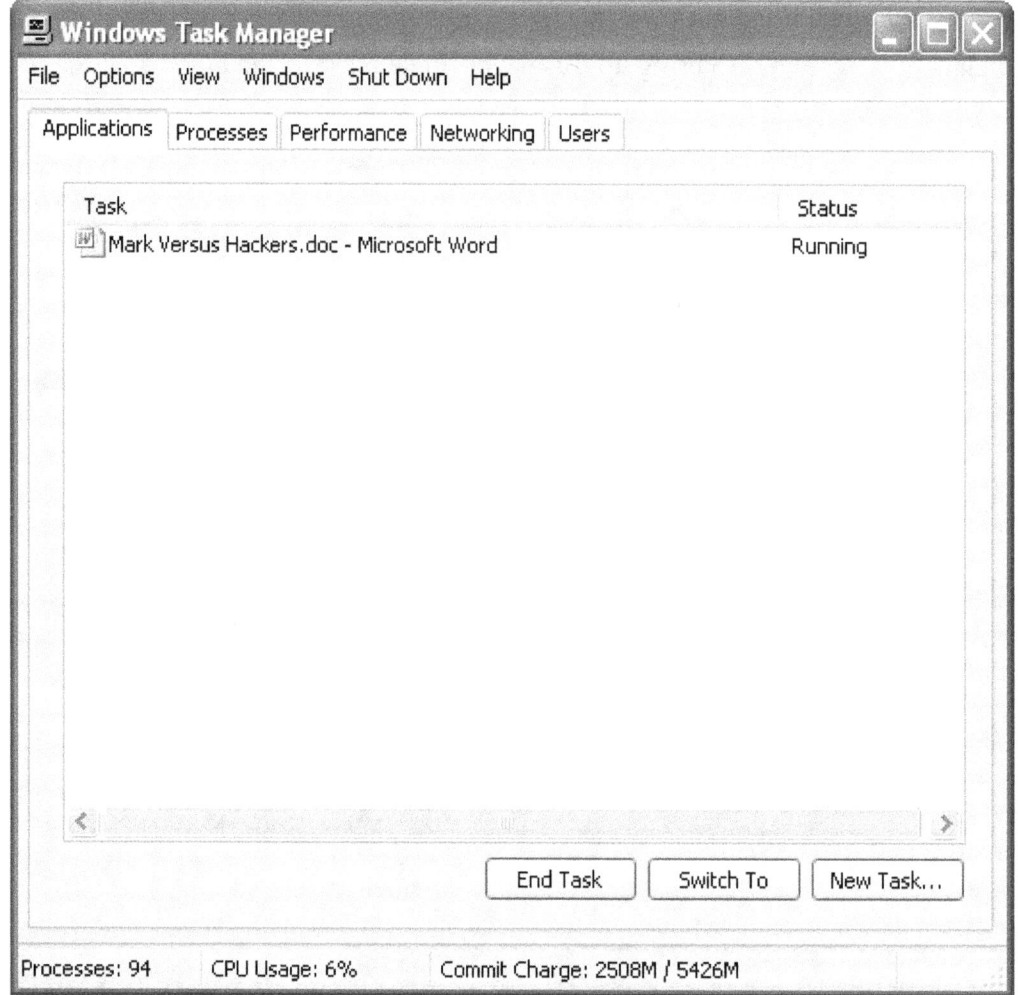

Windows XP - Figure 8

Under Windows 7 and above, it will look nothing like this – but use your common sense. (And go look at the section on your operating system.) What we want to look at is the "Processes" tab.

The Processes tab:

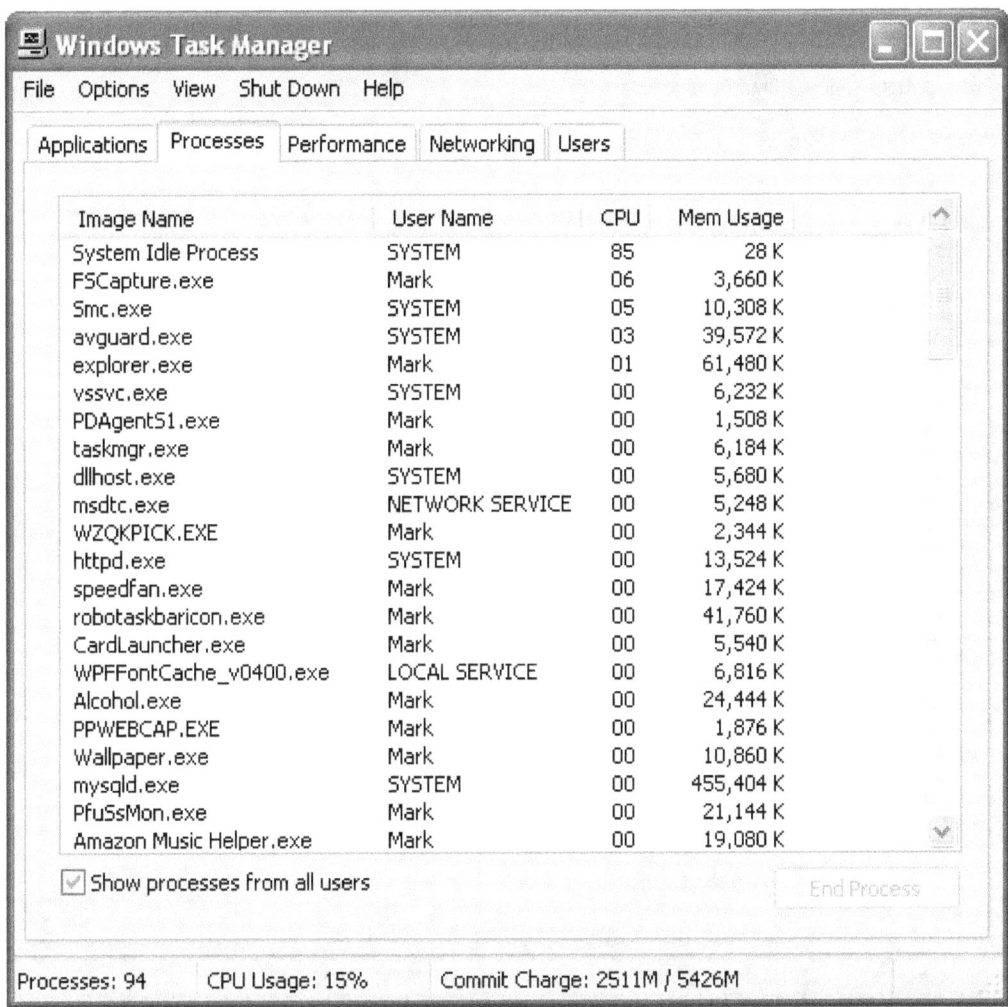

Windows XP - Figure 9

Here you can see everything that is running on your system. If you click on the "Image Name" area then everything will be displayed in an alphabetical list. If you click on the "User Name" everything will be listed by the user's name (like Mark in this instance or SYSTEM or NETWORK SERVICE). Here, I have the "CPU" column selected so I can see what is taking up most of my system's CPU. Notice that 85% of the system is sitting idle. Hackers will do things like give their programs low priority so they do not show up at the top of this dialog. You too can give a program low priority. All you do is to right single click on a line and the Task Manager will give you the option to do that. Is it a good idea to do that? Not really! Unless you know what you are doing you should not mess around with system processes. Unless you just like for your system to crash. As a system's programmer I can readily tell you I have crashed systems before by mucking around with priorities, killing off various programs, and so forth. That is how you learn to program a system. A lot of system crashes. But then you get better and only crash your system every **other** week. Or day. Or hour. ☺ How do you set the priority of a program?

Like this:

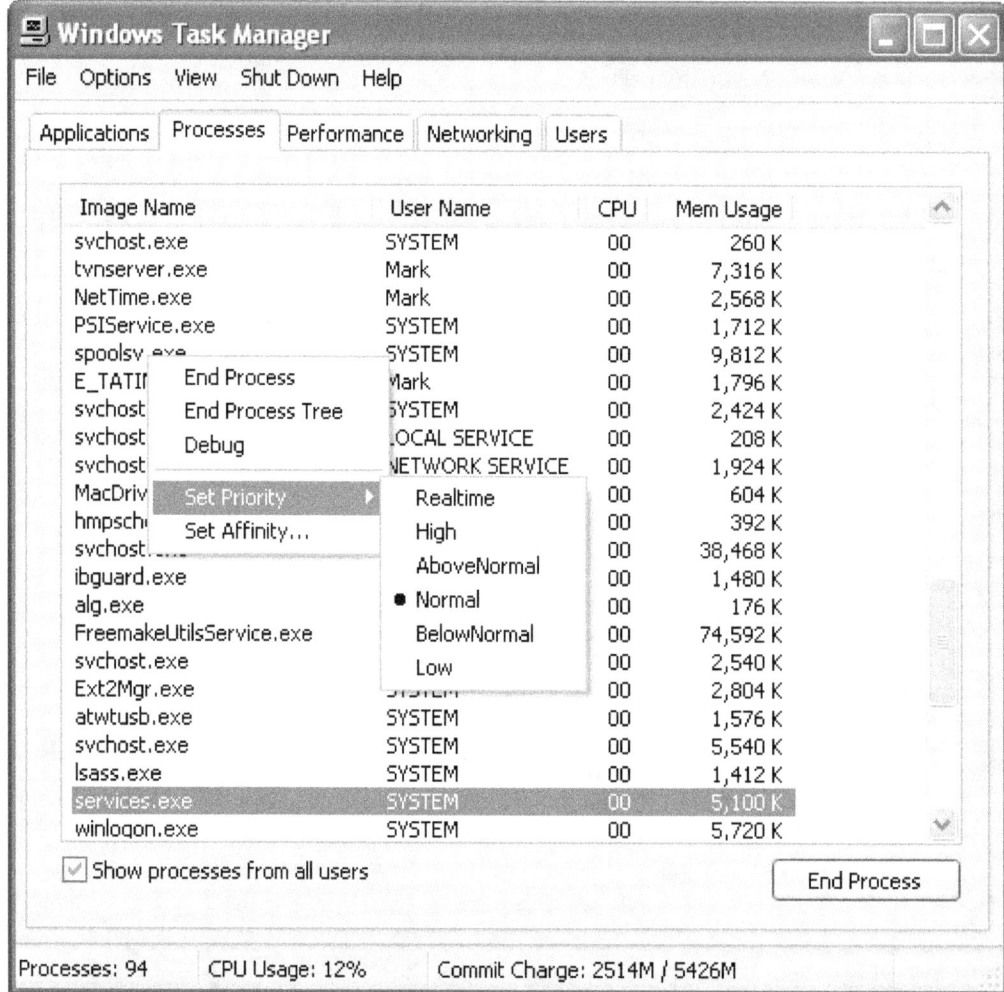

Windows XP - Figure 10

Notice you can also "End Process" or end a process (which is just another name for a program) as well. But notice that the different types of priorities range from low to Realtime. No one ever sets a program to be Realtime unless they have a very good reason to do so. But hackers will set their programs to run at a low priority so (as I said) you won't notice it. Like a program to monitor what you are doing.

Now you know how to bring up the Task Manager. You can read more about what all the Task Manager can do by going online and searching for information about the Task Manager.

HALF STEP #4 : TCPVIEW

TCP View is one of those programs you go "Wow! I didn't know that" after you have run it but after the first time you are going "Oh yeah, that again." TCP View is the only program I know of that could possibly make someone go insane because you are sitting there going "What the heck is all of this stuff doing?" Luckily, most (if not all) of what TCP View shows can be easily explained away. For instance, if you are running FireFox then all of the TCPView items that say they are from Firefox **are** from Firefox. Now – what they are doing is another thing. If you can not account for some part of Firefox that is running then that might be a area of concern. But you have to understand though that one website might spawn a huge number of TCP/IP connections. So just because there are a lot of one application's items sitting there – it doesn't mean something is wrong. You have to check each of the entries out. For me, I had a system once that actually was a ZOMBIE system and it was trying to attack a website. I managed to put a stop to it but it was a real eye opener that my system was doing this.

Ok. So how or where do you get TCP View? You get it from Microsoft. Yes, that really obscure place I mentioned before. Except this is the TechNet part of Microsoft. Those guys are pretty neat. Here is the link to TCP View:

https://technet.microsoft.com/en-us/sysinternals/tcpview.aspx

First, you have to download the file. It is a ZIP file so you need the 7-ZIP program in order to extract the files. OR – you can use the built-in ZIP program that is now in Windows. To extract the file just right single click and select the "Extract…" option. Once you have extracted everything what you should do is to move the new folder to some place like your "Program Files" folder. Or you can do what I did. I made a new folder called "Program_Files". Notice the underscore there? This lets me put programs such as the TCP Viewer program in to a folder with a familiar name – but which isn't protected against changes. In other words – there is no installer for TCP View and the normal "Program Files" folder doesn't like you just sticking things in to it. So if you make the "Program_Files" folder it looks just about the same but you can put programs that have no installer in to it. In any case, wherever you place the folder, you need to left double click on the Tcpview.exe file to run it. You will also have to agree to the EULA.

Then at last you will see something like this:

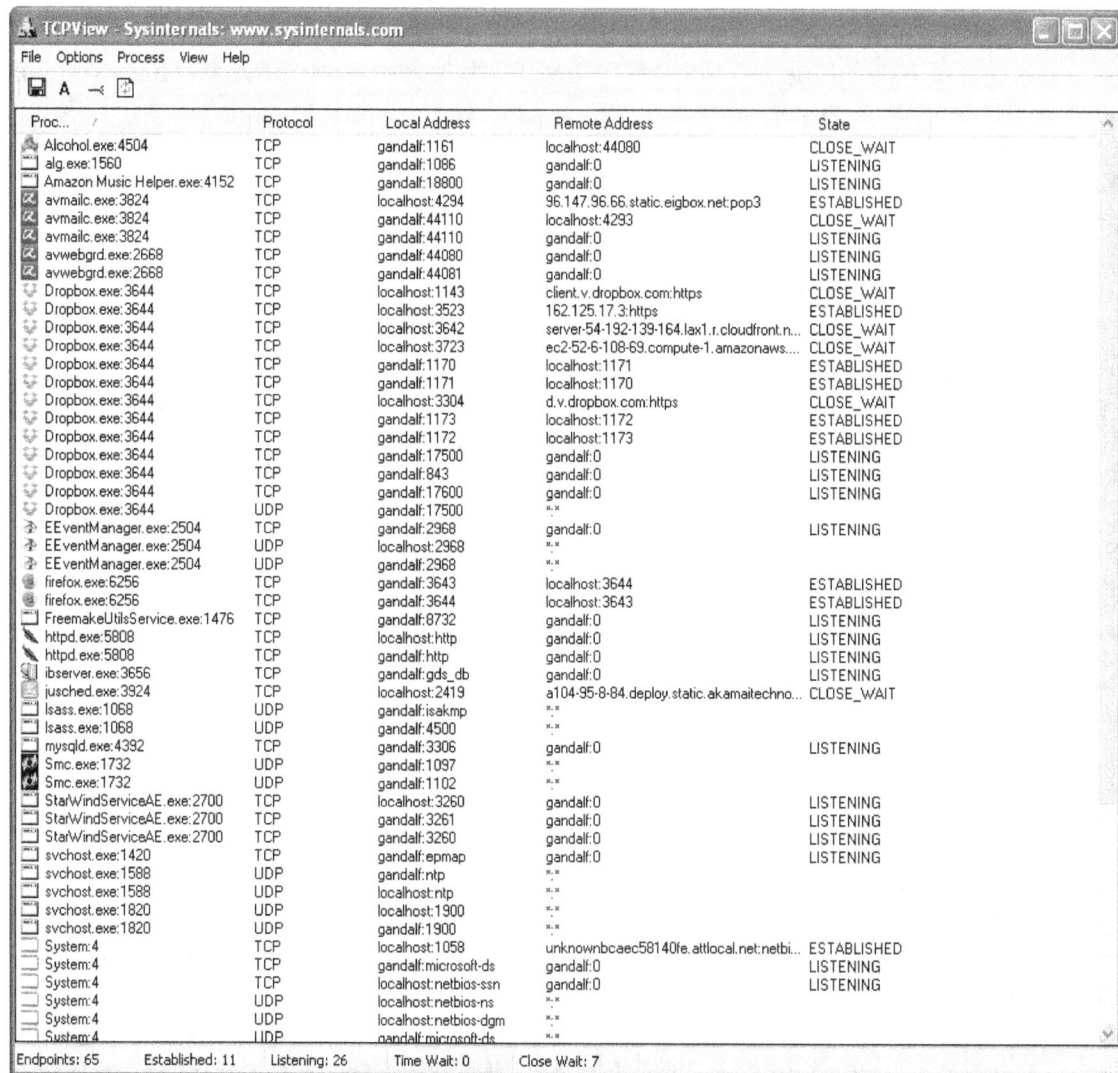

Windows XP - Figure 11

Here you can see that Avira is talking back to their server, Dropbox is talking back to it's server, Firefox is doing a little talking, Freemake (a free video converter program) is sitting there, httpd (Apache) is sitting there, and a lot of other programs are sitting there listening to see if there is anything coming back to them. Some of the connections say "ESTABLISHED" which just means they are connected. What you would want to look at here is there something that is running that you have no idea what it is. When I found out that my system was being used as a ZOMBIE it was because there was a "Local Address" which was coming from my computer to a "Remote Address" that I did not recognize. Basically, I did not recognize the program or where it was going to. So I looked them up, sent them an e-mail, and they said my computer was trying to attack them. I didn't believe it at first but afterwards I confirmed that my computer was attacking them and I put a stop to it. That is a bit outside of this book's scope though. So let's leave it at that.

What you need to know is – if TCPView suddenly stops. That is an indication that there is something wrong. Why? Because again, hackers do not want you to know they are using your system. So they will cause TCPView to stop running so you can't see which program is causing the problem. That is one of their tactics. So if you download this program, run it, and it goes away after a few moments – you may have a hacker using your system. The thing to do in that case is to get a good screen capture program ready, bring up TCPView, and capture the screen. Save that, scroll down some, and take another snapshot. If TCPView goes away, just bring it back up and scroll down faster to take the snapshot. Once you've gotten them – look them over for suspicious program names. It won't say "HackerHere" or "ImAGonnaHackYa" or anything like that but if you see a filename you have no idea what it is doing – you are going to need the Task Manager to kill the suspicious program. Then see if TCPView stays up and running. If you kill the program and TCPView stays up and especially if the suspicious program starts back up again and then TCPView goes away. It is a pretty good indicator that your system is being used by a hacker.

How can you find out about these suspicious programs? Simple. Just right single click on the program's line in TCP View and select "Process Properties". Like so:

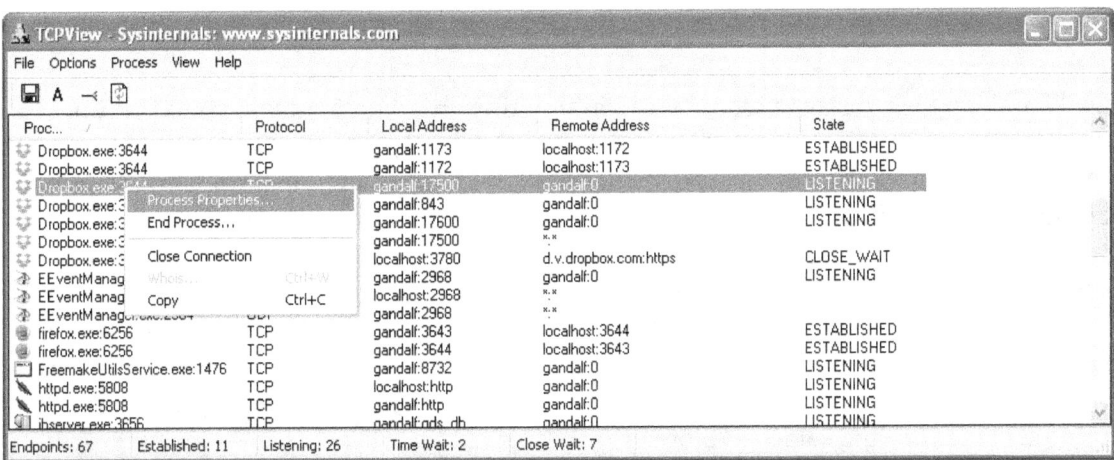

Windows XP - Figure 12

This will bring up a new dialog that gives you the entire path to where the program is located. Go there and DO NOT DELETE THE PROGRAM!!!! What you want to do is to move the program(s) to your desktop and then change the name of the program so it can't be automatically started again..

So first, here is what the "Process Properties" dialog box looks like:

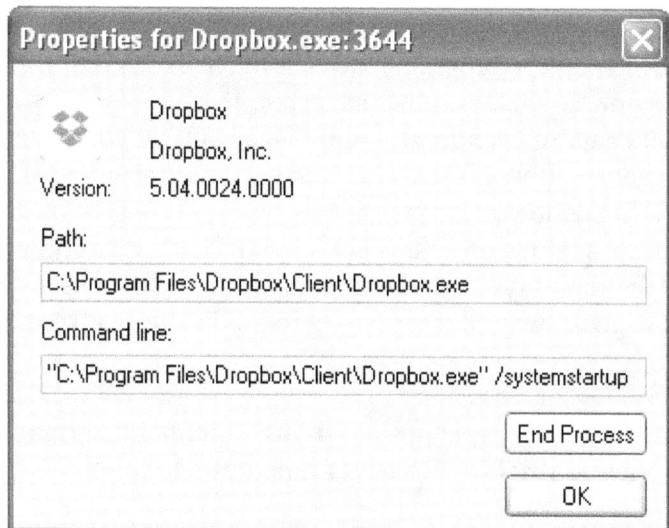

Windows XP - Figure 13

See the "Path" up there? That is where you can find this program. You just go to that directory and then drag that program off to your desktop. If it is the only program in that directory you can probably drag the entire directory off to the desktop and then go in to that folder on your desktop and change the name. That is to say, single left click, wait a second or two and then single left click the program again. This should allow you to change the name of the program. If you see the extension of the file then click at the end of the name and then use your arrow keys to move left four spaces so you are between the name and the type of file. (In the example above your cursor should wind up between the word "Dropbox" and the ".exe" part.) Just type a single letter (like "a") at this location. This makes it impossible for whatever is running the program to run it again because the name isn't the same anymore.

Did you notice that when I right single clicked in the list that there is an option to "End Process…"? That is the same as the Task Manager option. So you can use either Task Manager or TCP View's built-in command to stop a program from running.

In either case, you now have a way to tell if some hacker is using your system and to tell if something else is going on with your system. Like files are being copied or something like that. These are some of the tools you need to be able to tell something is wrong.

HALF STEP #5 : FOLDER OPTIONS YOU SHOULD USE

Here I am going to show you some things you should have with your folder options under Windows. First, you need to bring up the Control Panel again. Then go look for the Folder Options icon. Once you have found it left double click (or under Windows 7 and above left single click) on the icon. This will bring up the dialog box:

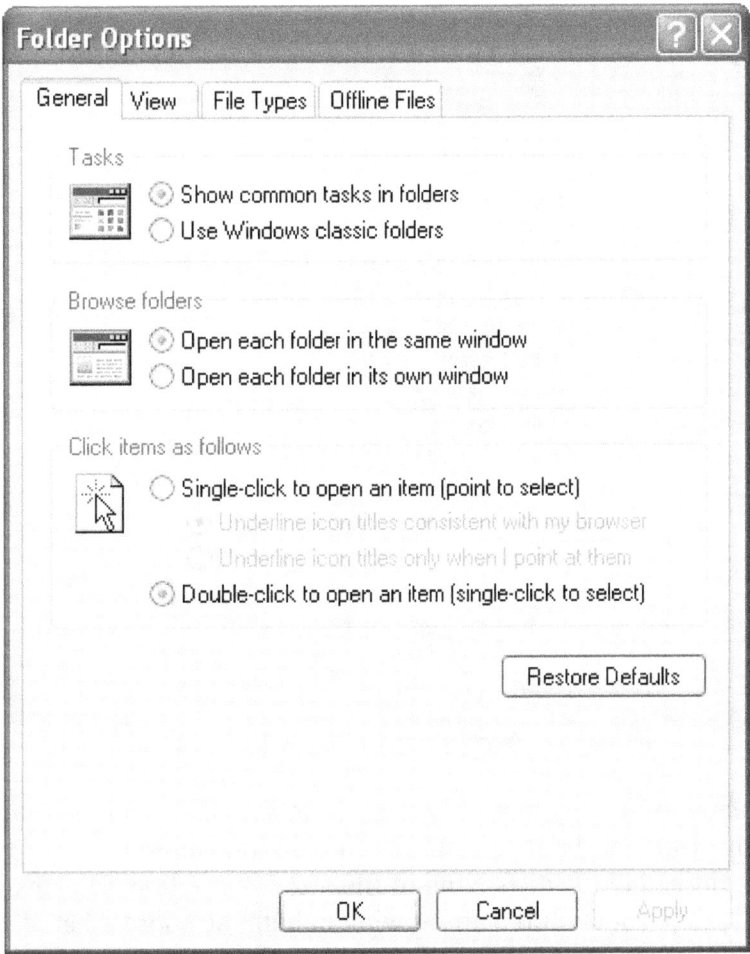

Windows XP - Figure 14

Your folder options should be set up similar to the above. If not, you might want to consider changing your options to match these as they were the default before Windows 7.

Next you want to click on the tab that says "View".

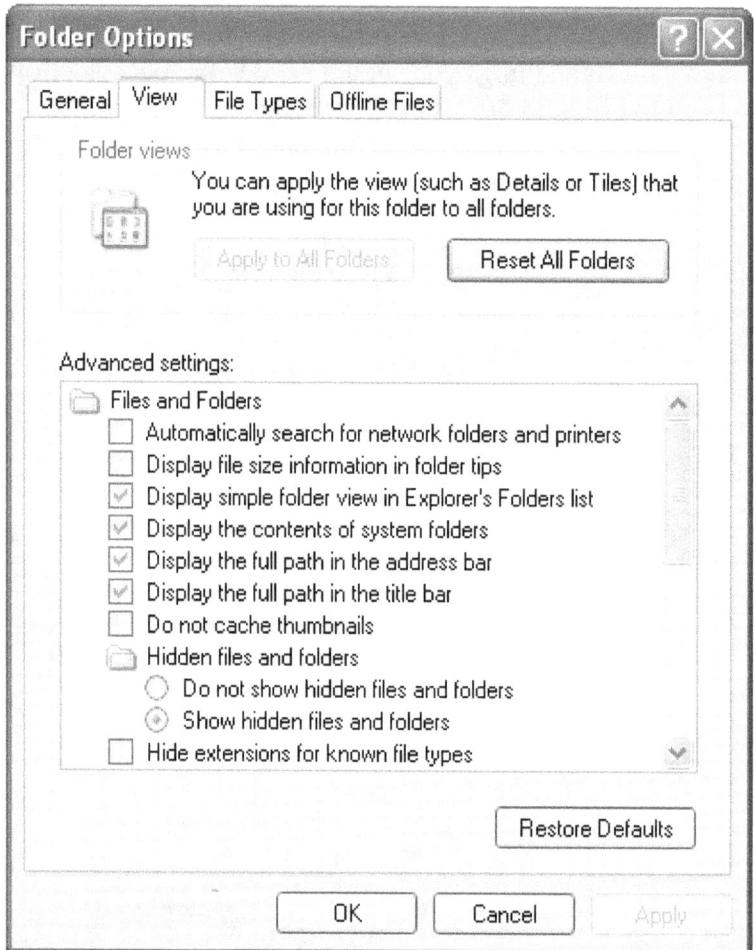
Windows XP - Figure 15

Notice that I have turned off to automatically look for folders and printers. I did this mainly because I would rather look for them myself. I also do not like those information bubbles that keep popping up so I turned of the displaying of file size information. The next four are fairly important. You really do want the full path showing in both the address bar as well as the title bar. In this way you always know EXACTLY where you are just by glancing at the title bar. I also have the "Do not cache thumbnails" turned off. Today's systems are so fast that it makes no sense to cache things like this. Note that the next section says to show hidden files and folders. Remember – it is YOUR computer and YOUR Operating System so why have it hide things from you? The last one that you can see in the above image is whether or not to hide known extensions. I ALWAYS want to know what extension a file has on it so I turn this option off.

Here is the next part of the options that are available to you:

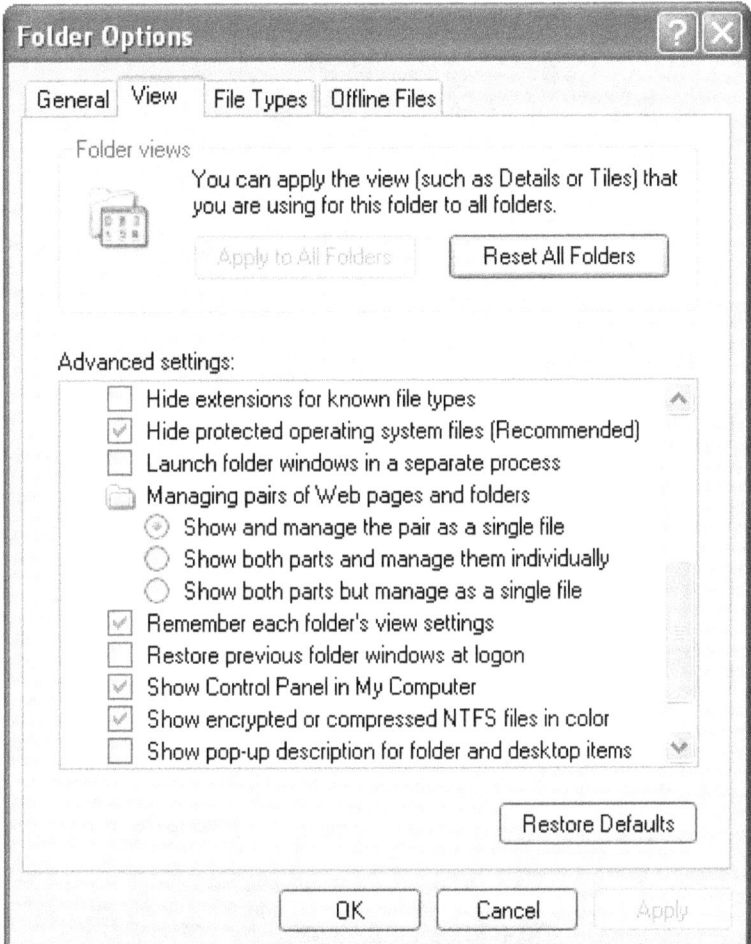

Windows XP - Figure 16

Here we see that the "Hide protected operating system files" is still checked. It makes me sleep better at night knowing that the files the system needs are not going to be accidentally deleted. I like having everything in one window so I do not select the next option. The same is true for managing pairs of Web pages and folders. I also want each folder to remember the settings I set so pictures always show up correctly as do documents. But I leave off the "Restore previous folder windows at logon" because I do not like having folders just popping-up for no reason. I do like having the Control Panel (which is just a folder anyway) to show up, I also do not mind having encrypted or compressed files showing but I do not like the pop-up descriptions of folders or other items.

The last little bit is the most important part.

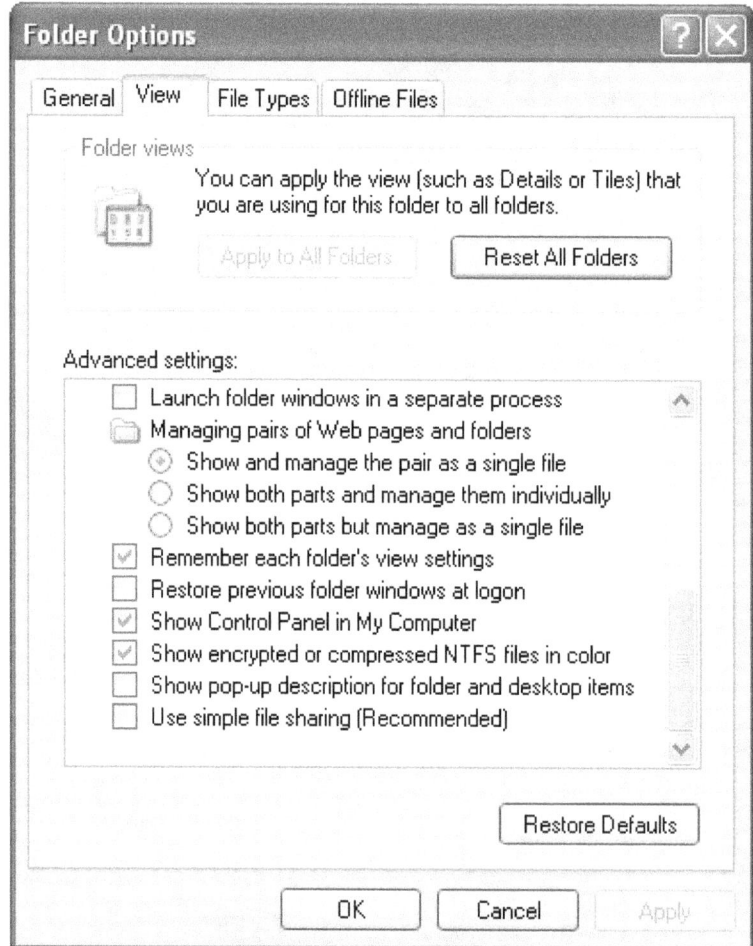
Windows XP - Figure 17

Notice that last line. It is HIGHLY recommended that you turn simple file sharing OFF. This is one of the ways hackers get to people is that they do not know that this is turned on.

Once you have made all of your changes, left click once on the "Apply" button and then left click once on the "OK" button. That's it! You are now set up on folder options. What about the "File Types" tab? That is to modify icons and what they mean. No need to mess with that. As you go along this list will increase automatically. What about the "Offline Files"? That is only to work with files stored somewhere on a network and is beyond the scope of this book. I do not use it so you may have to go ask someone else. But unless you are going to be totally wired to the internet all of the time – I'd forget about it.

The last thing I will say here is that if you watch, as we go along, most of the "Recommended" settings that Microsoft makes I say – "Do not use" and I have good reasons not to use them.

HALF STEP #6 : SYSTEM RESTORE

System Restore – do you need it? No. You do not. System Restore was a good idea but a bad implementation. That is to say – it is no more secure than any other file on your system. If a hacker gets onto your system, they probably have a program that infects your System Restore area so they can get back in the moment you, in your panic, attempt to do a System Restore. The same holds true for just about any virus produced in today's world. So should you turn it off? Yes. Turn it off. What if you need to go back to some way you had the system before? Let me tell you a few words of advice : CREATE BACKUPS ON AN EXTERNAL DISK DRIVE. I can not emphasize that enough. Especially the part about an EXTERNAL DISK DRIVE. Something you back your system up to and then disconnect it from your system. It is the **only** way to assure yourself your backup has **not been touched by a hacker or virus**. We will go into backups later. For now – go into your Control Panel->System program, Use the advanced options and completely turn off System Restore on all of your hard drives. Don't forget to first set the size of the System Restore down to the minimum. If you don't then the System Restore area will still keep that large of an area set aside – just in case you turn it back on again.

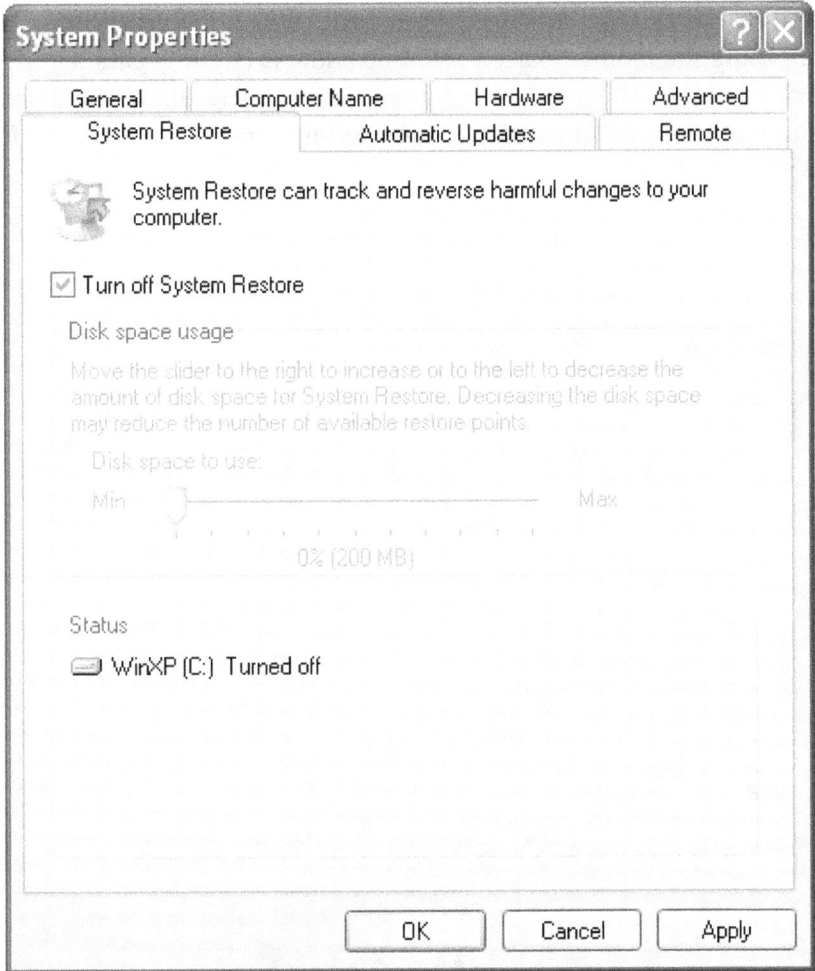

Windows XP - Figure 18

HALF STEP #7 : STOP AUTOMATIC REPAIR

This is taken from:

http://www.sevenforums.com/general-discussion/11336-disable-windows-startup-repair-default-option.html

I felt it to be very important to tell you how to stop the automatic repair feature that Microsoft put in to your operating system. Just like the System Restore feature – this is a good idea but a bad implementation. What Microsoft did was to make a special partition on your hard drive which contains a copy of your operating system. This is all good and fine **except** it can be gotten to by viruses and hackers both. So what happens is either the virus installs itself into this "secret" disk drive or a hacker puts his software in there. The problem is – **you have no idea this is even on your system.** So every time you boot your system – it restores the virus or hacker's software back onto your system. This happened to me. I could not figure out why a virus kept coming back. I couldn't figure out why my system kept getting infected over and over until I read about this on the Windows Seven forums. Thank goodness they are there! I haven't had a virus problem in years since I turned this off. Bad Microsoft! Bad! What they should have done is to encrypt everything using the motherboard's machine address (what is called a MAC address). I can hear it now "But what if I change out my motherboard?" The answer is to name the file in such a way that the encryption key becomes self apparent. There are ways to do that and still keep the contents of the file safe.

So how do you turn off the automatic repair feature? You need to go to Start->Accessories->Command Prompt and then right single-click on the "Command Prompt". Like so:

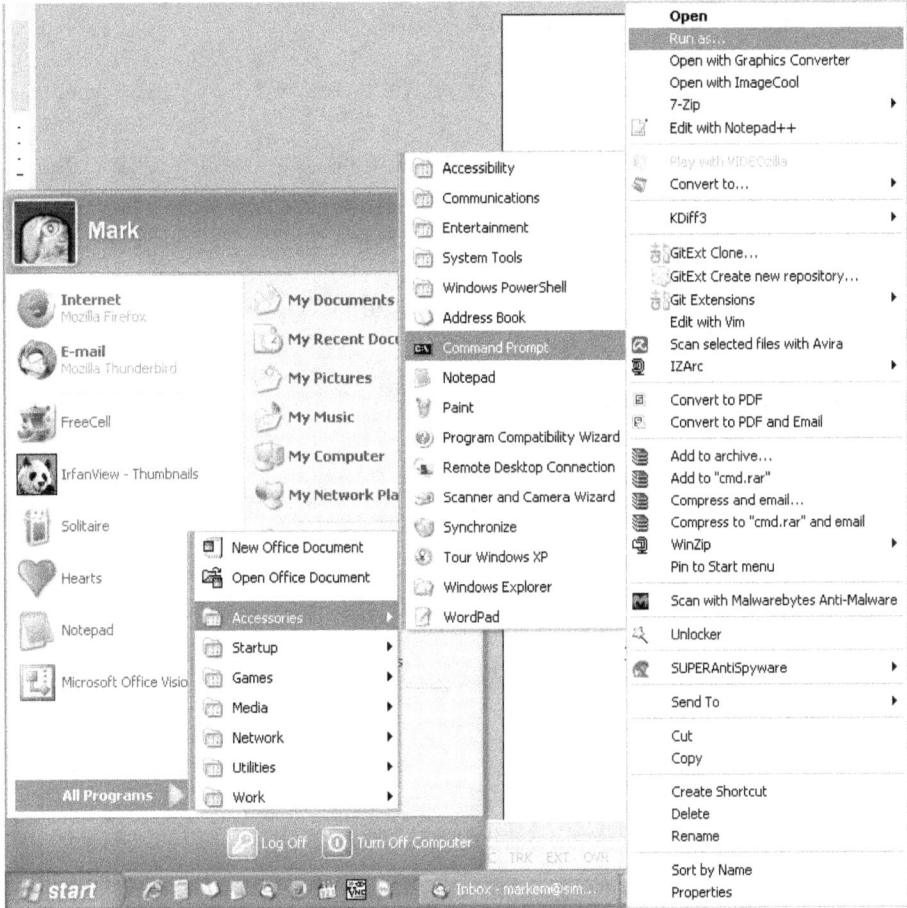

Windows XP - Figure 19

Select the "Run as…" (or on later versions it would say "Run as Administrator". You have to run as an administrator because otherwise the operating system simply dismisses your commands as not worthy of its attention. Or to put that another way – your request would be denied. Once you have a command prompt up and running just type in the following:

```
TURN OFF=> bcdedit /set {default} recoveryenabled No
```

This will turn off the automatic recovery. If you change the "No" to "Yes", that will turn it back on. However, someone on the forum stated that the above was not the ideal way to turn off automatic recovery. Instead, they said to use the following:

```
TURN OFF=> bcdedit /set {default} bootstatuspolicy ignoreallfailures
```

They also said the right way to turn back on automatic recovery was to do the following:

```
TURN ON=> bcdedit /set {default} bootstatuspolicy displayallfailures
```

Personally, to me, simpler is better. These last two commands also seem to say just to ignore or display failures but they do not say to "turn off" actually doing the automatic recovery. So I am not as confident in these commands as I am in the simpler "No" and "Yes" flags. You might want to use both. I did just to be on the safe side.

STEP #1 : FILE AND PRINTER SHARING

First, what is "File and Printer Sharing"? These are mainly used by businesses to be able to share files and printers among the employees. Do you need it at home? No. Will you not be able share your files or printers if this is turned off? No. You can still put a file onto a jump drive, Dropbox, Google Cloud, Microsoft One Drive, external hard drive, put it in an e-mail, FTP the file or any other method you would like to talk about with a file and give it to someone else. Also, if your printer is on your home network – then it is **STILL** on your home network and you can still get to it without any problem. The only difference is – no one can use **your** computer to do the sharing. In other words, if Billy turns off his Printer Sharing and Sally wants to print to his printer – she has to do it from **HER** computer and not Billy's computer. So no big loss there.

The way you get to this is to go to Start->Control Panel.

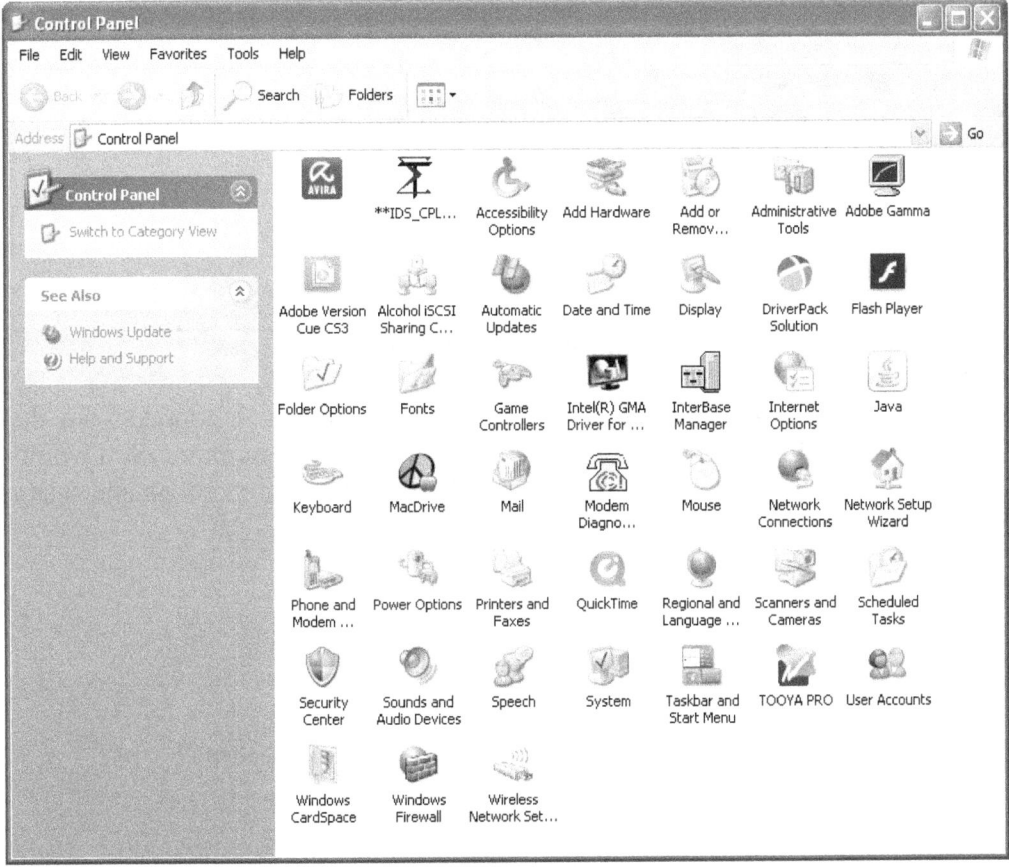

Windows XP - Figure 20

Here is my Control Panel again. Yours will be different. So now find the icon that is for working with your Network Connections. Under XP that is what it is called but under later operating systems it can be called by other names. Check out the screen shots for the other operating systems to see how to get to the networking section..

Here are my network connections:

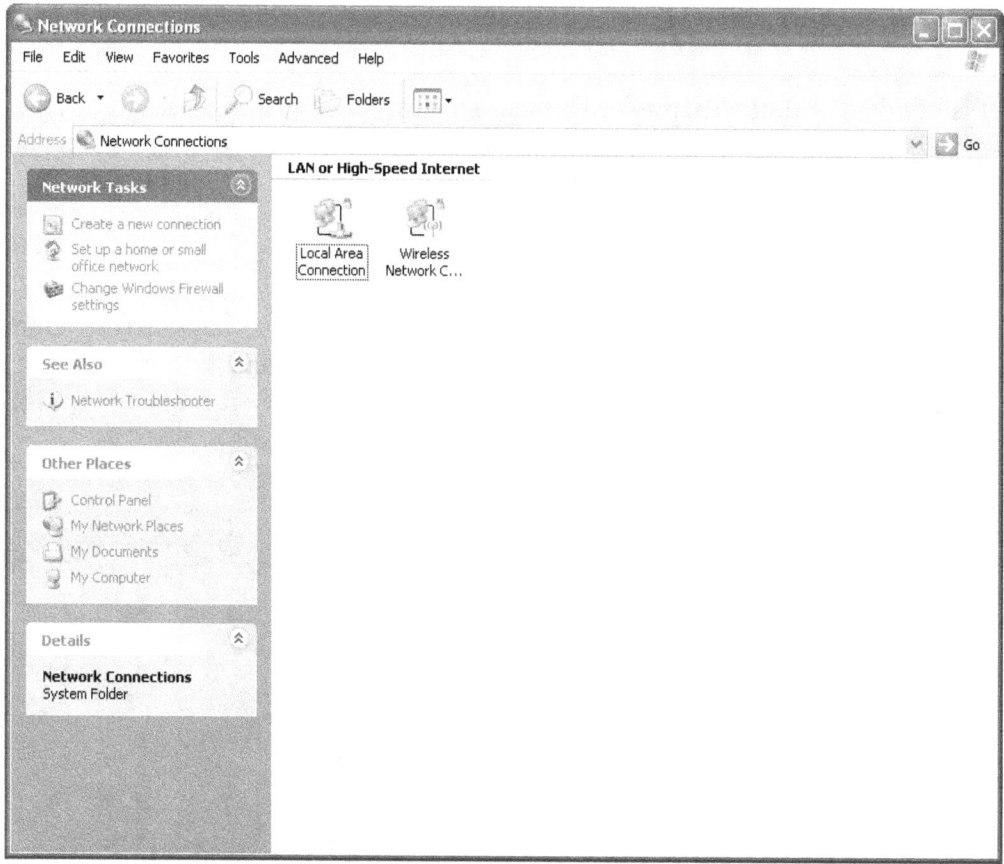

Windows XP - Figure 21

Here you can see the two types of connections I have. Select whichever connection is the current connection. In my case, I have an Ethernet cable hooked up to my computer. So I would select the one that says "Local Area Connection". You single-right click on that icon and select the "Properties" option

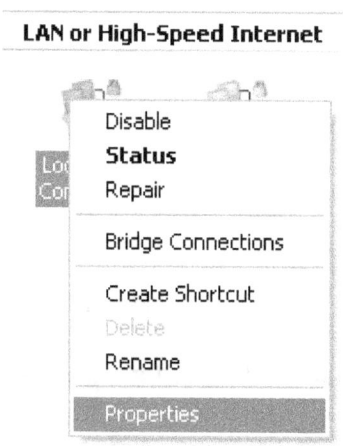

Windows XP - Figure 22

This will bring up a new dialog box.

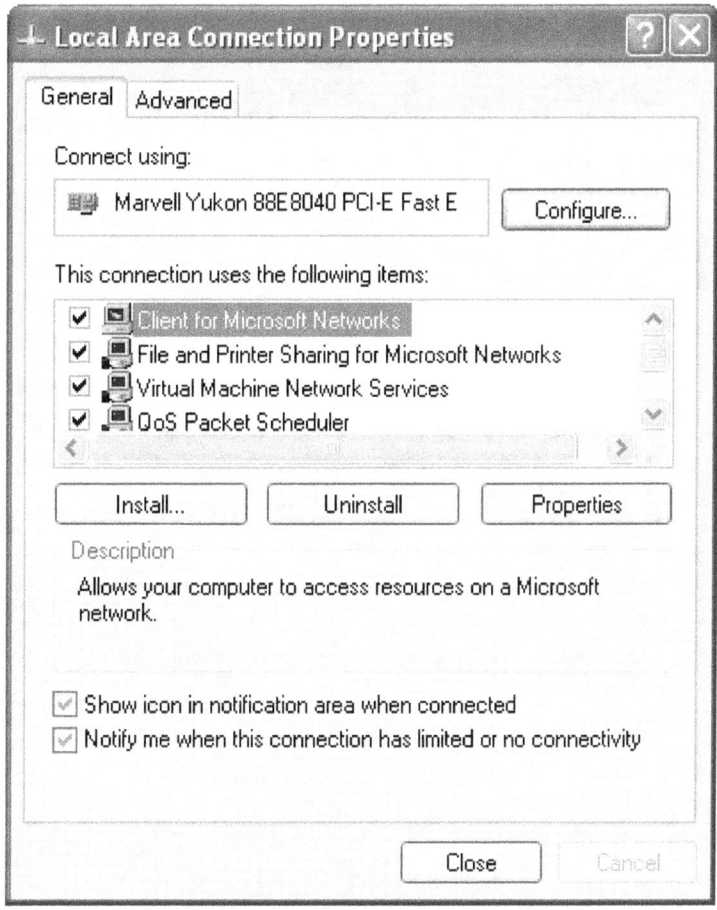
Windows XP - Figure 23

(Remember that what **MY** dialog box looks like and what yours looks like might be different.)

Now find the "File and Printer Sharing for Microsoft Networks" checkbox. Uncheck the checkbox. Once your system comes back from that highlight the "File and Printer Sharing for Microsoft Networks" and click the **Uninstall** button.

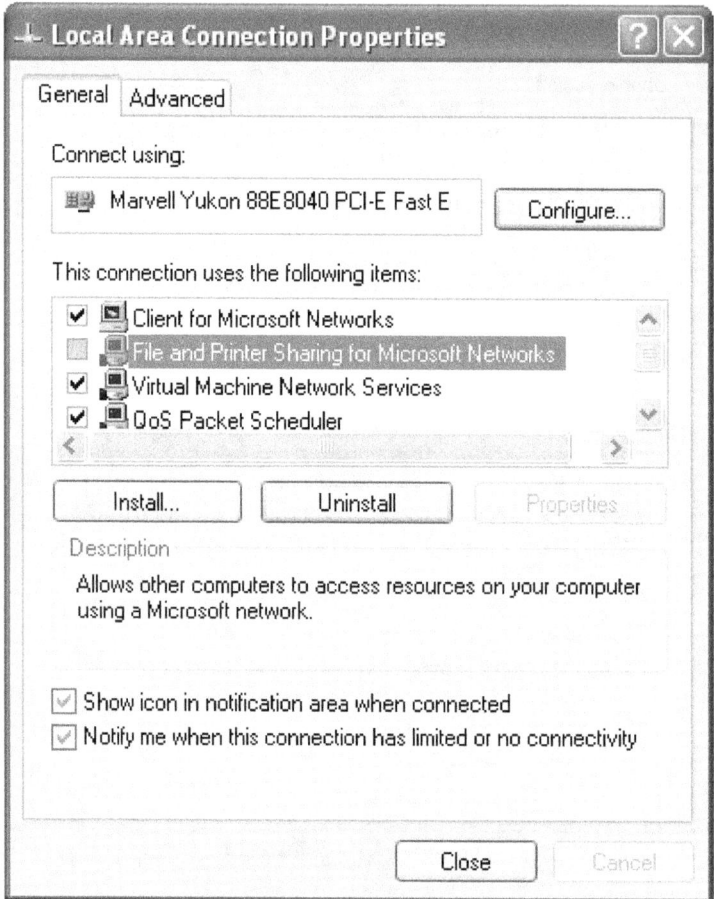

Windows XP - Figure 24

This will uninstall this option and leave your dialog looking something like this:

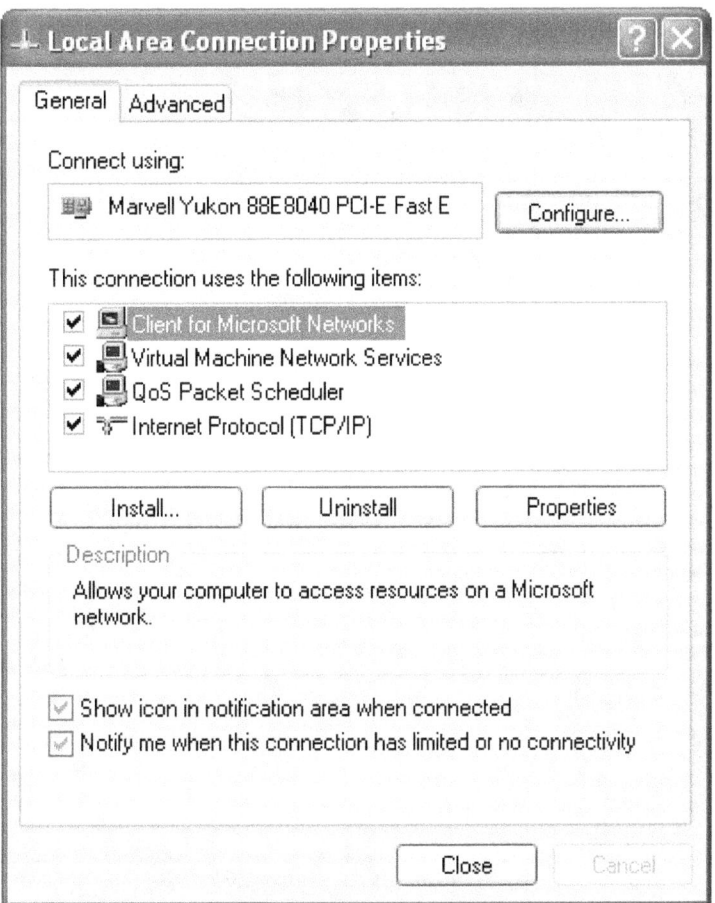

Windows XP - Figure 25

Then you just click on the **Close** button and you are through in this part. So what does this do? If you go to the dialog that shows all of your disk drives: (Which used to be the My Computer option.) You will see something like thia:

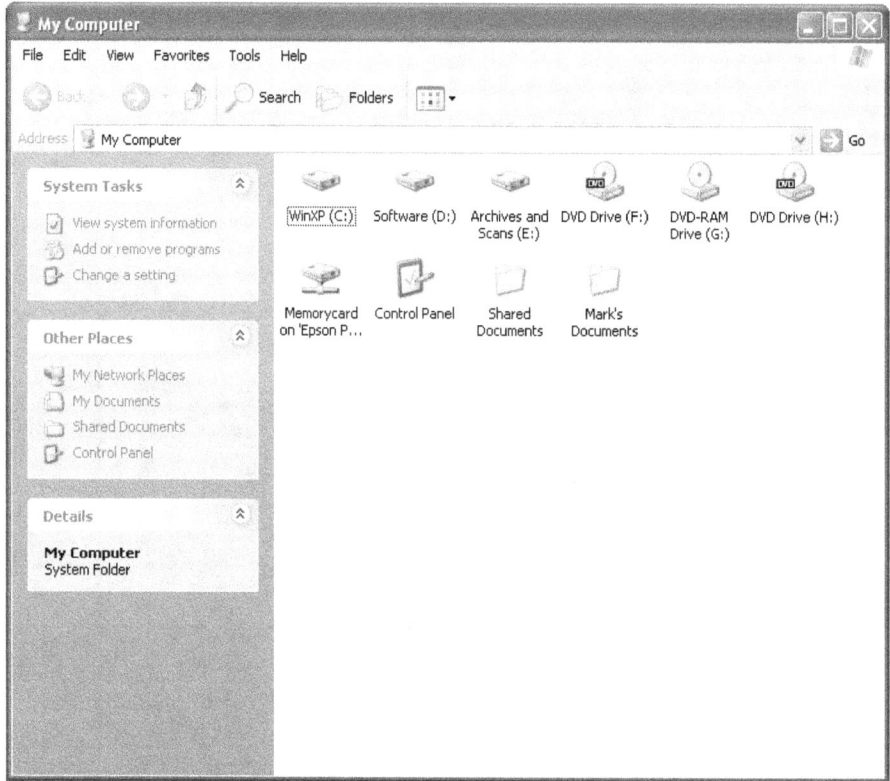

Windows XP - Figure 26

So here we have WinXP, Software, Archives and Scans, and more items. If you now right-single click on a disk drive you will see a pop-up menu. Select the "Properties" option from the bottom of that menu to get the Properties dialog box to come up:

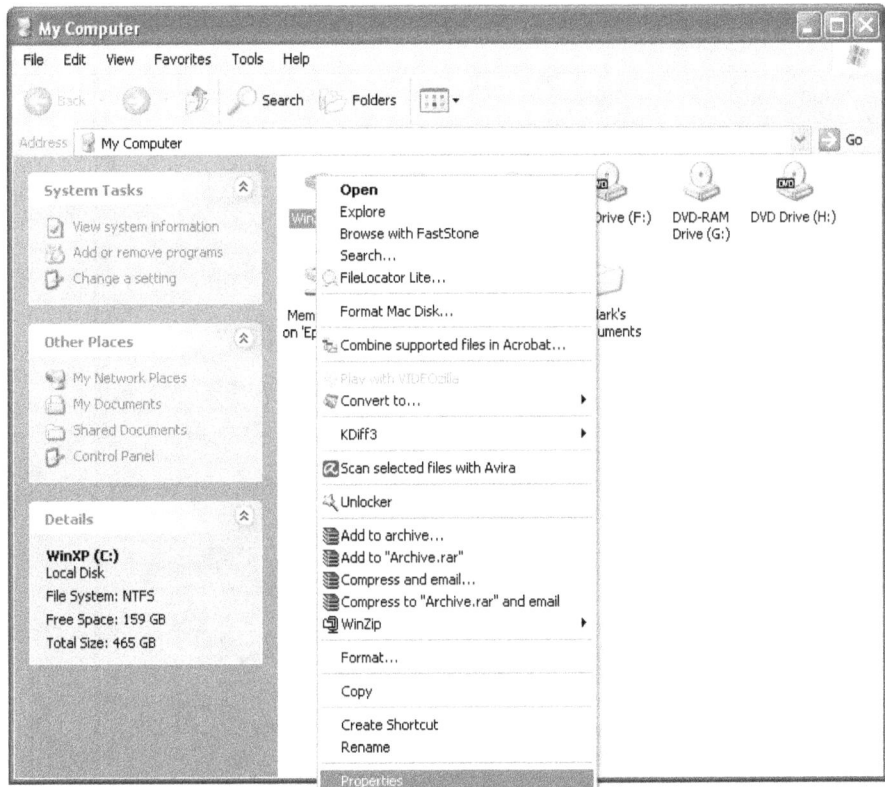

Windows XP - Figure 27

When this dialog comes up it should look something like this:

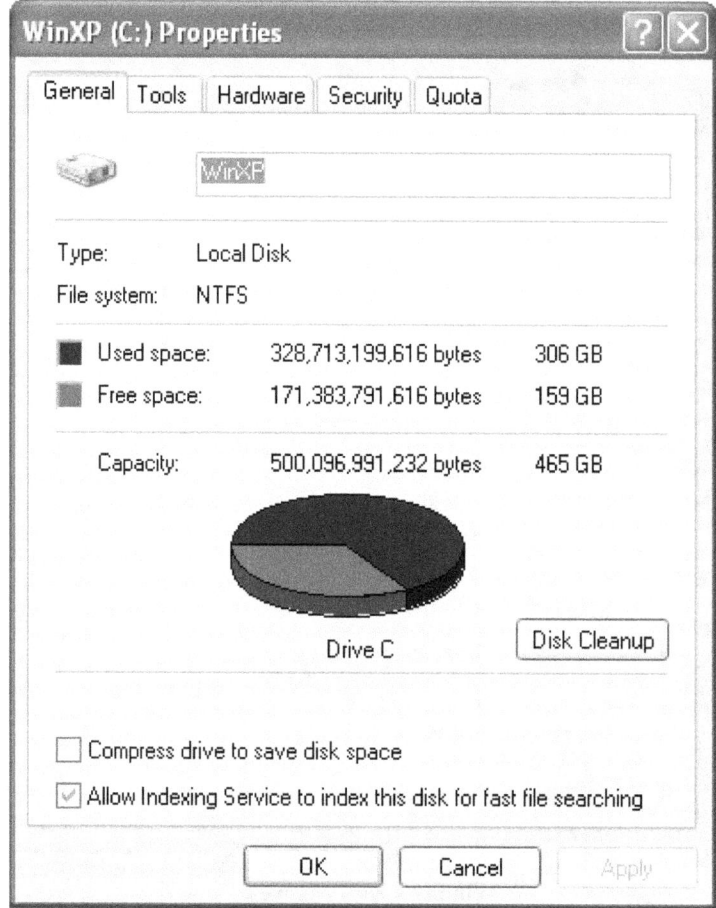

Windows XP - Figure 28

Only on mine one of the tabs is missing. This is the "Sharing" tab. Also, if you wait a few minutes it will disappear off of your dialog box also. This is because you have gotten rid of file sharing. Now, why would you want to get rid of file sharing? Because it is one of the ways in which hackers can get all of your stuff without you ever even knowing they were doing it. That's right. File sharing sounds like a great thing but actually the way Microsoft made it work means that it is more suited to an office environment (with someone who monitors your network) and not a home environment (where no one monitors the network). If you had, before turning off file sharing and uninstalling it, come and looked at this dialog you would have had the sharing tab on it. Under the sharing tab you would probably see that your main hard drive (the C: drive) was being shared. IF A HACKER had set things up on your system so they could get to everything on your hard drive then you would have seen that not only was your hard drive shared but **YOU** would not have been able to remove it. Or if you managed to remove it – it would be back the next time you rebooted your computer. It is as simple as that. They are controlling your hard drive and you are not. But now that you have turned off file sharing and uninstalled that component – no one can share your hard drive. Which is a good thing.

But what about if you need a file from someone or you want to give them a file? Use a jump drive or send it to them via e-mail, DropBox, Google Cloud, Microsoft's One Drive, use FTP (File Transfer Protocol) or some other way. Better to use that than to let hackers onto your system.

So is this it? That's all? Well, that's all for this – but we are not through yet. Not by a long shot. Ready for Step #2? Ok! Here we go!

STEP #2 : THE GROUP POLICY PLUG-IN

Ok, so you have taken your first step and stopped hackers from stealing your files via the file and printer sharing "feature" that is a huge backdoor for hackers. Now we are going to be going in to how the system's security works and we are going to make it so no one can log in to your system except you. In order to do this we first have to download (if you have the HOME version) the group policy plug-in. This is the plug-in that Microsoft left out and which is so very important in order to keep the system clear of hackers.

If you have the Professional version or any of the other versions go to your Control Panel and then the Administration Tools and see if you have the Local Security Policies plug-in. If you do then you can skip down to Step #3. Otherwise, continue reading.

First, go to the following website:

http://drudger.deviantart.com/art/Add-GPEDIT-msc-215792914

Way over on the far right you will see a thin rectangle that says "Download" with a green arrow next to it. THAT IS THE LINK TO DOWNLOAD THE FILE. Not any of the other giant buttons that say "DOWNLOAD"!!!!! Those are just come-on buttons. Look for and find the right button and click it. Now, the file is an archive which means you have to get the files out of the archive in order to run them. This is a 7-Zip archive which means that if you do not have the 7-Zip program installed then you will not be able to unarchive the file. So use your favorite download site or go to

http://www.7-zip.org/

and download it from there. Otherwise locate the 7-Zip program on your favorite download website and download it to your computer. Note that there is a 32bit version and a 64bit version. So get the right one.

Before going any further it is important to remind you that we are doing administrator type tasks so you **always** need to run these programs as an administrator. You do by that right-single clicking on the installer and select the "Run as administrator" or the "Run as…" menu option. In the second version (which is on Windows XP) it will ask who to run the program as. Tell it to run it as yourself. Why yourself? Because most people are running their systems as the administrator and don't even know it. That's why hackers want to take over your account. Because if you are the administrator on your computer and they can take over your account….

Here is a screen capture of me running the 7-Zip program as an administrator.

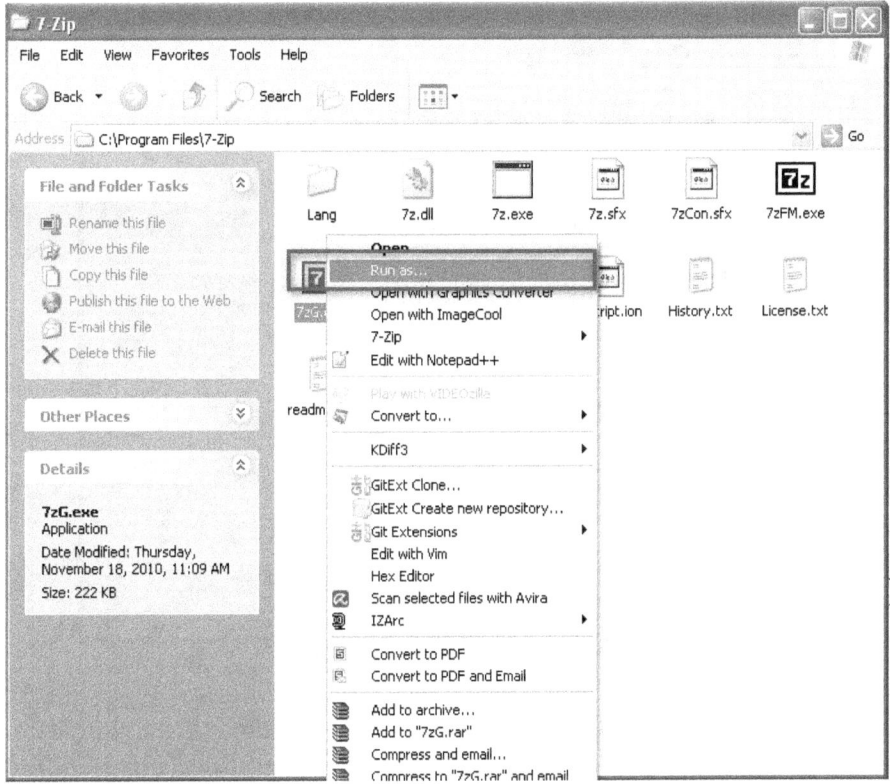

Windows XP - Figure 29

As you can see – I'm having to use the "Run as…".

On Windows XP this will bring up a new dialog box that says:

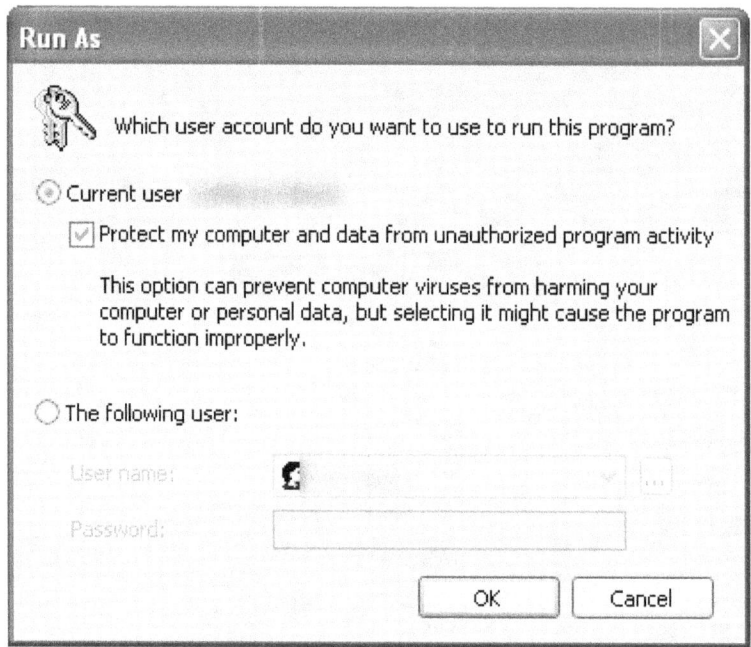
Windows XP - Figure 30

So you leave it selected as "Current User" because it is most probable that you are an administrator on your own system. The weird thing is – if you don't do this step the files will still be installed – but they won't work. By telling the installer to run as an administrator you are also giving it permission to activate the files it installs. Got it? Good! Let's continue.

Going back to the website where you downloaded the Group Policy Editor, there is a notice for 64bit users after the download link. It reads:

Windows 7 x64 Users:
You must go to the SysWOW64 folder and copy the "GroupPolicy", "GroupPolicyUsers" folder and the "gpedit.msc" file into the System32 folder.

What they mean is – once you have downloaded the program, unarchived it, and run it – the program will put everything into one directory. For 32bit systems this is the System32 folder (which is the right place to put this). For 64bit systems though, it puts everything into the SysWOW64 folder. Both folders are found in the WINDOWS folder. So on 64bit systems you have to go find the C:\WINDOWS\SysWOW64 folder and **copy**(Don't just move them because they have to be in BOTH directories on a 64bit system.) the files "GroupPolicy" and "GroupPolicyUsers" over to the C:\WINDOWS\System32 folder. Then do the same for the gpedit.msc file in the SysWOW64 folder.

Once you have done this you are ready for the next step. Wait! What was that? HOW do you know if you have a 32bit or 64bit system? That's easy! All you do is – first bring up the Control Panel via the Start->Control Panel.

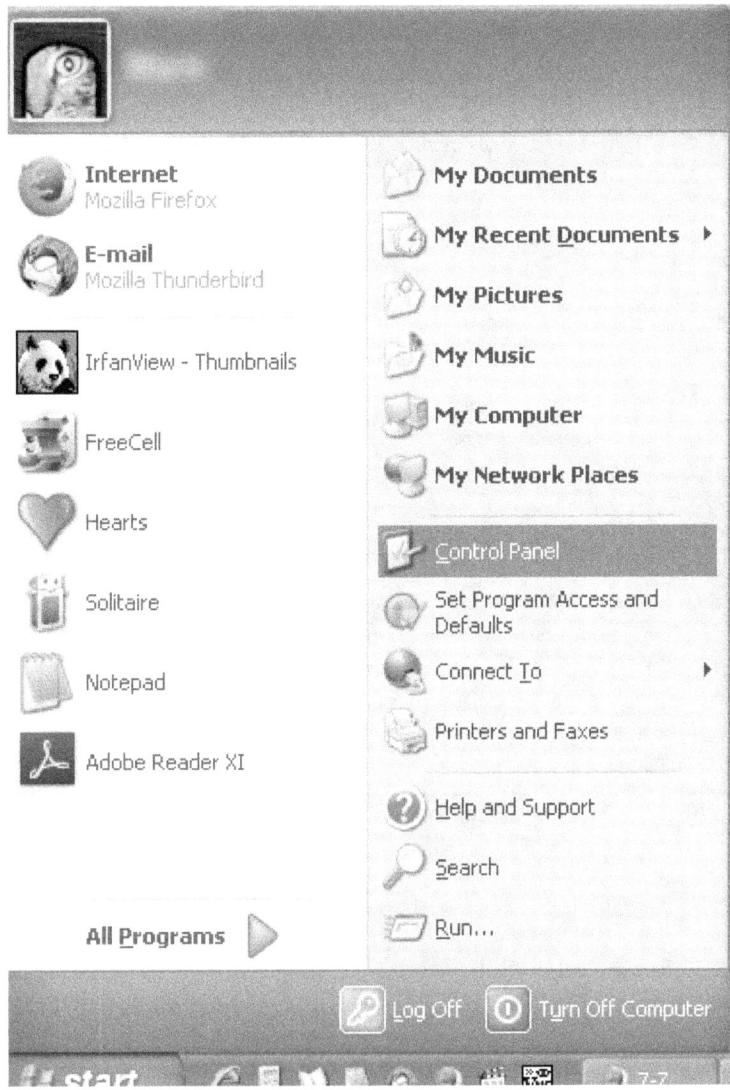

Windows XP - Figure 31

And then the Control Panel dialog box will display:

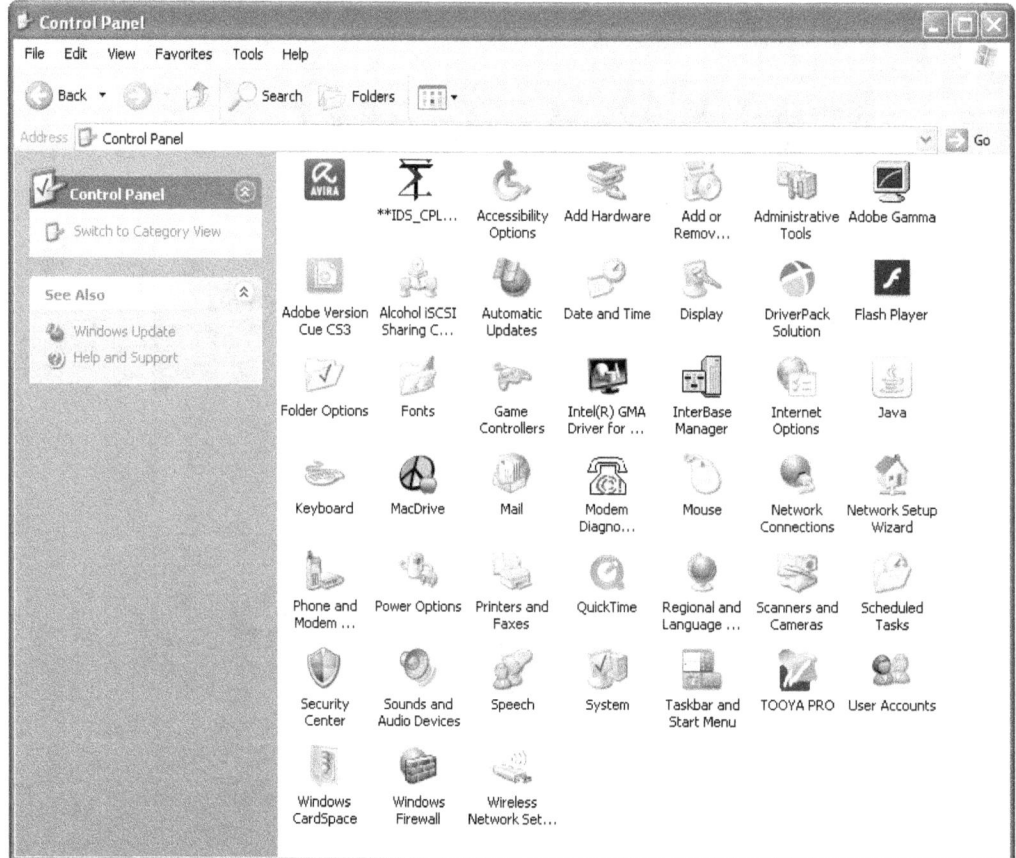

Windows XP - Figure 32

Next you select the "System" icon.

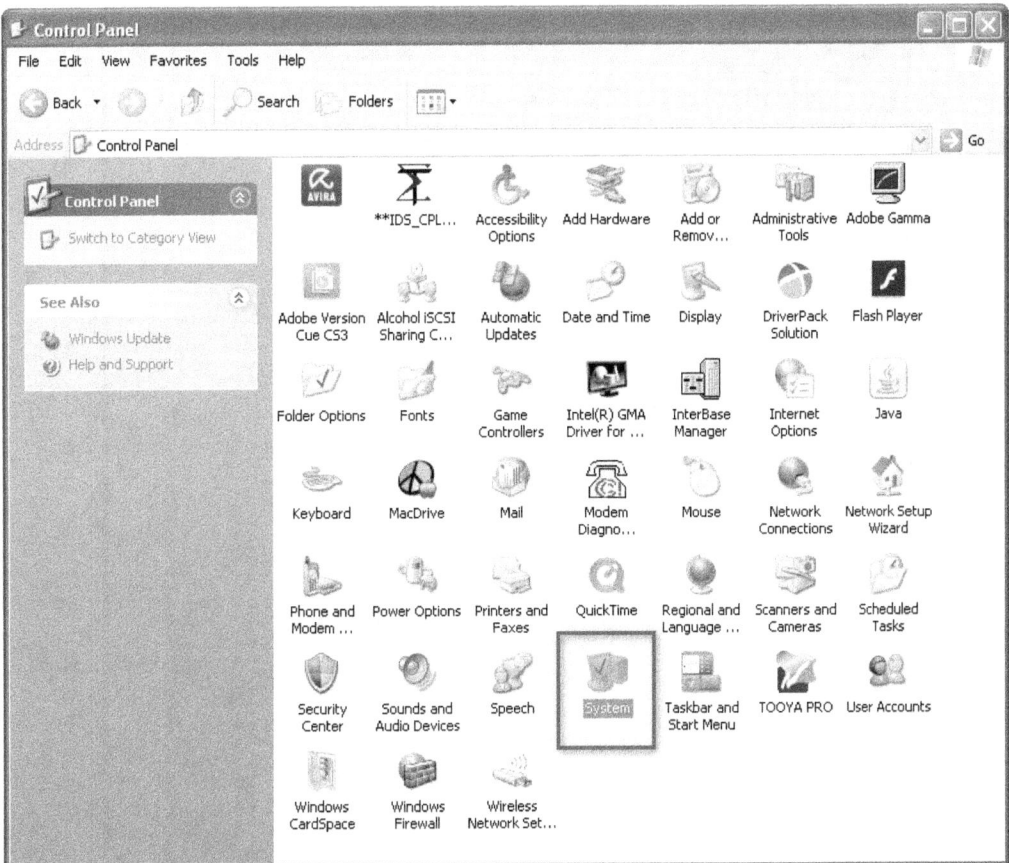

Windows XP - Figure 33

Left double-click on that icon to bring up information about your system.

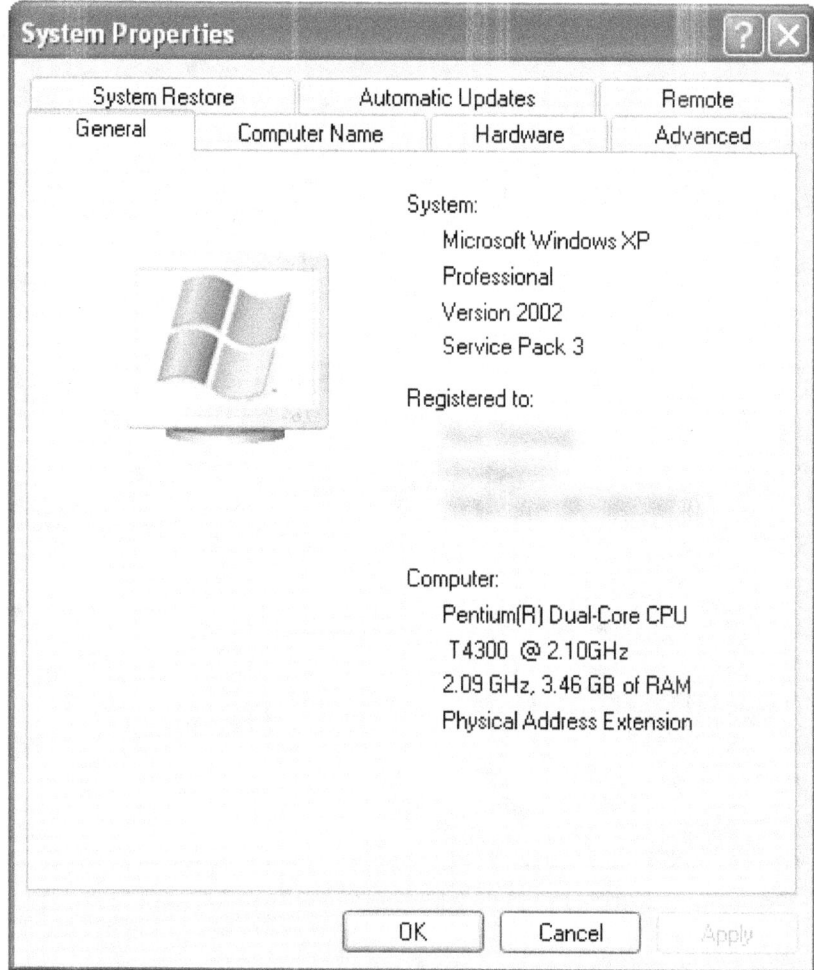

Windows XP - Figure 34

In Windows XP's case if you have a 32bit operating system it doesn't say anything. If this were the 64bit version then it would say this was a 64 bit operating system. You can also visit this webpage at Microsoft:

https://support.microsoft.com/en-us/kb/827218

Scroll down a bit and it will automatically tell you which type of OS you are running. The website also tells you how to do this manually. Please ignore all of the fear mongering messages on the website. Although support from Microsoft has stopped that does not mean that Windows XP no longer works and Microsoft does still send out updates occasionally.

Ok! So far you have downloaded 7-Zip and the Group Policy Editor (if you have the HOME version of Windows). You also now know whether you have a 32 bit Operating System (OS) or a 64 bit OS. You've already learned quite a bit! Let's go to the next step.

STEP #3: INSTALLING THE GROUP POLICY PLUG-IN

Ok. So first we turned off File and Printer Sharing, then we downloaded the Group Policy Editor. Or did you? If you have any other version other than the HOME version of Windows – you skipped Step #2. What you need to do now is to skip down to Step #4. Because this section just tells you how to get the Group Policy Editor up and running if you had to download it. Alright? Great! Let's go!

Once you have downloaded and installed the Group Policy Editor in your Windows directory you are ready to try to run it. This is also a simple task. What you want to do is to locate the Command Prompt program (called just COM usually). You do this by left single clicking the Start button and either using the "Run…" dialog box or by finding the Command Prompt program inside of the Accessories submenu.

Windows XP - Figure 35

Remember that we have to run everything as an administrator. So you would right single click on this menu entry and select the "Run as administrator" or "Run as…". Otherwise nothing will work.

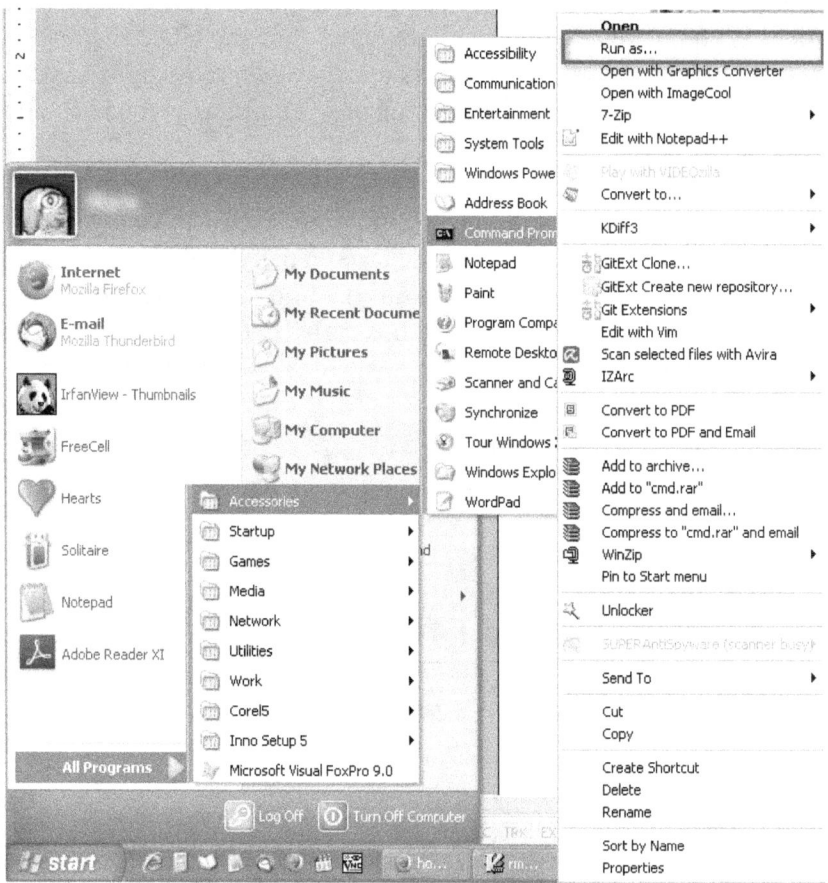
Windows XP - Figure 36

This will bring up a command window so you can type things in to it.

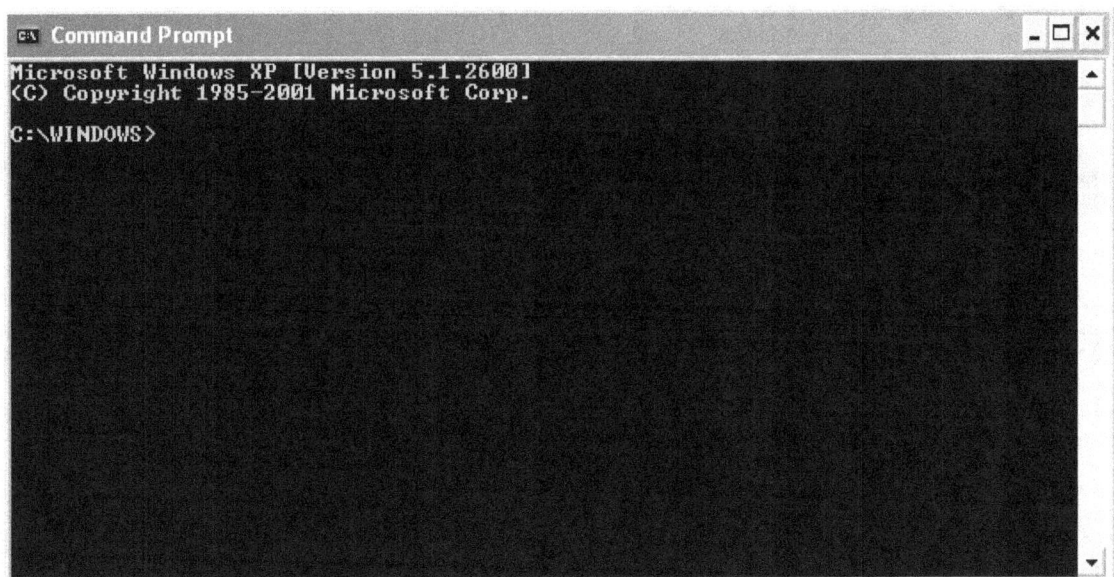

Windows XP - Figure 37

What you do here is to type in gpedit.msc followed by a return (or Enter).

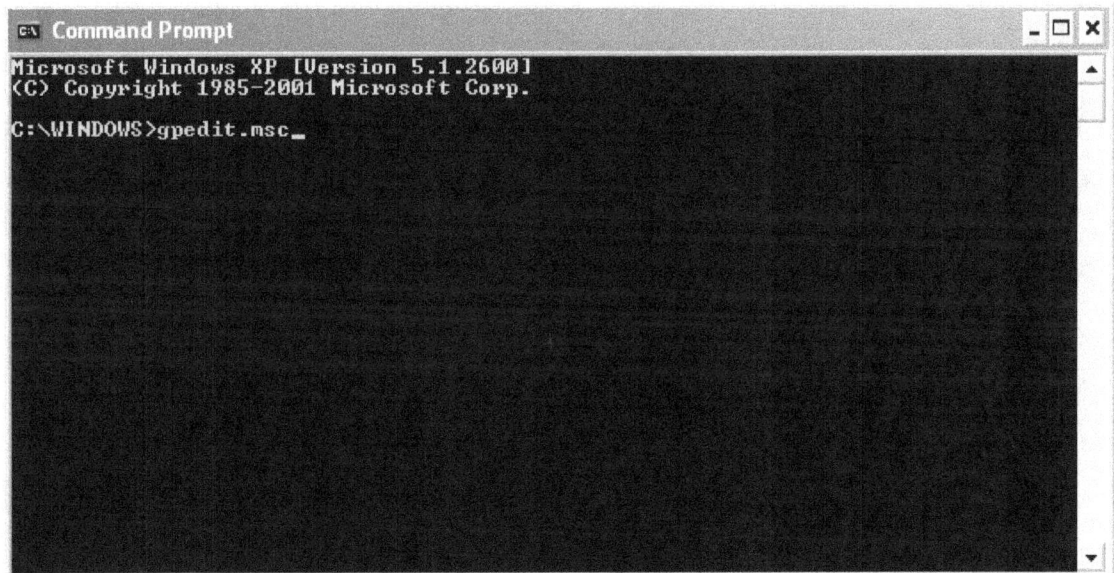

Windows XP - Figure 38

When you press the Enter/Return key the Group Policy Editor should show up. If it doesn't then you either did not run the setup program to set things up as an administrator or you didn't copy all of the files you needed from the SysWOW64 folder like we showed you how to do.

I have to add that SOMETIMES you have to run the gpedit.msc from the "Run…" part. For unknown reasons – sometimes the Command Prompt just won't run gepedit.msc. Instead, it says it can not find it. So if that happens – try using the "Run…" option.

If you DID do everything right then the Group Policy Editor should come up.

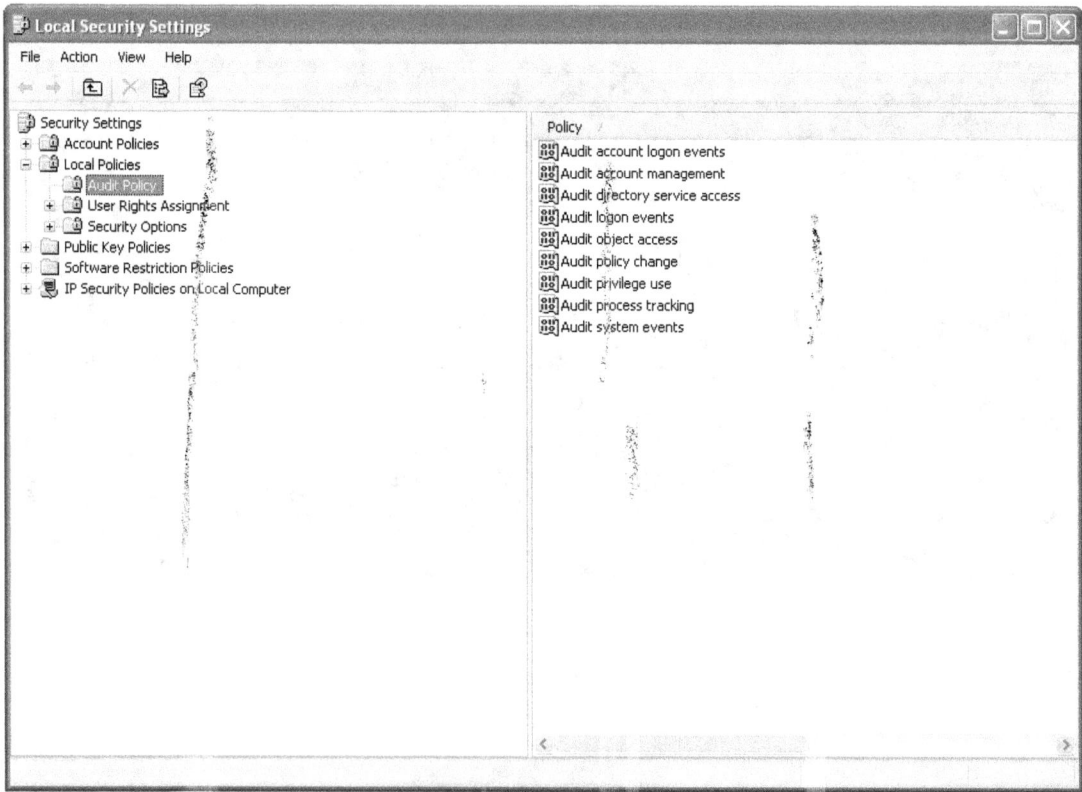

Windows XP - Figure 39

Here I am cheating a bit. Since I have Windows XP Professional already installed I can not just run gpedit.msc. I have to go through the Local Security Policies tool in the Administrative Tools folder. But what you see should look the same or similar.

STEP #4 : USING THE GROUP POLICY PLUG-IN

Ok, if you skipped Step #3 because you do not have the HOME version of Windows. Then what you should do is Start->Control Panel->Administrative Tools->Local Security Policy. That was the short-hand version of what to do. The longer version is to click on the Start button, find the Control Panel again, let the system bring up the dialog box (or window), look for the Administrative Tools folder and then find the Local Security Policy icon and left double click on it. This should bring up something that looks like this:

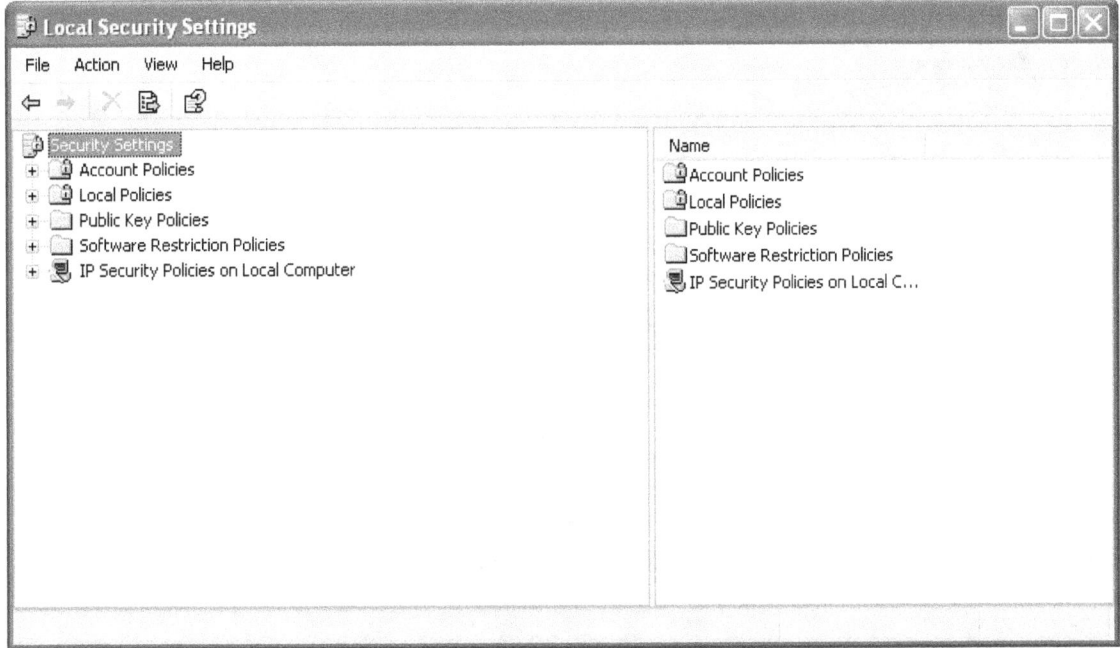

Windows XP - Figure 40

If you are going through the Group Policy dialog box, it should look like this:

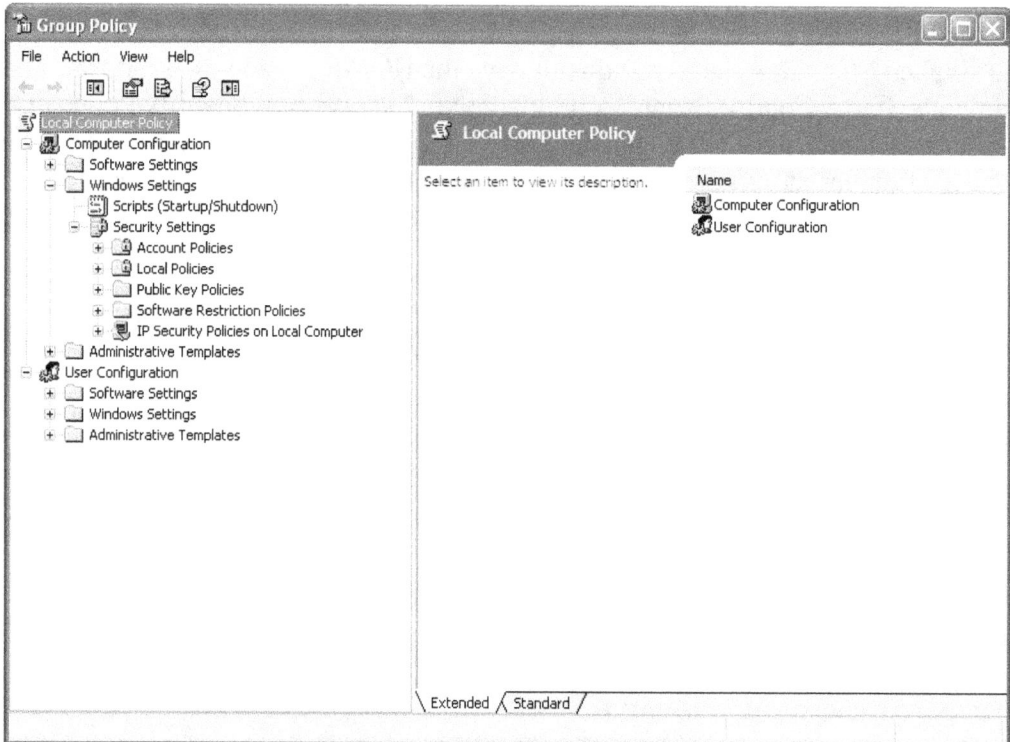

Windows XP - Figure 41

Note that you have to open the Computer Configuration tree entry, then the Windows Settings tree entry, then the Security Settings tree entry before you get to the Local Policies tree entry.

So that is Group Policy Editor->Computer Configuration->Windows Settings->Security Settings->Local Policies in shorthand notation.

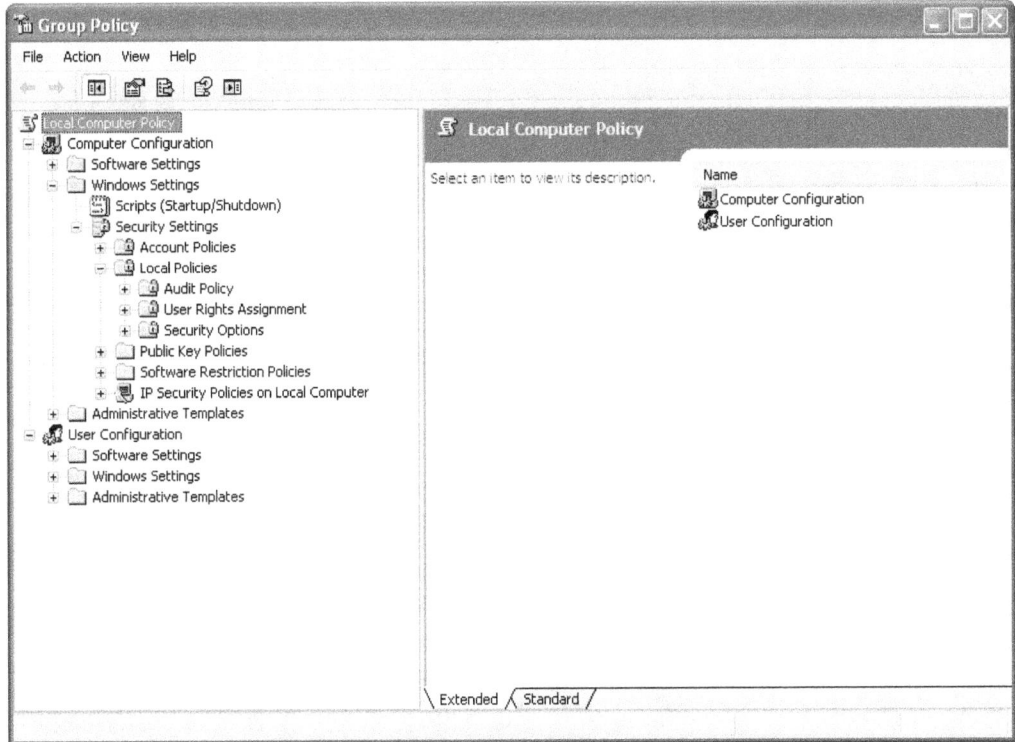

Windows XP - Figure 42

Here is where most of our changes are going to take place. There are two areas we will work in. The first is the Local Policies area and the second is in the Account Policies area. What we are going to do is to restrict who can or can not get onto your system from the network and we are also going to change some policies so your account is monitored and harder to log in to. Will this affect you? Yes it will. Will it be difficult to log in? No, it won't.

For our first set of changes you will need to click on the "User Rights Assignment" option. Here is what you should see:

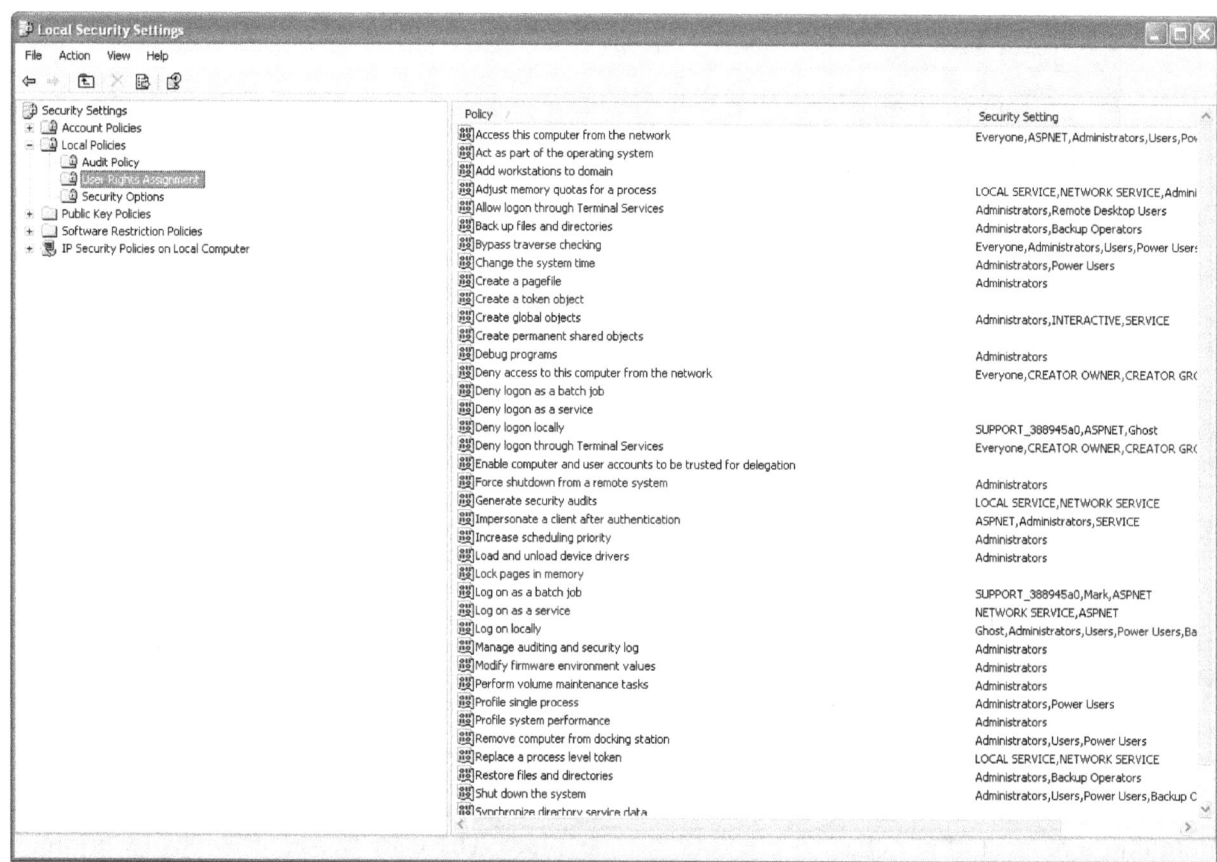

Windows XP - Figure 43

Your set up may look different. That's ok. If you look at the first line it will say something like "Access this computer from the network" on the first column and it will have a list of accounts that can do so on the right column. We are not interested in that list – it is just an example of what you will see.

What we are interested in is the line that says "Deny access to this computer from the network". This entry overrides the other entry. What we are going to do is to make it so NO ONE can get to your computer from the network. (Or does it? More on that later.) To change this value you left double click on the RIGHT HAND column.

This should bring up a new dialog box that will look something like this:

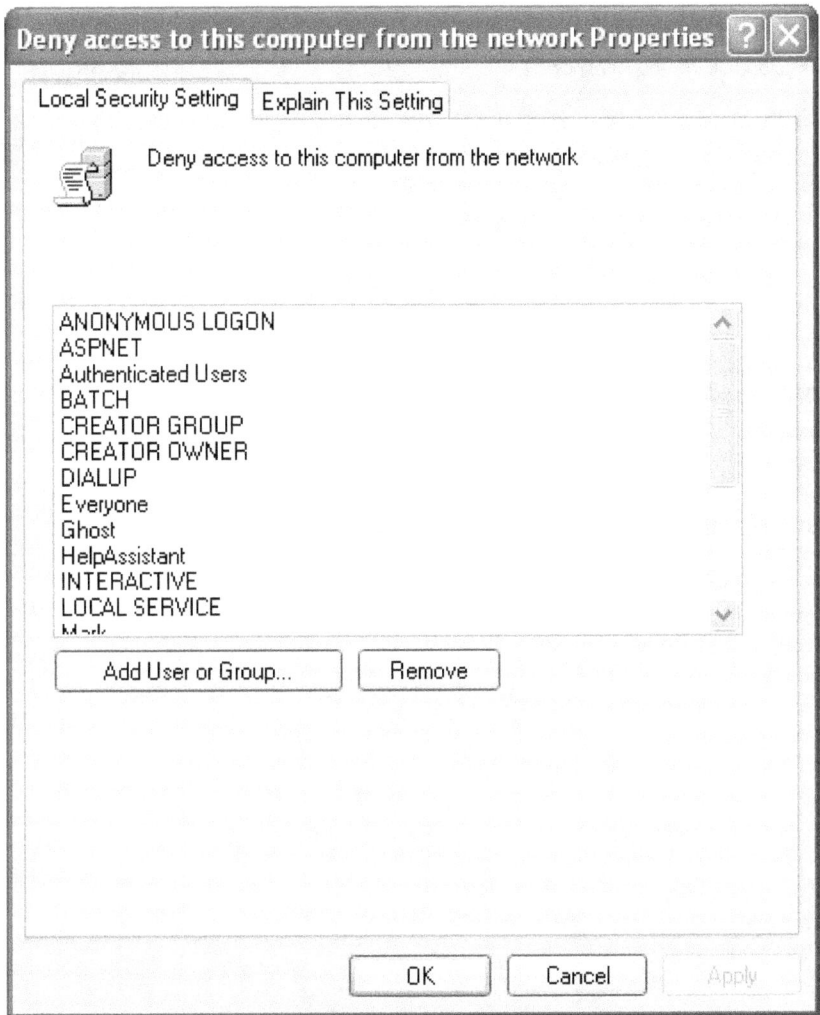
Windows XP - Figure 44

Now, on my screen it already has all of the accounts put into it. Yours should be blank. What you do next is to click on the "Add User or Group" button. This will bring up another dialog.

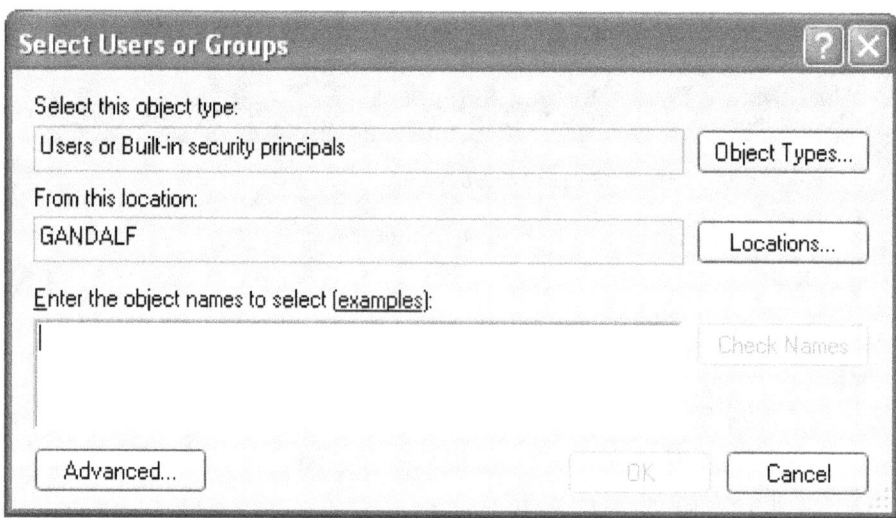

Windows XP - Figure 45

This dialog is just an intermediary dialog. Now click on the "Advanced" button.

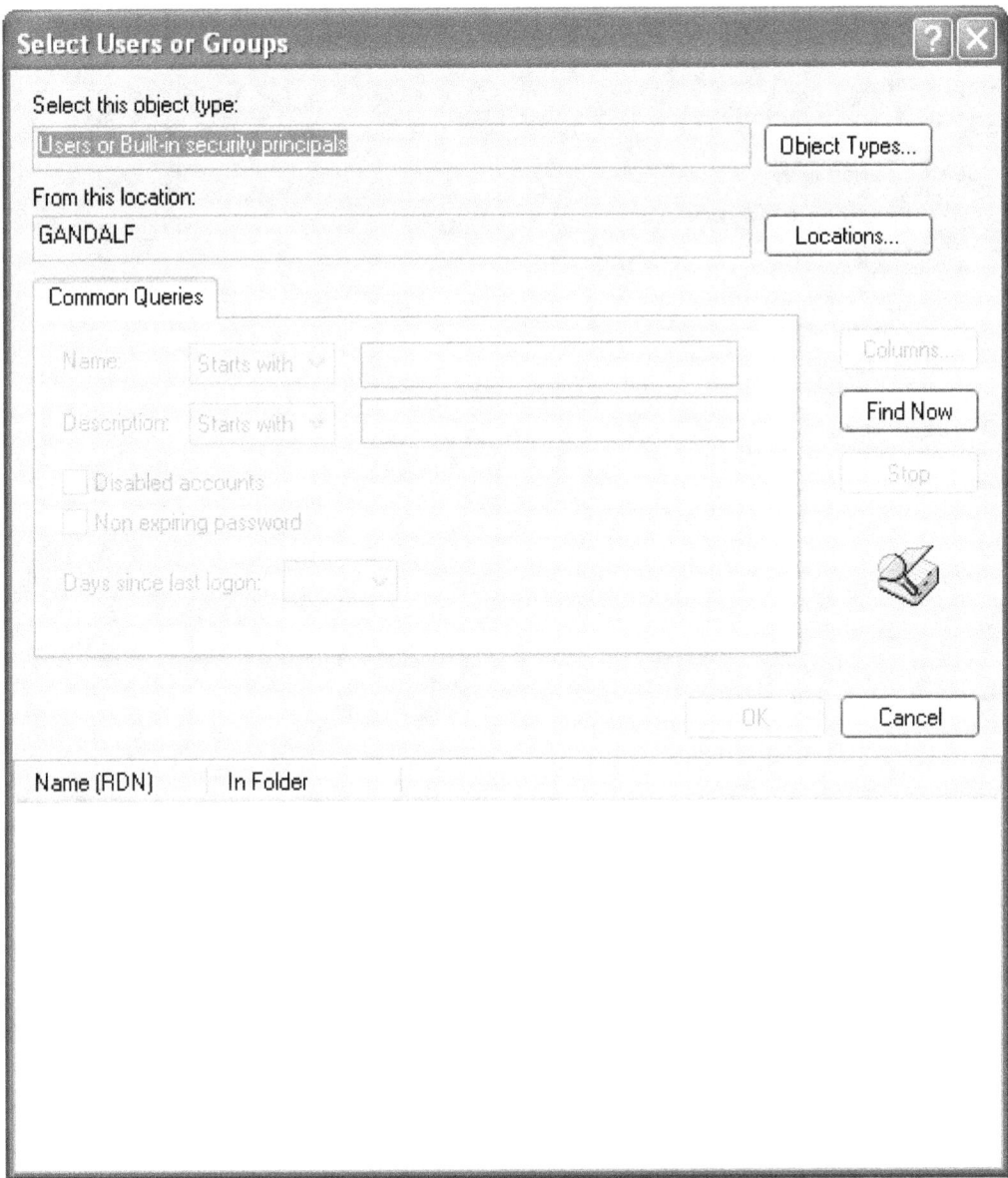

Windows XP - Figure 46

So now you have yet another dialog box. I'm sure you are thinking this is a lot of steps but we are almost finished.

Click on the "Find Now" button.

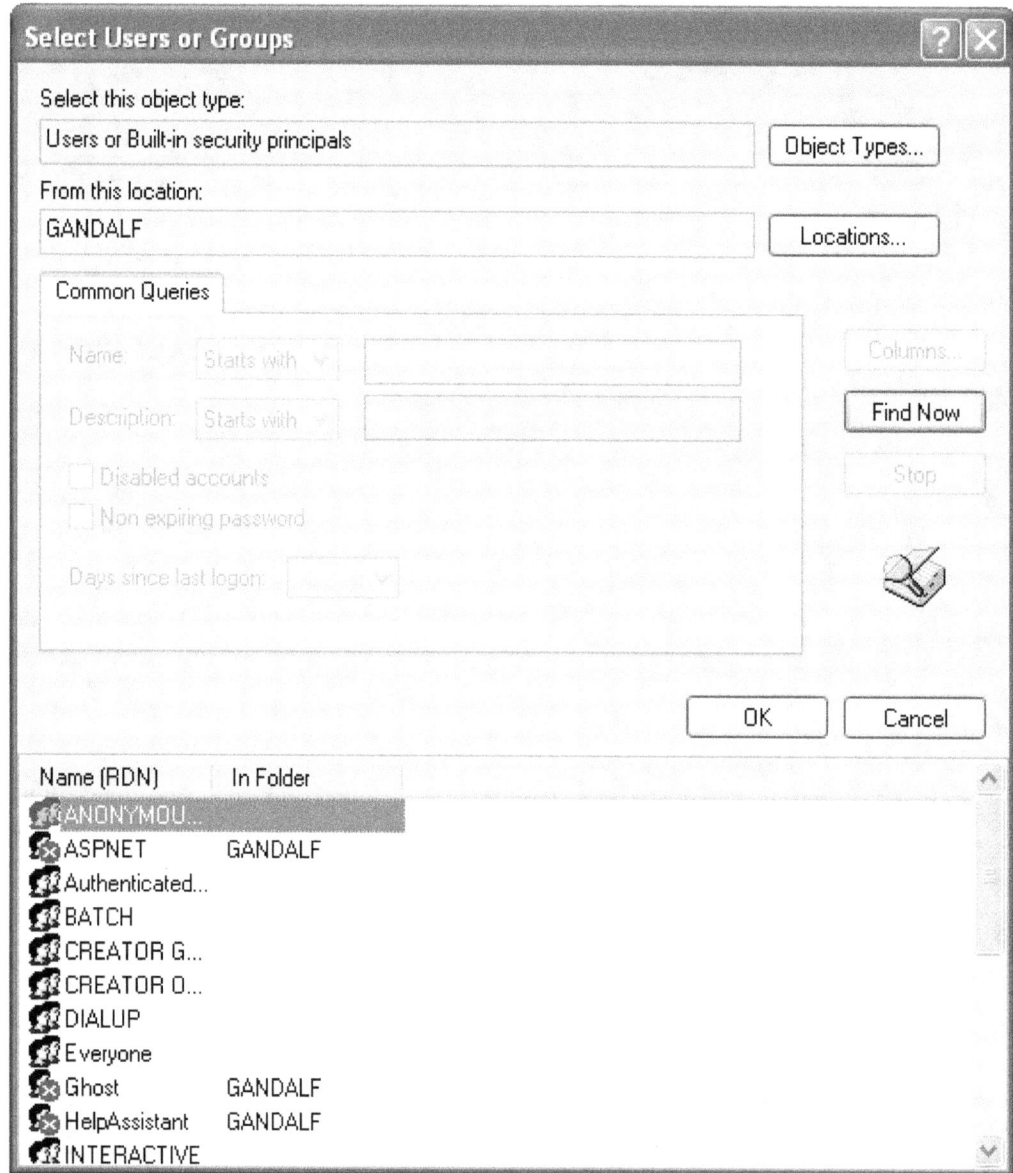

Windows XP - Figure 47

And HEY! No new dialog box! But now you see at the bottom of the window a list of EVERY account on your system. Quite a few of them aren't there? Yeah, that's what I thought too. What you want to do is to use the scroll bar on the right to scroll to the bottom of this list, hold down your shift key and select the last entry.

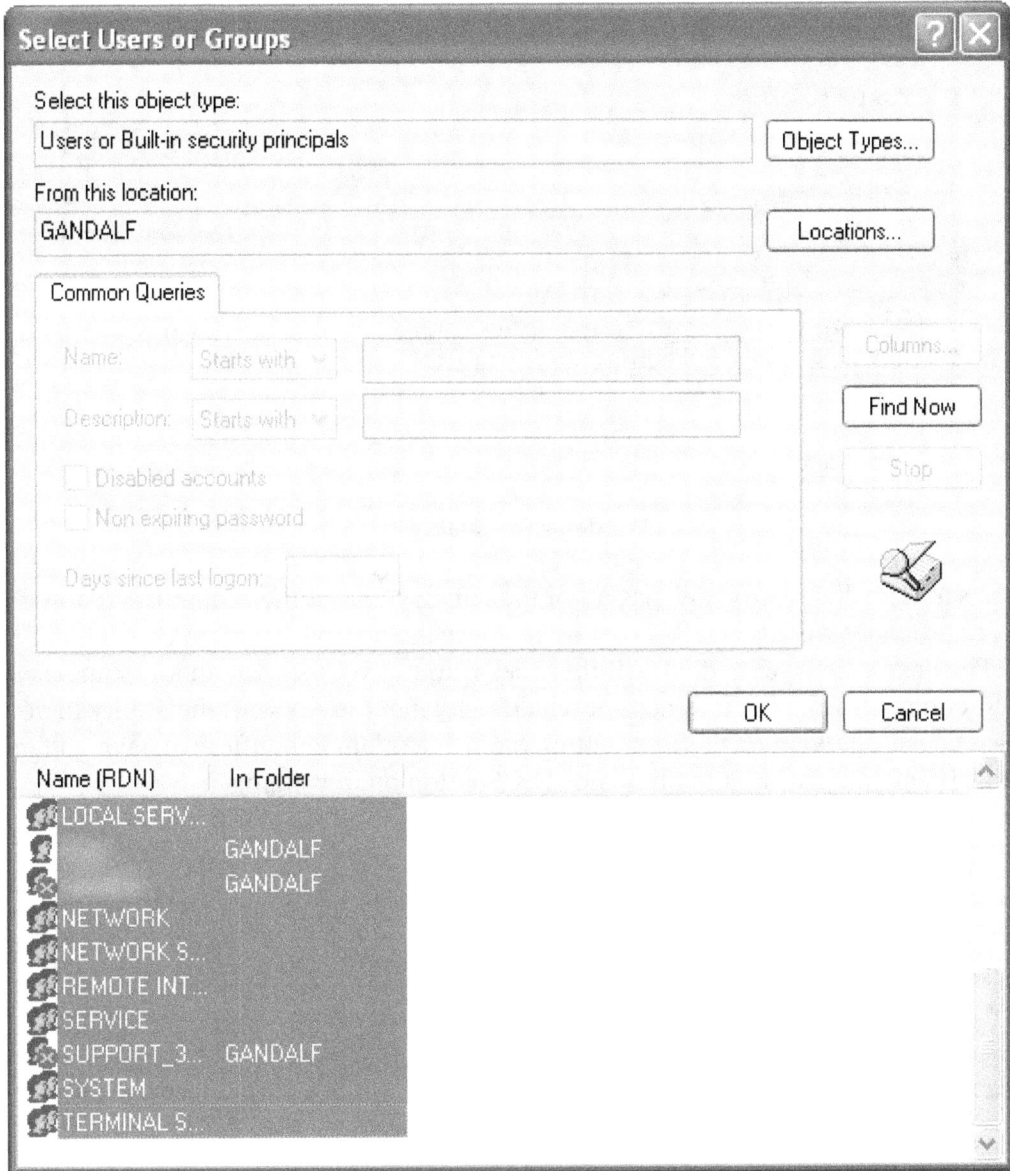

Windows XP - Figure 48

So now you have selected all of the accounts. Click the "OK" button. At this point – we actually haven't done anything yet. It is not until you get to the last dialog box and either click the "Apply" button or the "OK" button that anything happens. When you click on the "OK" button on this dialog box it just loads all of those accounts in to a list.

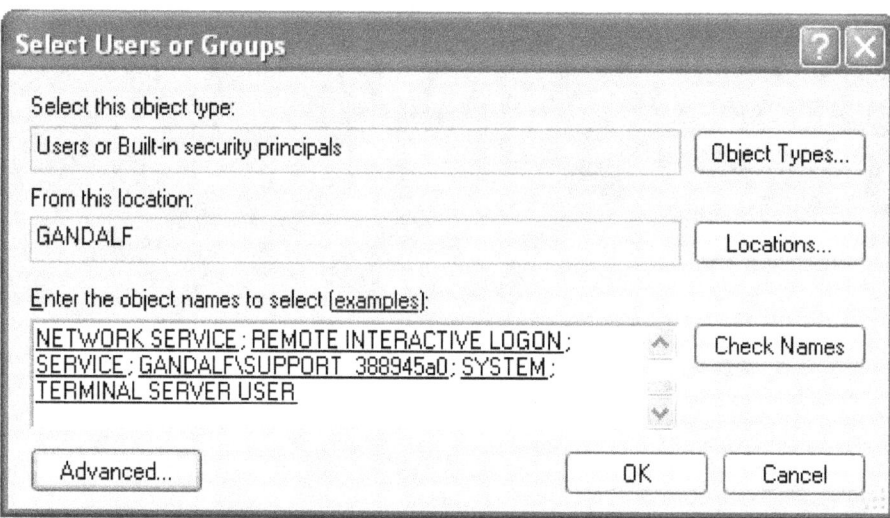

Windows XP - Figure 49

As you can see. The dialog box now has all of the names of all of the accounts. At about this time you are probably wondering "If I do this will it make it so >I< can't even get on to my system?" The answer is – yes and no. All this does is to tell your system that if someone tried to get on your computer from the internet – it would deny them (even you) the ability to do so. But actually – it doesn't prevent YOU from getting on. I'll explain later after we have gotten through this. At this point you just want to click the "OK" button on this dialog.

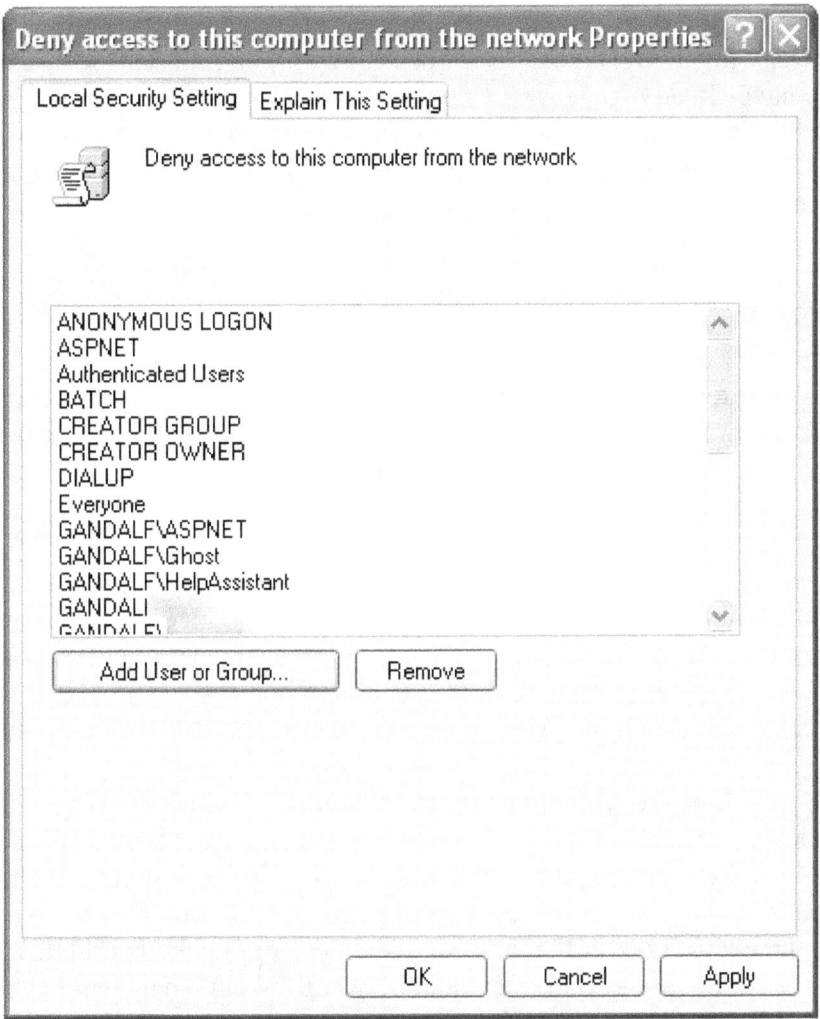
Windows XP - Figure 50

And here we are back at the first dialog. (Notice that I have blurred out my account id. Not that it is all that hard to guess it – but I just did it.) Ok. So the moment of truth has come. Either click the "Apply" button followed by the "OK" button or just click the "OK" button. The scary time is here! But – nothing happened. Did it? You can still run that game you like to play or bring up a word processor or do anything else. Nothing has changed for you – or has it? What has changed is if you got on another computer and tried to log in to this computer – you should no longer be able to do that. But, as I keep saying, I will show you how to get around that problem later on.

For now, after you have clicked on the "OK" button, look down a bit farther on the left column and you will see the "Deny logon through Terminal Services". This is the second half of how we are going to lock up your system to keep hackers out. The first one we just did says no one can get on over the network. The second one says no one can use the terminal program called MSTC (which everyone else calls RDP) to get on to your system. We want to turn this off so a hacker can not get in through that back door. RDP is a really nice program but it can also be used to get onto your system. So you go through the same exact steps to set this up to block hackers as you did for the previous option. When you are through, continue on to the next paragraph.

Ok! So you've made it past the second part of this step. You might have noticed there are other entries like the "Deny logon as a batch job" or the "Deny logon as a service" we don't mess with these because we have already made it so no one can just logon to your system. Since they can't log on at all – we don't have to worry if they are trying to do so as a service or batch job. This is not to mention the fact that some system services need to be able to logon as a batch job or service. So best to leave those alone. Next step – Security Options.

Security Options

The Security Options are found on the far left under the User Rights Assignments tree entry we just worked on. You click the little plus sign to open them up. They are similar to the User Rights Assignments in that they act the same way. In other words you left double click on the right column and that opens a dialog box where you can do something.

Here we only want to do two things. 1)Change the administrator's account name, and 2)Change the Guest account's name. If possible we also want to disable both of these accounts but mainly we want to change the names of these accounts. This is also a gigantic hole in your security with Windows because all systems come with the main administrator's account set to "Administrator" and the guest account set to "Guest". Yes. It is really dumb of them to do that – but they do.

So first left double click on the "Accounts: Rename administrator account" and give it a unique name that has at least one number in it and some special character if it will take a special character. Don't try to be smart about it and don't try to be sly about it. Don't change the nane to aDmiNistrator because that just doesn't do a lot of good. My favorite way to do this is to take a pet's name, pick three letters out of that name, pick a niece or nephew's middle name, add that to what you already have. Put some kind of symbol between the pet's name and your nephew's name OTHER THAN a period or dash. Now pick your favorite radio station and use that at the end of the name. If you want to then use a hint you can say something like "my pet ran over to see my nephew while we listened to the radio". Ok – you haven't given away your pet's name (it could be anyone's pet really) or which nephew/niece you are talking about and you haven't said what radio station you like but at the same time it tells you exactly what you called it. The only thing that doesn't tell you is what symbol you used but if you are smart you'll figure a way out to put that in too.

So after you have changed your administrator's account's name – change the Guest account's name also. Once you have done that, if it is possible (sometimes it is not) change the status of both accounts to being disabled. (This should be the first and second lines.) Now they no longer are the default names and no one can log in to them. You are getting safer all the time! Good job! Now we want to look at the Audit Policy.

Audit Policy

This is found just above the User Rights Assignment tree entry on the left hand side of the dialog box. What we want to do here is to set any/all lines that talk about logging in to your system to monitor all FAILURE attempts. So there should be two of these. "Audit account login events" and "Audit logon events". Why are there two that seem to say the same thing? I don't know. I didn't program Windows. All I know is – they are there. Now, what I did was to turn on all but three of these. I did not turn on "Audit object access", "Audit process tracking", and "Audit system events". When I originally had them on there were just too many events going on. So I scaled back to just the essentials. Once you have set these up to monitor all failures you want to open up the "Account Policies" tree entry.

Account Policies

I did not find the need to set up the Password Policy. Once the hackers are locked out you should not have to worry about your password unless you do something like let a virus take over your system. But then you would have more things to worry about than just a password. So instead, left single click on the "Account Lockout Policy".

In businesses, they give you three tries and then lock you out for thirty minutes to an hour. But this is your home computer. We do want the hacker to be locked out after three tries but we don't want you to have to wait forever to get back in to your system. So left double click on the "Account lockout threshold" and then set it to only three tries. This will pop up another dialog that asks if you want to automatically set the "Account lockout duration" and the "Reset account lockout counter after" entries. Let it go ahead and do those.

Next, left double click on the "Account lockout duration" and set it to five minutes. This might also cause another dialog box to pop up asking if you want to set the "Reset account lockout counter after". If it does ask – tell it - it is ok to do so. If not, then go set the "Reset account lockout counter after" to be five minutes also. Now, a hacker has no idea if your computer is a part of a business or if it is just your personal computer. So the hacker will think you have set it up to lock them out for thirty minutes. This is one of the signs a hacker is attacking your system. When we go and look at the Event Logs you may see someone trying to log in to your system other than you. (I see the SYSTEM account trying to log in to my personal account a lot.) That is a hacker doing that.

So we have now come to the end of working with the Group Policy Editor. You can now close this dialog box. The next step is to go to the Event Viewer Logs and let me tell you about that.

STEP #5 : THE EVENT VIEWER LOGS

By this time you should be an old hat at getting to the Control Panel and then the Administrative Tools. Do so and then left double click on the Event Viewer icon.

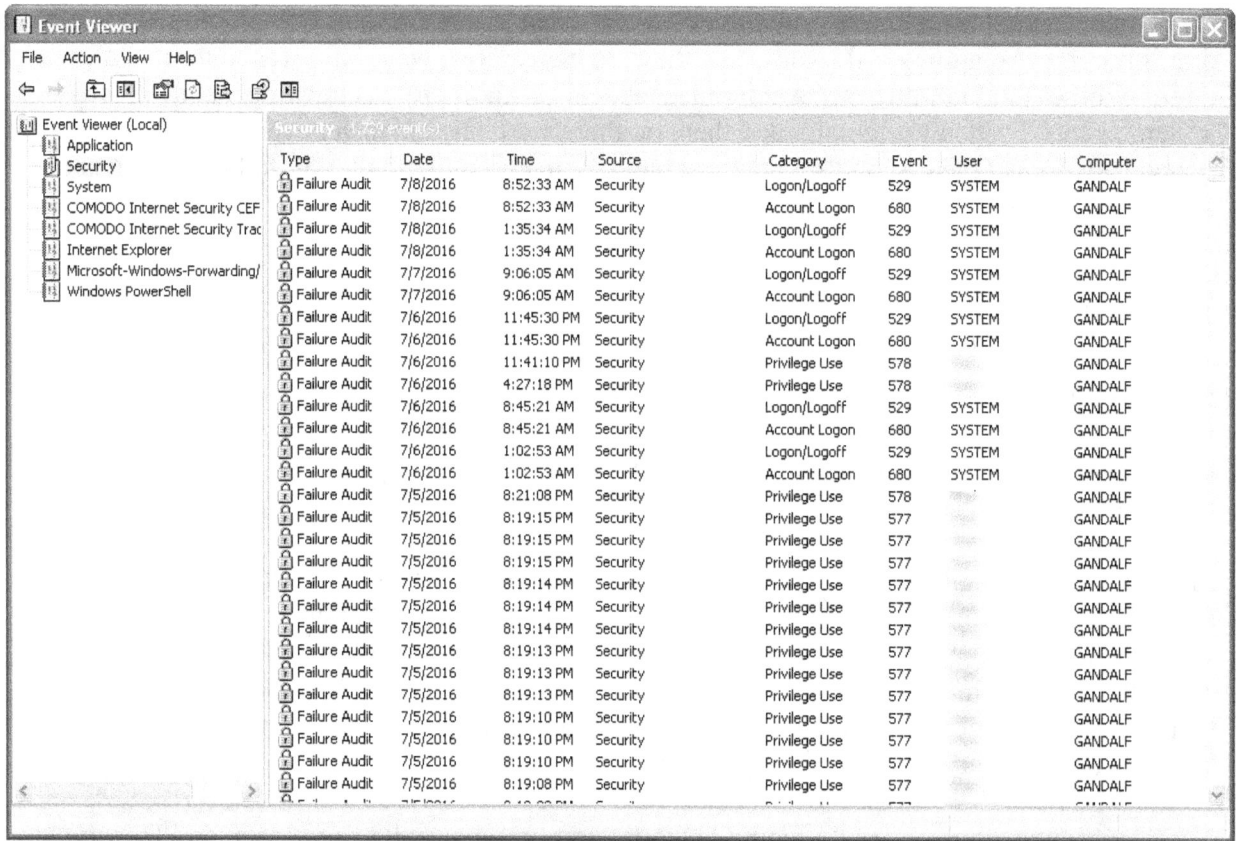

Windows XP - Figure 51

Here I have selected the "Security" option on the left. As you can see, there is a list of "Failure Audit"'s running down the left side. But what I want to draw your attention to is the ones that say "Account Logon" and "Logon/Logoff" which have the "SYSTEM" User trying to log in. Say what? Why is the SYSTEM account trying to log on to my system? It isn't. That is a hacker trying to break in to my system.

If you left double click on one of the lines you will get something like this:

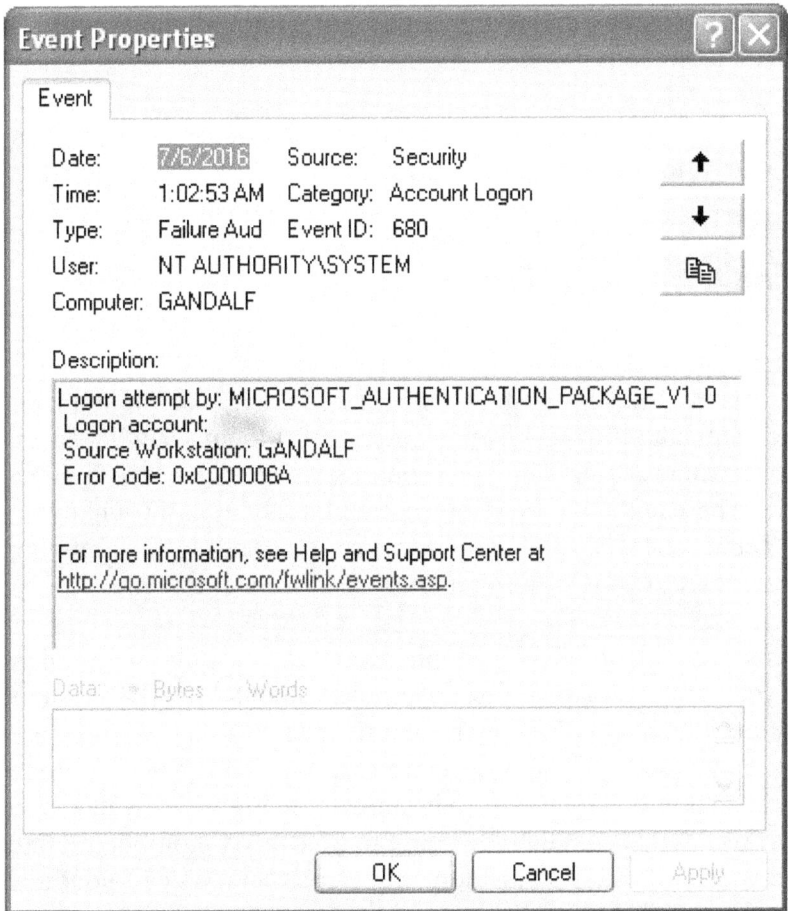

Windows XP - Figure 52

Notice the blurred out area? That is my account someone is trying to log in to. On the next line up from this one it tells me that SYSTEM was trying to log in to my computer via the internet. These options can be found as "Logon Type"'s and if you go to

http://www.windowsecurity.com/articles-tutorials/misc_network_security/Logon-Types.html

That webpage will tell you all about the various types of logons. Some are good (like type '2' is 'interactive' which is another way of saying you are typing from the keyboard) others are not so good (like type '3' which is from the network). You can get lost trying to figure out where each and every login comes from. But basically you can categorize everything in to two separate areas: 1)It is being done ON your computer, or 2)It is being done from a different computer. All of the #1 things are good. If you didn't authorize someone to get on to your computer over the internet then all of the #2 things are bad. So here we again meet the "Batch" and "Service" logon types (both are good), while such things as #8 (Network Cleartext) are not so good. The people at the website given above do a very decent job of telling you which are which.

Ok. Now you are going "But I don't see anything." That's because most hackers are active at night after 1:00am until around 5:00am. This is in your local time. So if you live in California it would be later to me living in Texas. Usually though, you have to give it a few days in order to actually catch someone trying to get in to your system.

One last thing. After you have made all of these changes it is always a good idea to reboot your system once. This will knock anyone who is already on your system off and it will also make it so they can't get back on to your system.

Are we through yet? No. I just wanted to get this major part out of the way. Now we will go through some other steps to help protect your system.

STEP #6 : REMOTE DESKTOP

Just like many other things – Microsoft made it so anyone can use the Remote Desktop Program (or RDP for short) to log in to your system. Once they have hooked up via RDP they can send a Control-Alt-Delete command to your system which can let them see what account is logged on. Once a hacker knows what account name to use all they have to do is to figure out your account's password. There are even programs that will let them know what your password is or to reset it to some default value. That is why it was so important to first get your system set up to not allow anyone to log in to your system remotely. But we are not done yet.

Remote Desktop is something only techy people need. Anyone at home usually doesn't need to have this. Even if you get some remote person to help you out with your system – they do not need Remote Desktop. There are other, more secure programs that could be used which we will talk about later. For now – let's get rid of Remote Desktop. If Remote Desktop is turned on then you have two ways to get to it. The first is to bring up a dialog where you can see your disk drives. Under Windows XP this is done by going to Start->My Computer. Under later OS's there is a folder on your task bar. You just left single click on it and a folder dialog pops up. Then you click on "This PC" in the path area and the screen will change to show all of your disk drives, CD drives, DVD drives, and other thing. You would then right single click on your "C:" drive and select "Properties" from the pop-up menu. Then you look for the "Remote" tab and select it. Uncheck any/all check boxes so nothing is selected. Click "OK" and you are through there.

Next, select Start->Control Panel yet again. Look for the System icon and left double click it to bring up the System Properties dialog box.

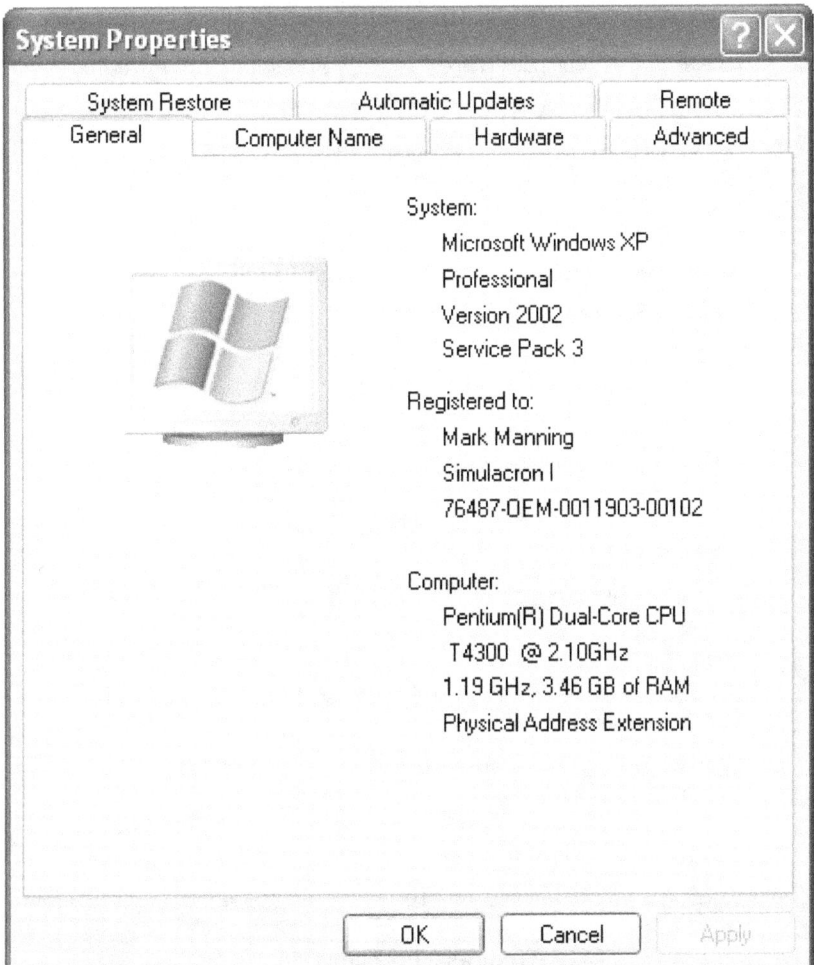
Windows XP - Figure 53

See the "Remote" tab on the top-left? Left single click it.

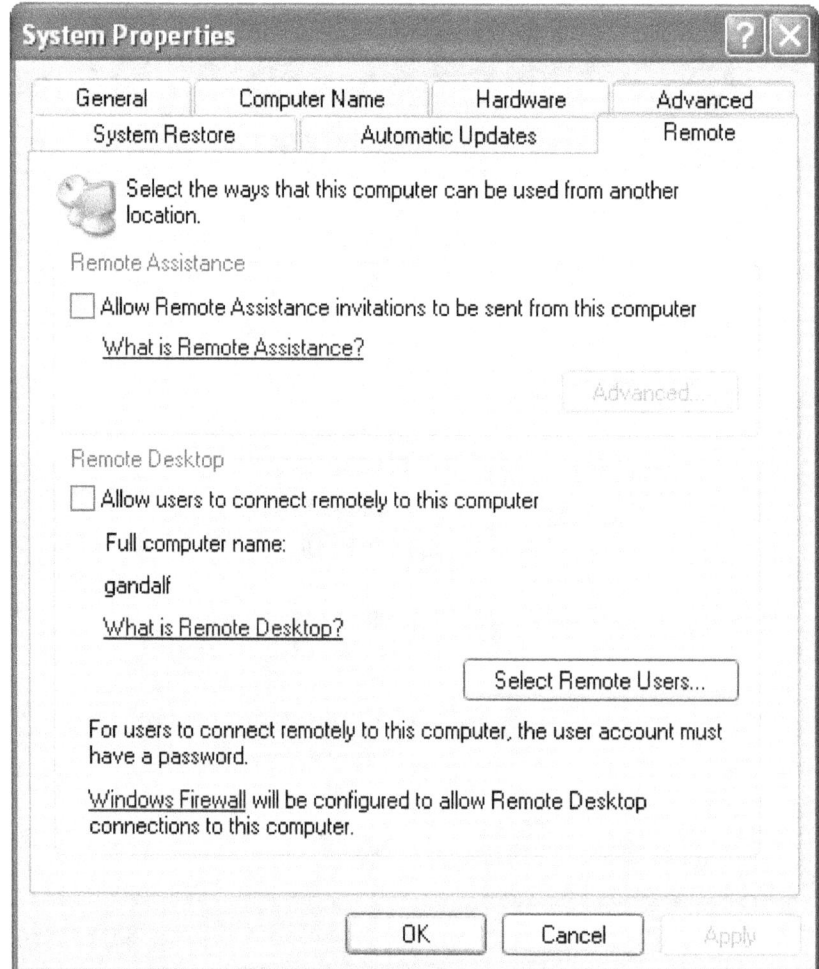

Windows XP - Figure 54

Now, I have already unchecked everything but yours should still be checked. Uncheck both the top and the bottom checkboxes.

But wait! Before you uncheck them, left single click on the "Select Remote Users" button.

Windows XP - Figure 55

Make sure you do not have anyone in the list above. If there is someone's account there you probably want to remove them (if it isn't you or someone you set up already). Once you have removed everyone click on the "OK" button and close this dialog box. Then unselect both the top and bottom buttons. This will make it so no one can RDP to your system and it will also remove the capability of someone using the Remote Assistant methods to get on to your system.

But wait again! There is an "advanced" button next to the Remote Assistance checkbox. Shouldn't we look at that?" Why – yes we should. So before you uncheck that box left single click on the "Advanced" button.

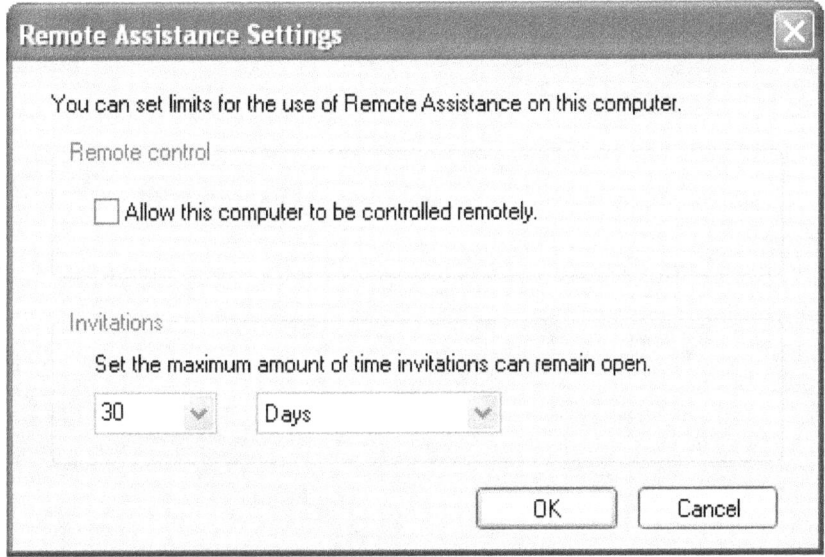

Windows XP - Figure 56

Note that there actually IS something here we should uncheck. The "Allow this computer to be controlled remotely". You really do not want that to happen. So uncheck that checkbox and then click the "OK" button.

So NOW uncheck the button on the Remote tab area and then left single click the "Apply" button at the bottom as well as the "OK" button. Now you won't have any more worries about someone trying to remotely login to your system.

Let me take a moment out here to say : IF SOME NUT JOB CALLS YOU UP SAYING THEY ARE FROM MICROSOFT AND YOUR SYSTEM HAS A VIRUS – Don't believe them. They are hackers just trying to dupe people into letting them on to their computer. Be smart – tell them you work for the FBI and your boss would like to speak to them. If they stay on the line just set the phone down for a few minutes or just hang up on them. Don't fall for their malarkey.

So let's see. What else is there to tell you? We have turned off Remote Desktop…ah! How to get in to your system even though we've put up all of these blockades.

STEP #7 : LOG IN REMOTELY TO YOUR SYSTEM

Ok. So now we have set up your system so NO ONE can log in – right? Right. Unless we want them to be able to log in. You see, although no one can get IN to your system, you can get OUT of it. Everything that worked before still works now. But now >YOU< have to make it so someone can come in to your system. How to do this? There are two main programs that will let you do this. The first is a VNC program. What is a VNC program? A Virtually Networked Computer or VNC for short is a way to set up your computer so you can log in to it remotely. My favorite is TightVNC. You can download it from their website

http://www.tightvnc.com/

You will want the latest version and when you install it BE SURE TO DO THE FULL INSTALL. This is because that will install both the viewer as well as the server. The next thing to do is to right single click on the V at the bottom-right of your screen (or if you hide your icons it might be in your hidden icon area.

Windows XP - Figure 57

It should ask you for the password you gave it when you were setting it up. Once you have the dialog up:

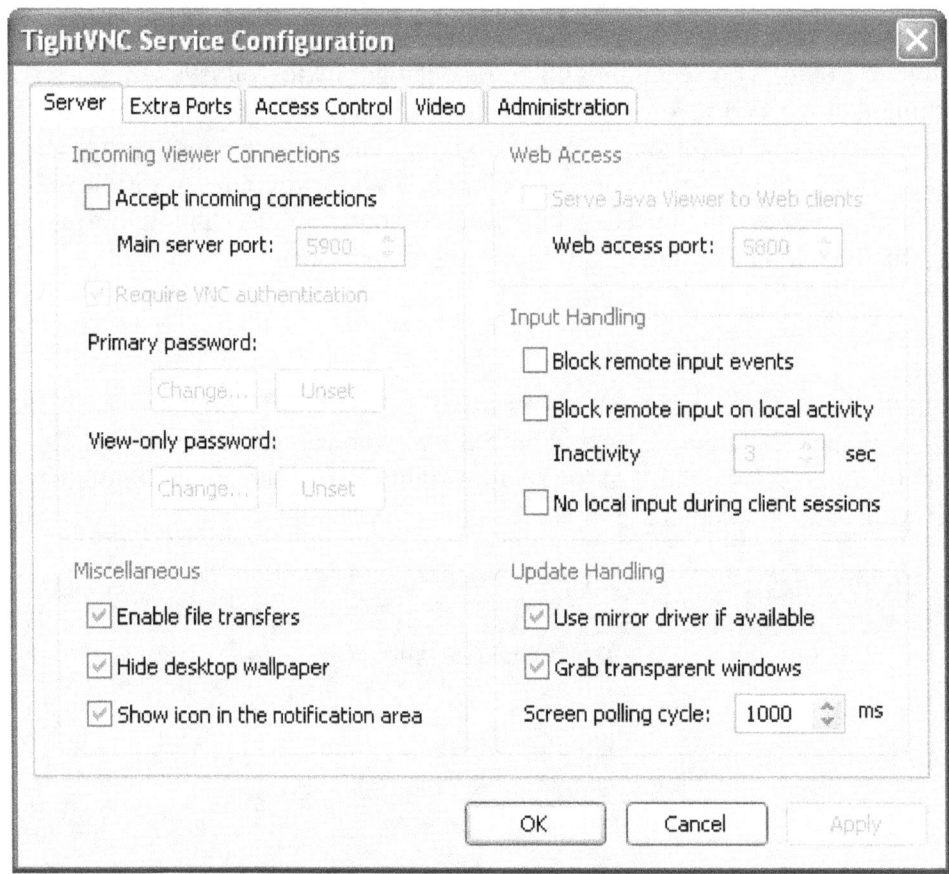

Windows XP - Figure 58

You want to make sure you have a Primary password so no one can just get on for free. (Kind of defeats the purpose of locking up your system if you don't do that!) And you also want to put a password on the "View-only" aspect of TightVNC. After all, you don't want anyone to watch what you are doing do you?

Notice though, that I also have the "Accept incoming connections" UNCHECKED. Only if I check this box can someone get on to my system with TightVNC. Or can they? Look on the right hand side of the dialog box. See that "Web Access" option? Uncheck it too. No need to allow someone to type in something like http://192.168.1.375 and suddenly get onto your system via the internet.

Next, go to the "Access Control" tab.

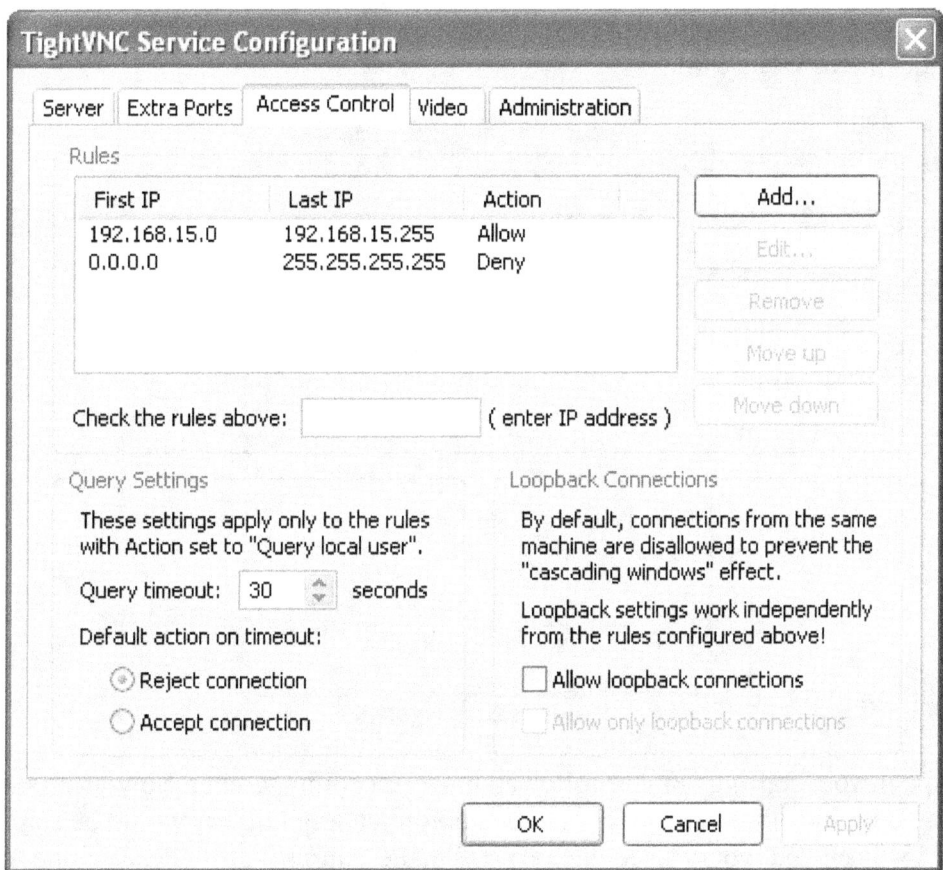

Windows XP - Figure 59

See how I have this set up? All you do is to left single click on the "Add" button and it will come up with a small dialog of its own.

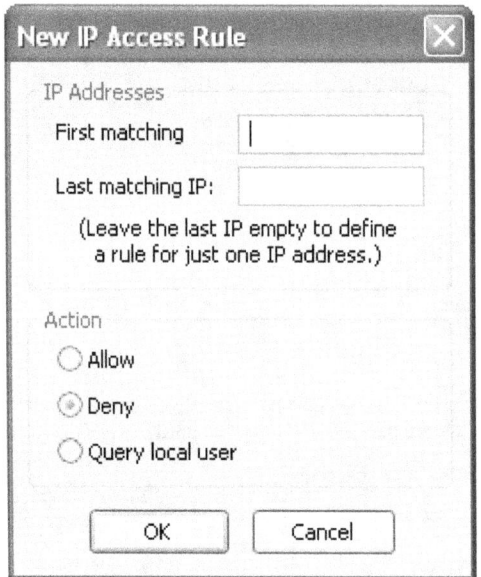
Windows XP - Figure 60

Here you type in your starting number followed by your ending number. So your first set of numbers would be something like 192.168.1.0 and your ending number would be something like 192.168.1.255. Then you would select the "Allow" radio button. This means anyone who's TCP/IP address was in that range can get onto your system WHEN you select the "Accept Incoming Connections" button on the first tab. The idea here is that you set it so only people on your private network can get on.

So the next thing you do is you want to say that no one else can get on to your system. So you do another "Add" but this time you start with 0.0.0.0 and you end with 255.255.255.255 along with leaving the "New IP Access Rule" set to "Deny". So what you are saying is – no one anywhere else can get on to this system. So now your system is fairly hard to get on to – but wait –there's more!

Click on the last tab. The "Administration" tab. What you will get is this:

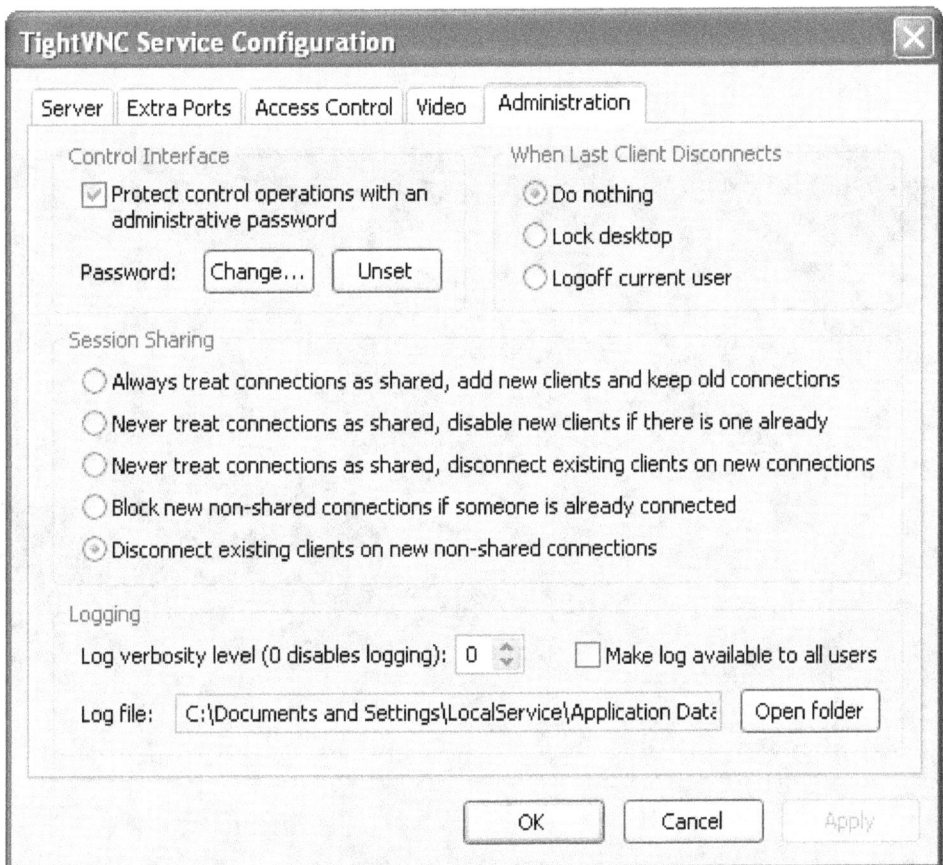
Windows XP - Figure 61

Ah ha! Aren't you glad you looked? Here is yet another place to put in a password. Set it to something strong but remember – you can only use eight characters. Notice that I have the "Do nothing" selected for when the person logs off but also note that it doesn't say just one person logs off but that when the LAST person logs off.

Now, for me, I have the last option in the "Session Sharing" section selected. In this way I would know immediately that someone else had tried to log on to my system. However, you may prefer the one above it which blocks anyone else from using your system if you are already connected to it. This might be better for you. Notice too that you can have TightVNC log who is doing what on your system. A very useful feature.

When through you just close the dialog by left single clicking on the "OK" button and TightVNC is now ready to accept incoming connections (if you have activated that). In order to actually USE TightVNC though you will need to go find the folder it was installed in to (usually C:/PROGRAM FILES/TIGHTVNC) and find the CLIENT program. (The SERVER is what is sitting there waiting for you to connect.) You just left double click on the TightVNC Client program and it will ask you for the TCP/IP address of the computer you want to connect to.

But wait! How do we know what our TCP/IP address is? That is really simple. Remember us talking about bringing up a Command Prompt window? Go back to that part and bring it up again. Now just type in:

```
C:>ipconfig/all
```

at the command prompt and it will show you all sorts of information. Like this

Windows XP - Figure 62

What you look for in this (because your system could have a lot of information) – is where it FIRST says "IP Address". If your set-up is a lot like other people's setups, then it will probably be something like mine which reads

```
IP Address. . . . . . . . . . . . : 192.168.1.115
```

So my IP address is what I would type in to the TightVNC dialog box.

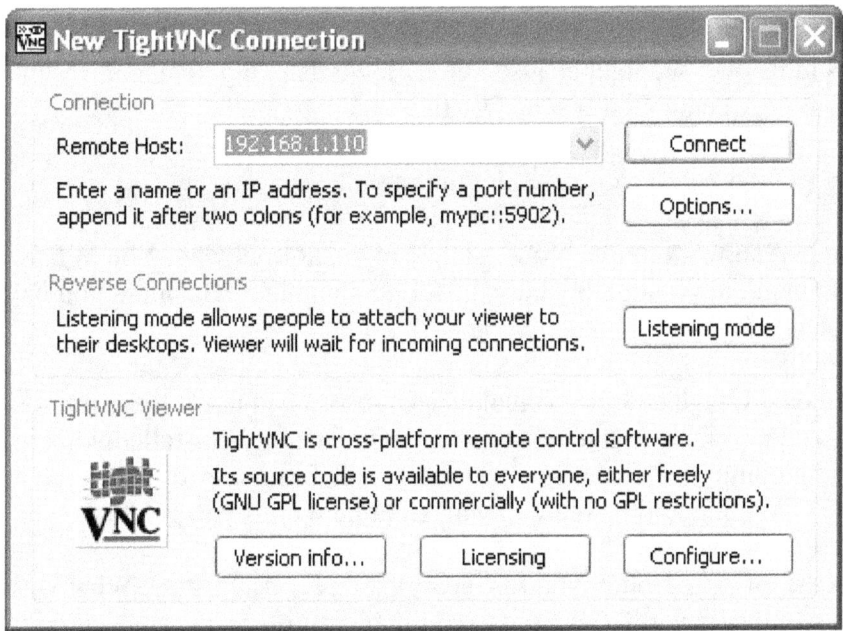

Windows XP - Figure 63

In this case though, I was typing in the address for the computer at 192.168.1.110. Then you just click on the "Connect" button and a connection is made and you are then logged in to that computer.

So see – that's one way to log in to a remote computer even if it is locked up.

STEP #8 : TEAMVIEWER

I am putting this in its own section because TeamViewer is really nice and it is even more secure than TightVNC. To get TeamViewer – just go to

https://www.teamviewer.com/en/download/windows/

and download the Windows version. You install it in the normal way. You WILL be asked if you are going to use TeamViewer for a business or for personal use. Business you pay for the program – personal is free.

So select the Personal Usage and the normal usage (so you can use it to go out to one of your other computers or let someone on to your computer). Once it is installed you are now ready to log in to a different computer. But first – you did install TeamViewer on the OTHER computer – didn't you? No? Well, go do it. We will wait right here until you get back.

Ready? Ok. On the other computer you run TeamViewer and....what? What was that? What's the use of having TeamViewer if you have to run it every time you want to use it? Well, THAT feature is one of the reasons TeamViewer is more secure than TightVNC. Because you have to run it each and every time you want to use it. This means no hacker can break in to your system if TeamViewer hasn't be run yet. So run it and write down the ID number it gives you as well as the password.

Now – every time you run TeamViewer again it will change the ID number and password on you. Again, this is to keep your system secure. Just write down the two numbers and you will be ready to log in to your other computer (or even a friend's computer).

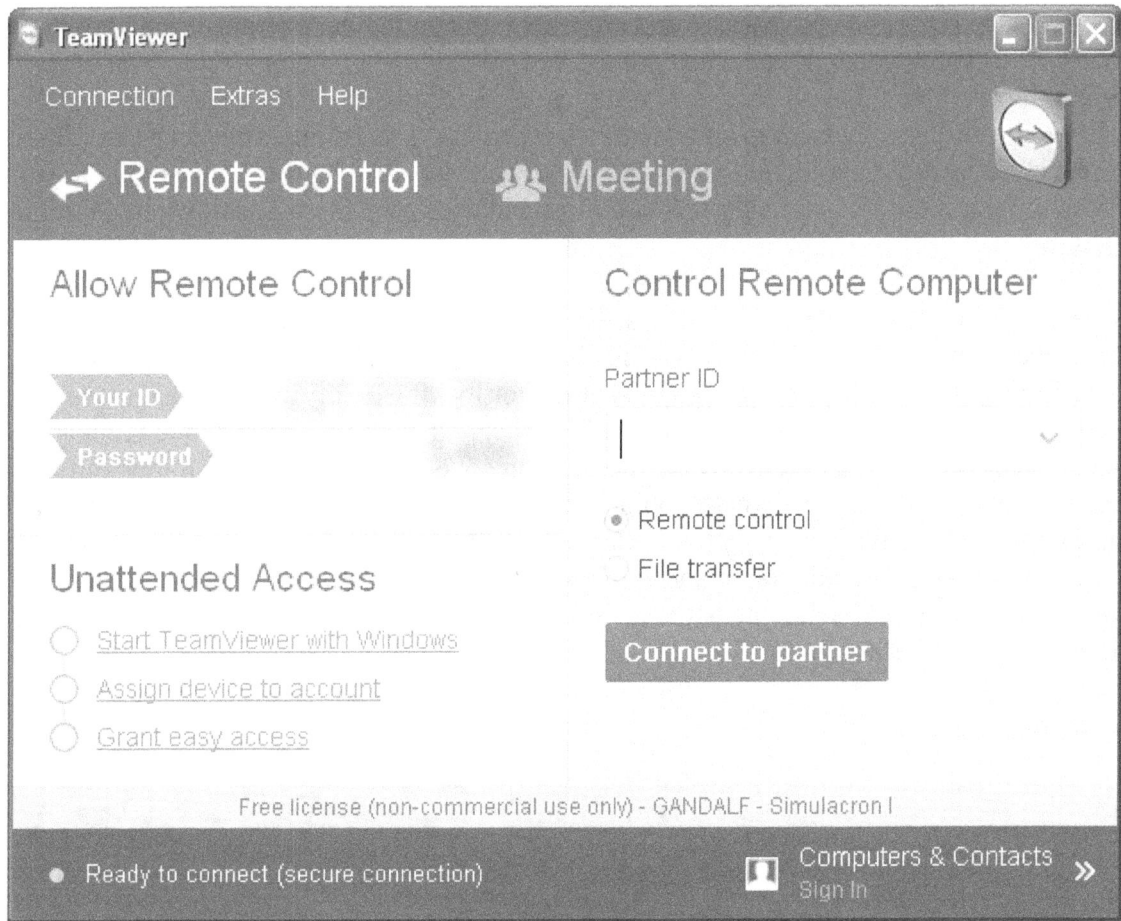

Windows XP - Figure 64

So you can see a blurry 227 as the first three digits. Then there is a space with a few more digits, space, more digits, and then a group of digits for the password. Where it says "Partner ID" you put in the first set of digits from the computer you want to connect to and press return. This will bring up a second dialog that asks for the password. You type in the password and then TeamViewer will connect the two computers.

Ok. So why is this a better route to go than TightVNC? First, TightVNC only uses a maximum of eight characters. TeamViewer uses nine. TightVNC keeps the same password until you change it. TeamViewer gives you a new password each time. Next, TightVNC is on all of the time. So if a hacker does get on he/she can turn on the web access and log off. Since TightVNC doesn't even make the screen flash when you log in with it – you won't even know that a hacker has gotten onto your system.

TeamViewer on the other hand really lets you know that it is there. You get a banner across the top of your screen and a large tab area on the right side of the screen. Now these can be put away – but you always know someone has tried to get on or did get on with TeamViewer. That is a lot better than how TightVNC handles everything. I am hoping that TightVNC takes notice of how TeamViewer works and modifies the program so it has better security in the future.

FINI!

Well – that's it! I hope you have a safe and enjoyable computing experience. Once your system is locked up – I know you will. One last thing. As I said at the beginning of this book – there are programs out there that will track everything your kids do on their computer. It will show you exactly what websites they went to and what they typed in – everything. The bad part of these programs is – hackers can use them to watch you as well. So don't let this happen to you. Don't use those programs unless you really feel you must and then keep the usage down to a mnimum if possible.

Since I have done these things my Windows XP system has sped back up and is running really nicely. But as you saw in my Event logs – the Hacker is still trying to break back in to my system. In fact, the hacker has gotten so mad at me for locking up my systems that they have crashed our router repeatedly. We have AT&T. So I called them up and talked to them about the hacker. They checked and said "Yeah, there is someone logging in to your router and crashing it. When I asked them what I could do about it they said "Nothing". Actually, I am in the first stages of modifying the way the router works. I am going to close the back door AT&T left on the router so they could log in and is the way the hacker is getting on to the router, and then I'm going to make it so no one but us, in our house, can get on to the router. Then it will be goodbye to Mr. Hacker for good.

Mark Manning

Screen shots for Windows Vista

Windows Vista Figures

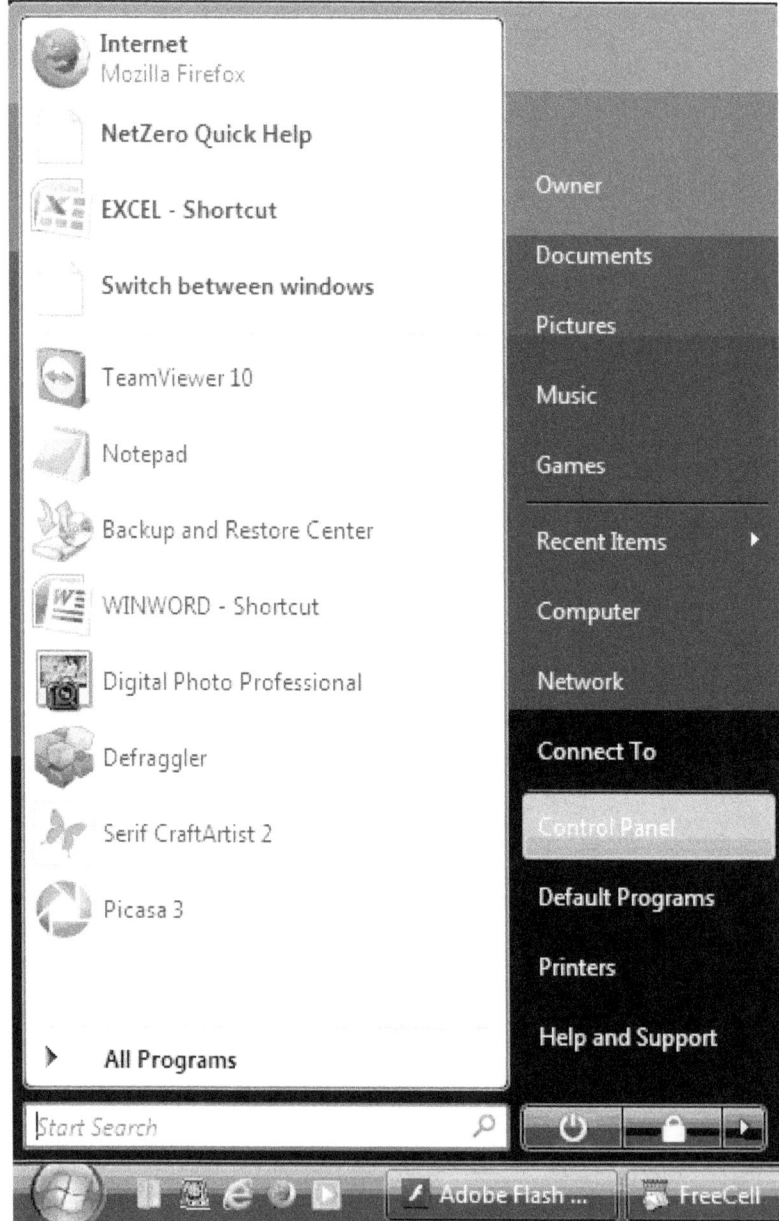

Windows Vista - Figure 1

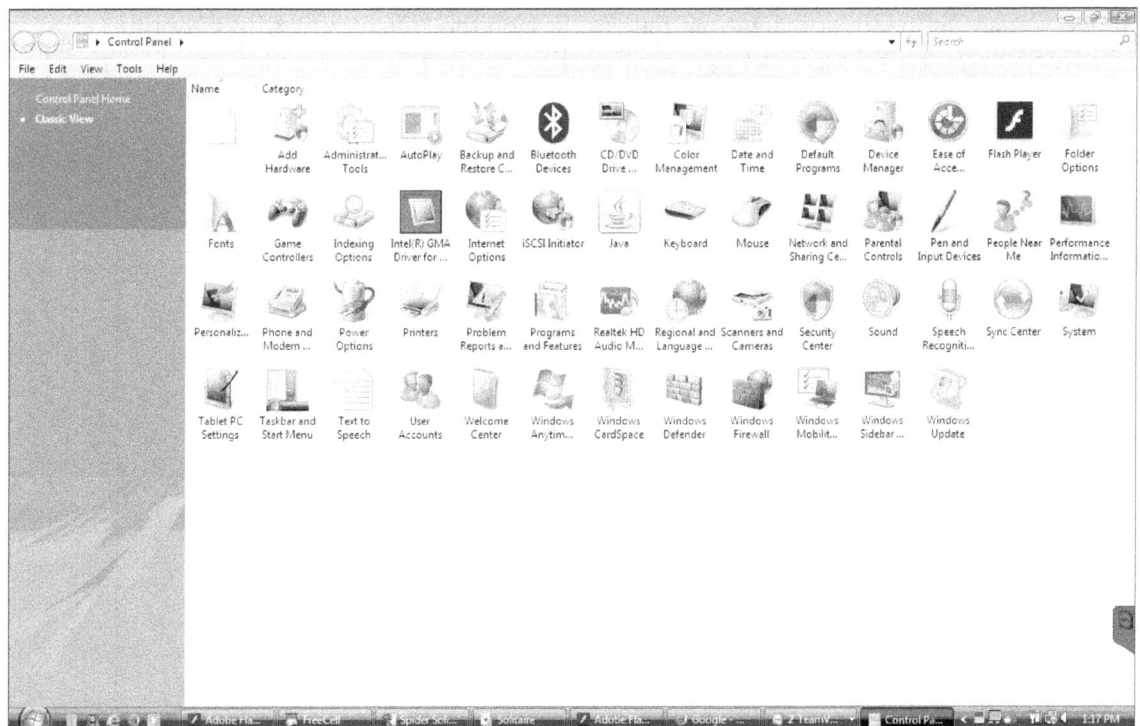
Windows Vista - Figure 2

Under Vista and the newer operating systems, instead of seeing an icon named "Display" – you instead click on the Personalization icon.

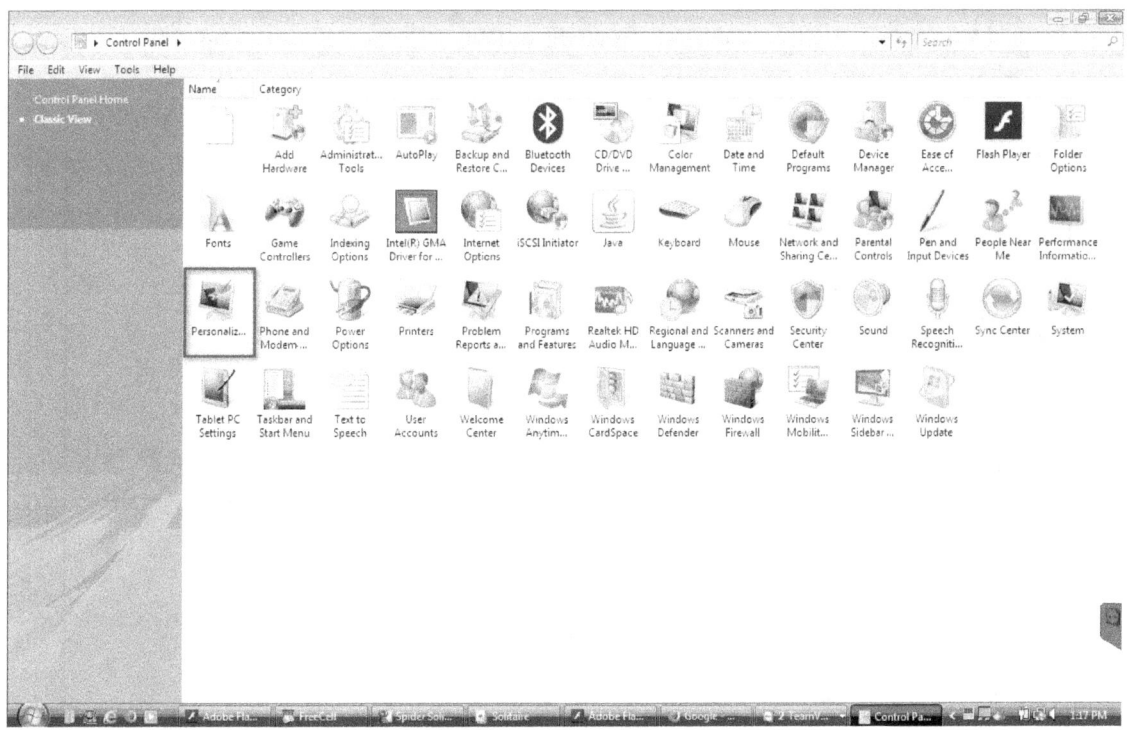
Windows Vista - Figure 3

Once you are in the Personalization dialog, click on the "Display Settings" option.

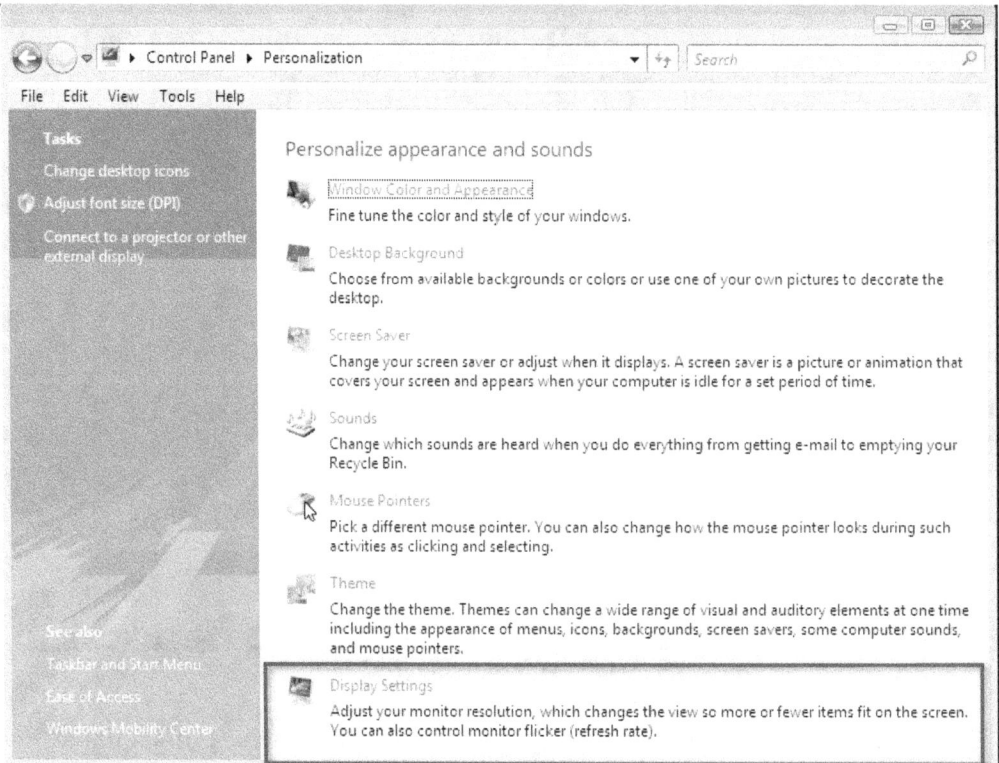

Windows Vista - Figure 4

In our case though, we want to work with the Screen Saver program.

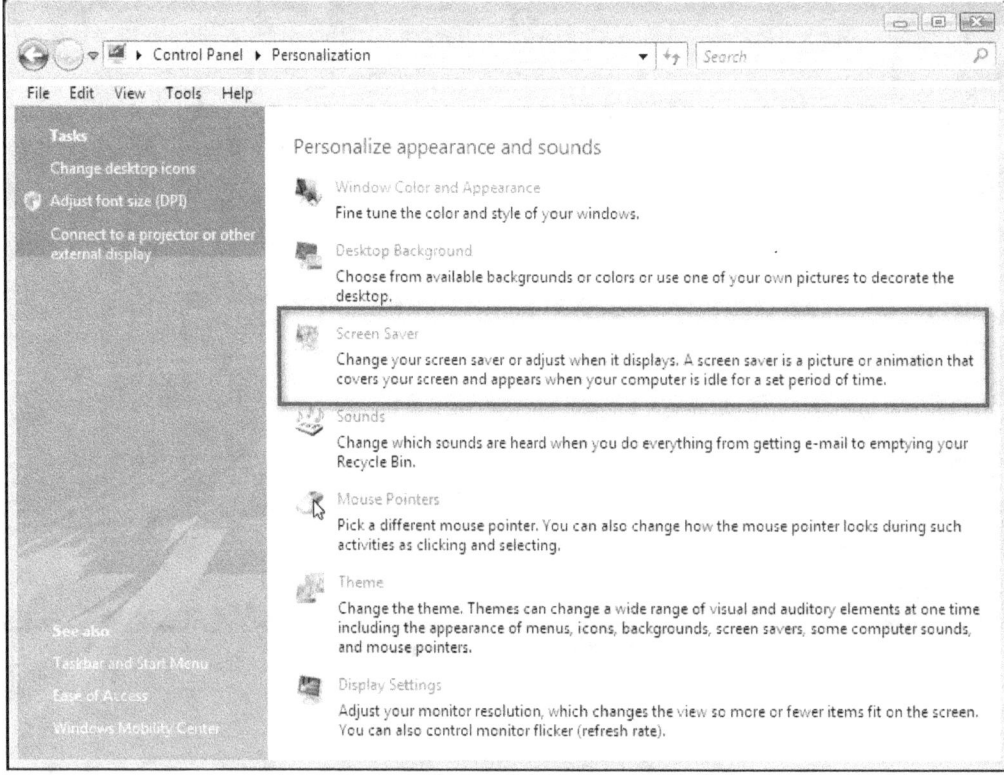

Windows Vista - Figure 5a

And here you have the Screen Saver display which looks almost like the Windows XP Screen Saver dialog.

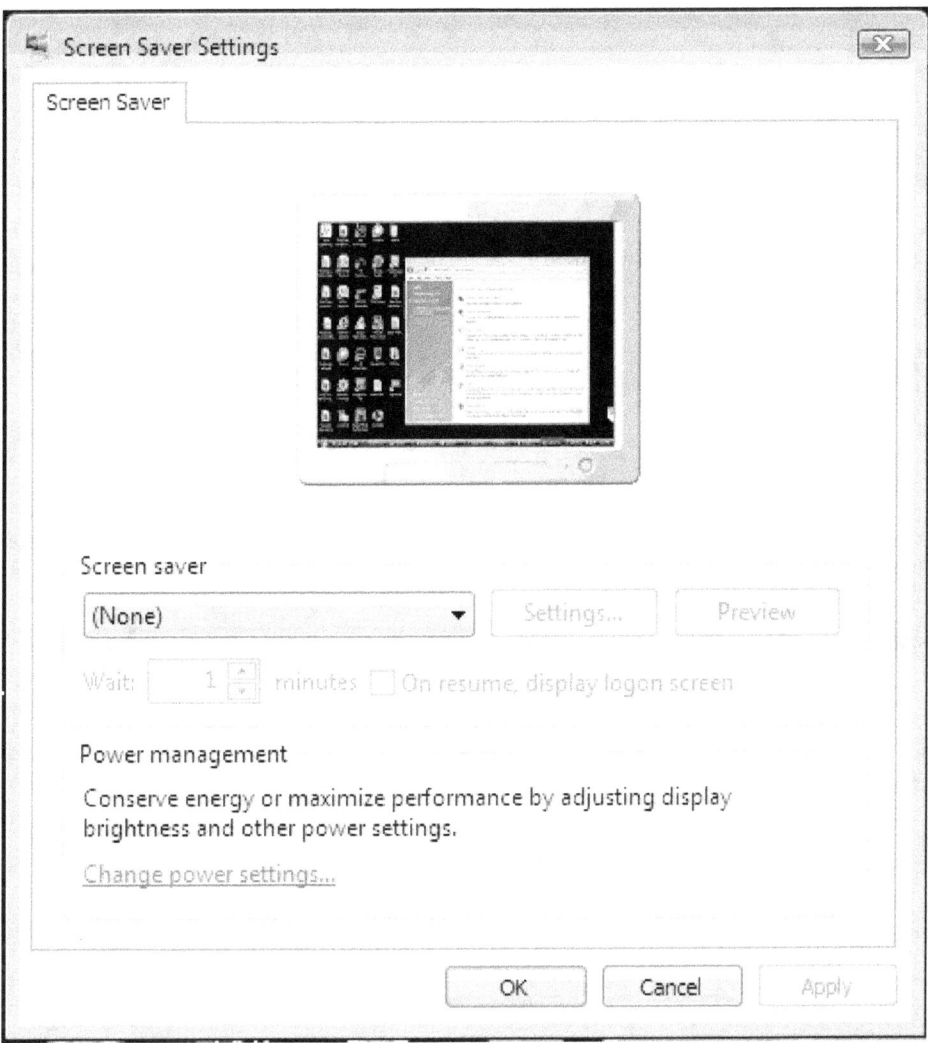

Windows Vista - Figure 5b

Mark Versus Mr. Hacker.doc

In order to get to the Power Options, you have to go back to the Control Panel and select it from there.

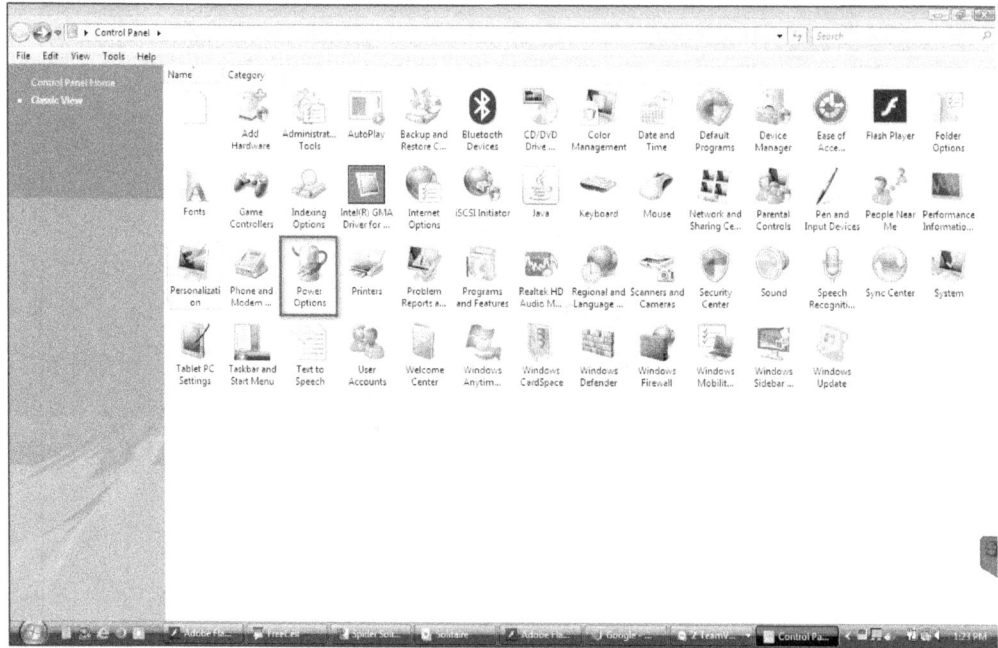

Windows Vista - Figure 6a

Note that under Vista, 7, 8/8.1, and 10 you first have to say
Which Power Plan you want to modify.

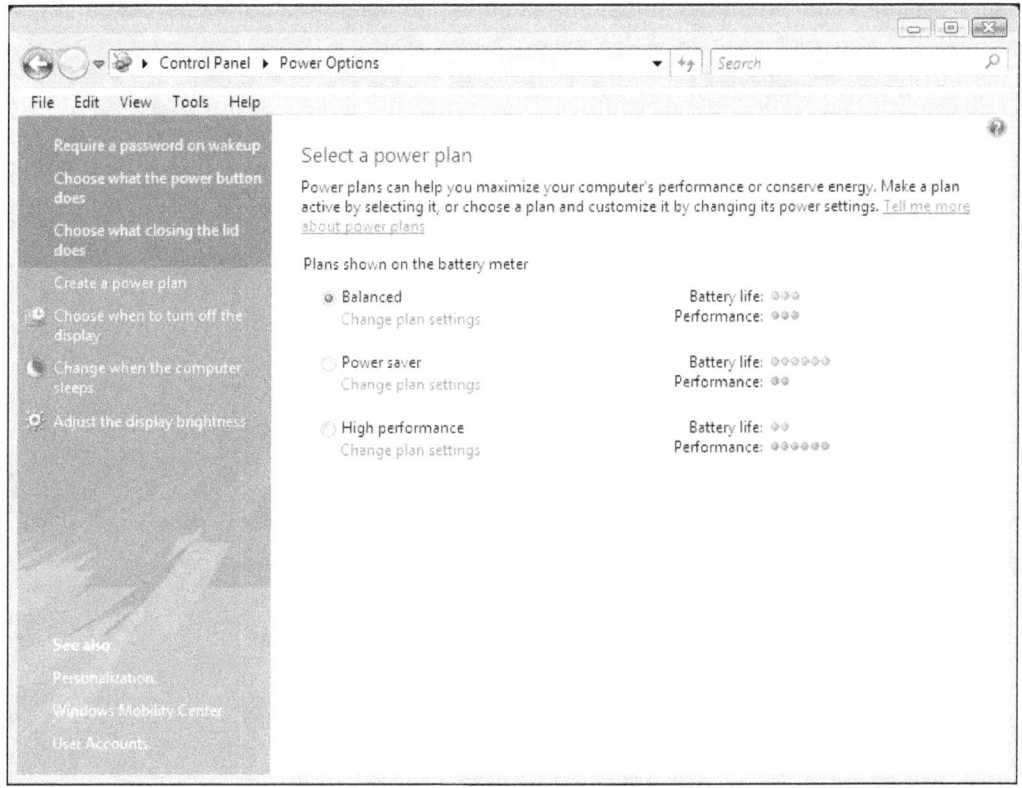

Windows Vista - Figure 6b

Once in the Power Plan area, change your time to turn off your display to be 30 minutes and to never shut down the computer when it is plugged in. Notice the "Change advanced power settings" link. We are going to use that next.

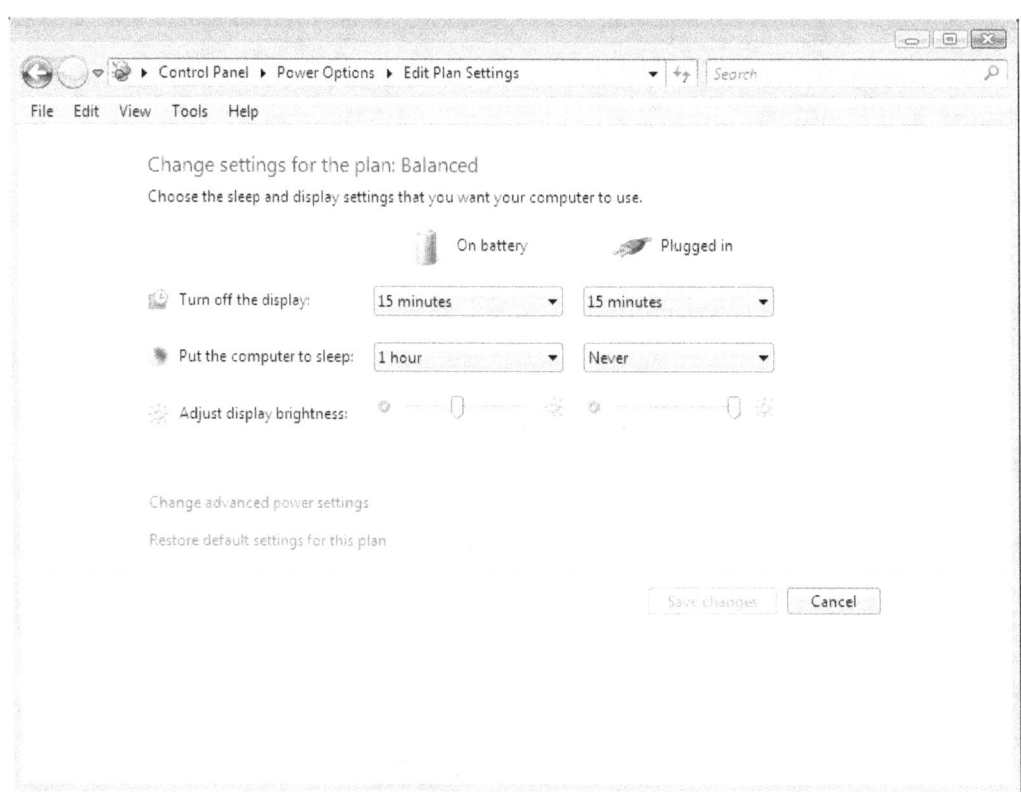

Windows Vista - Figure 6c

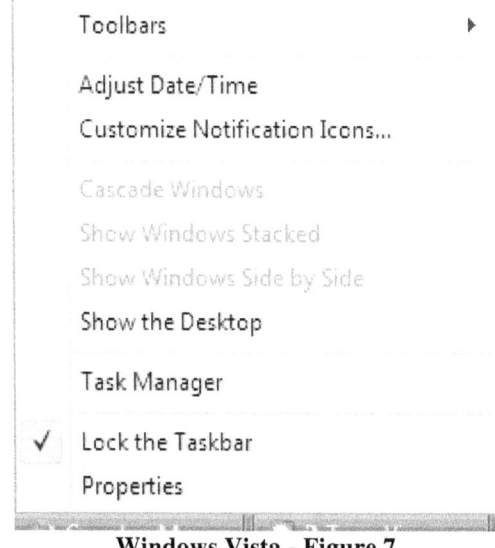

Windows Vista - Figure 7

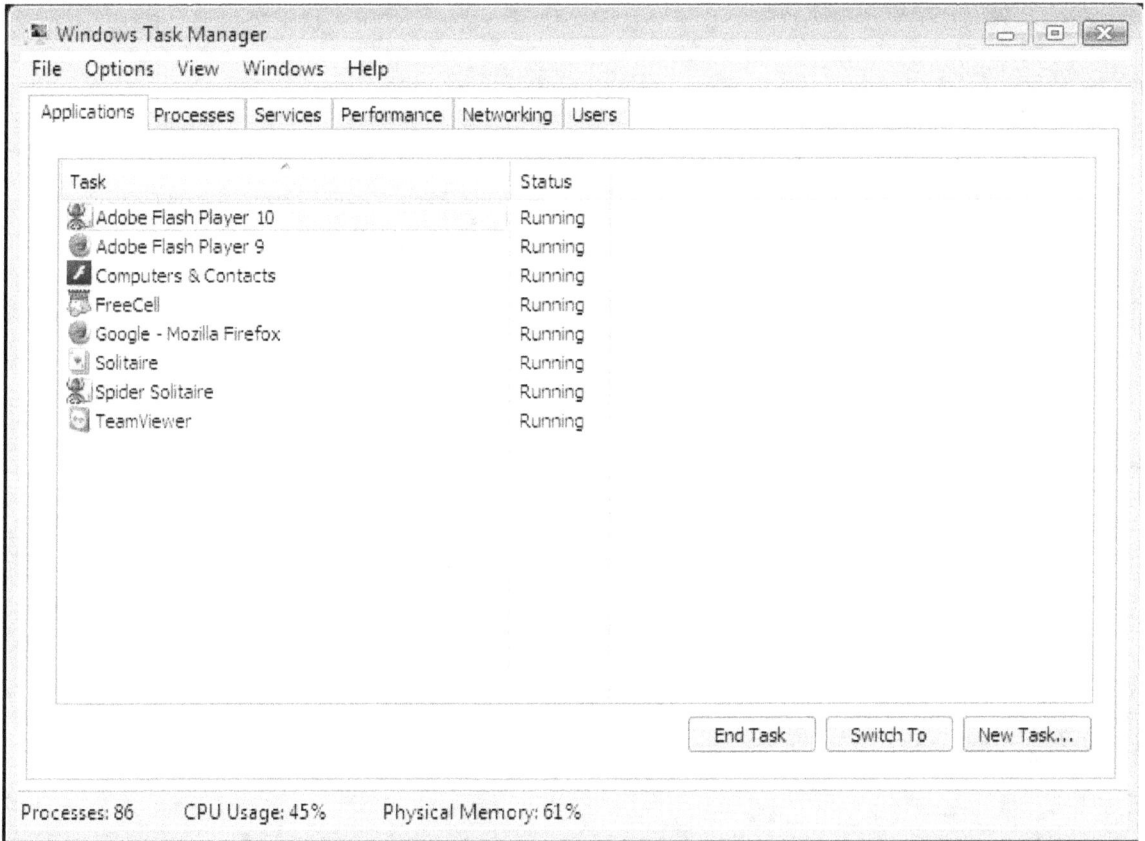
Windows Vista - Figure 8

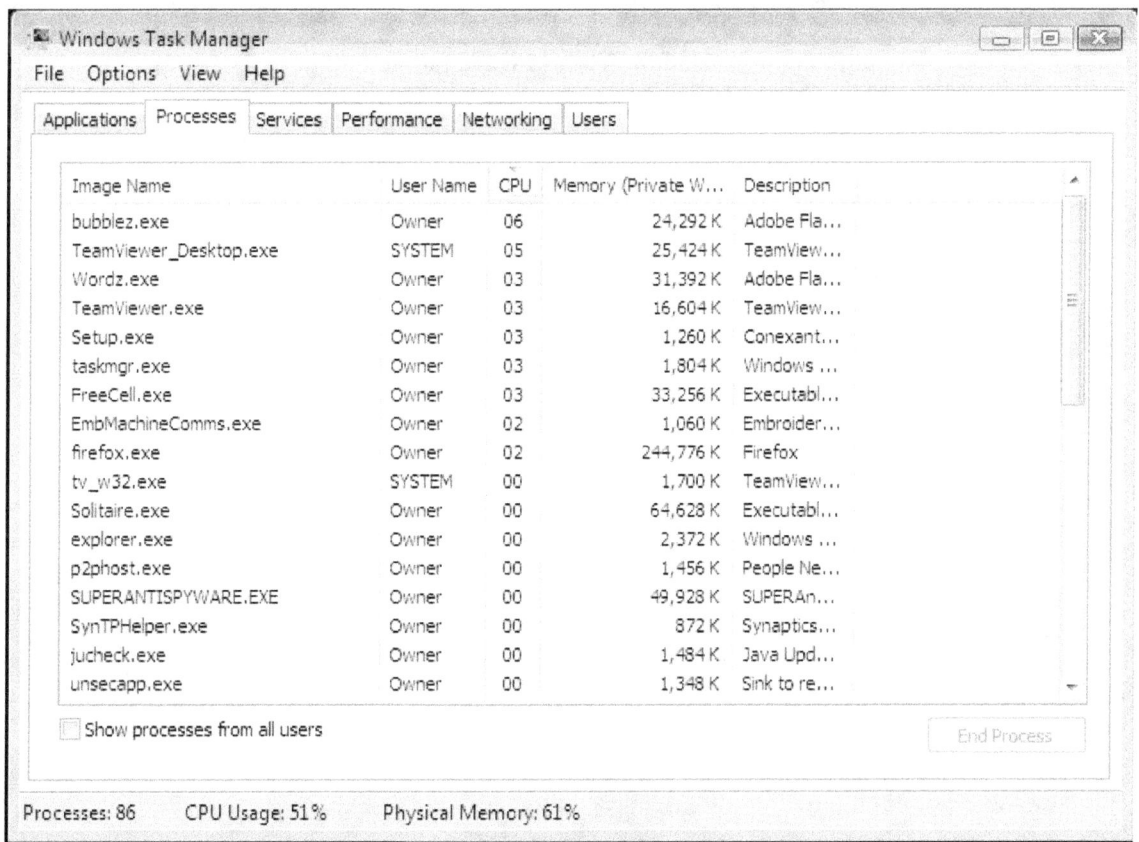
Windows Vista - Figure 9

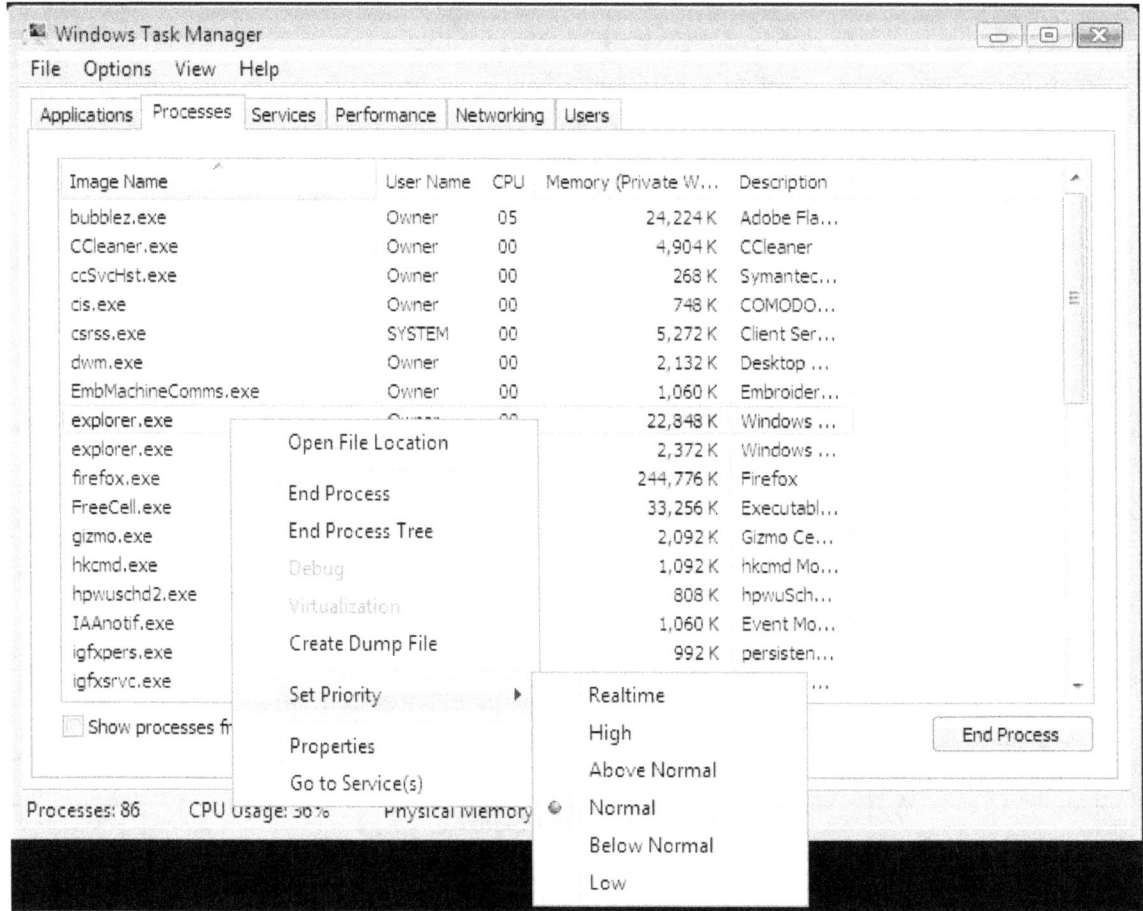

Windows Vista - Figure 10

Mark Versus Mr. Hacker.doc

Since TCPView looks the same on all platforms – here is the Windows XP version.

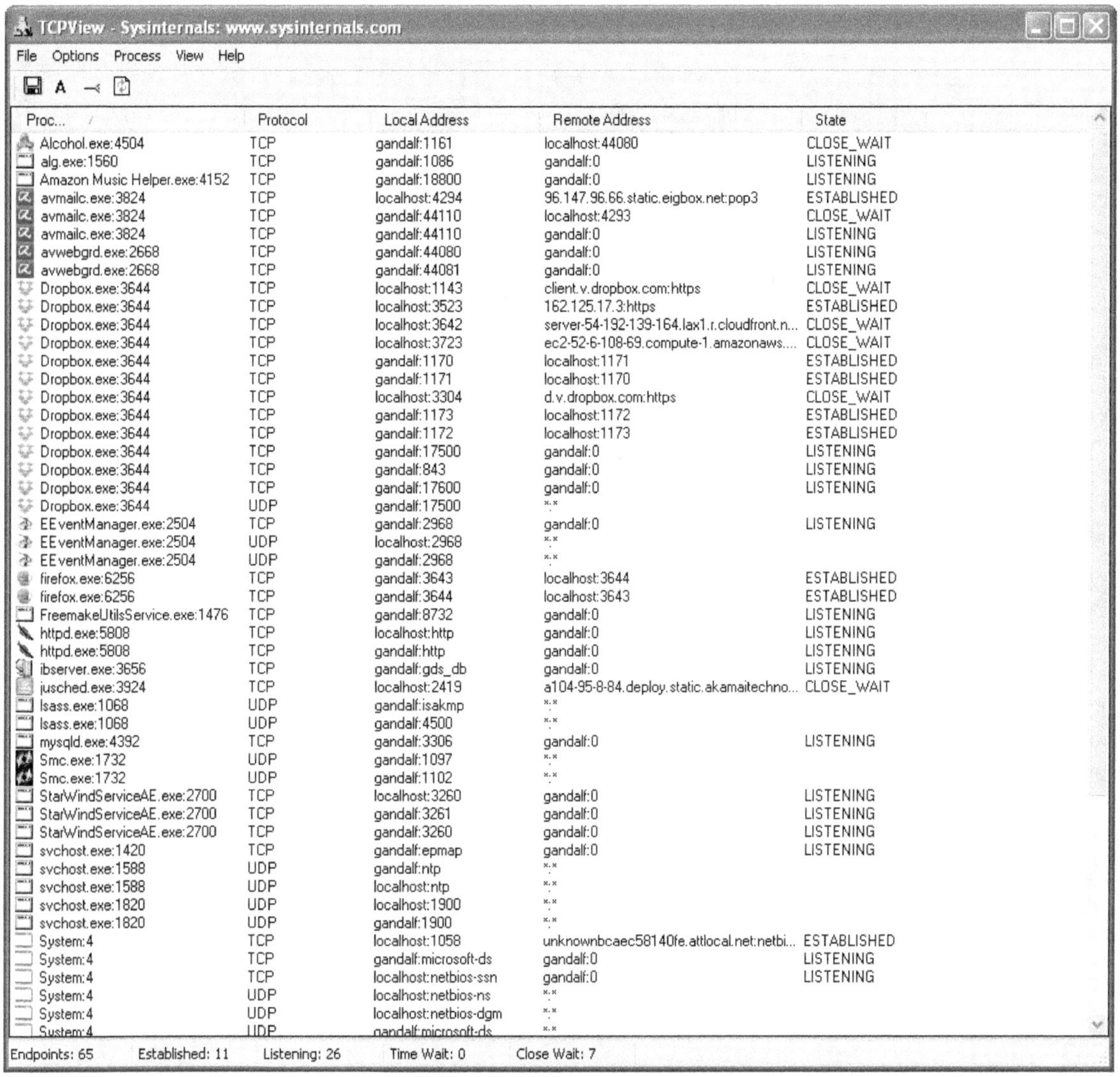

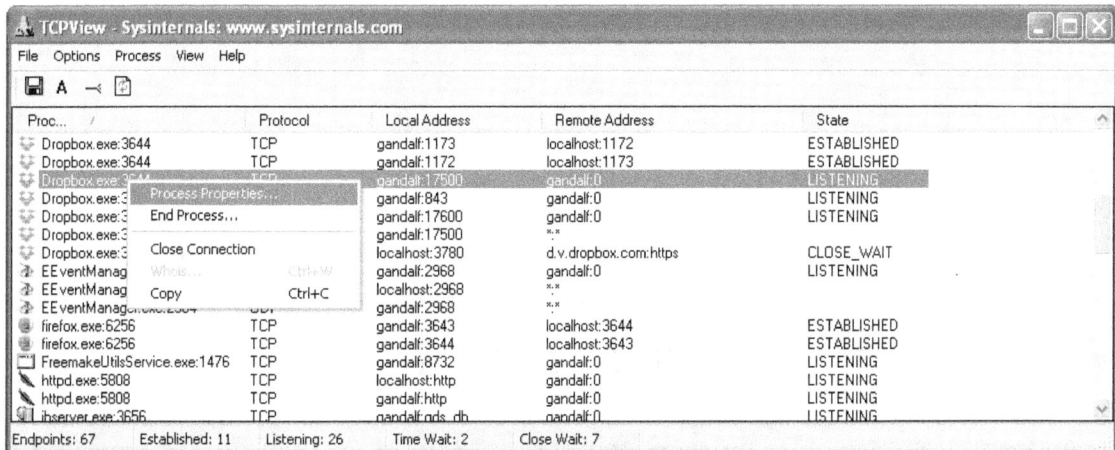

Windows Vista - Figure 11

Windows Vista - Figure 12

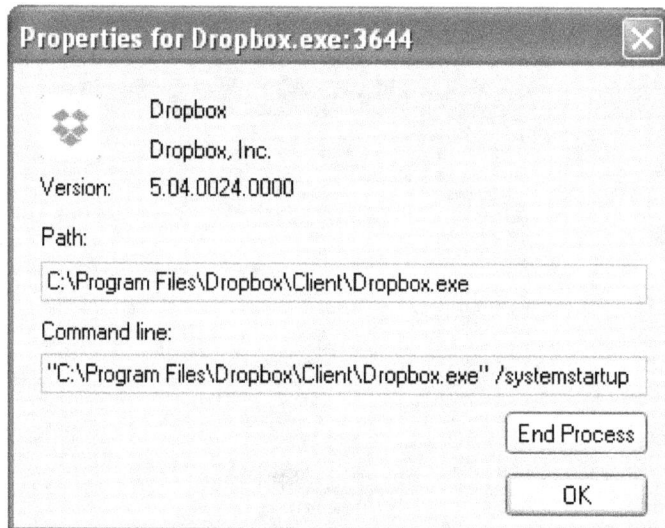

Windows Vista - Figure 13

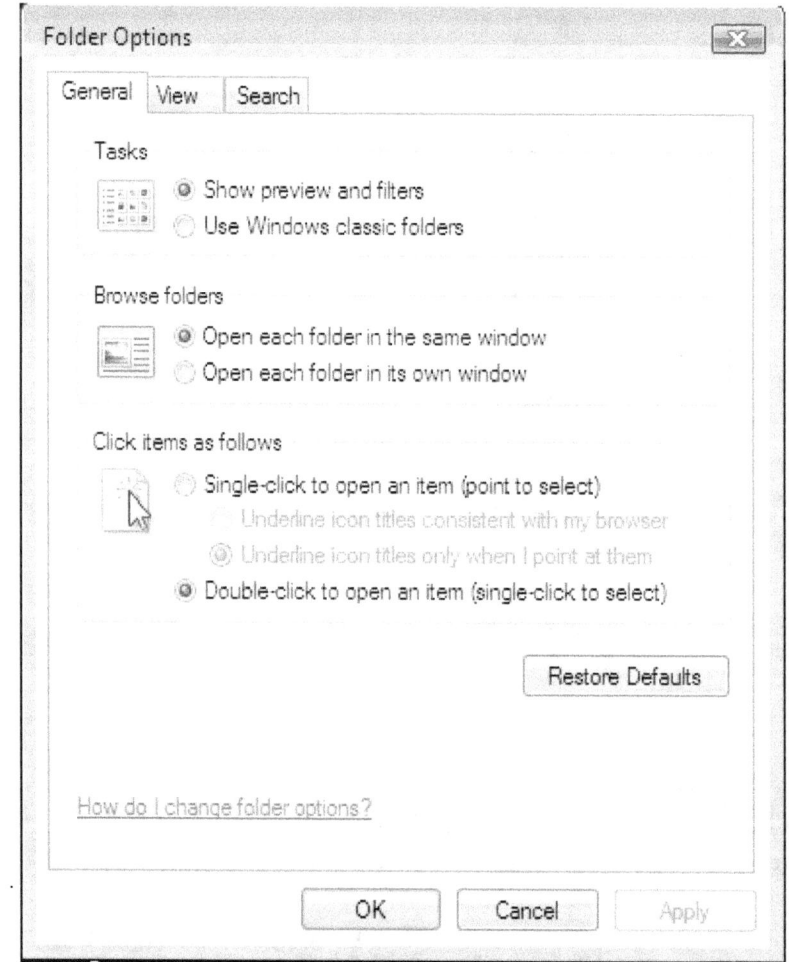

Windows Vista - Figure 14

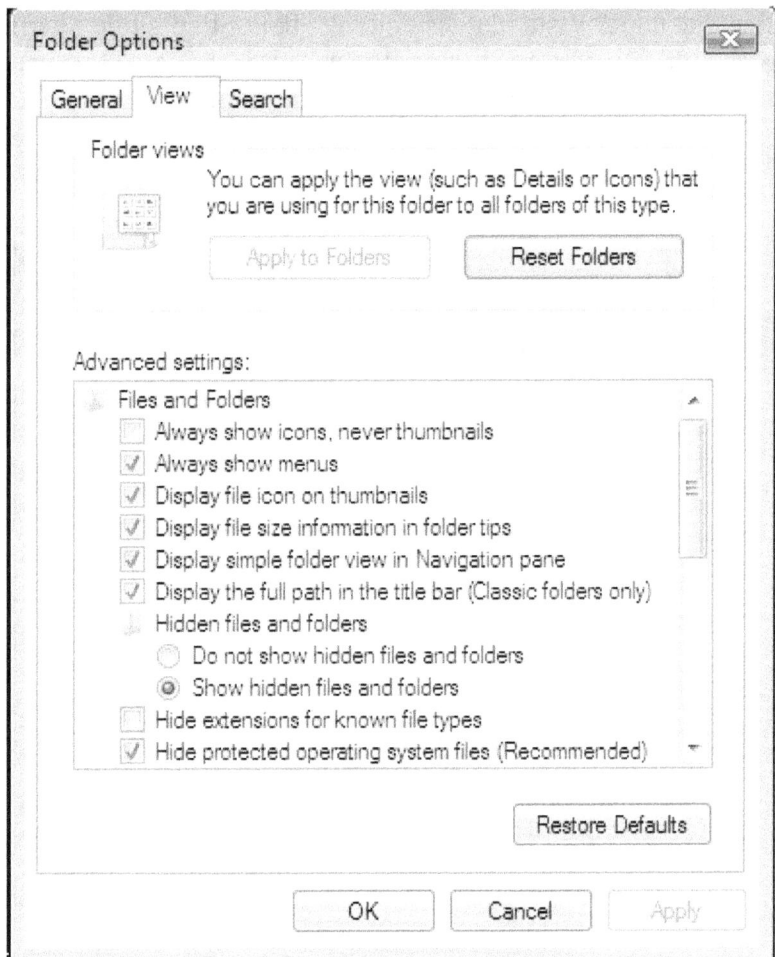

Windows Vista - Figure 15

Notice that under Vista there is nothing about Simple File Sharing. Instead, there is just a "Sharing Wizard". It is the same program. Microsoft just changed the name.

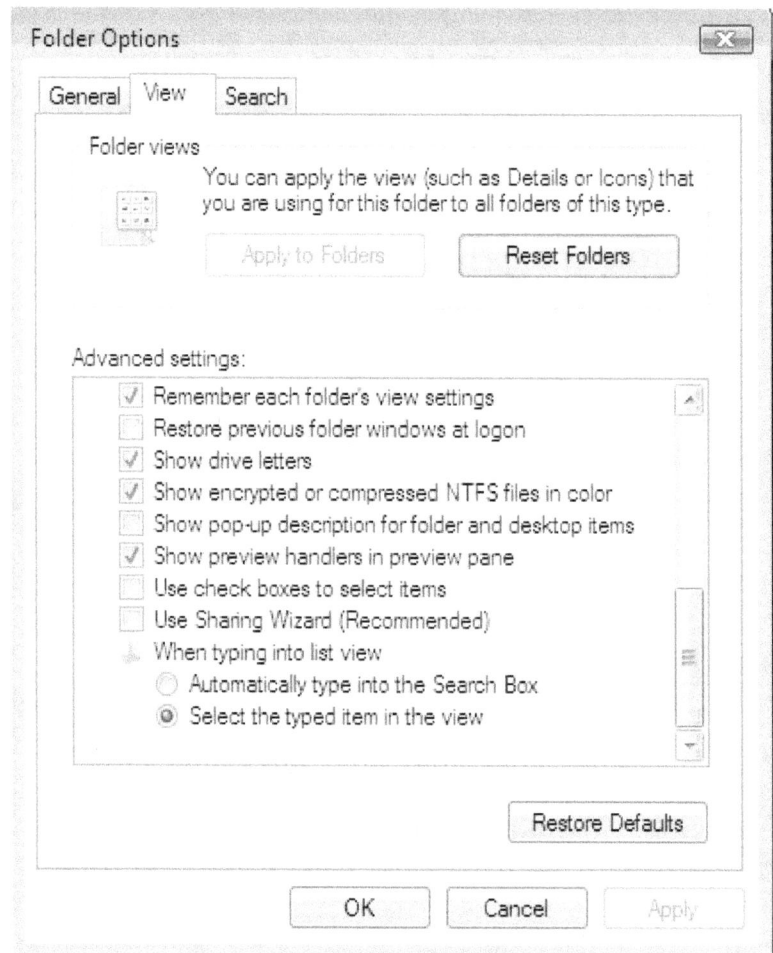

Windows Vista - Figure 16-17

Mark Versus Mr. Hacker.doc

In order to get the to System Restore area you first have to go to the control panel and then left click on the System icon.

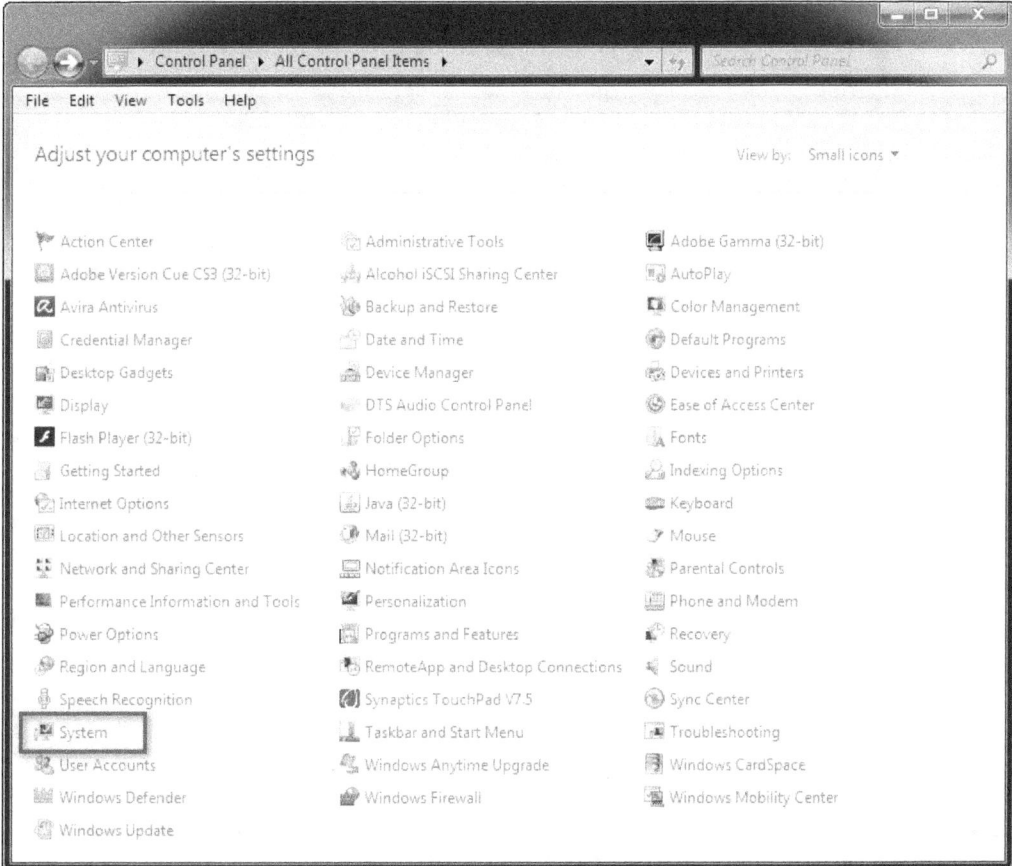

Windows Vista - Figure 18a

Mark Versus Mr. Hacker.doc

In the System dialog box, select the "Advanced system serttings".

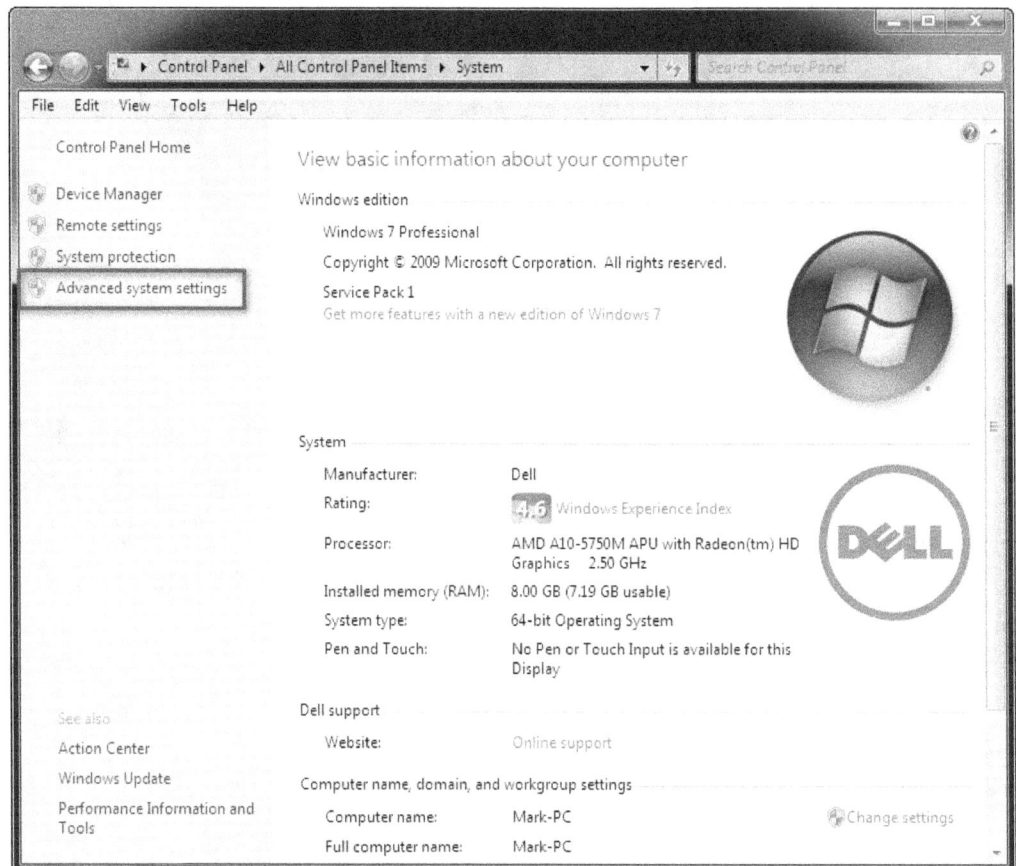

Windows Vista - Figure 18b

Here you can see that the System Restore is turned on for the Local Disk (or C: Drive). Use the Configure button to change this.

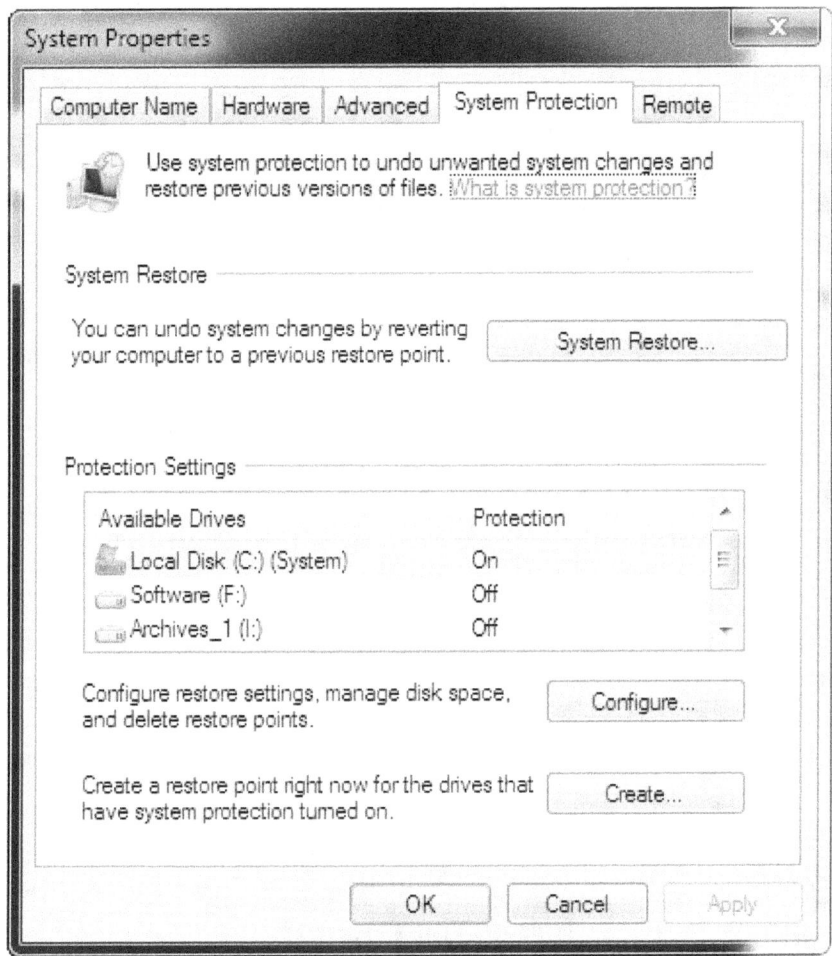

Windows Vista - Figure 18c

Here is what the dialog looks liked after you have pushed the Configuration button.

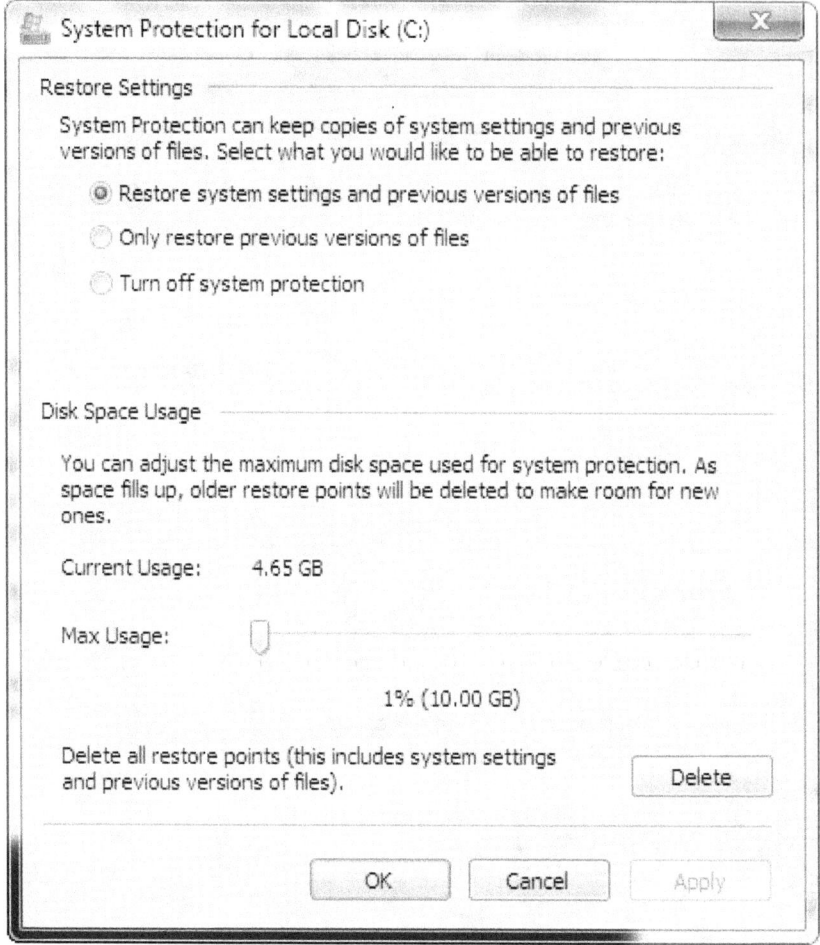

Windows Vista - Figure 18d

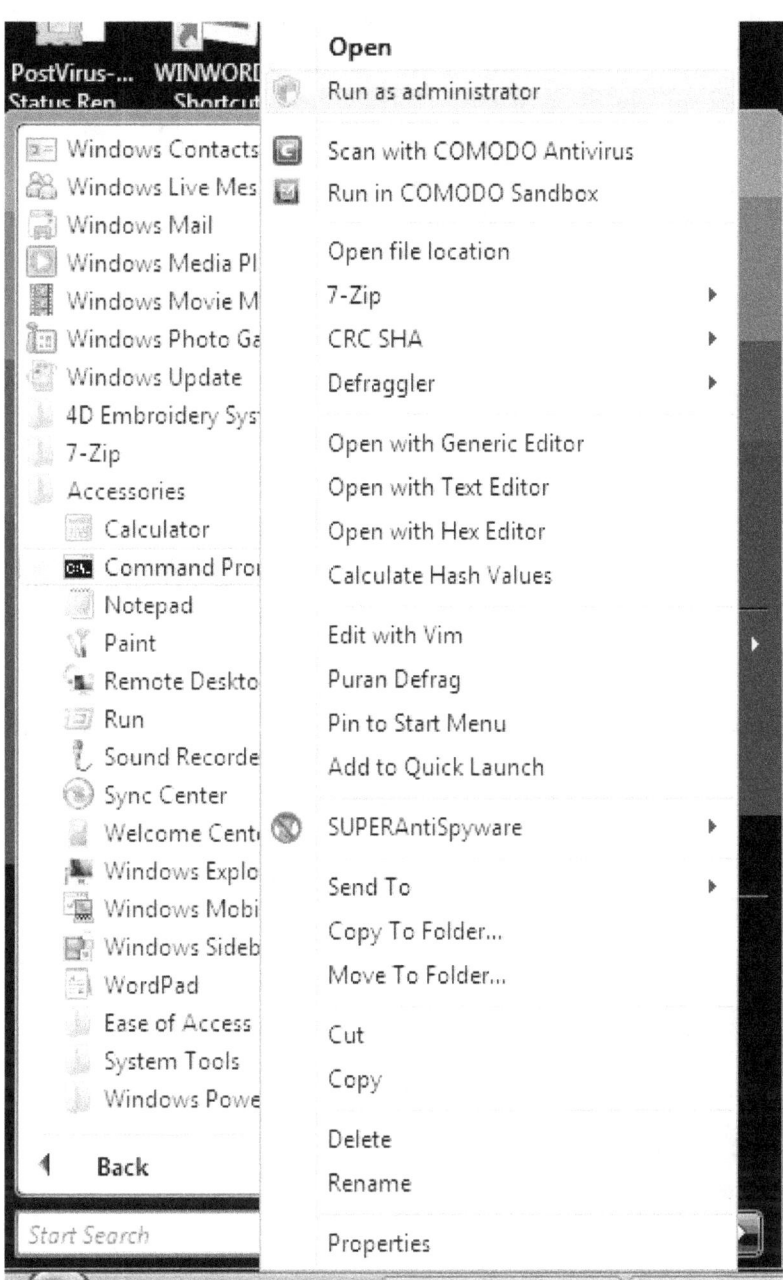

Windows Vista - Figure 19

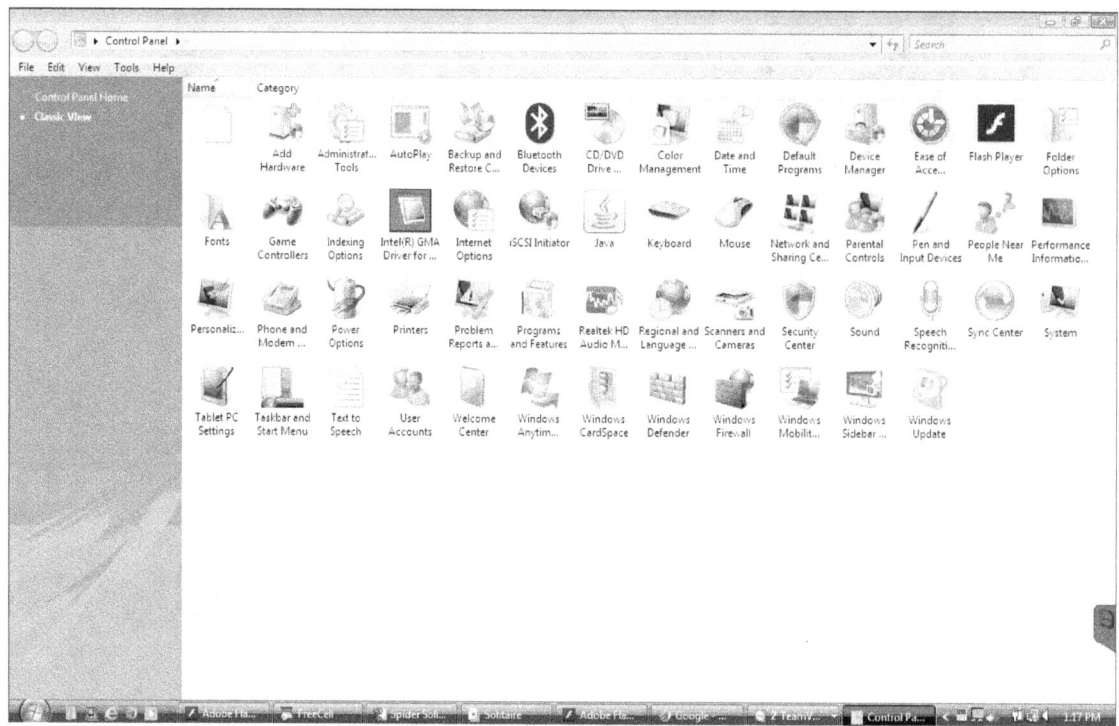
Windows Vista - Figure 20

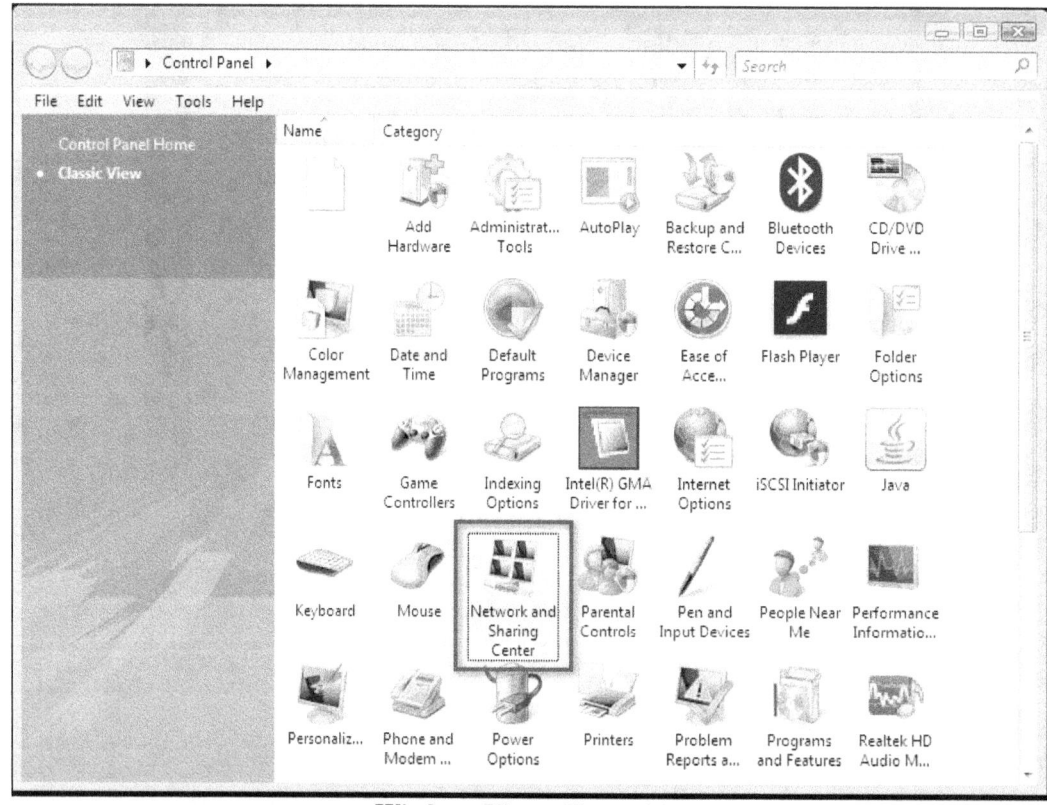
Windows Vista - Figure 21a

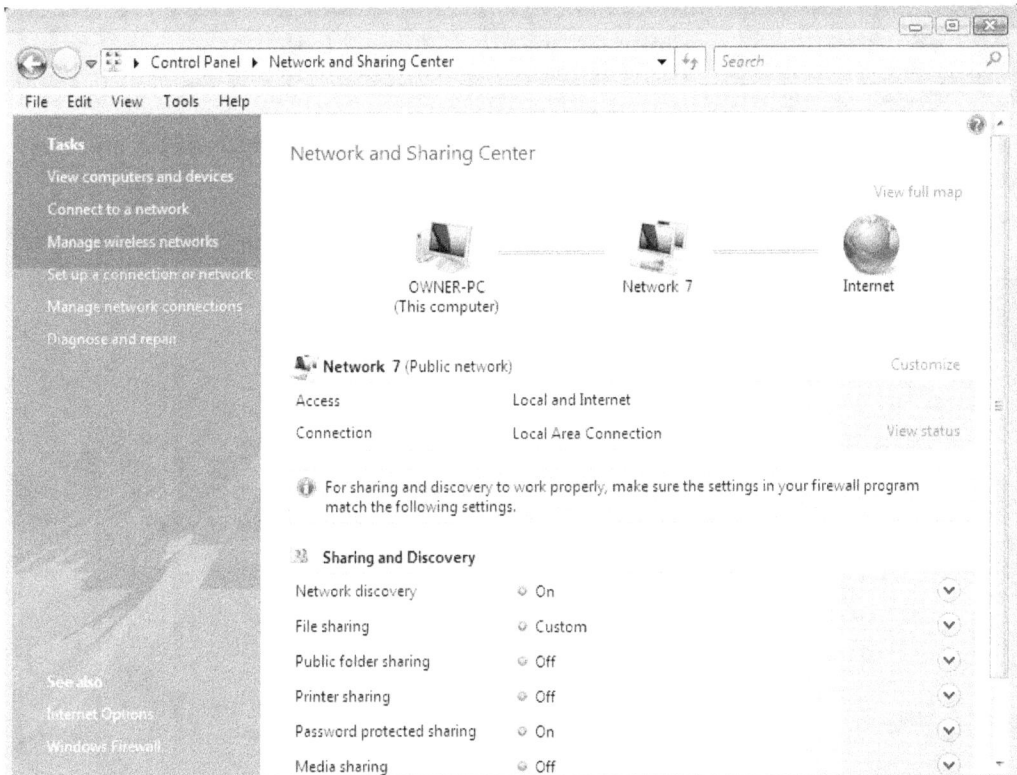
Windows Vista - Figure 21b

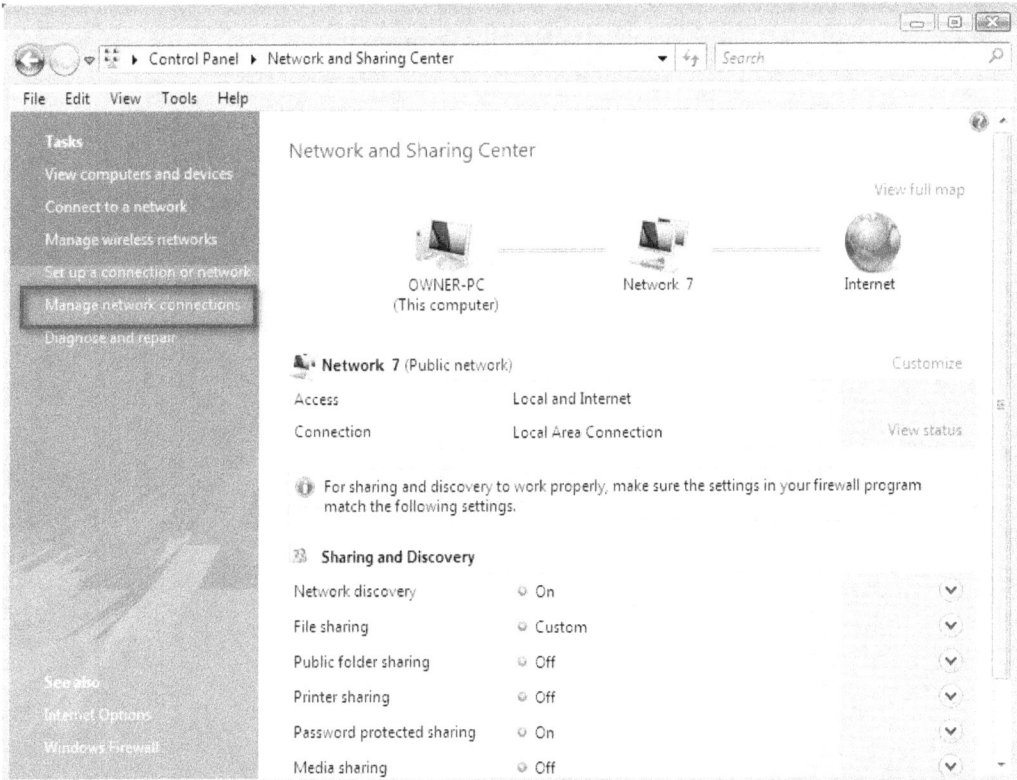
Windows Vista - Figure 21c

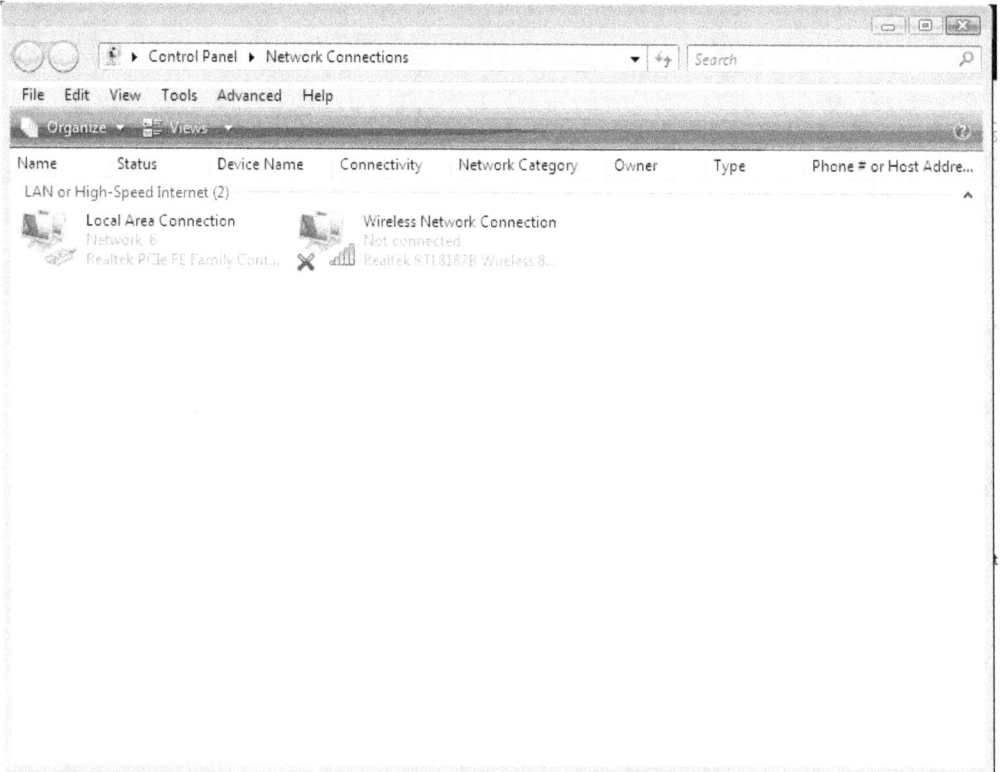

Windows Vista - Figure 21d

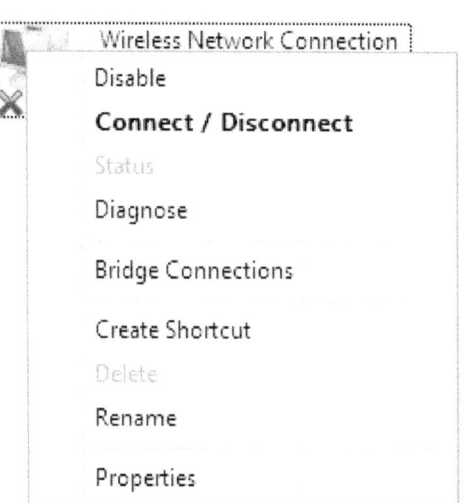

Windows Vista - Figure 22

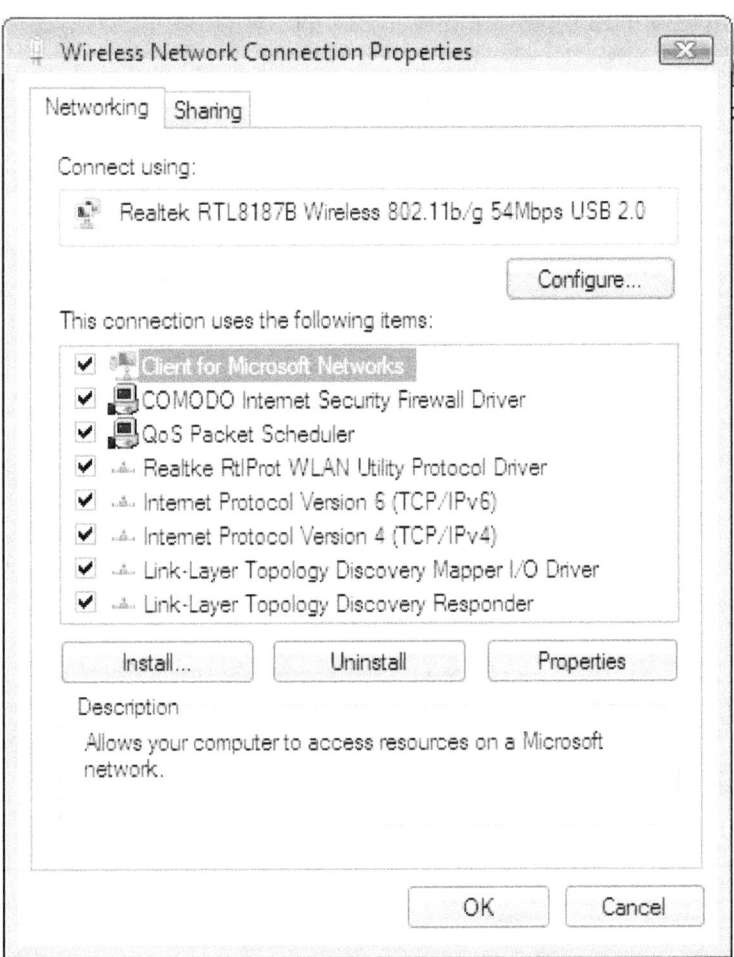

Windows Vista - Figure 23

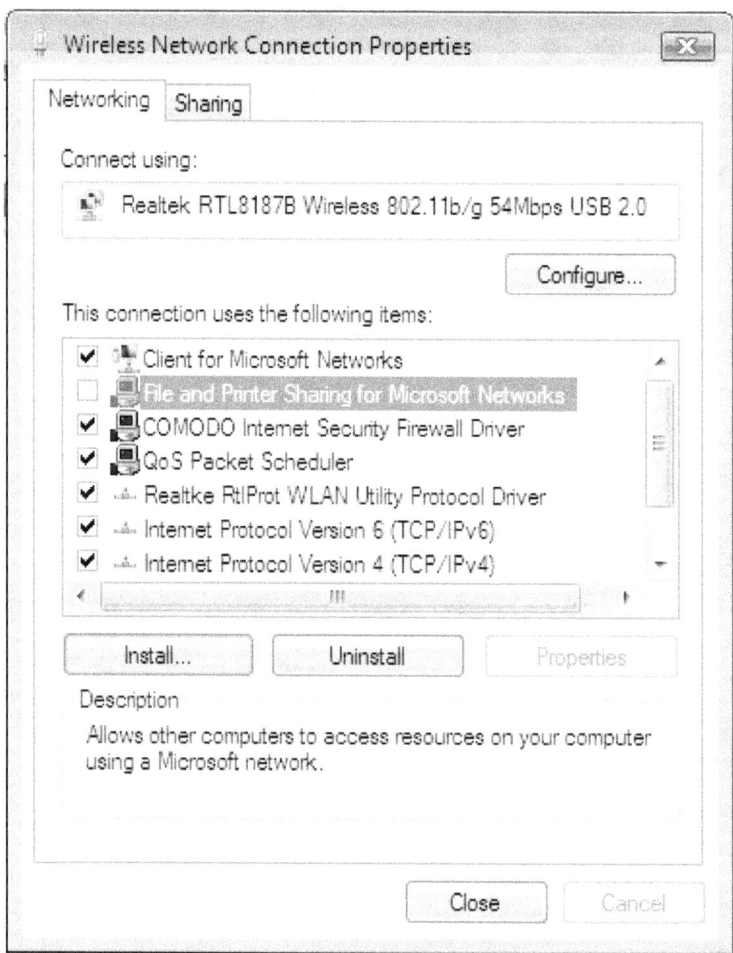

Windows Vista - Figure 24

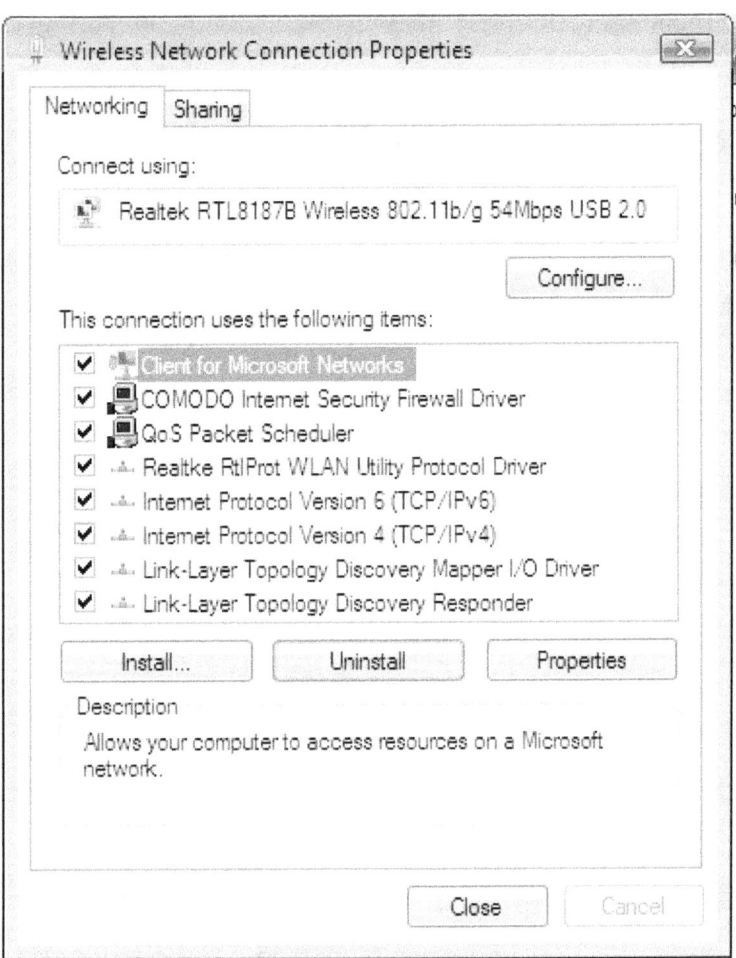

Windows Vista - Figure 25

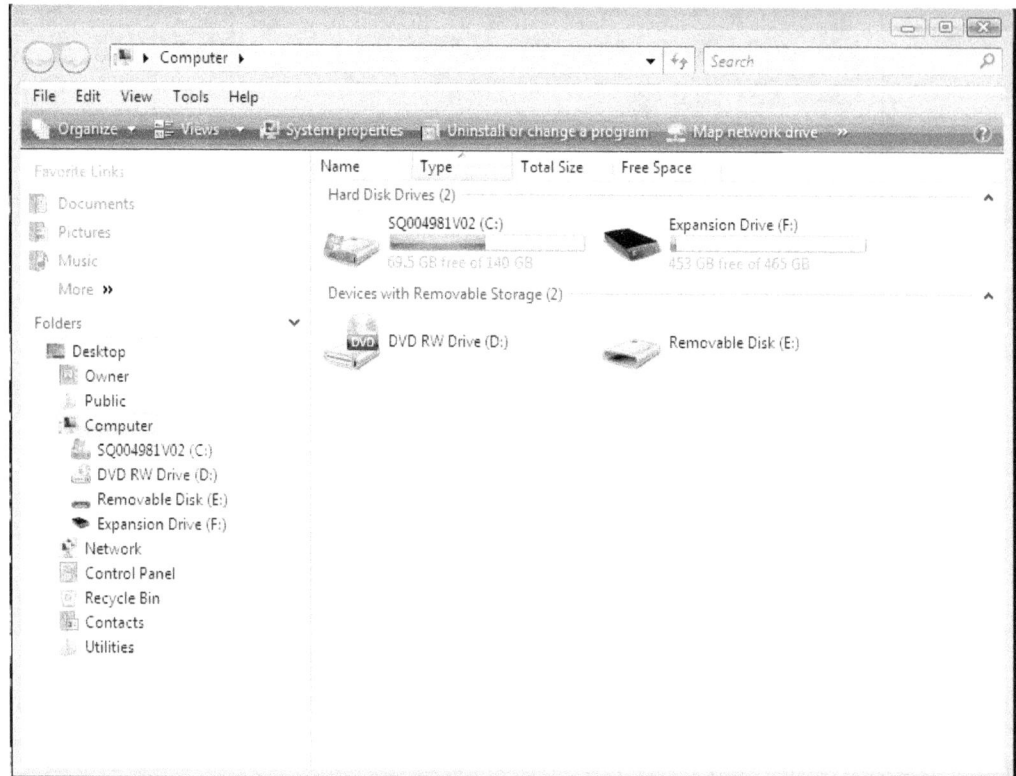

Windows Vista - Figure 26

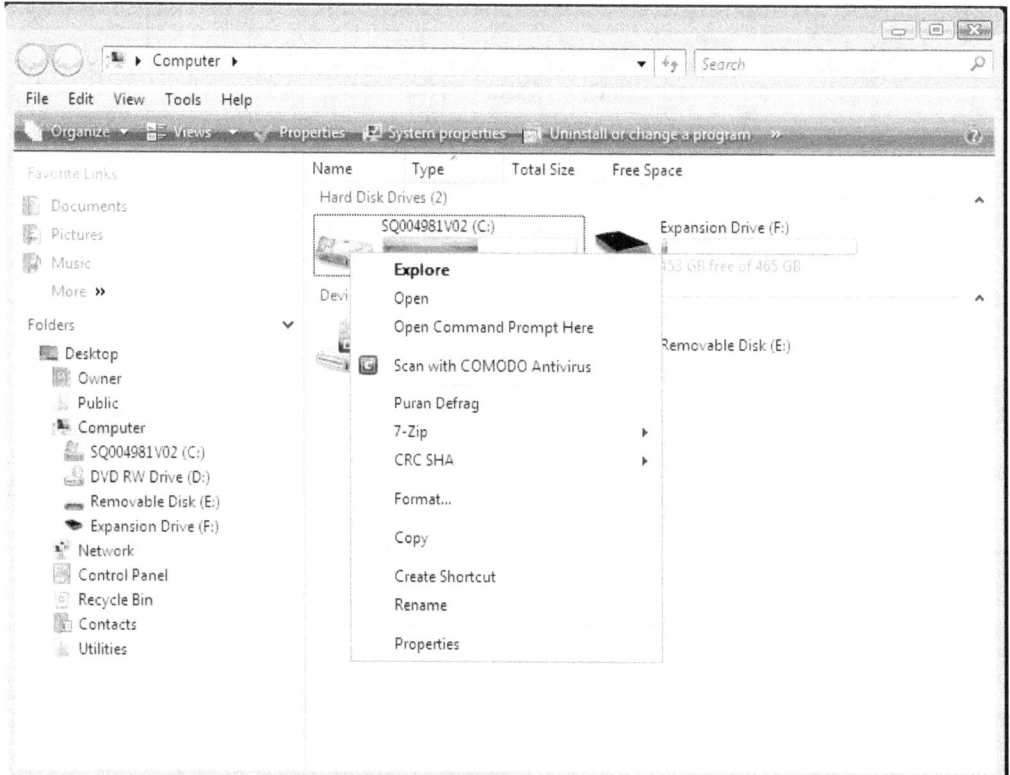

Windows Vista - Figure 27

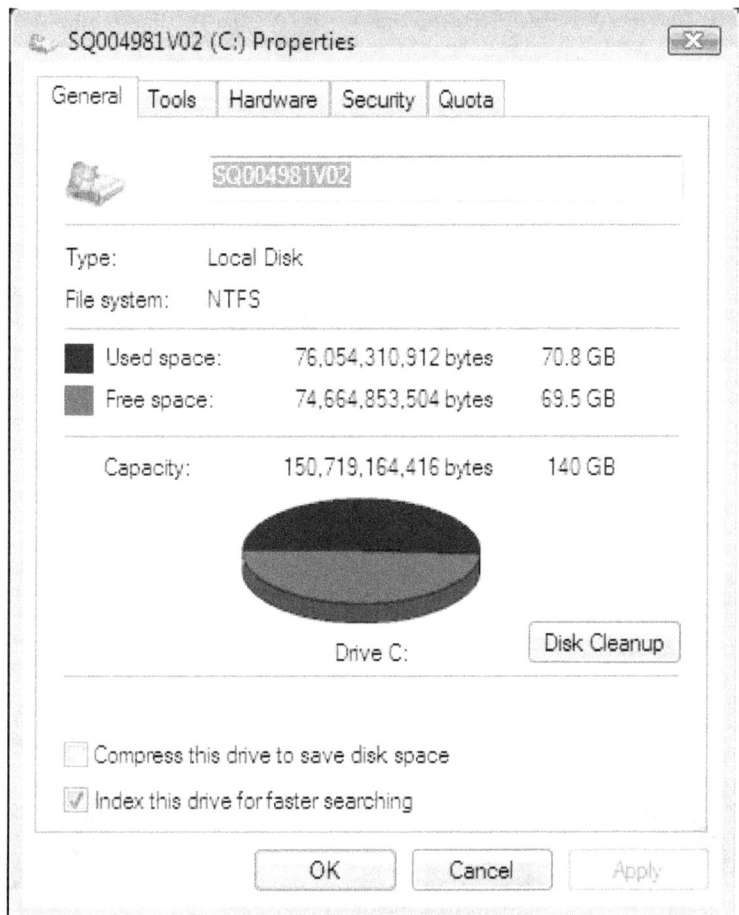

Windows Vista - Figure 28

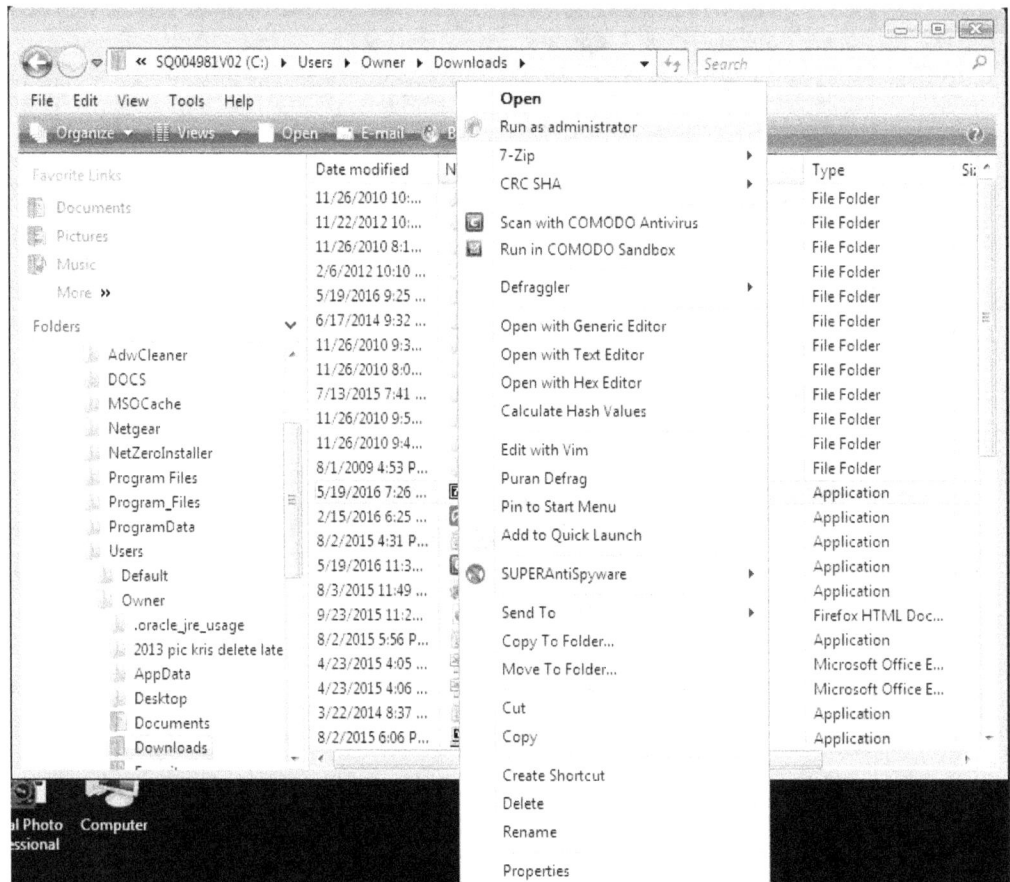

Windows Vista - Figure 29

Windows Vista – Figure 30 omitted because Vista doesn't do that.
It just runs as an administrator.

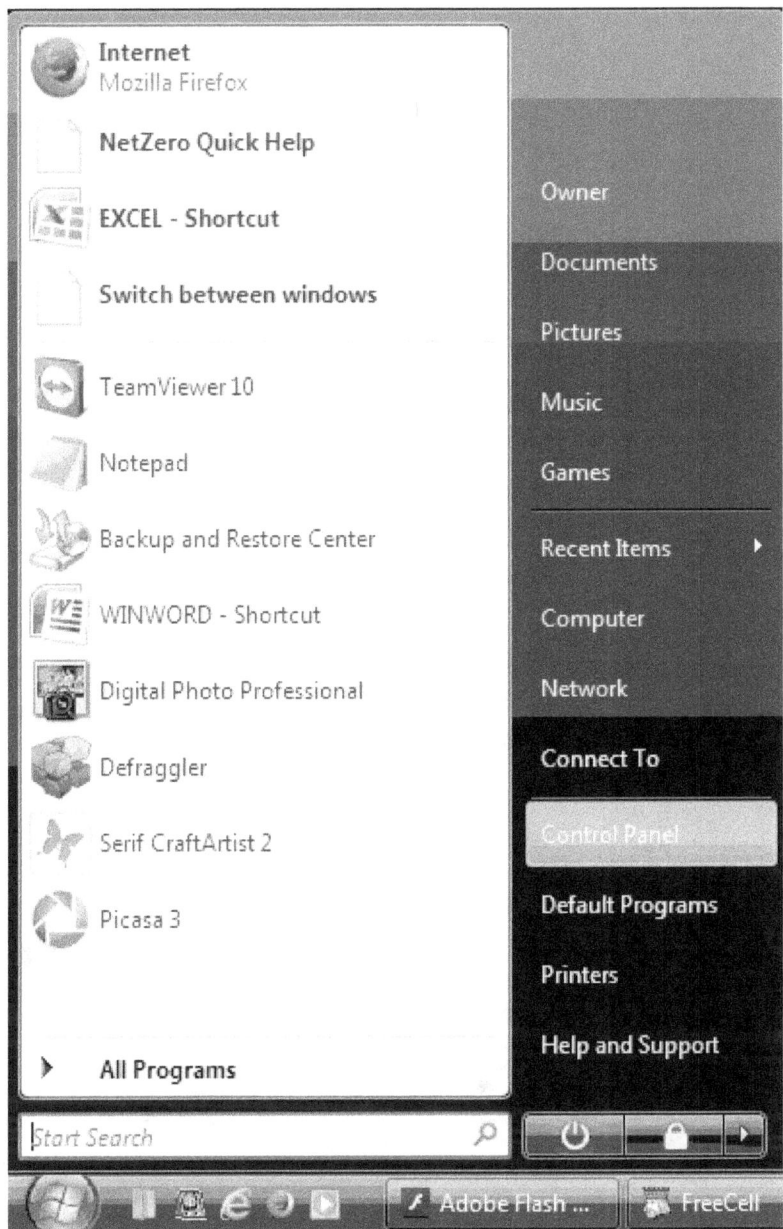
Windows Vista - Figure 31

Mark Versus Mr. Hacker.doc

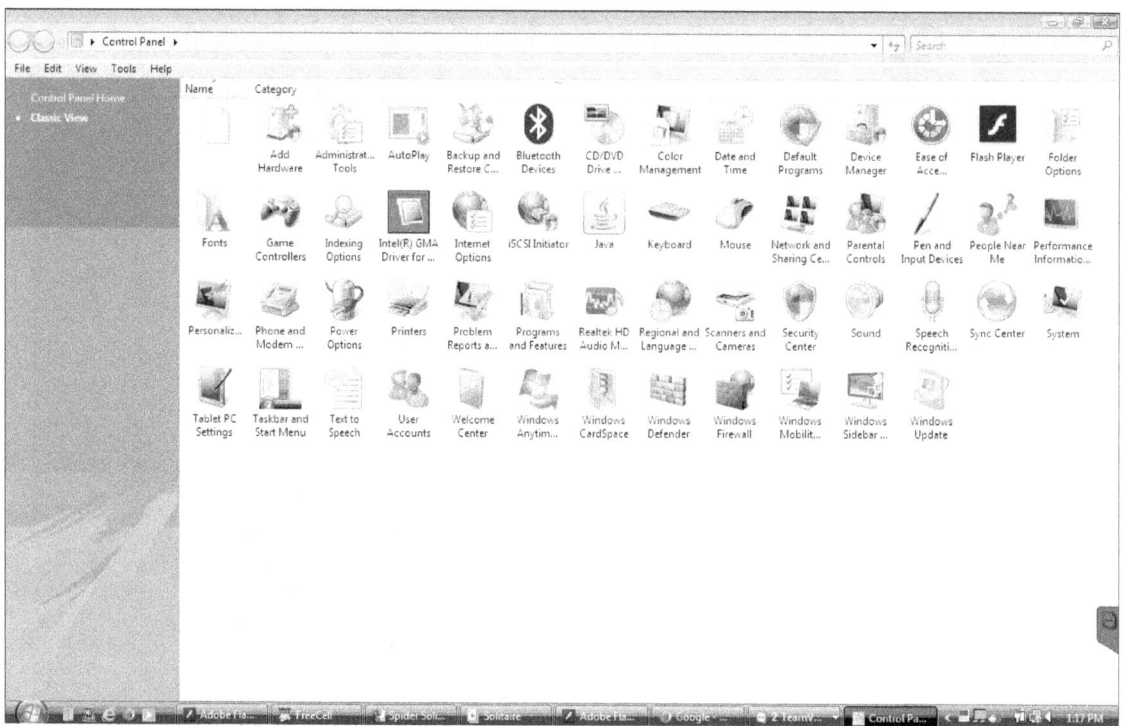
Windows Vista - Figure 32

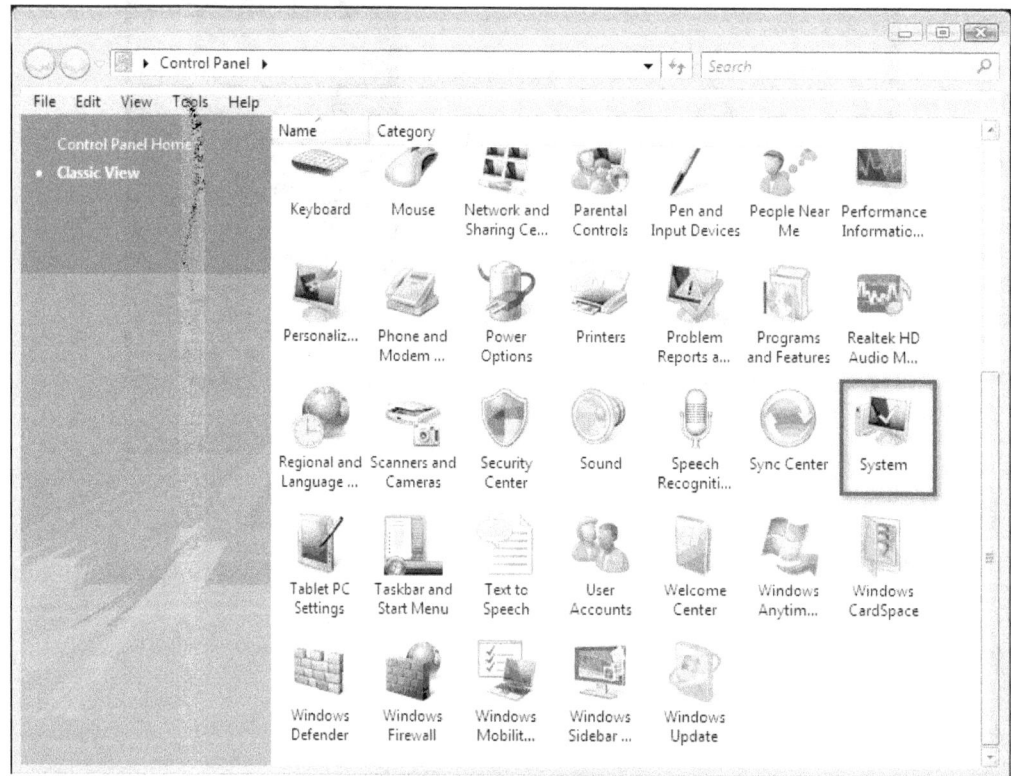
Windows Vista - Figure 33

Mark Versus Mr. Hacker.doc

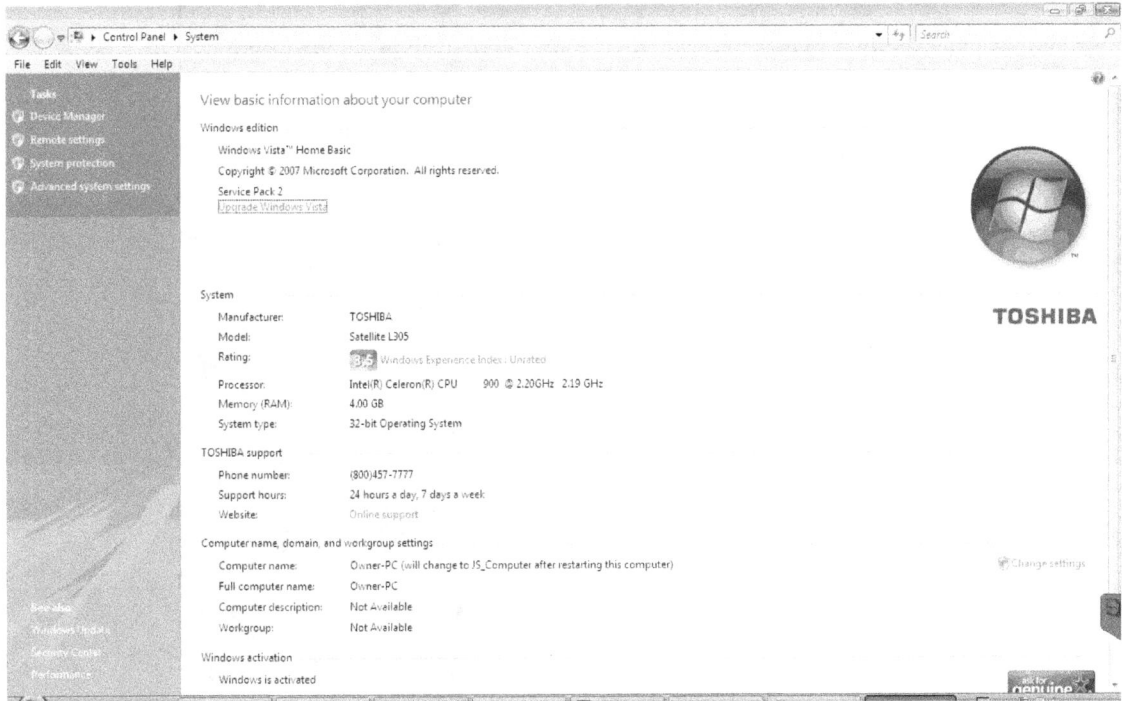

Windows Vista - Figure 34

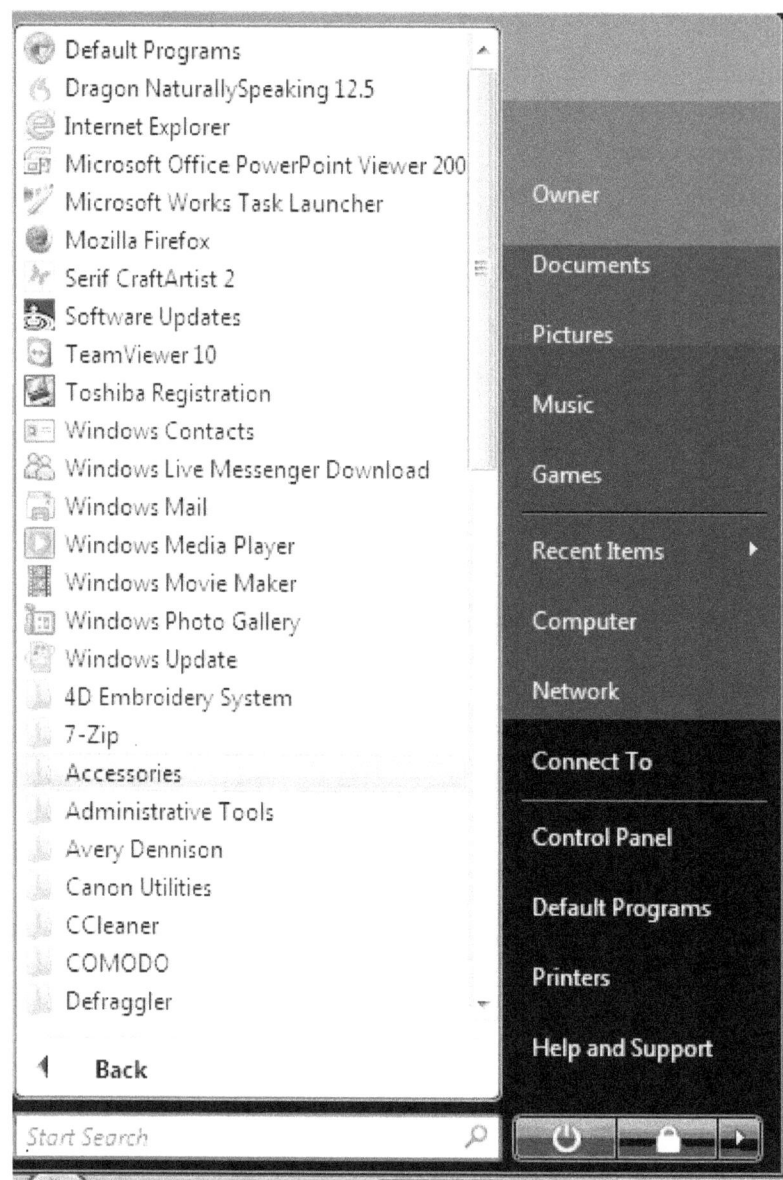
Windows Vista - Figure 35

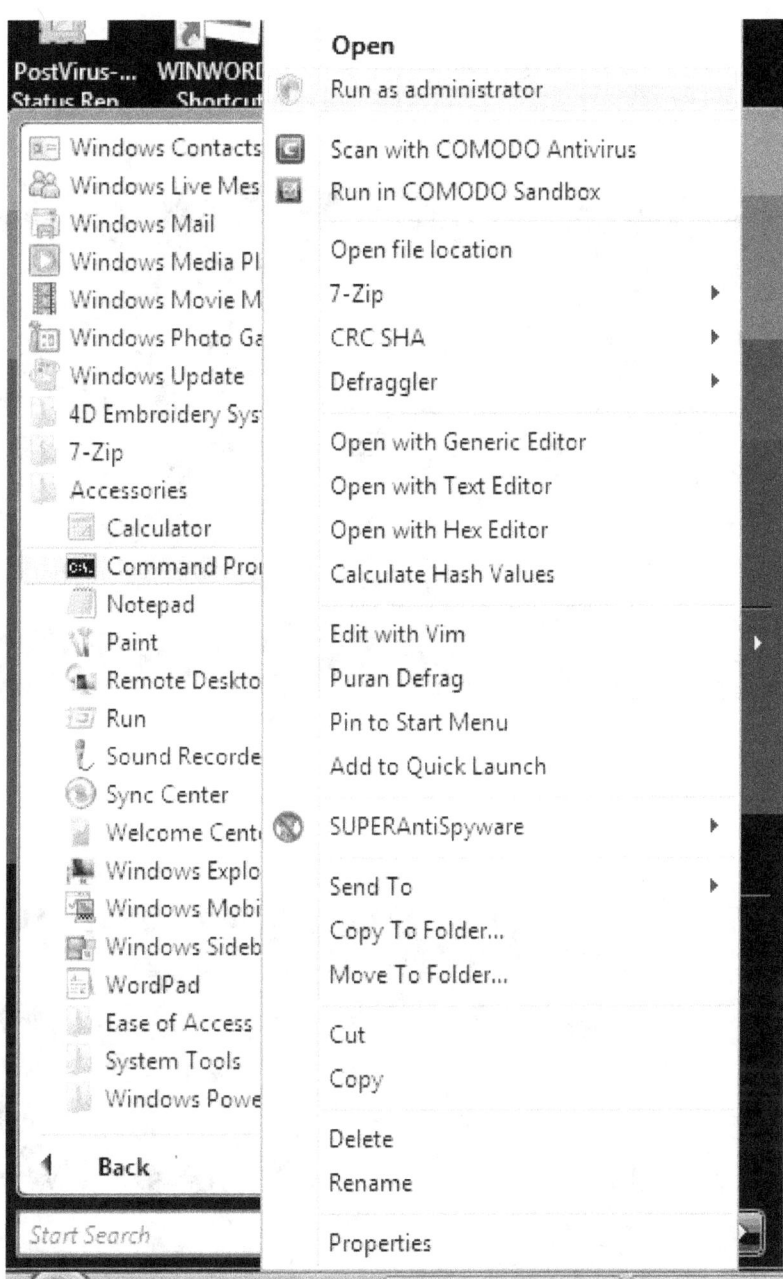

Windows Vista - Figure 36

Mark Versus Mr. Hacker.doc

Since The Command Prompt is the same on all versions of Windows; here the is Windows XP version again.

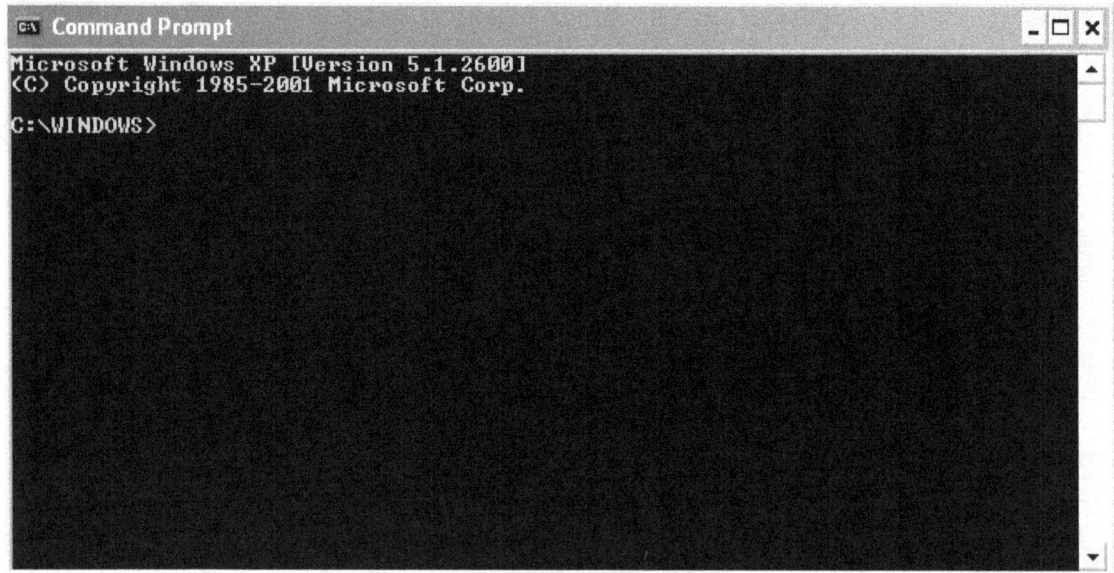

Windows Vista - Figure 37

Just like above – here is the Windows XP version.

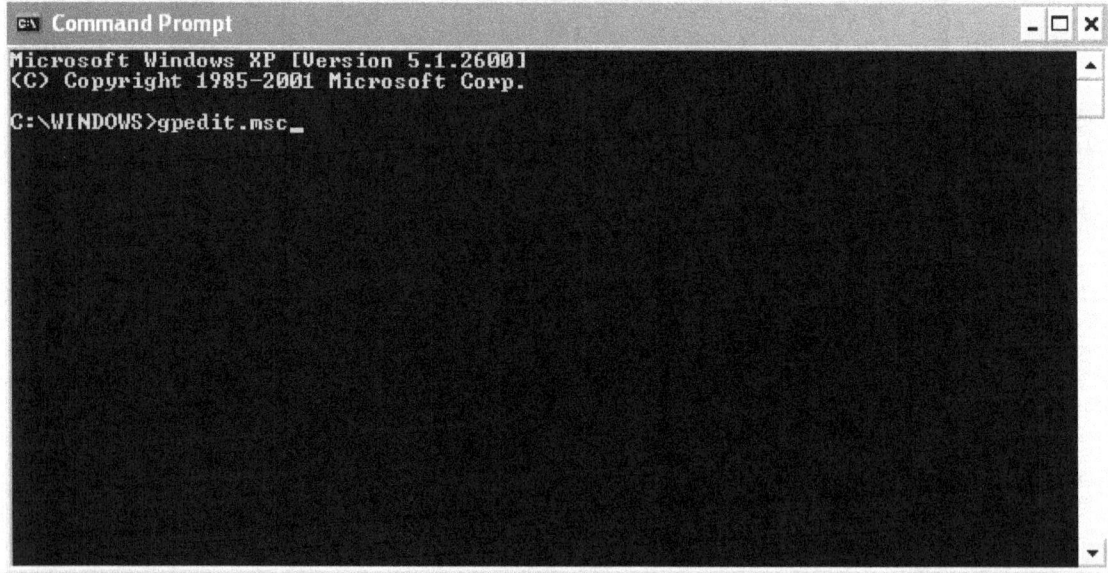

Windows Vista - Figure 38

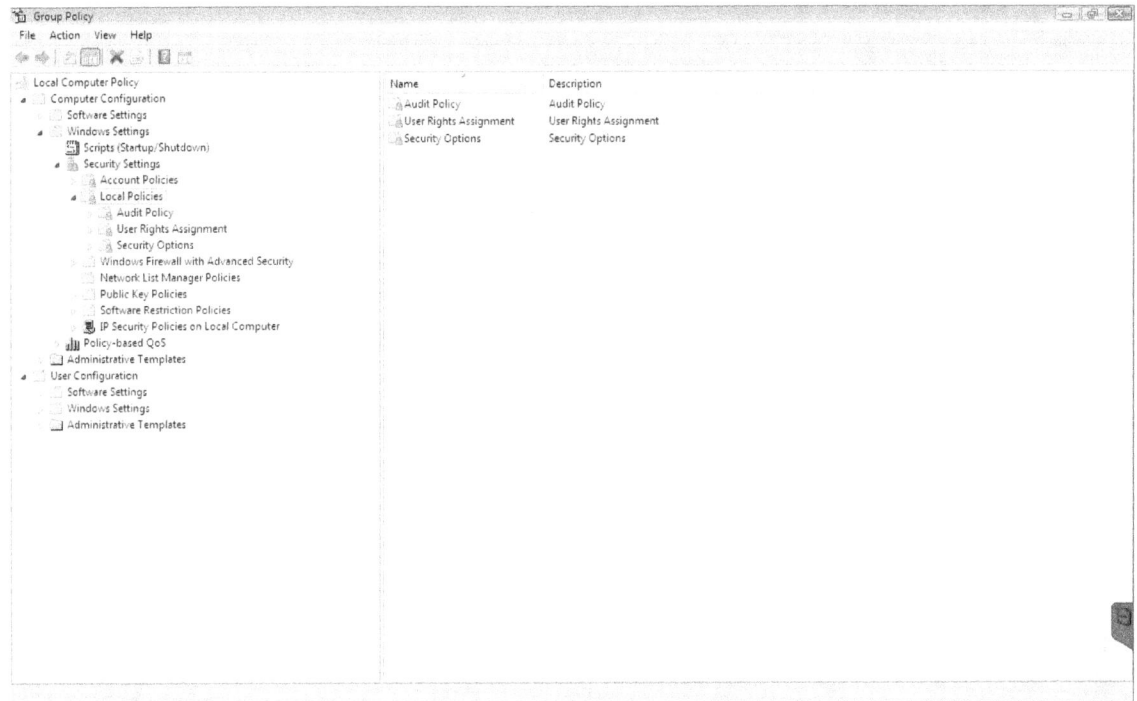

Windows Vista - Figure 39

Windows Vista - Figure 40

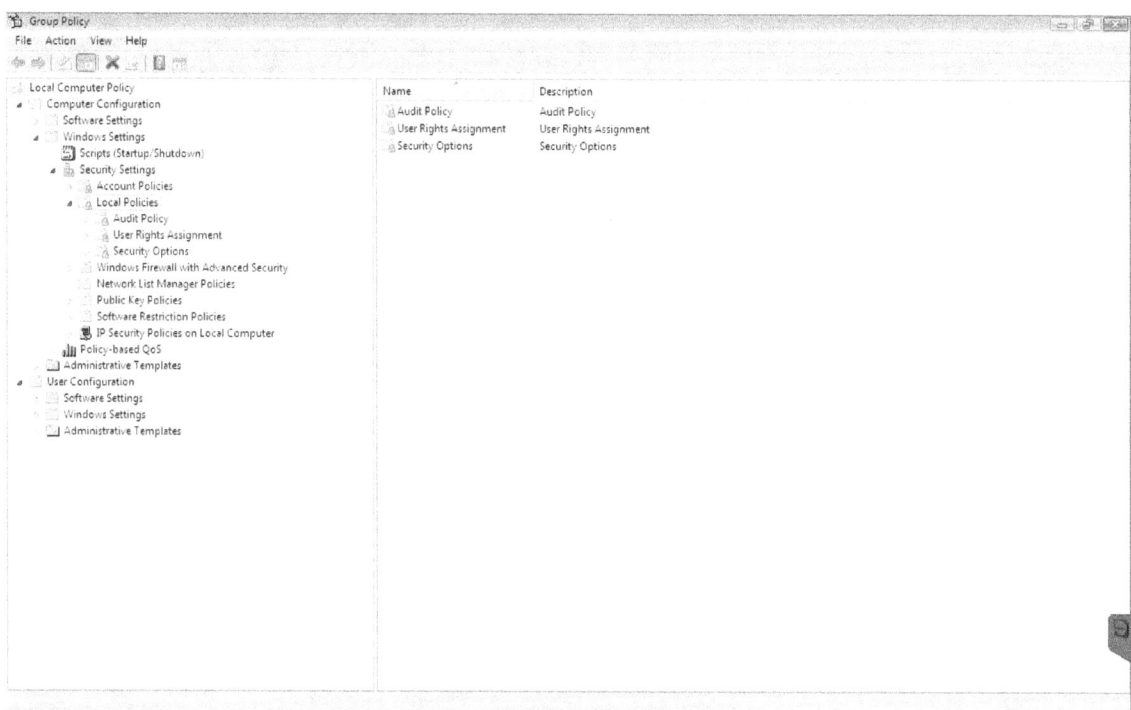
Windows Vista - Figure 41

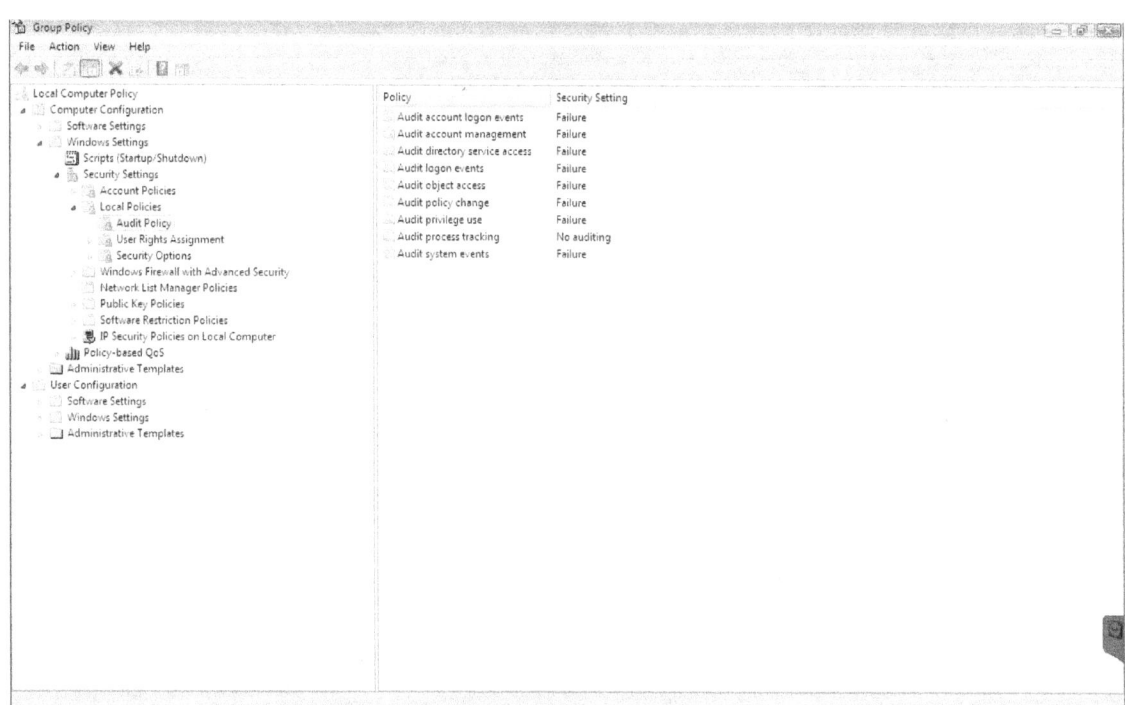
Windows Vista - Figure 42

Mark Versus Mr. Hacker.doc

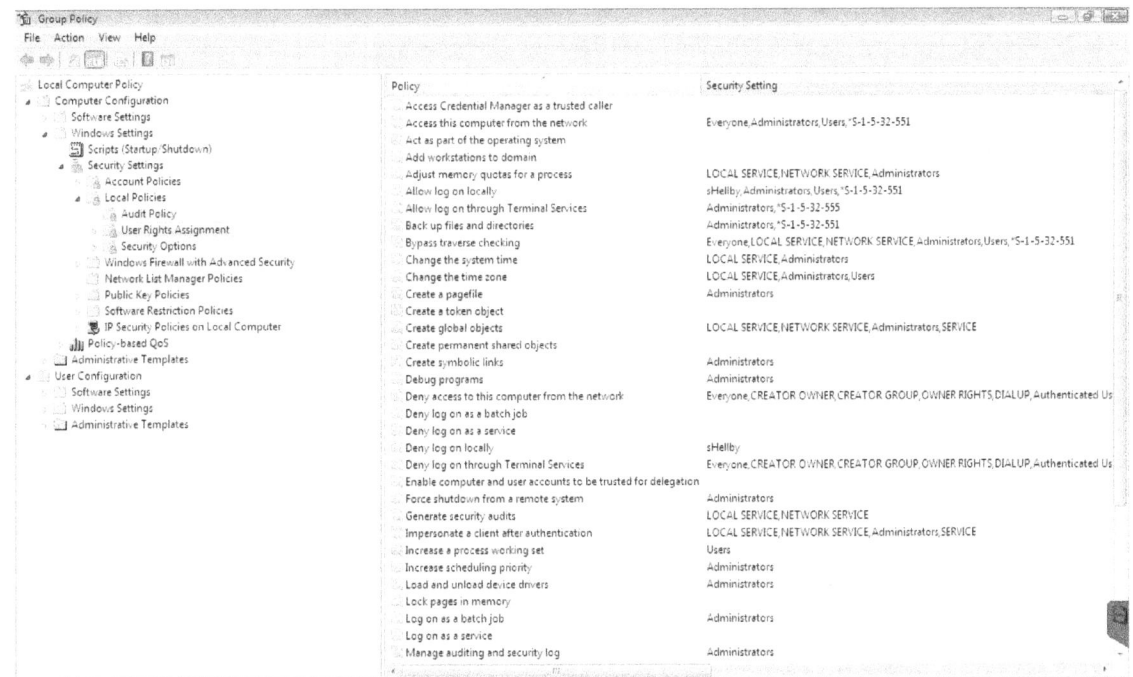

Windows Vista - Figure 43

Windows Vista - Figure 44

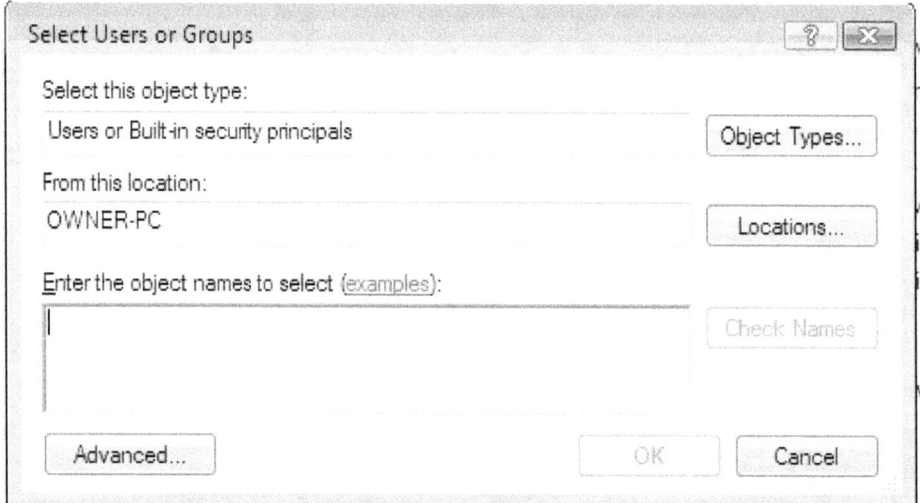
Windows Vista - Figure 45

Mark Versus Mr. Hacker.doc

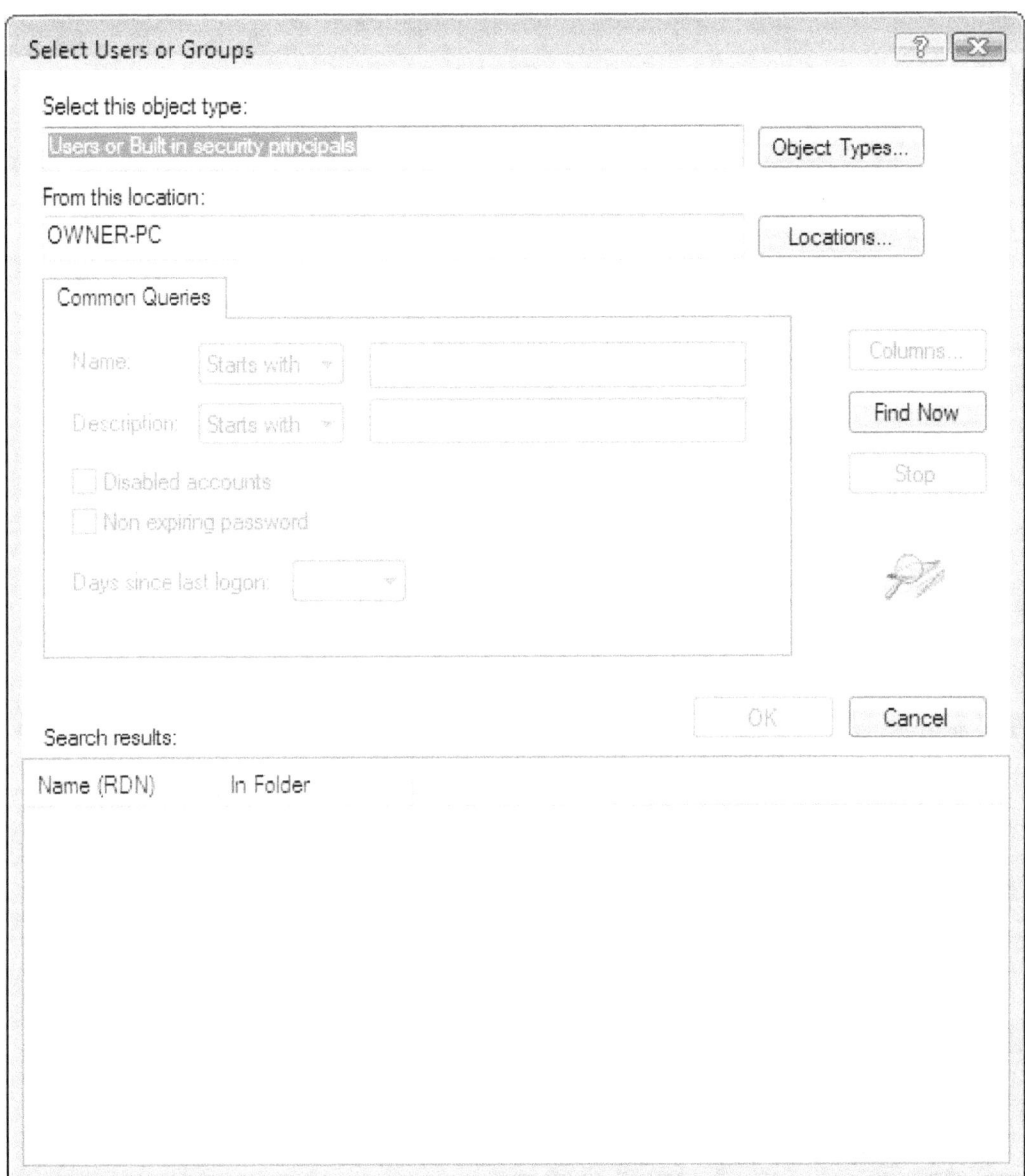

Windows Vista - Figure 46

Mark Versus Mr. Hacker.doc

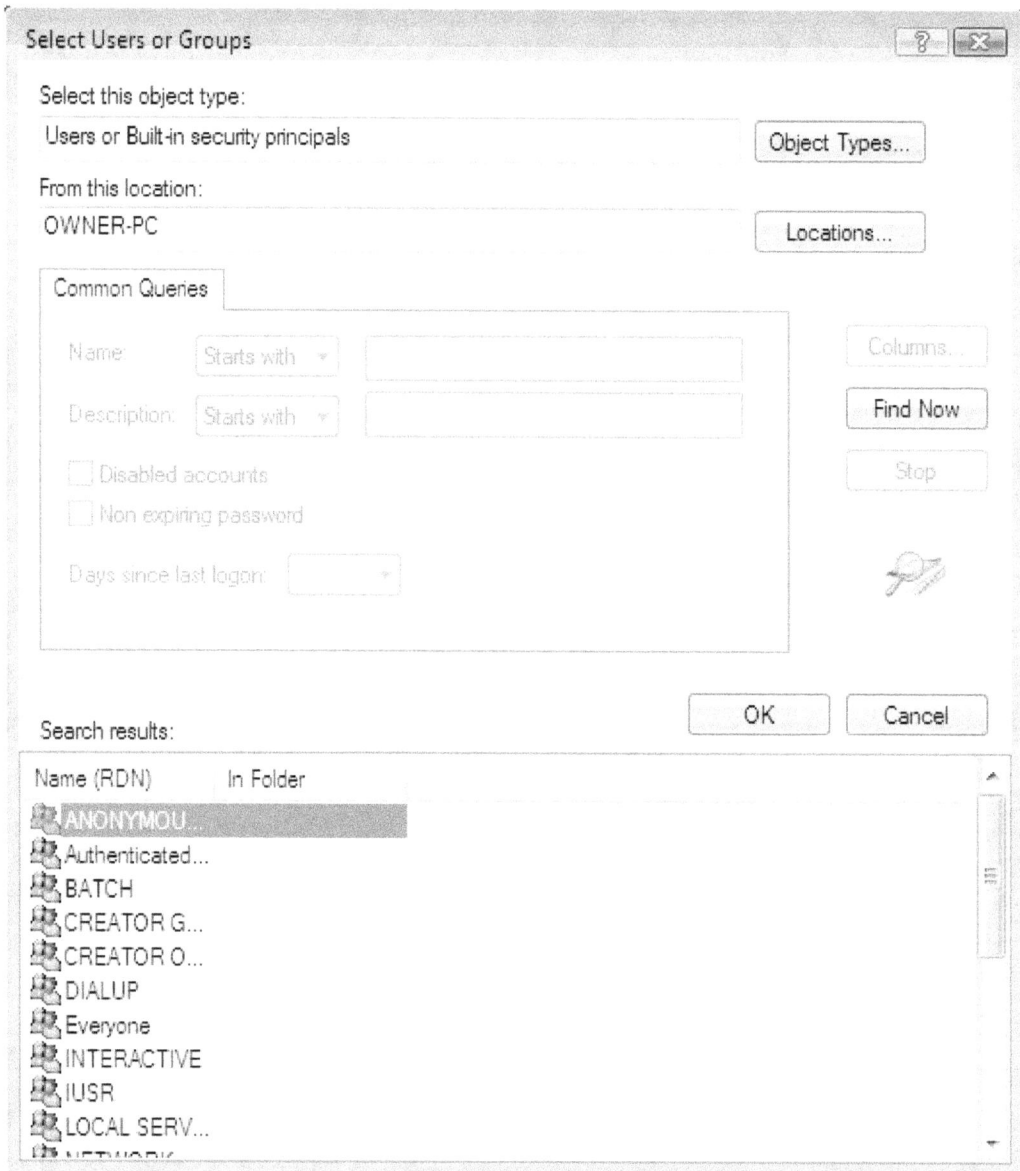

Windows Vista - Figure 47

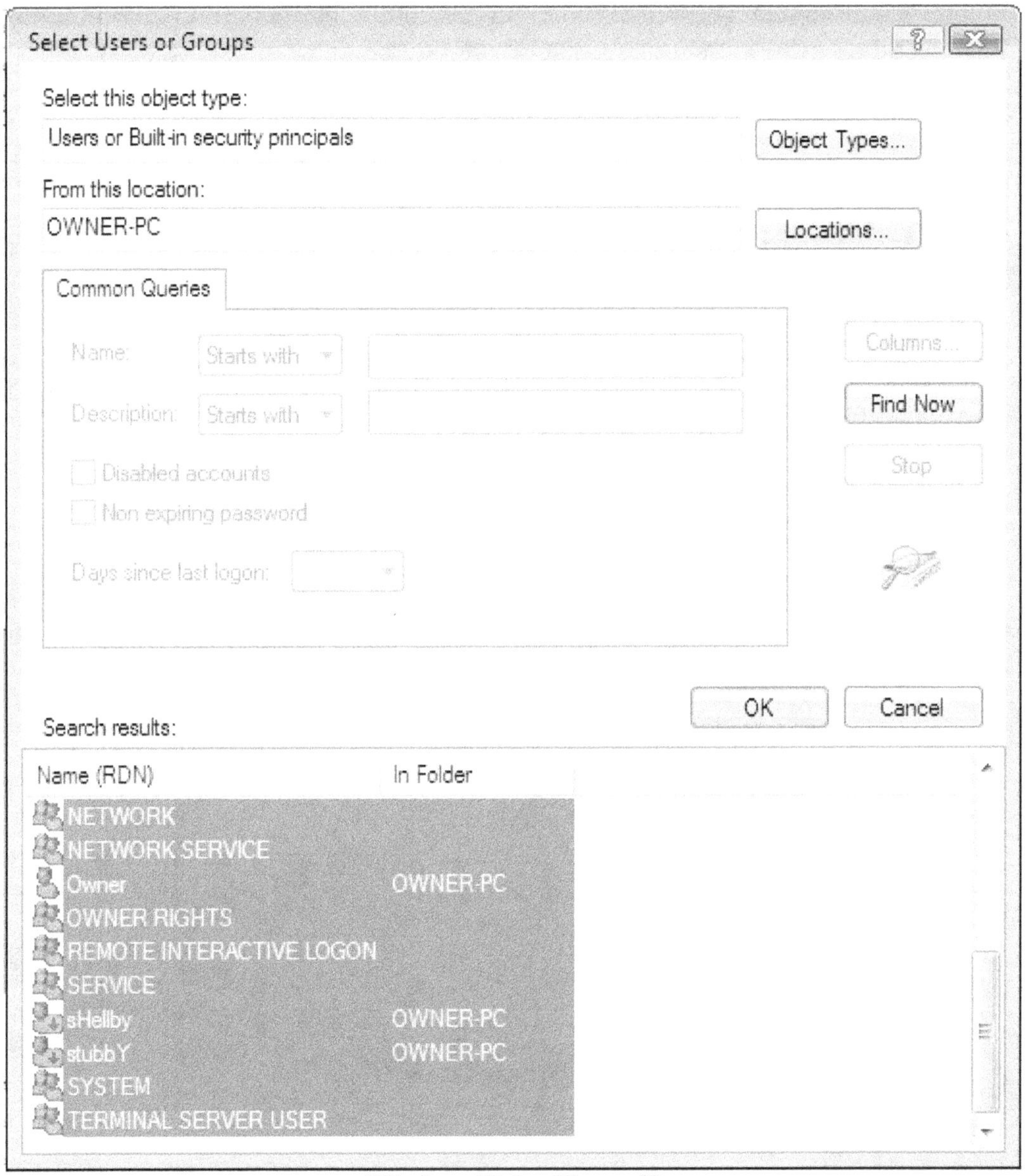

Mark Versus Mr. Hacker.doc

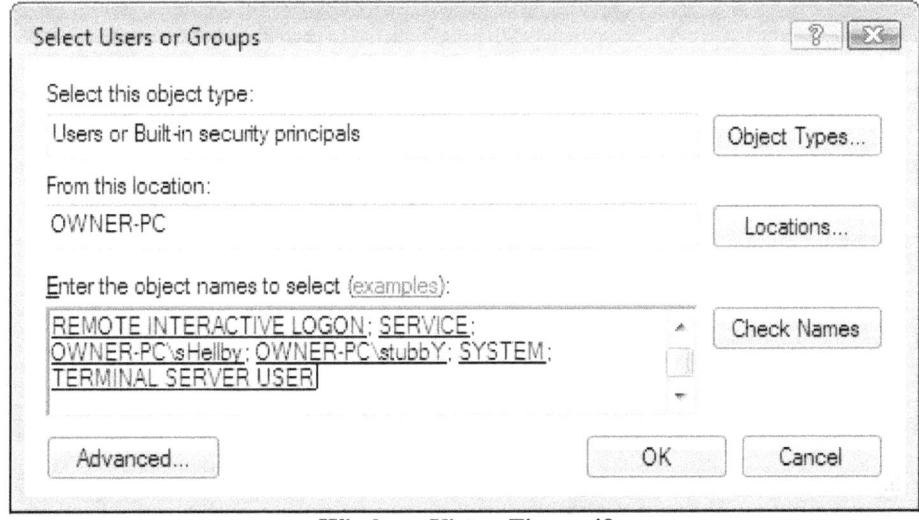

Windows Vista - Figure 48

Windows Vista - Figure 49

Windows Vista - Figure 50

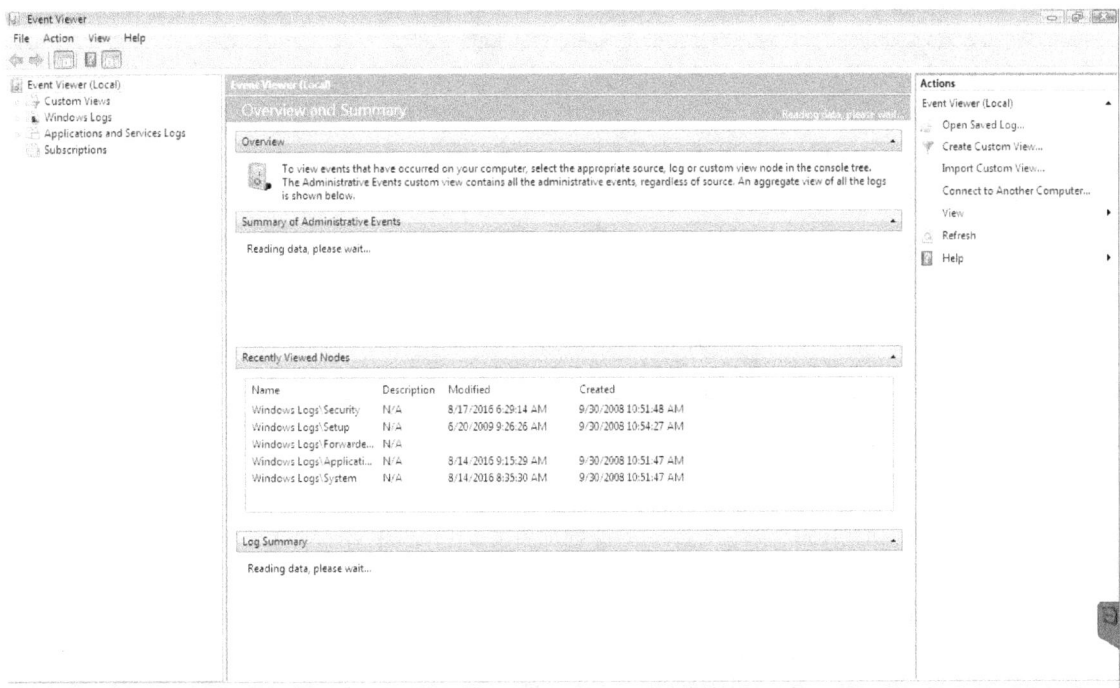

Windows Vista - Figure 51a

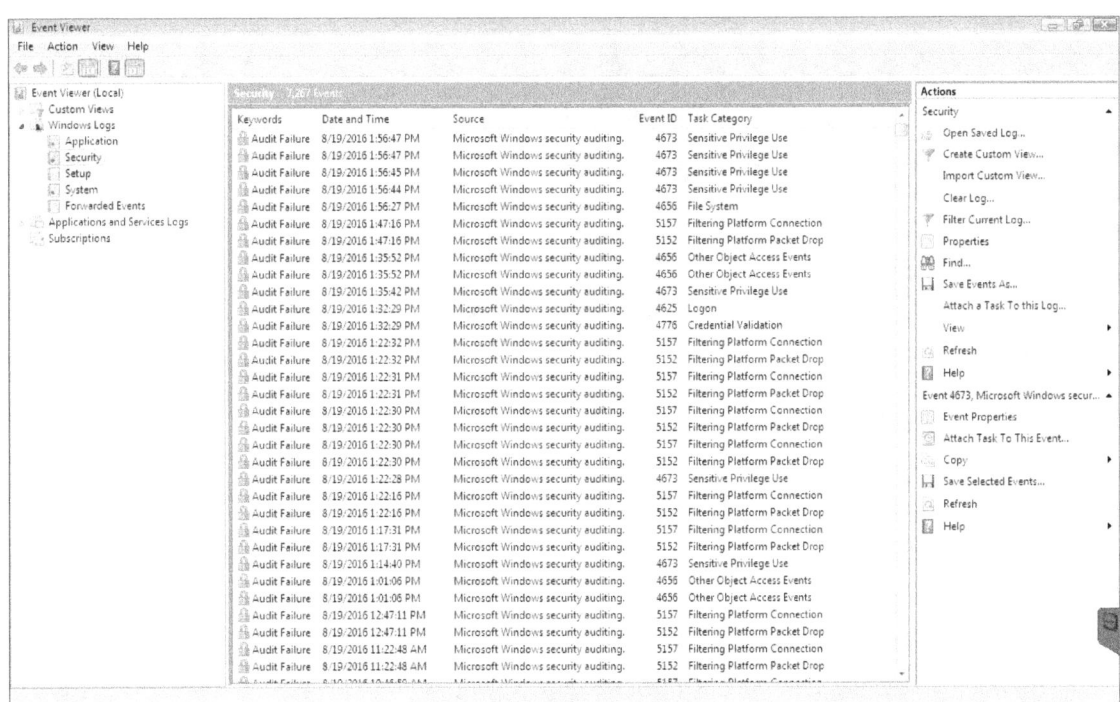

Windows Vista - Figure 51b

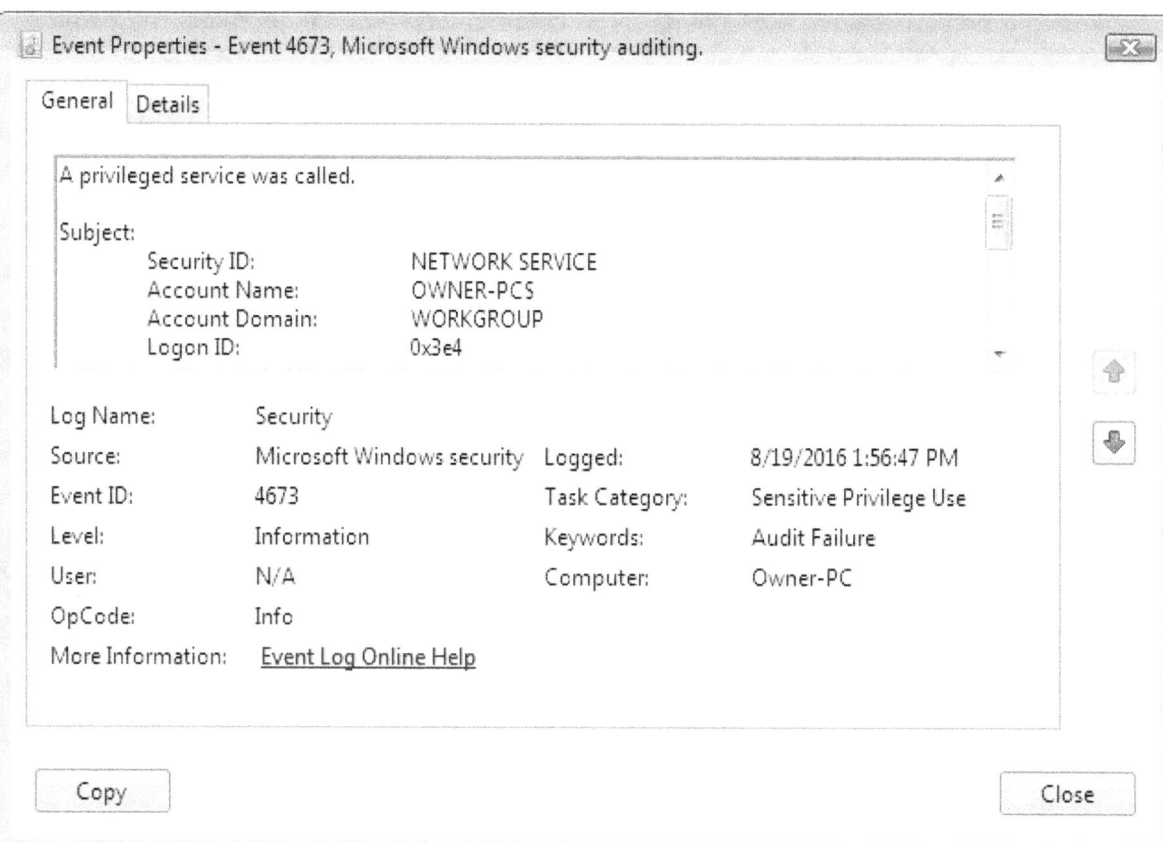
Windows Vista - Figure 52

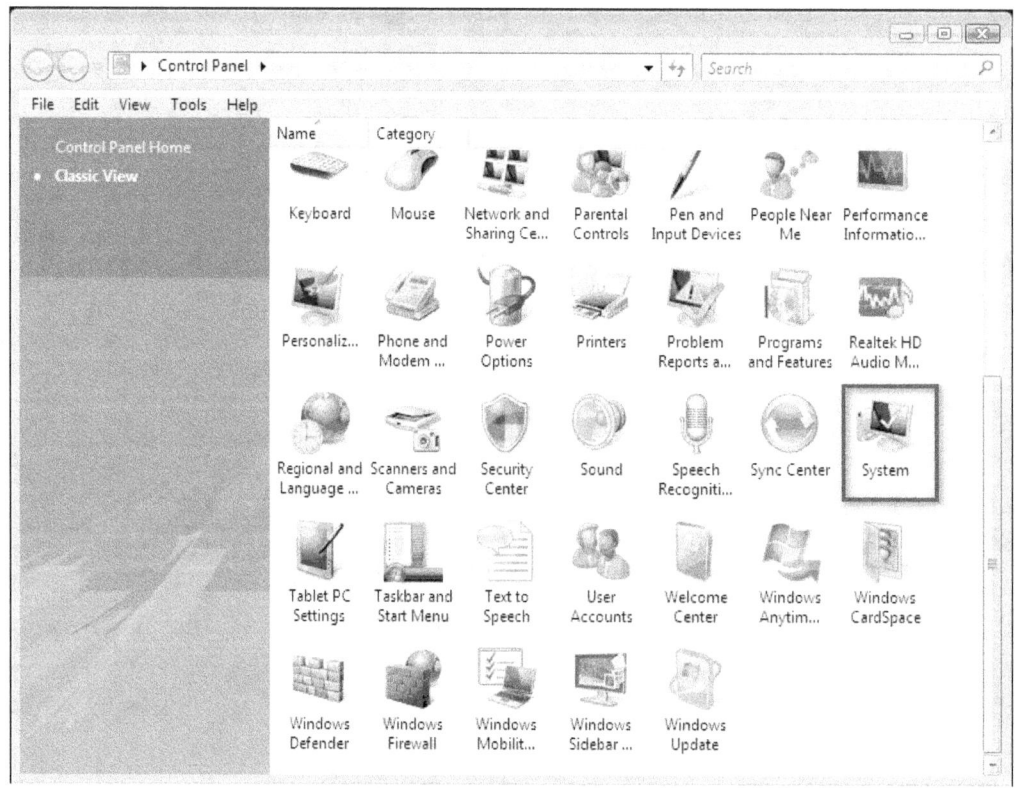
Windows Vista - Figure 53

Mark Versus Mr. Hacker.doc

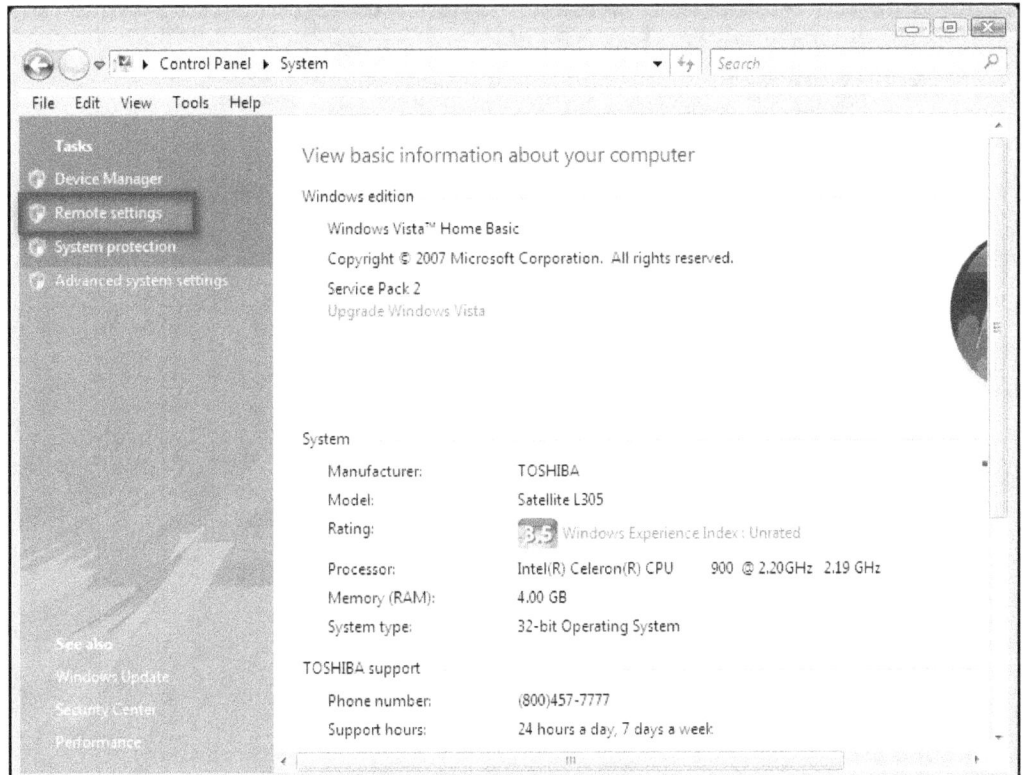
Windows Vista - Figure 54

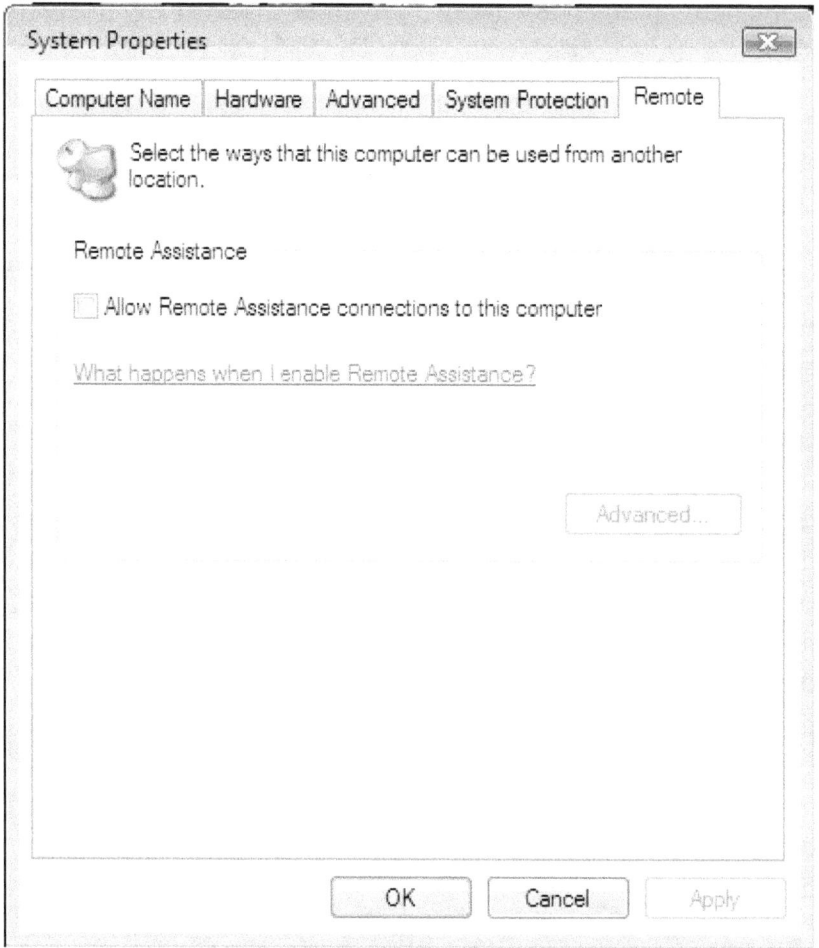
Windows Vista - Figure 55

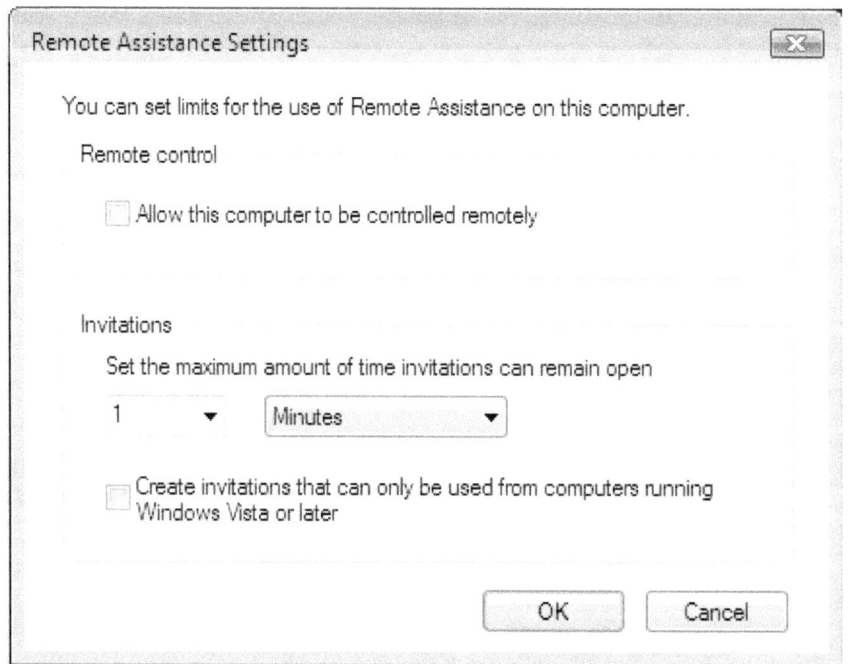
Windows Vista - Figure 56

Mark Versus Mr. Hacker.doc

All other figures deal with external programs to Windows
so use the figures provided from #56 on to the end of the book.

Have fun!

Mark Versus Mr. Hacker.doc

Screen shots for Windows 7

Windows 7 Figures

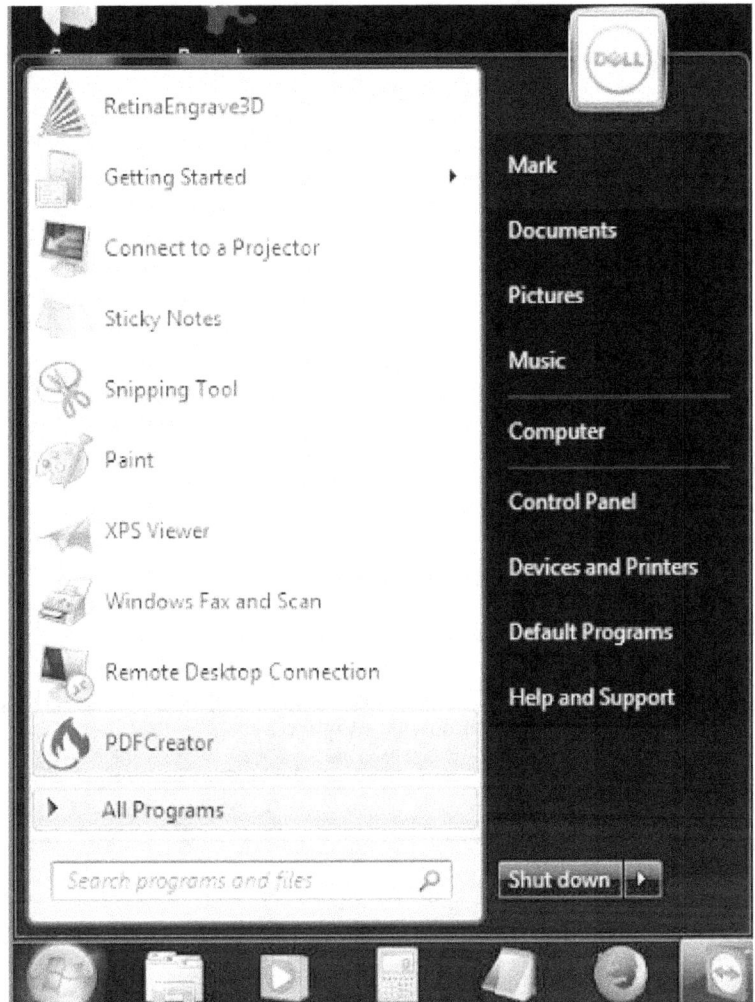

Windows 7 - Figure 1

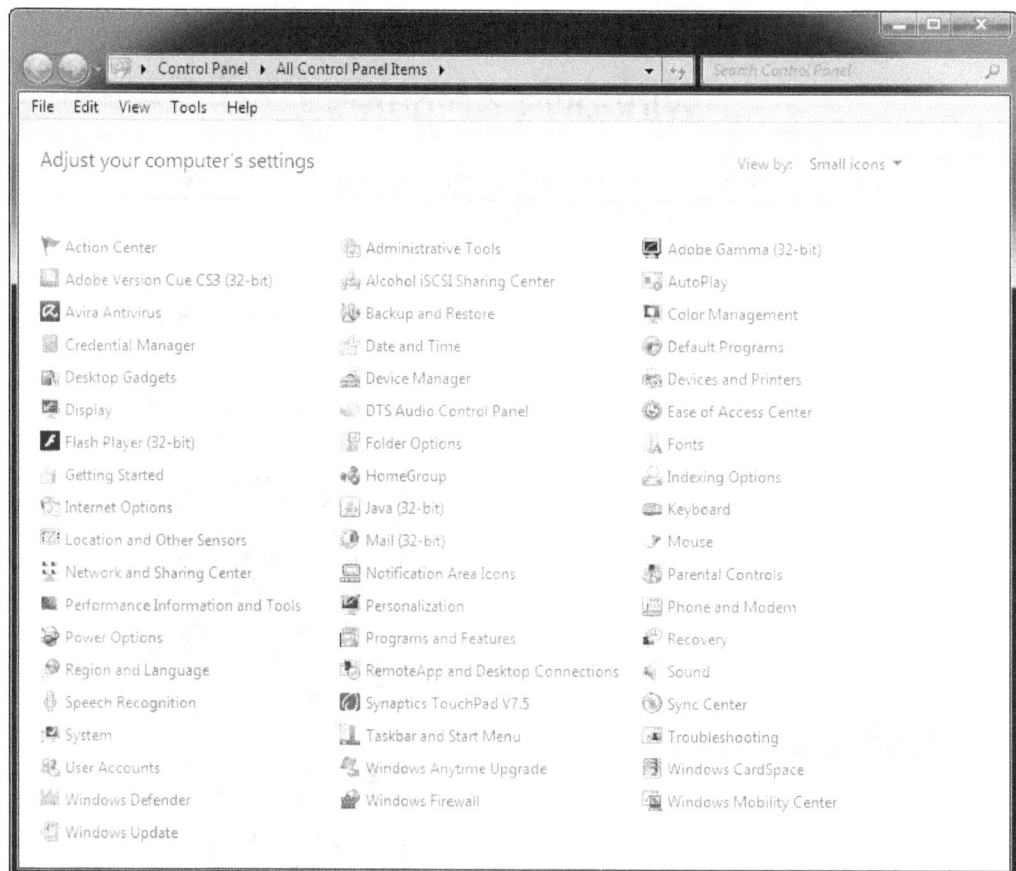

Windows 7 - Figure 2

Under Vista and the newer operating systems, instead of seeing an icon named "Display" – you instead click on the Personalization icon.

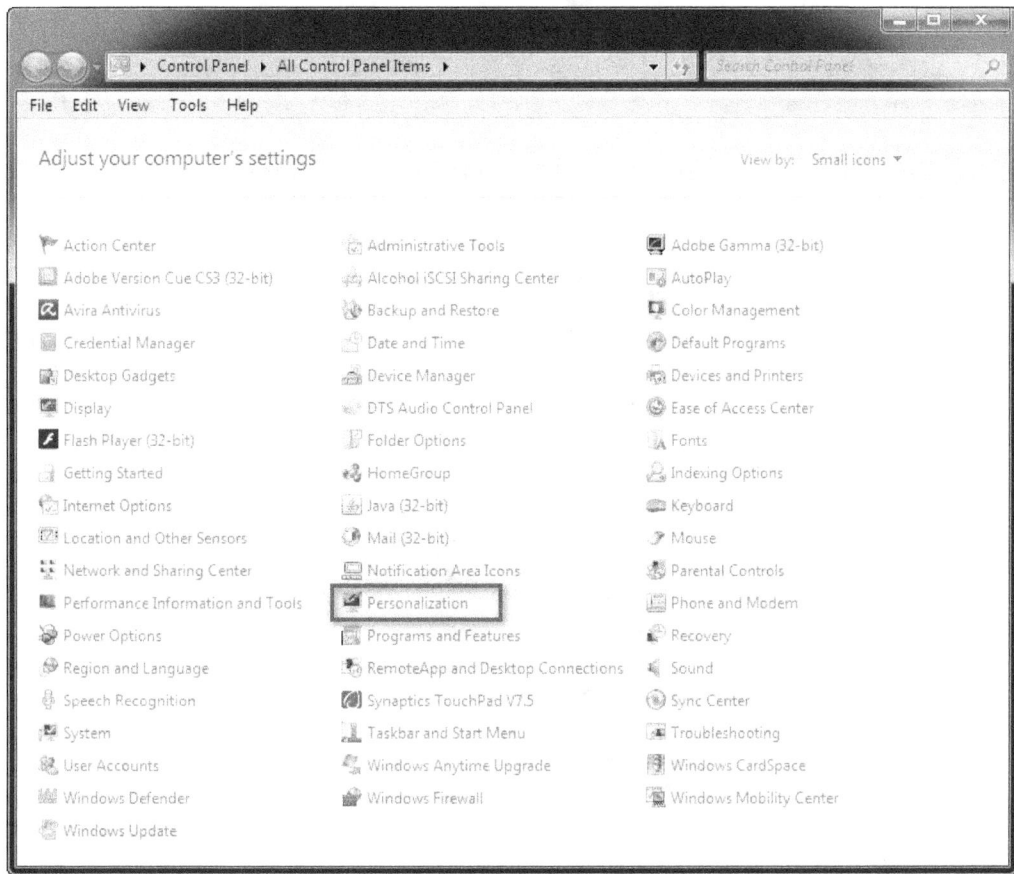

Windows 7 - Figure 3

Unlike Windows Vista – under Windows 7 the
Screen Saver option is a part of the Personalization dialog.

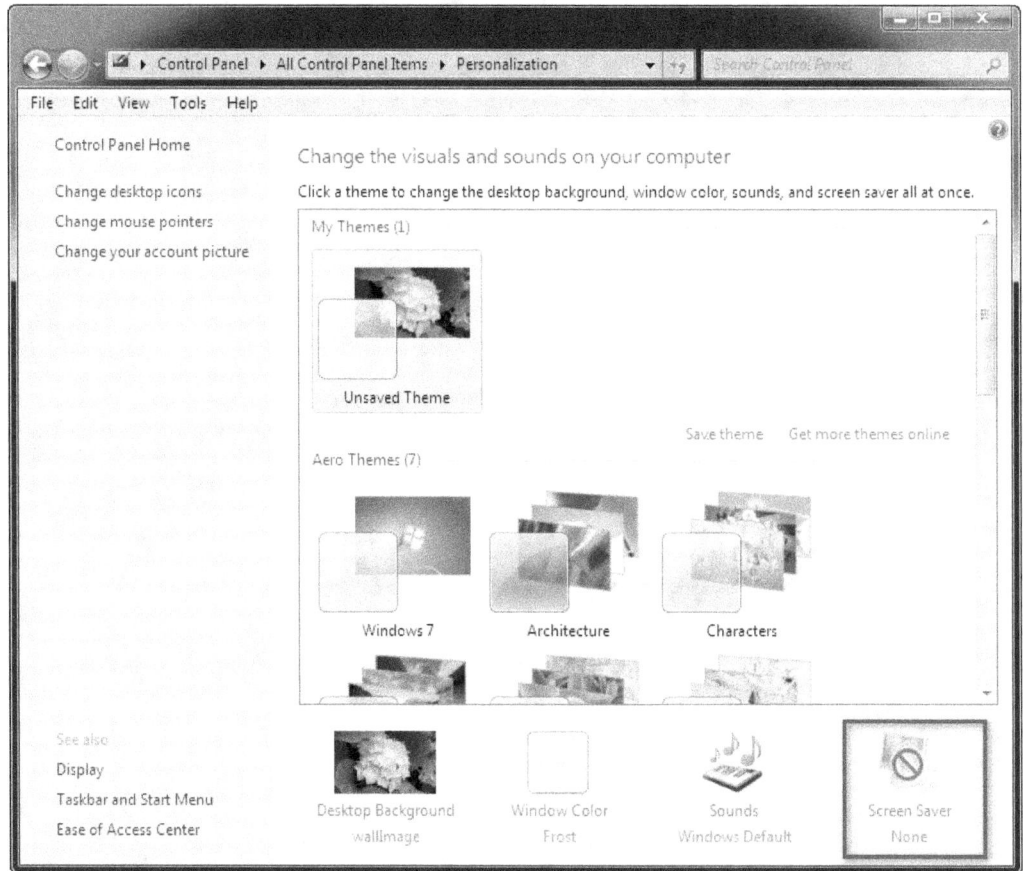

Windows 7 - Figure 4

Mark Versus Mr. Hacker.doc

And here you have the Screen Saver display which looks almost like the Windows XP Screen Saver dialog.

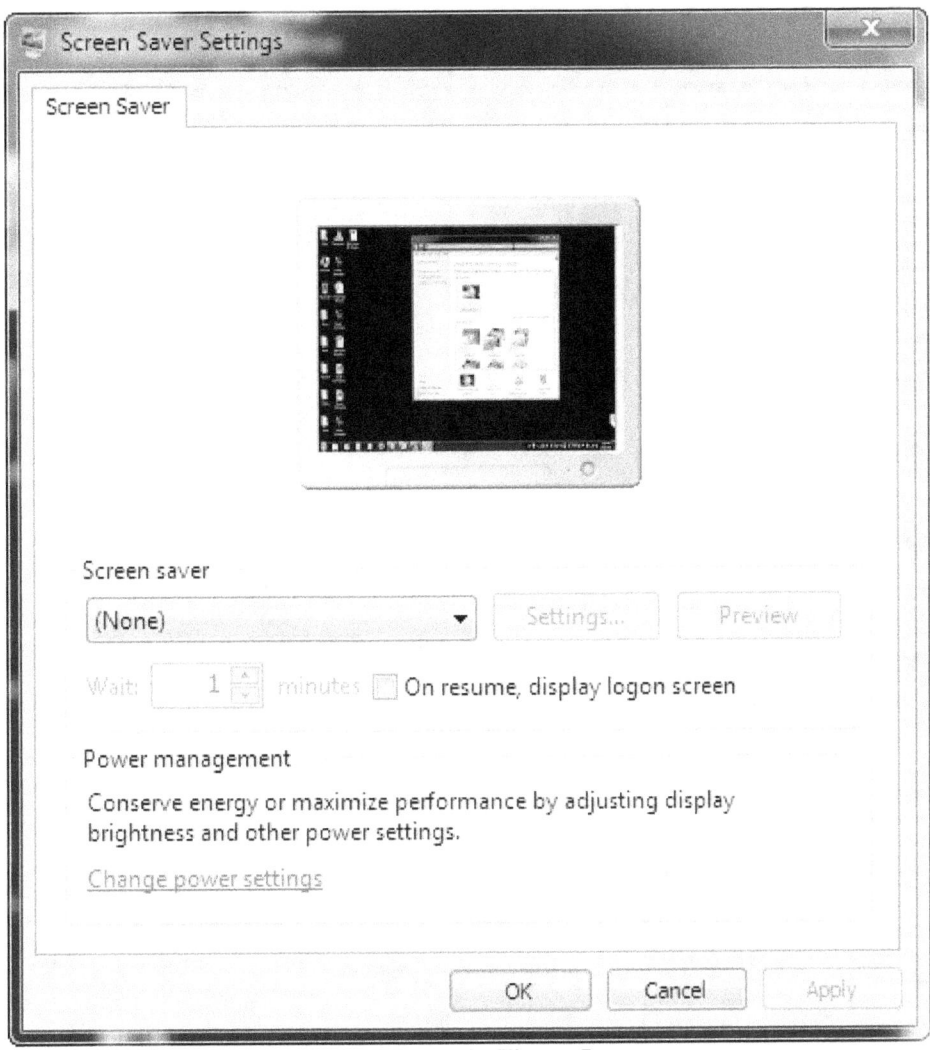

Windows 7 - Figure 5

Mark Versus Mr. Hacker.doc

In order to get to the Power Options, you have to go back to the Control Panel and select it from there.

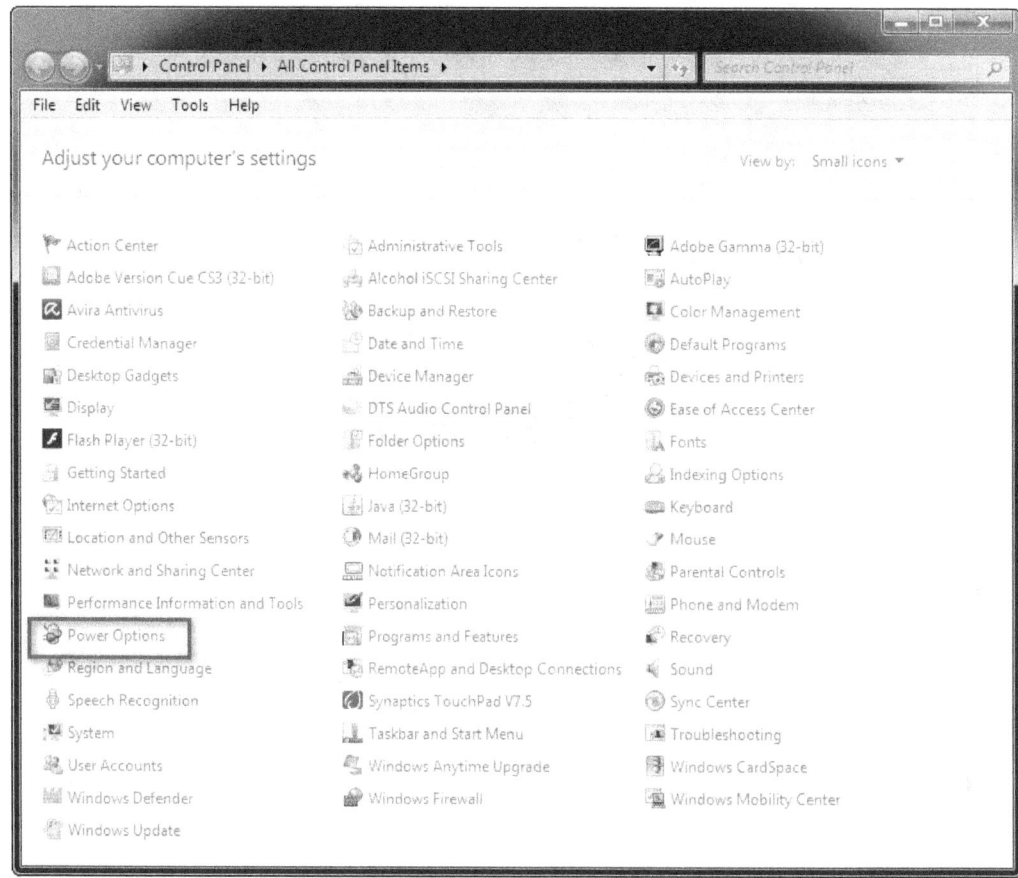

Windows 7 - Figure 6a

Page 133

Note that under Vista, 7, 8/8.1, and 10 you first have to say
Which Power Plan you want to modify.

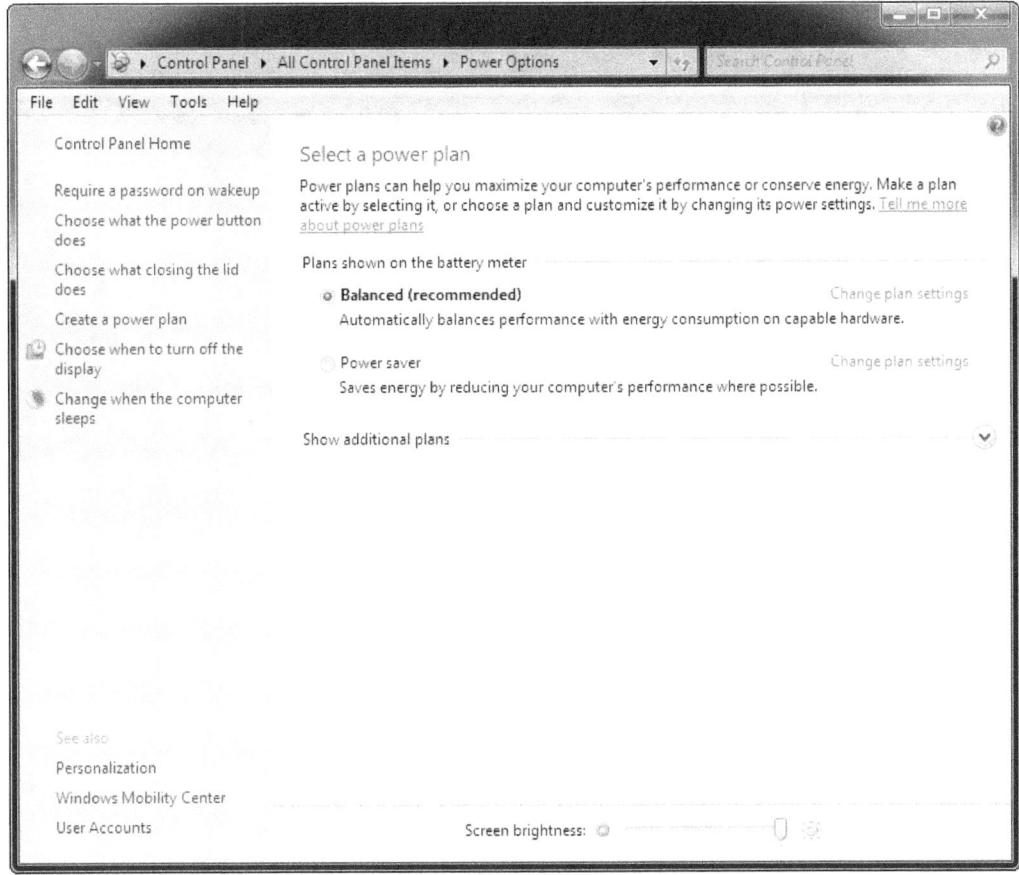

Windows 7 - Figure 6b

Once in the Power Plan area, change your time to turn off your display to be 30 minutes and to never shut down the computer when it is plugged in. Notice the "Change advanced power settings" link. We are going to use that next.

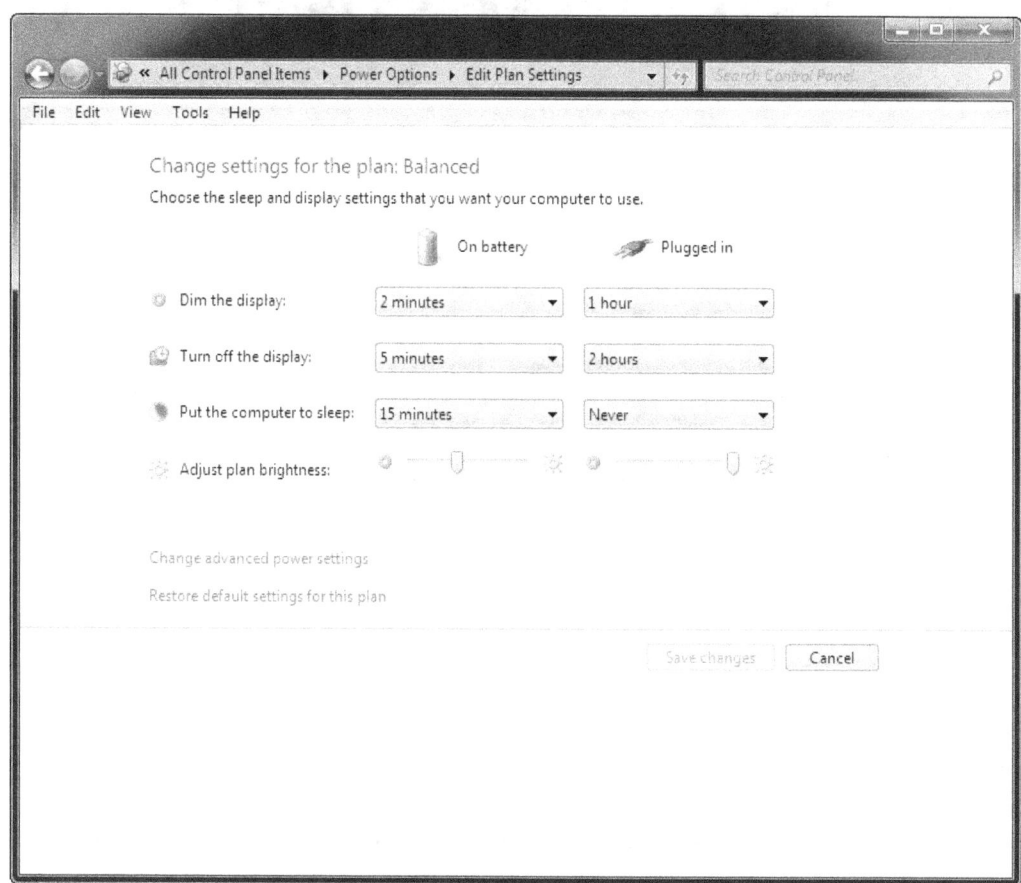

Windows 7 - Figure 6c

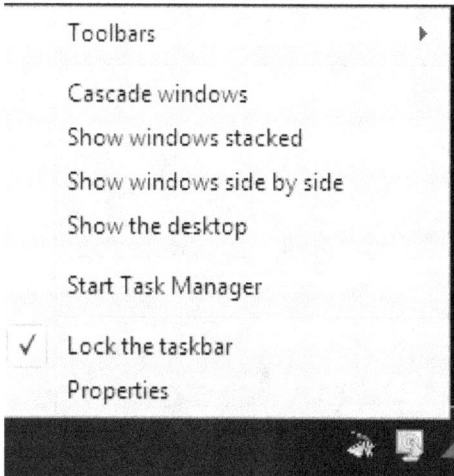

Windows 7 - Figure 7

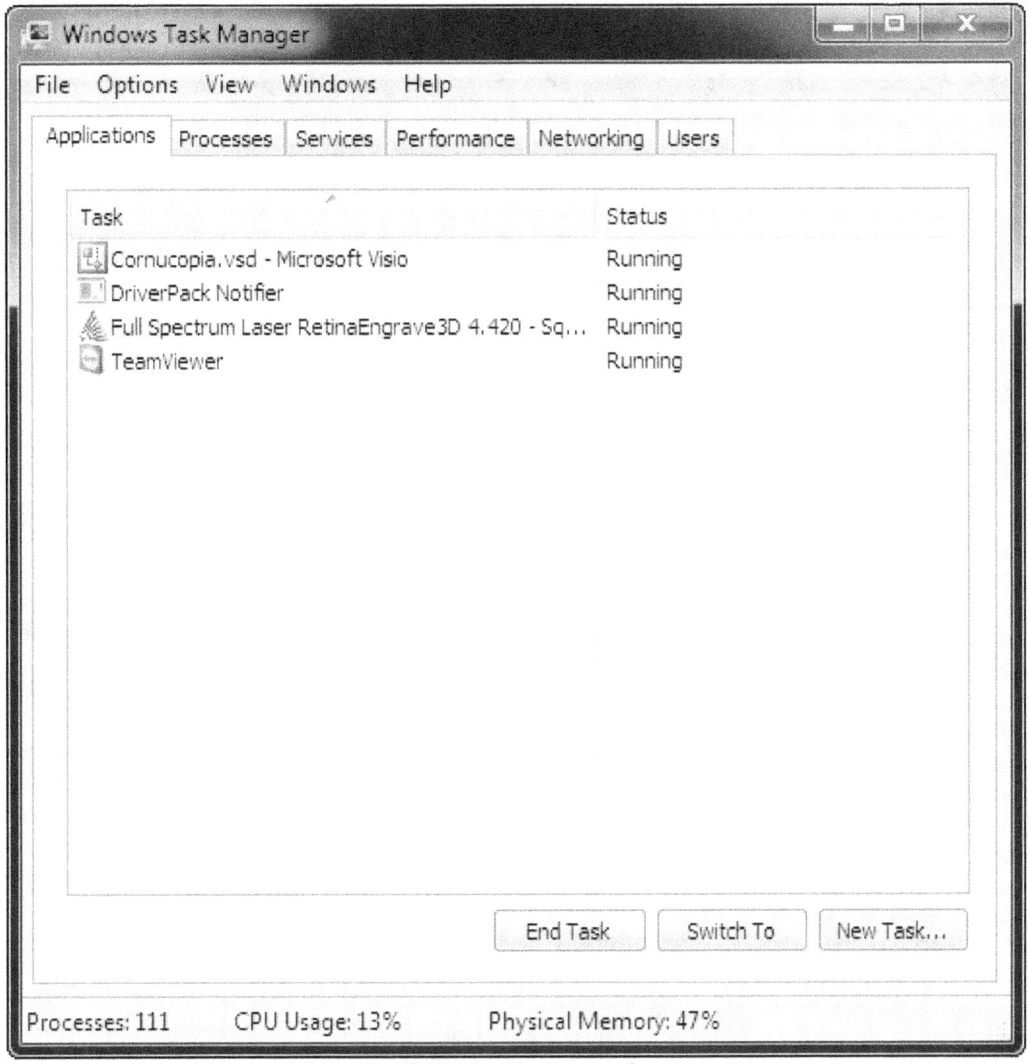

Windows 7 - Figure 8

Mark Versus Mr. Hacker.doc

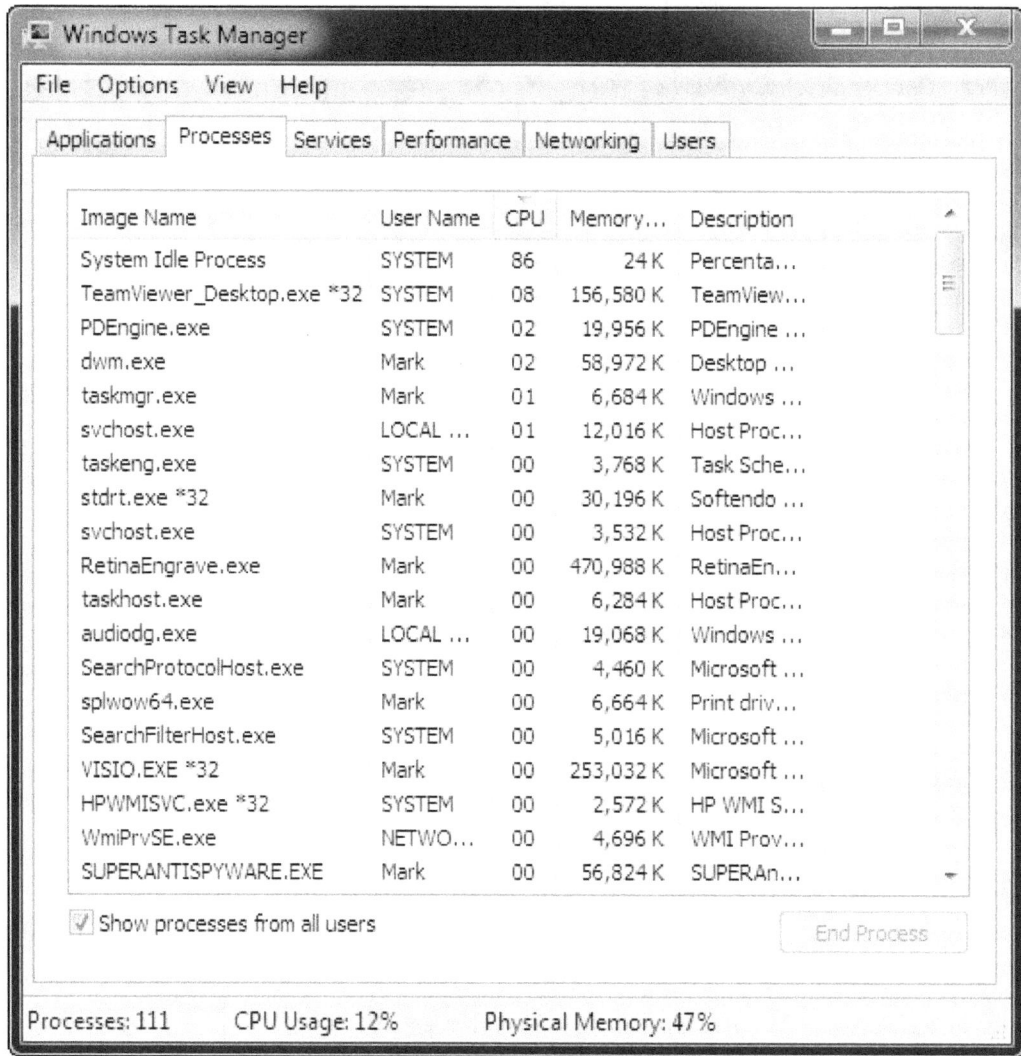

Windows 7 - Figure 9

Mark Versus Mr. Hacker.doc

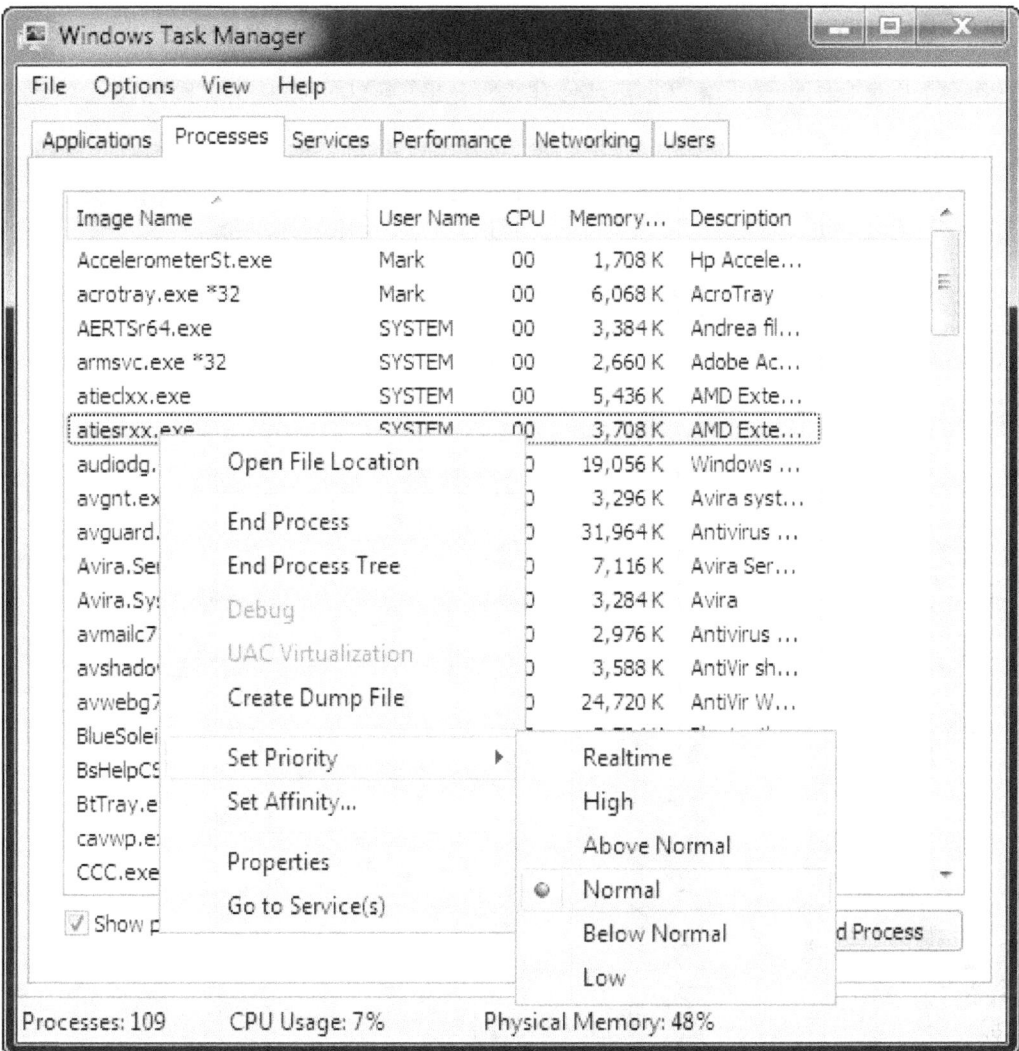

Windows 7 - Figure 10

Mark Versus Mr. Hacker.doc

Since TCPView looks the same on all platforms – here is the Windows XP version.

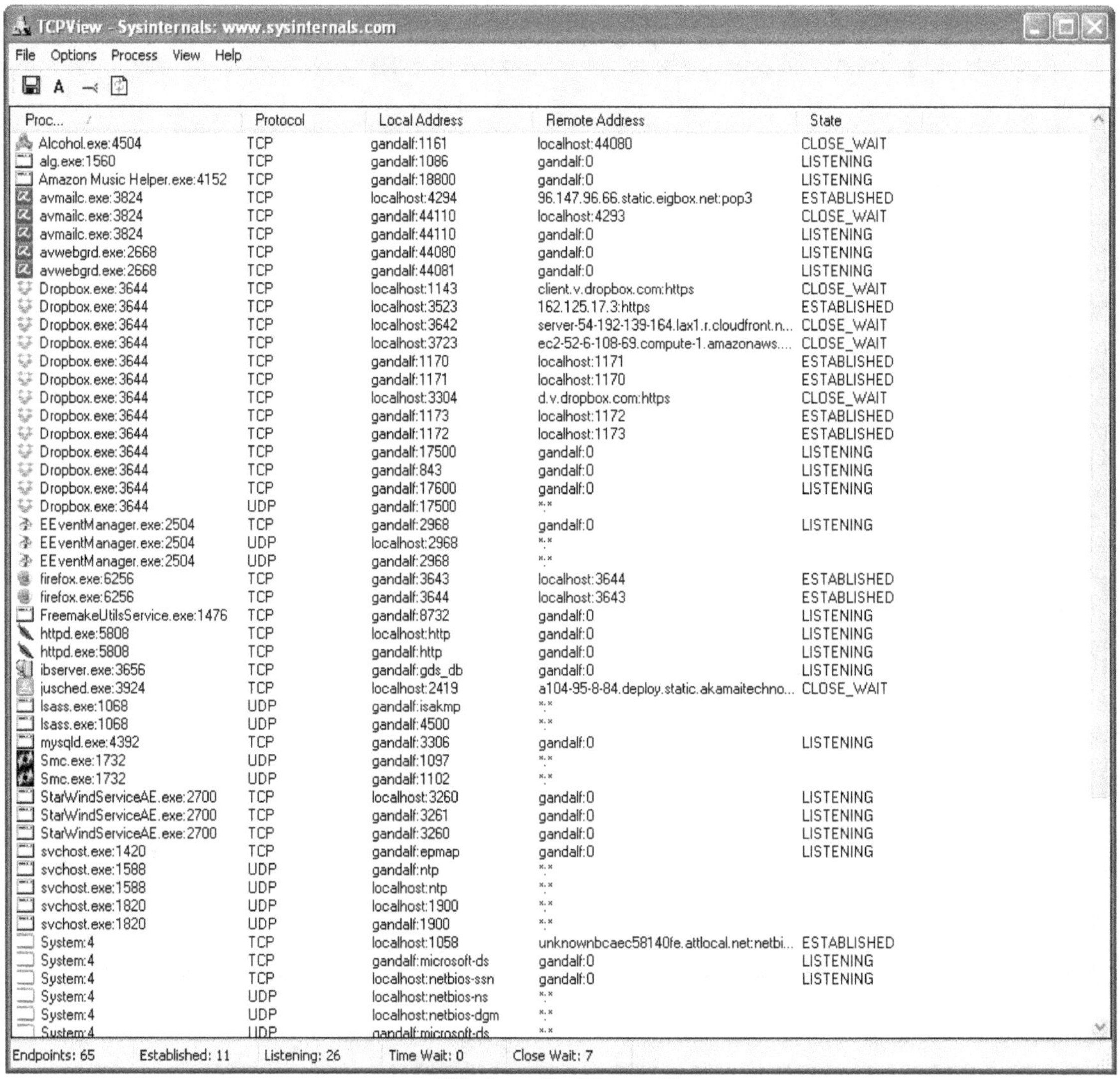

Windows 7 - Figure 11

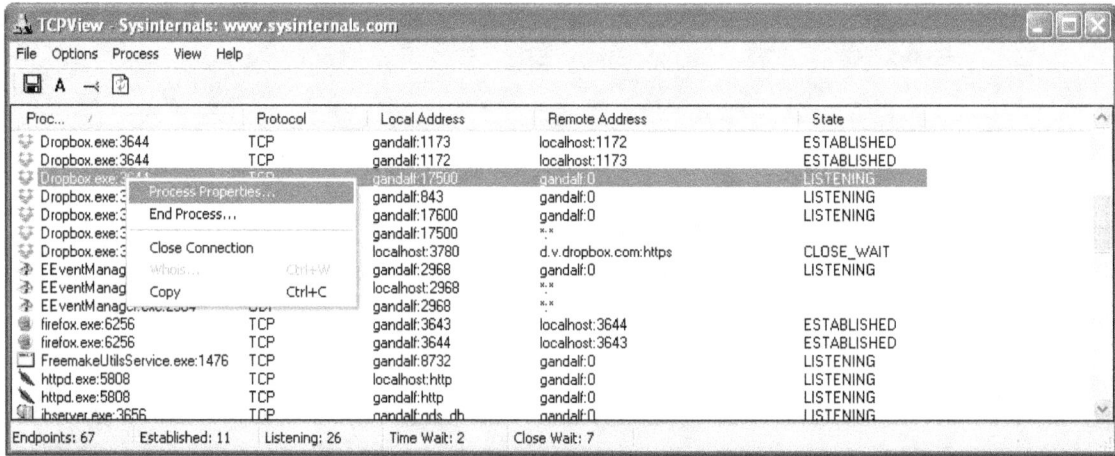

Windows 7 - Figure 12

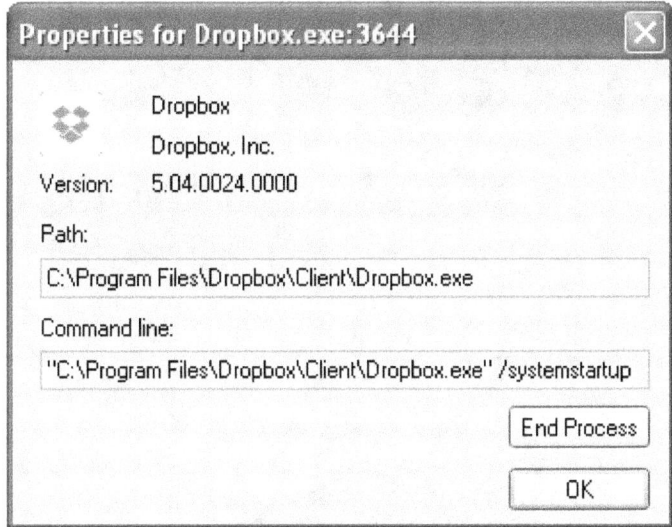

Windows 7 - Figure 13

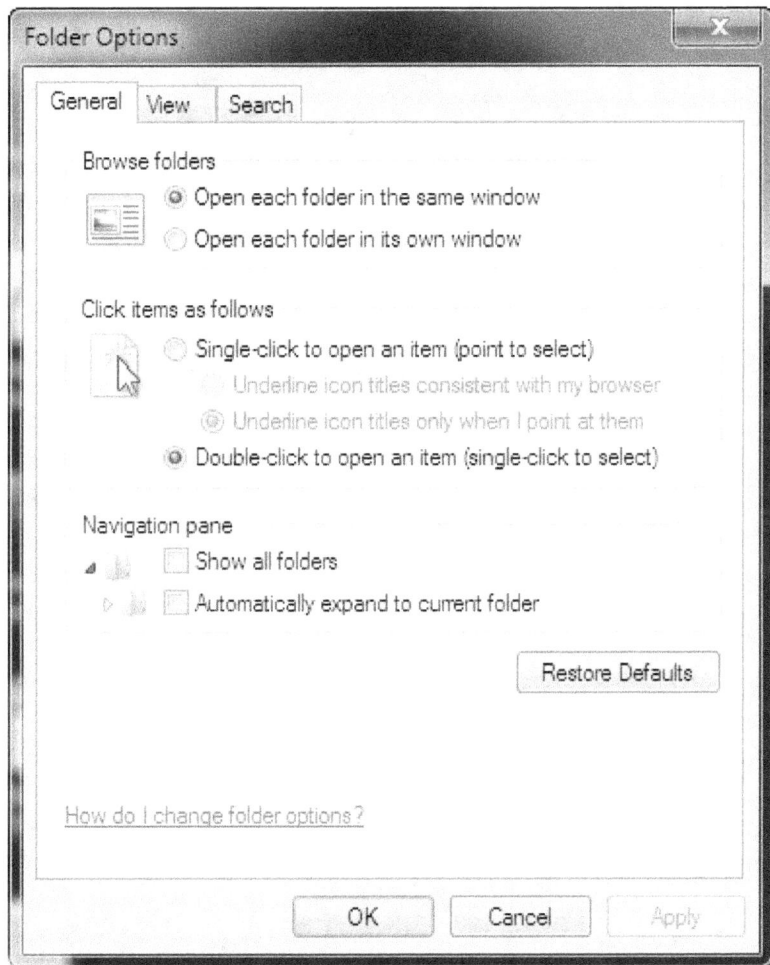

Windows 7 - Figure 14

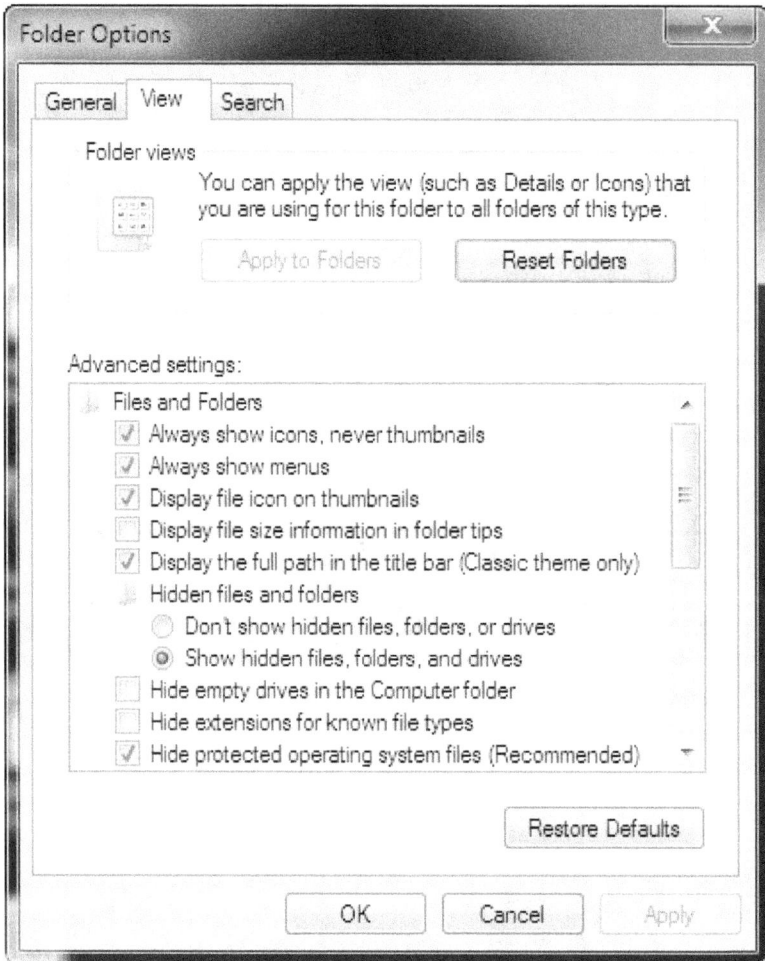

Windows 7 - Figure 15

Notice that under Windows 7 there is nothing about Simple File Sharing. Instead, there is just a "Sharing Wizard". It is the same program. Microsoft just changed the name.

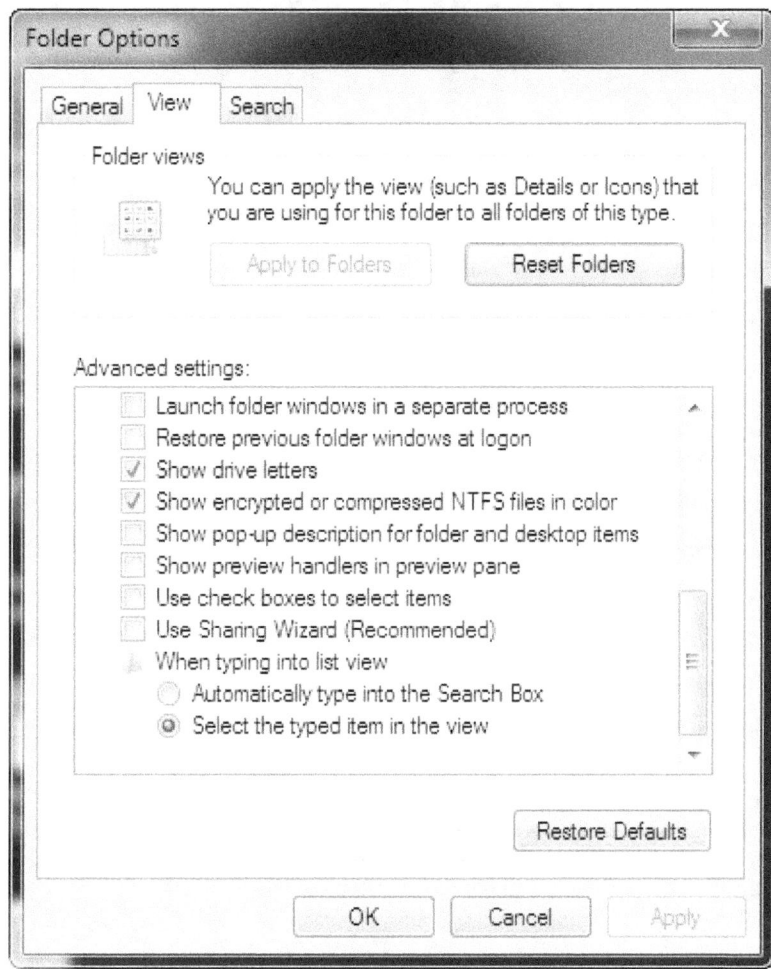

Windows 7 - Figure 16-17

Mark Versus Mr. Hacker.doc

In order to get the to System Restore area you first have to go to the control panel and then left click on the System icon.

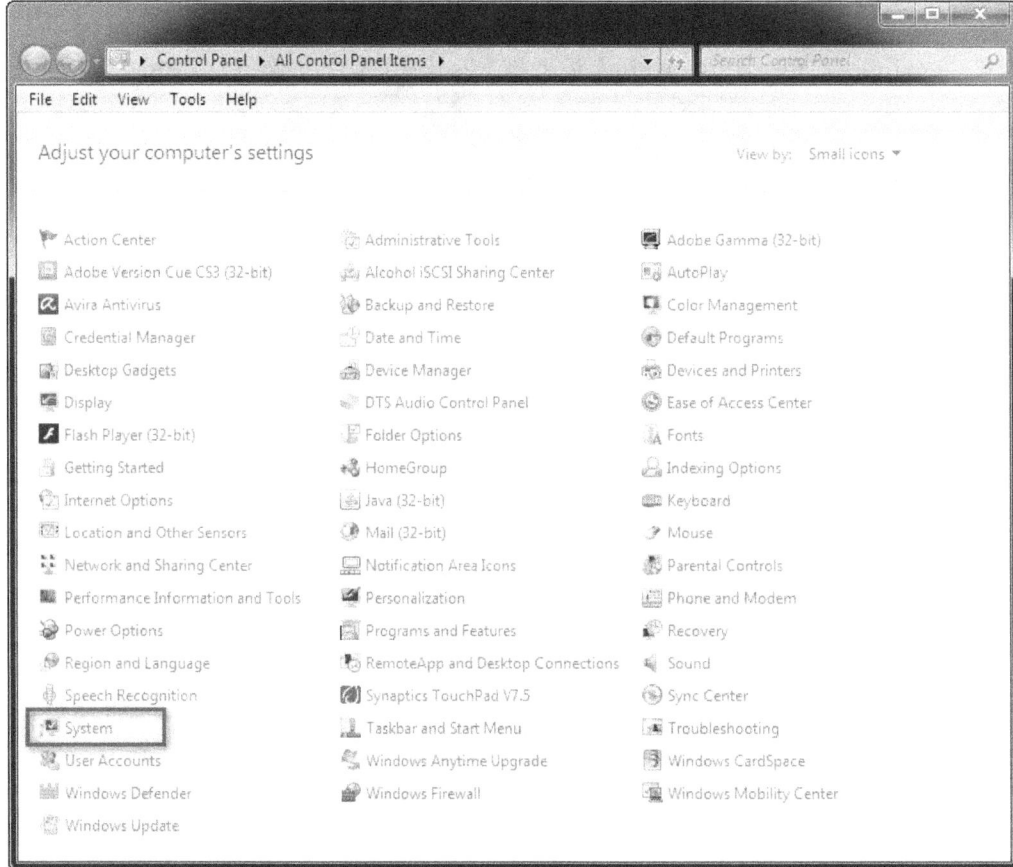

Windows 7 - Figure 18a

In the System dialog box, select the "Advanced system serttings".

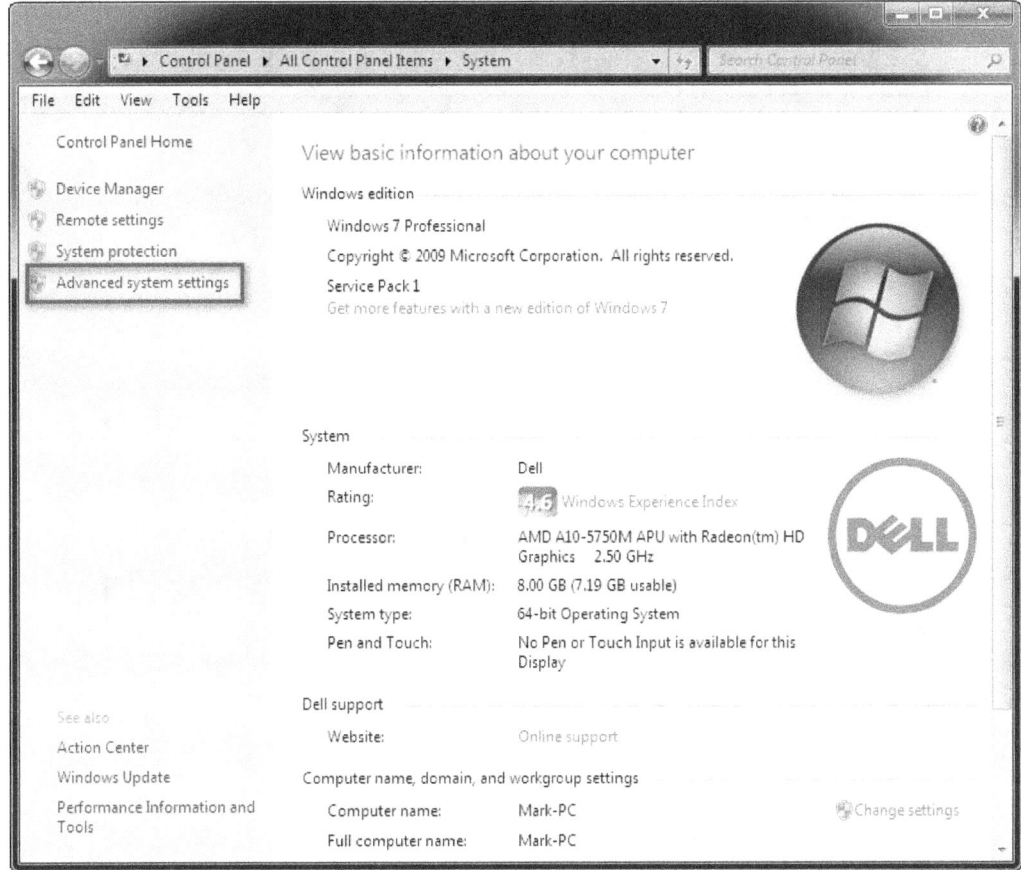

Windows 7 - Figure 18b

Under Windows 7 Microsoft changed the tab from "System Restore" To "System Protection". Use the Configure button to change this.

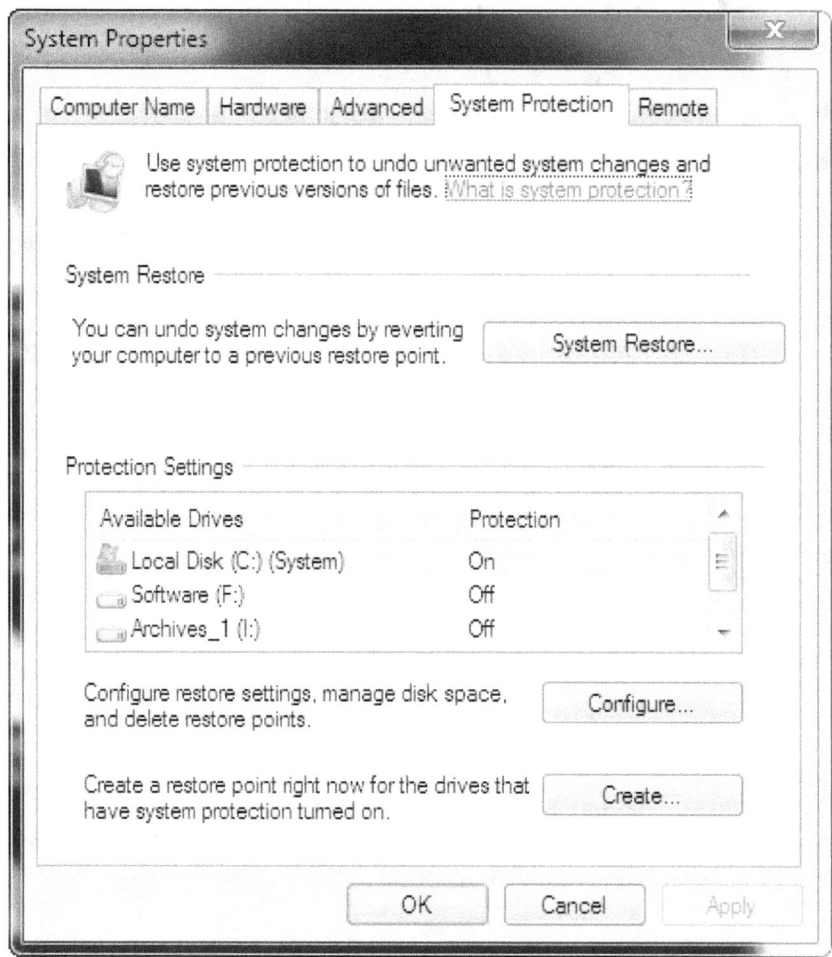

Windows 7 - Figure 18c

Here is what the dialog looks like after you have pushed the Configuration button.
You should turn off the "System Protection" and instead make a backup
on an external hard drive and then store that hard drive in a safe place.
Then when you need it – you can restore the system from the external hard drive.

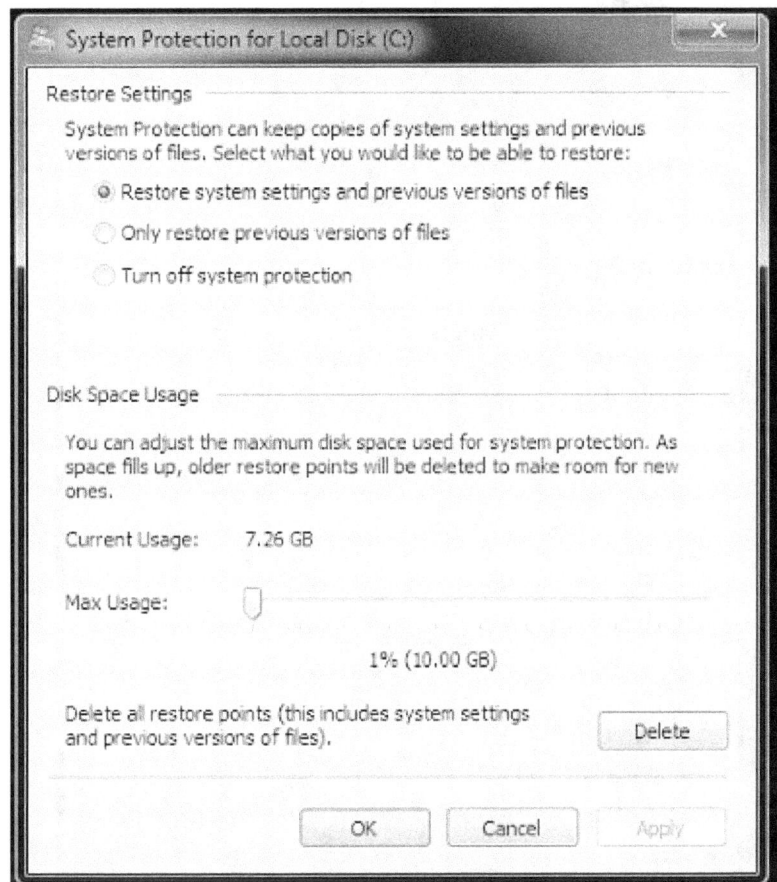

Windows 7 - Figure 18d

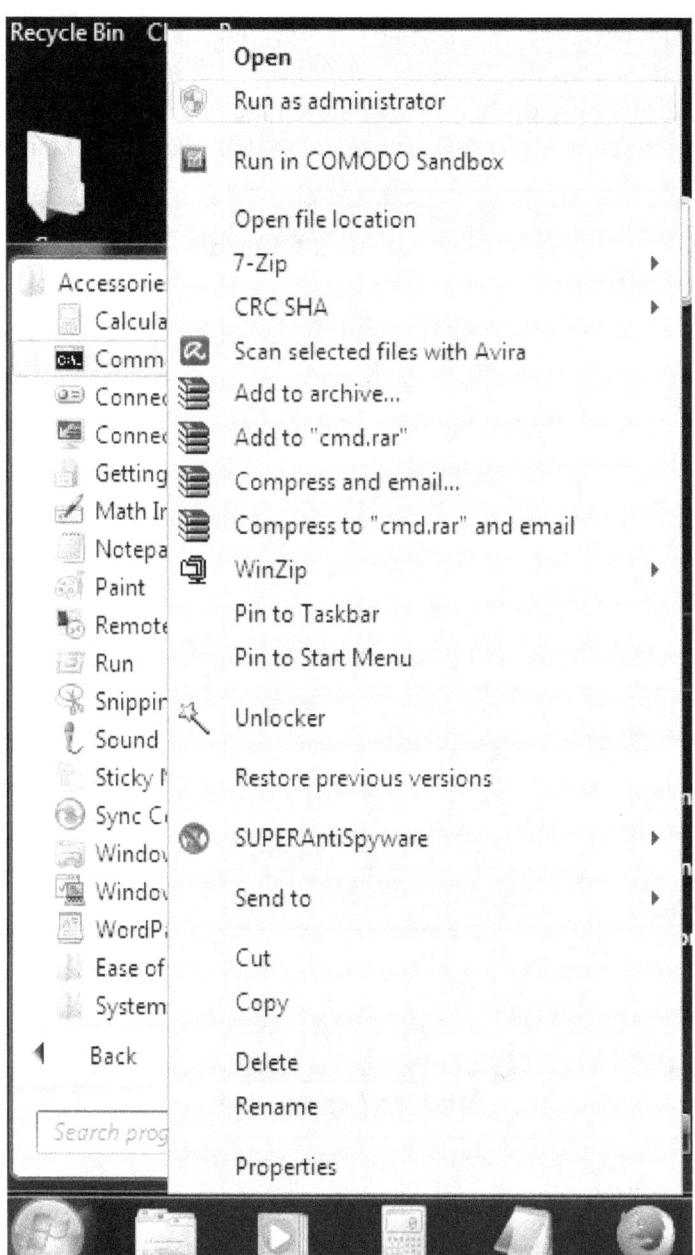

Windows 7 - Figure 19

Mark Versus Mr. Hacker.doc

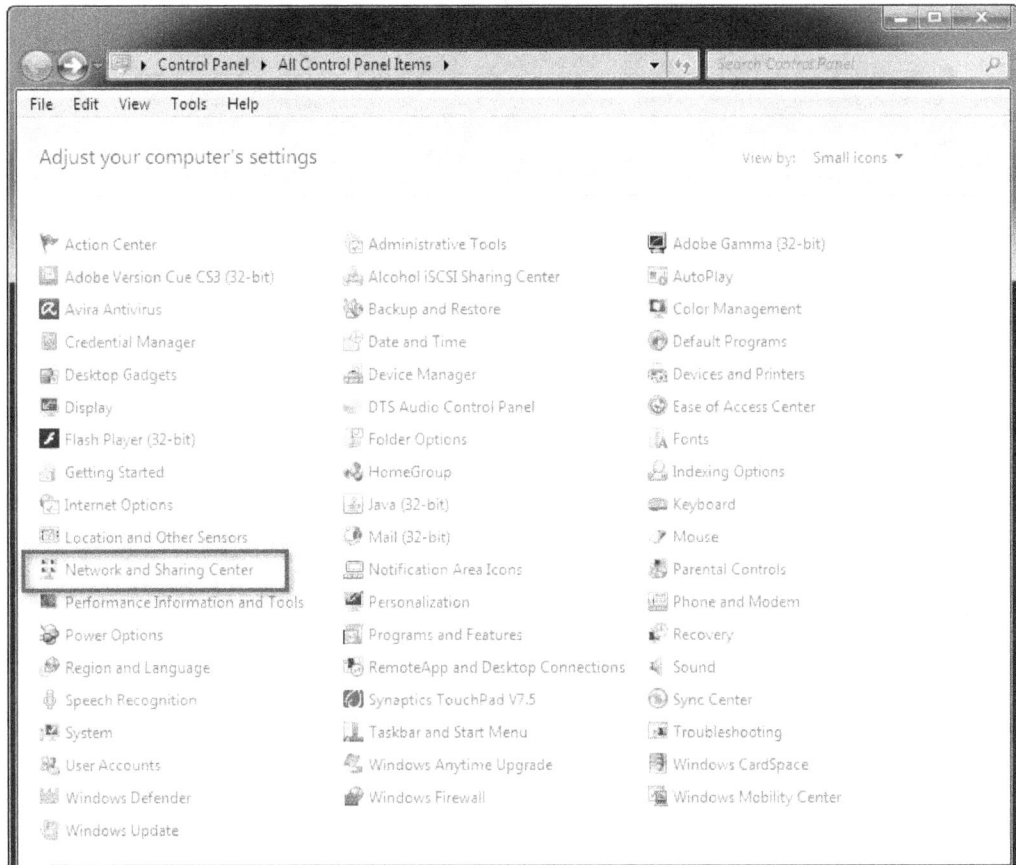

Windows 7 - Figure 20

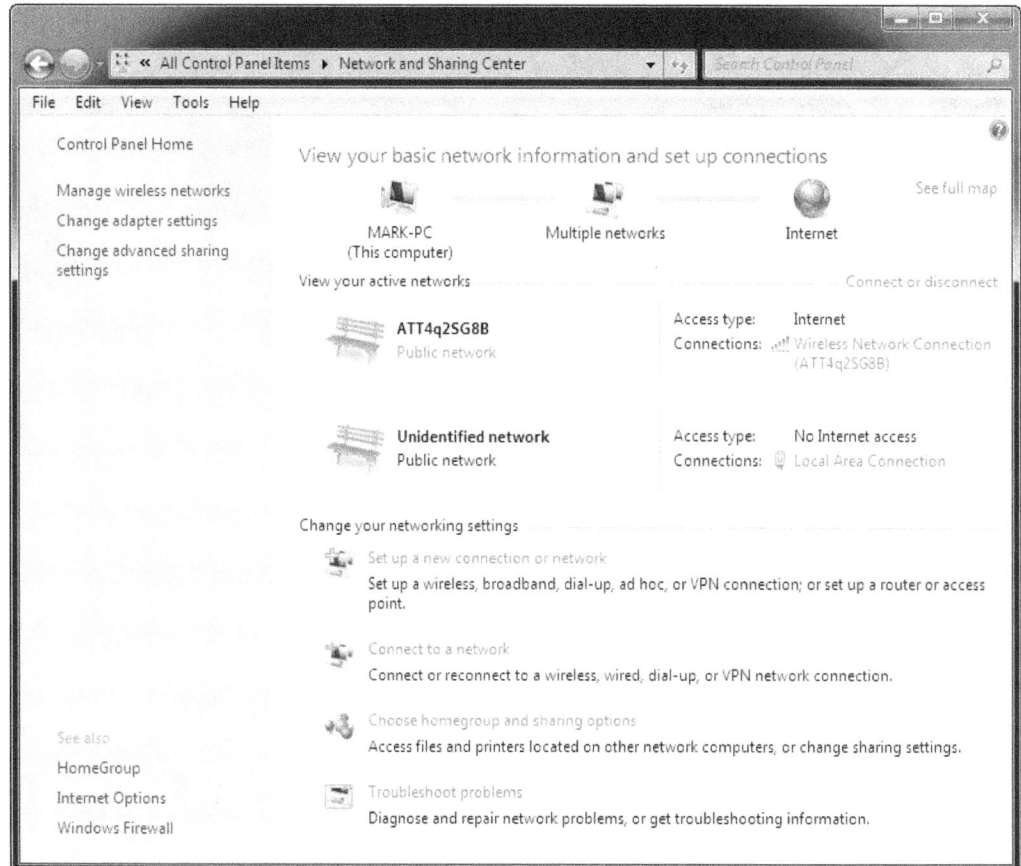

Windows 7 - Figure 21a

Mark Versus Mr. Hacker.doc

You can get to it via the "Manage wireless networks".

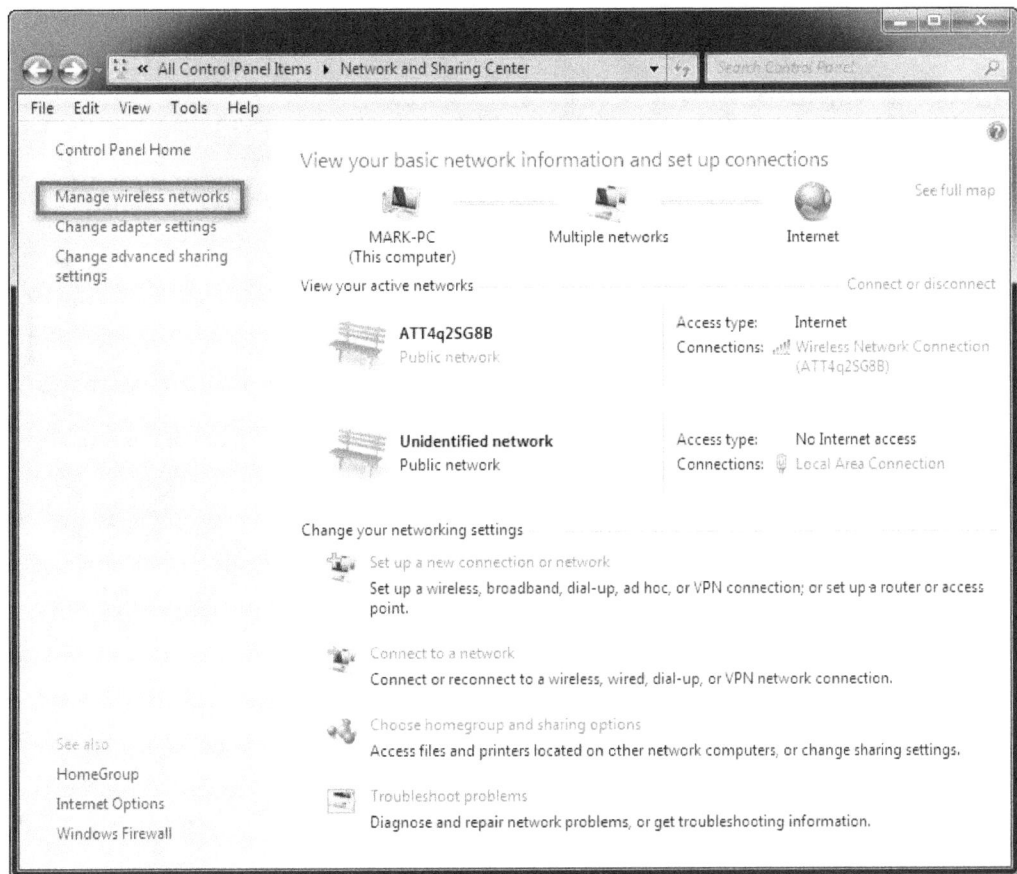

Windows 7 - Figure 21b

Mark Versus Mr. Hacker.doc

Here is an alternative way to get to the networking information.

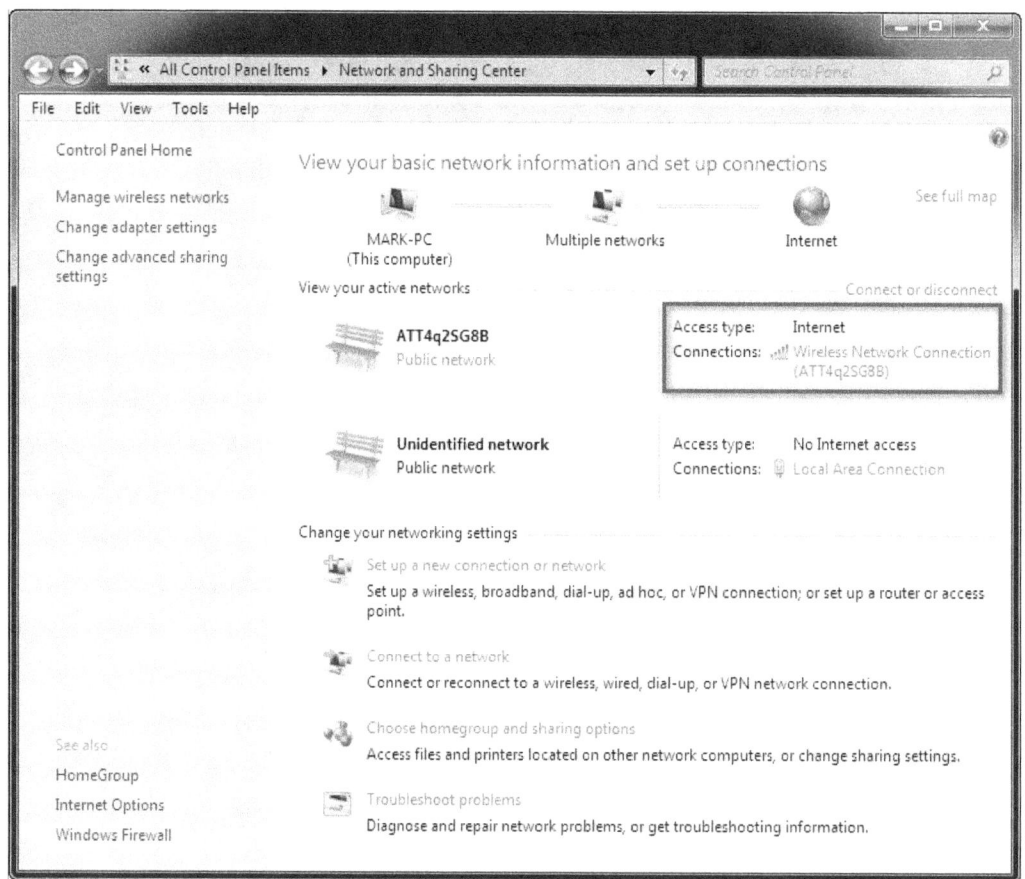

Windows 7 - Figure 21c

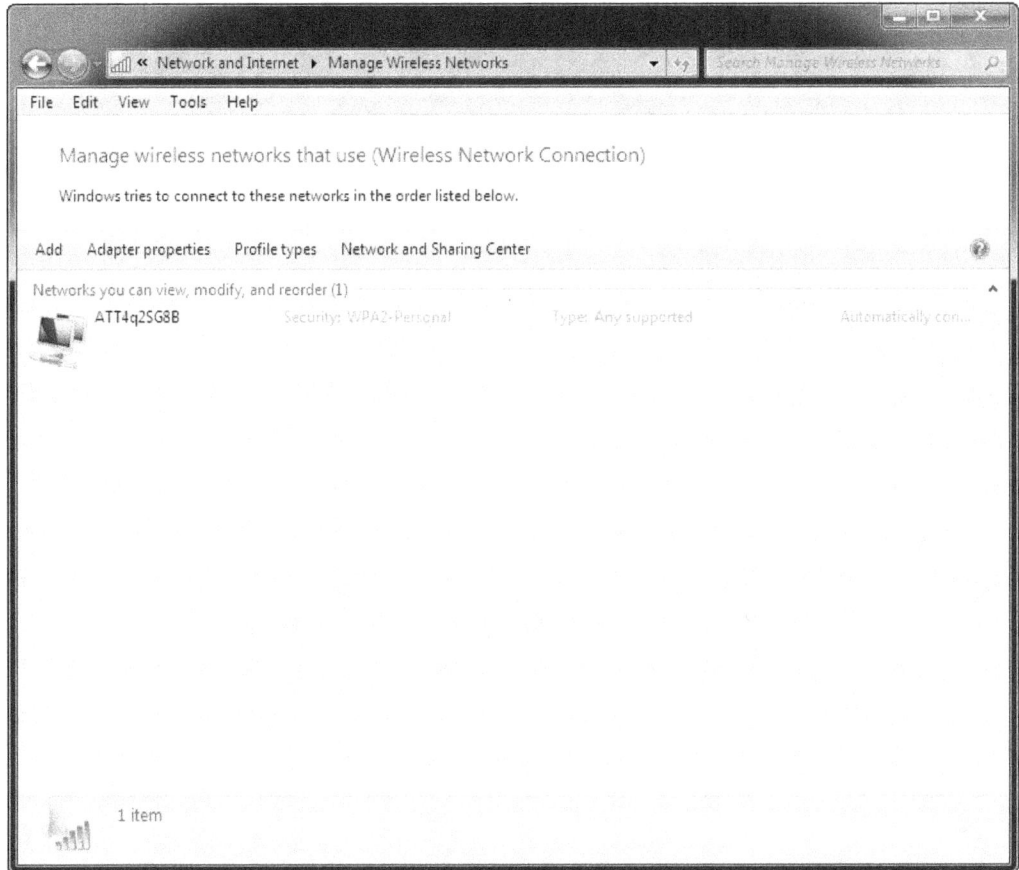

Windows 7 - Figure 21d

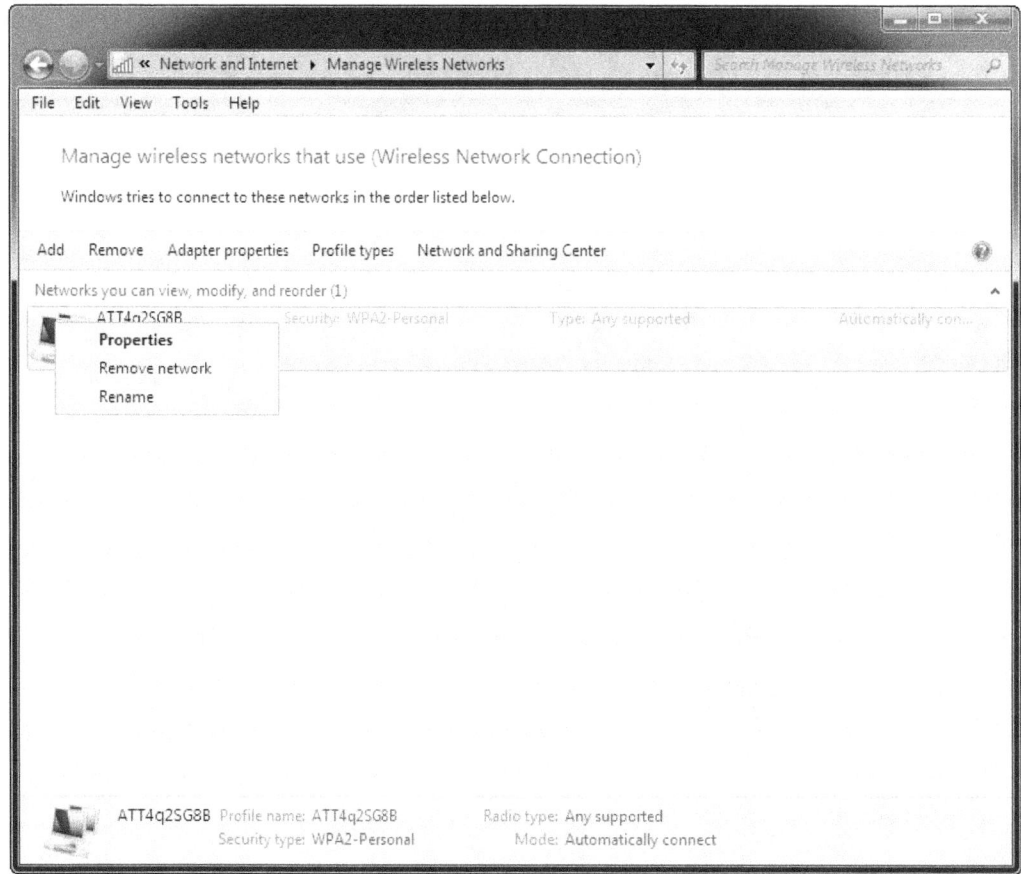

Windows 7 - Figure 22

Be sure to click on the "Properties" button
and not the "Wireless Properties" button.

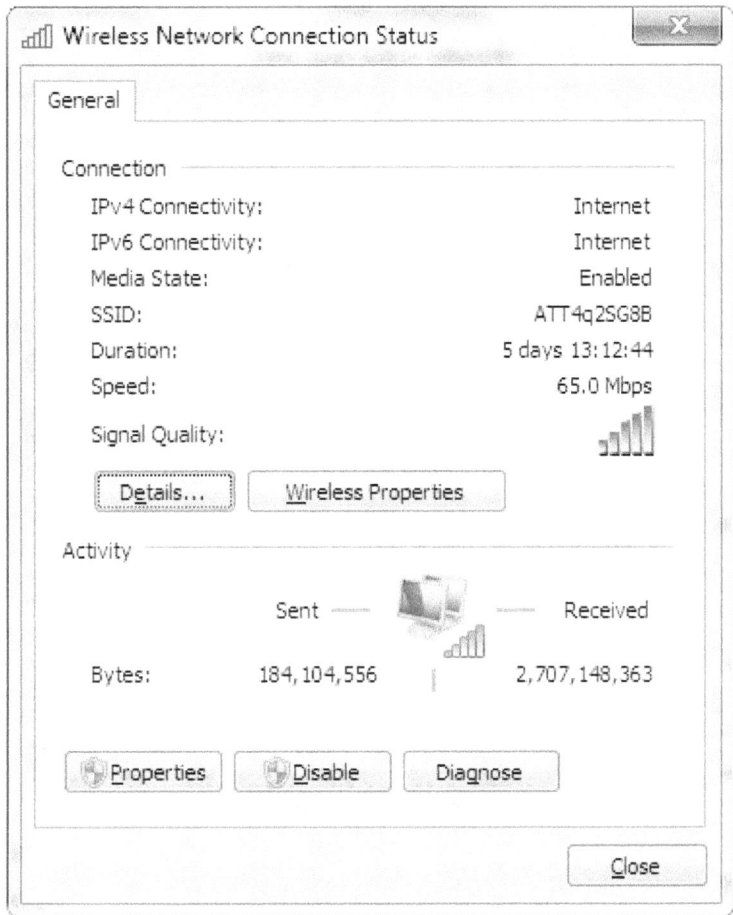

Windows 7 - Figure 23a

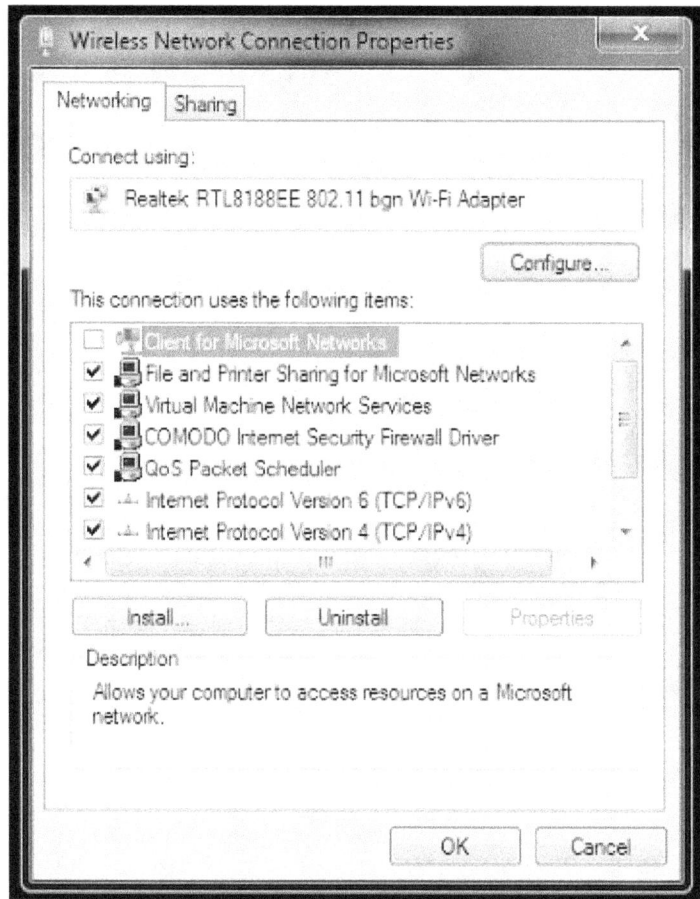

Windows 7 - Figure 23b

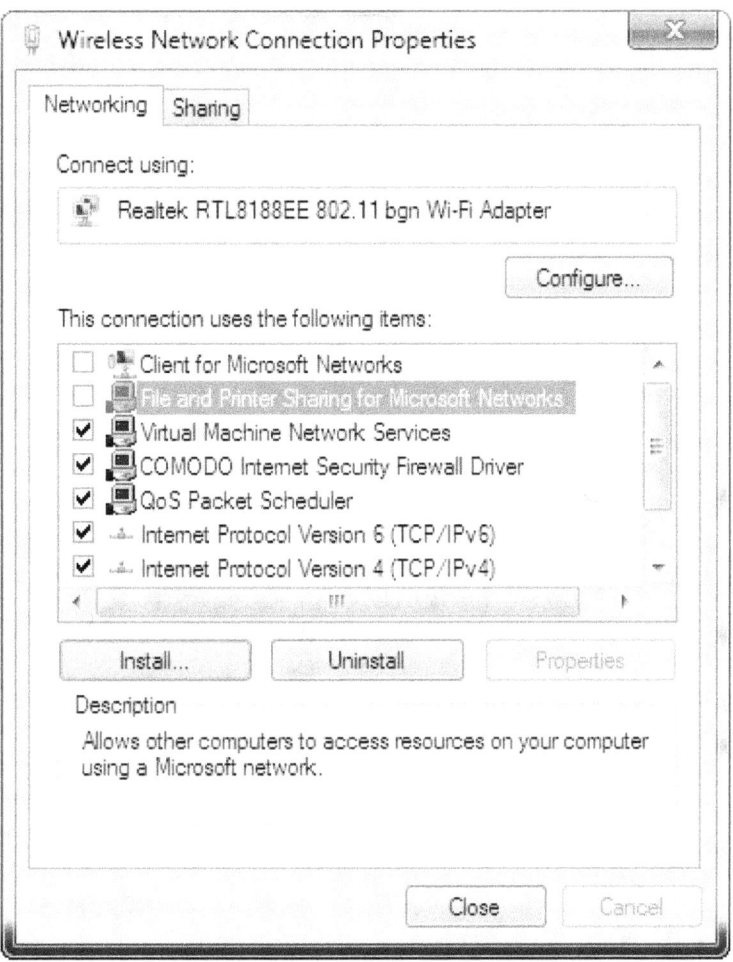

Windows 7 - Figure 24

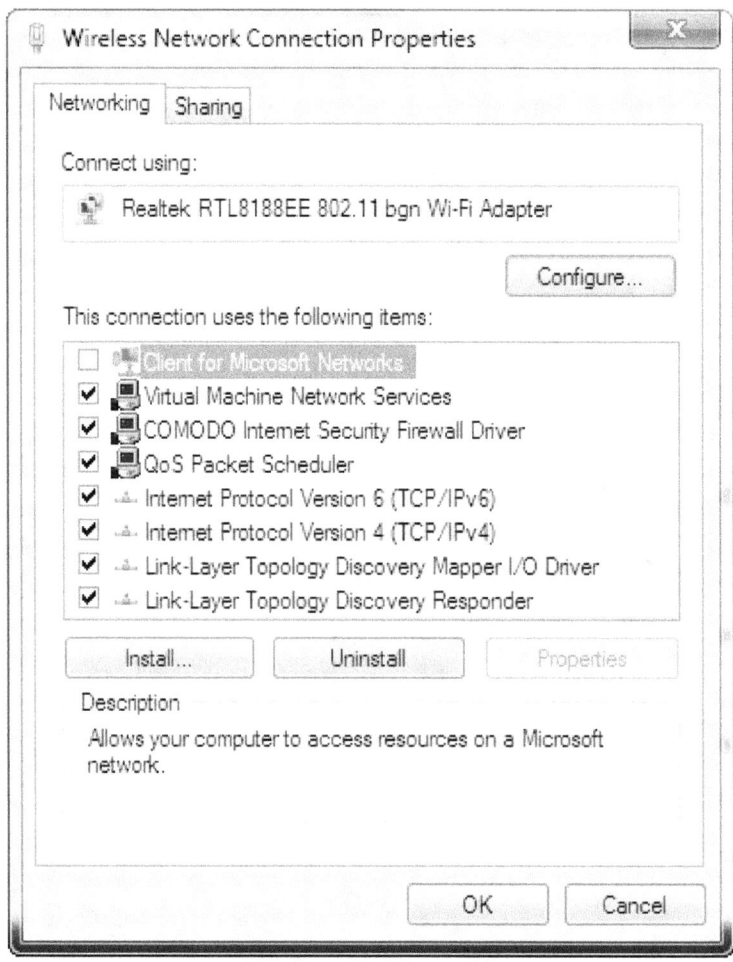

Windows 7 - Figure 25

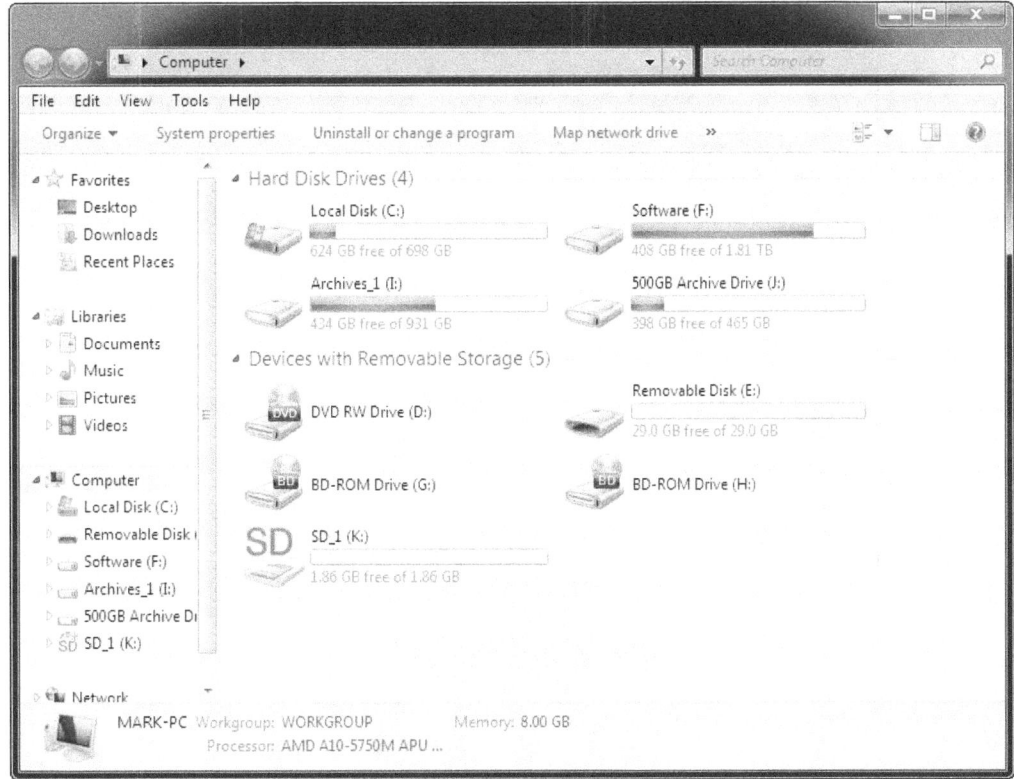

Windows 7 - Figure 26

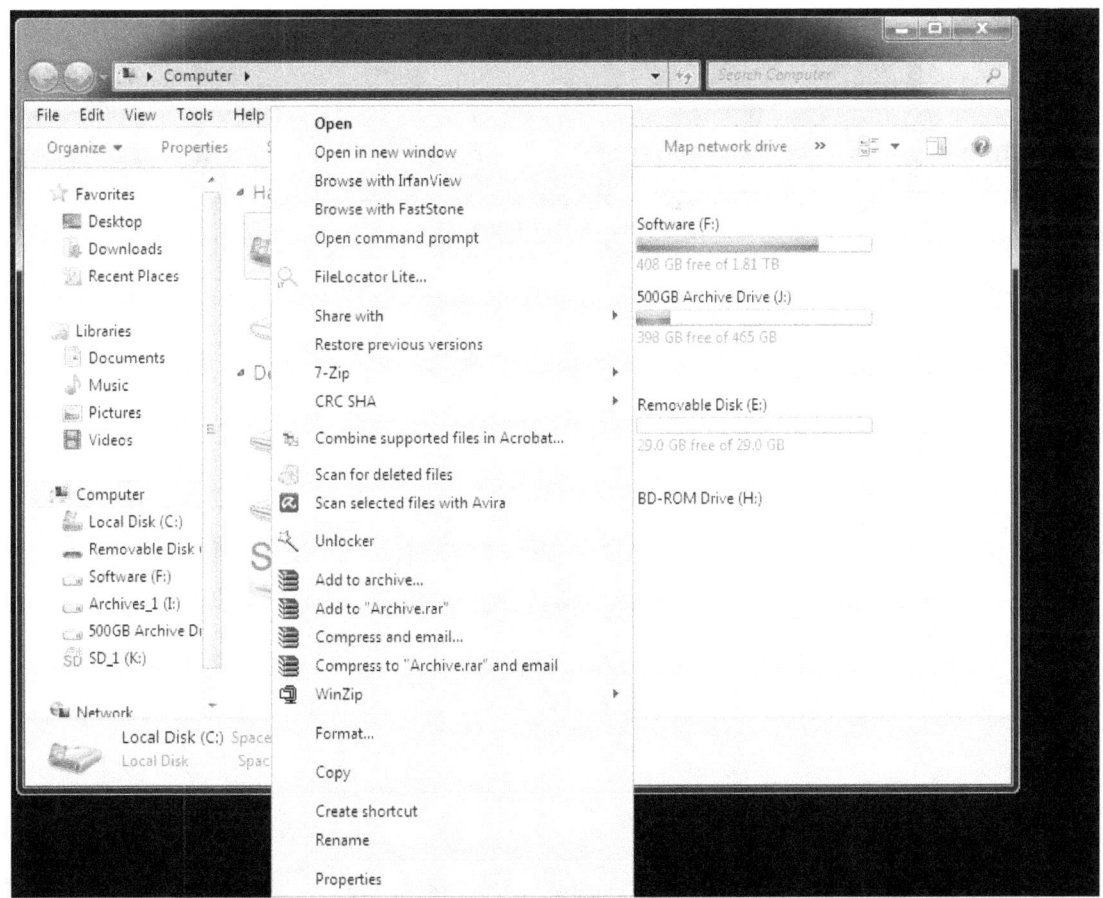

Windows 7 - Figure 27

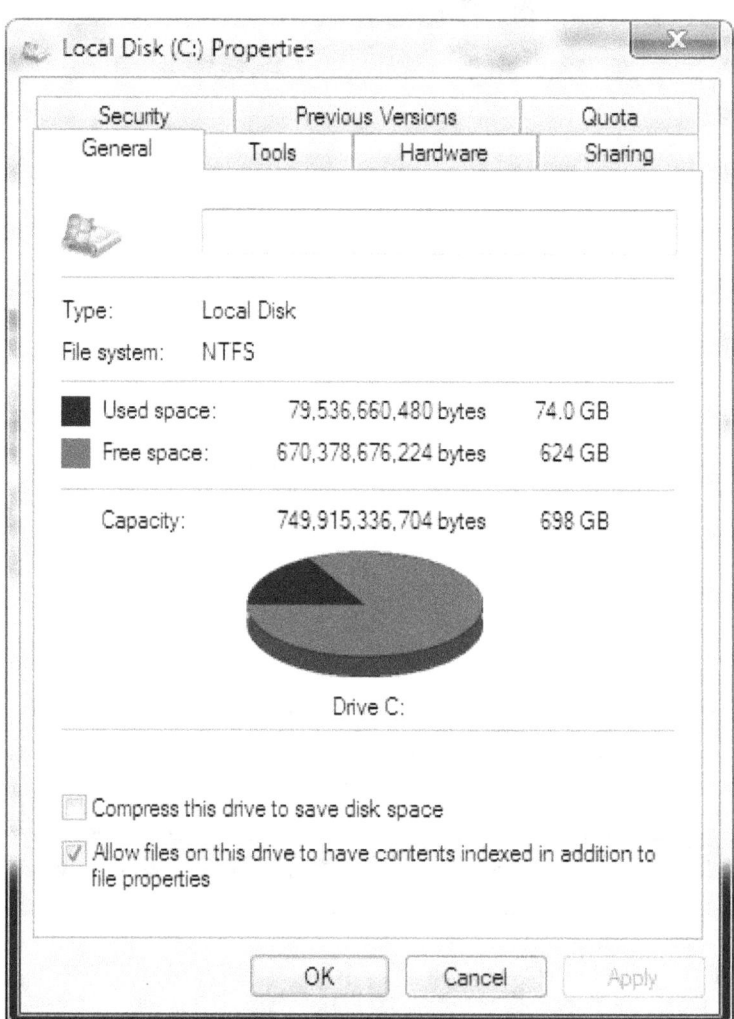

Windows 7 - Figure 28

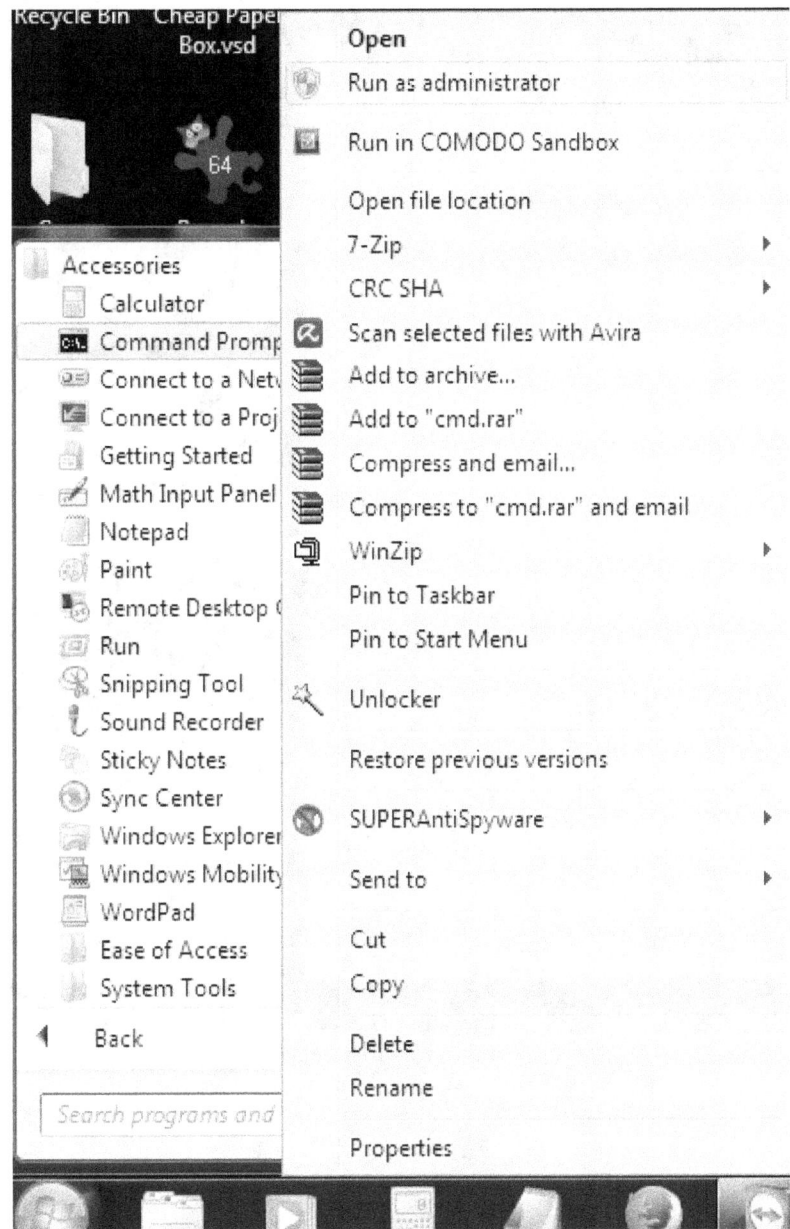
Windows 7 - Figure 29

Windows 7 – Figure 30 omitted because Windows 7 doesn't do that.
It just runs as an administrator.

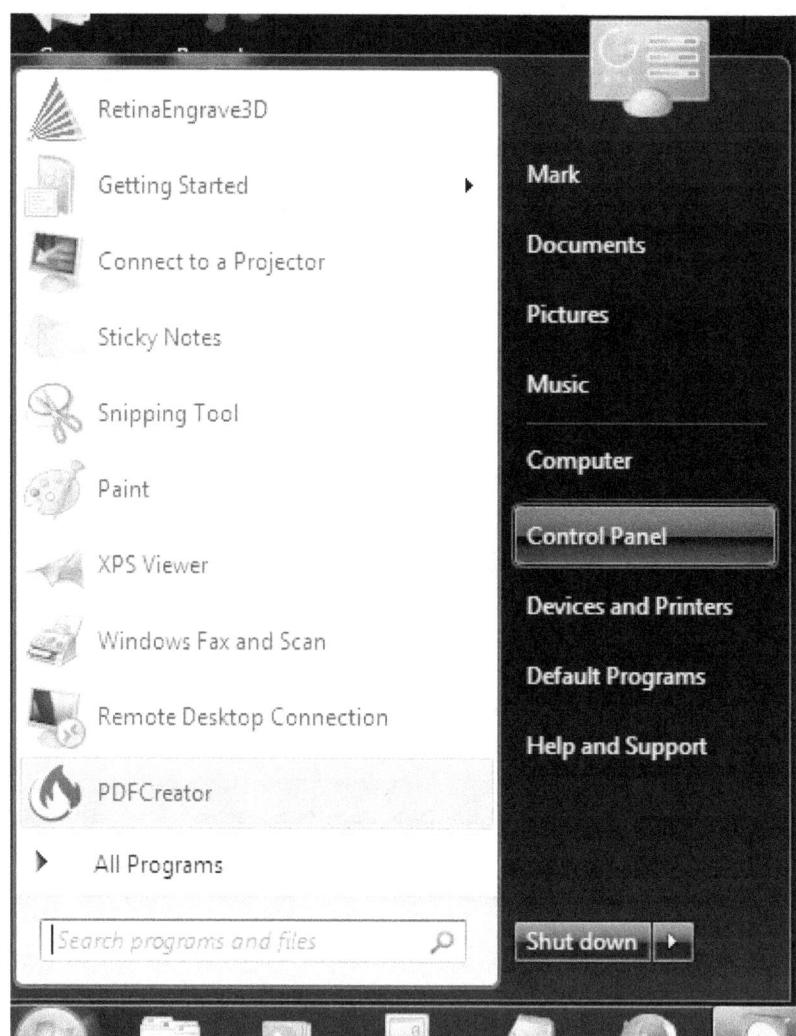

Windows 7 - Figure 31

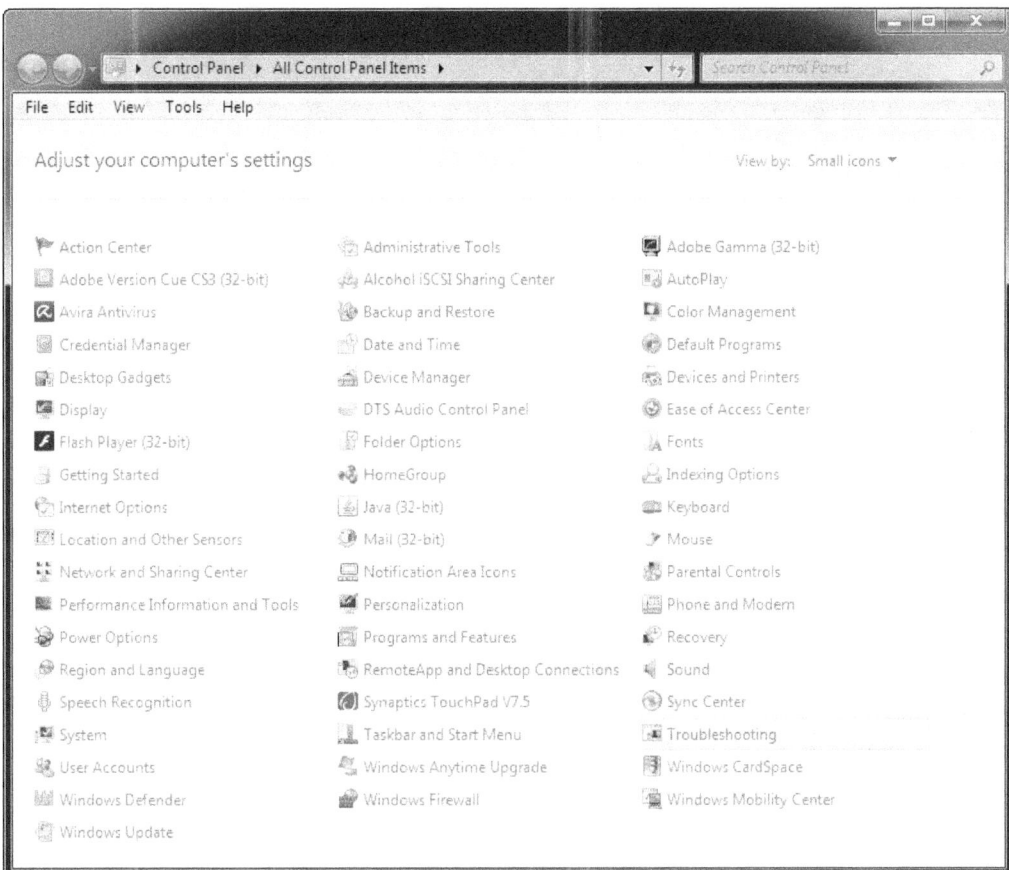

Windows 7 - Figure 32

Mark Versus Mr. Hacker.doc

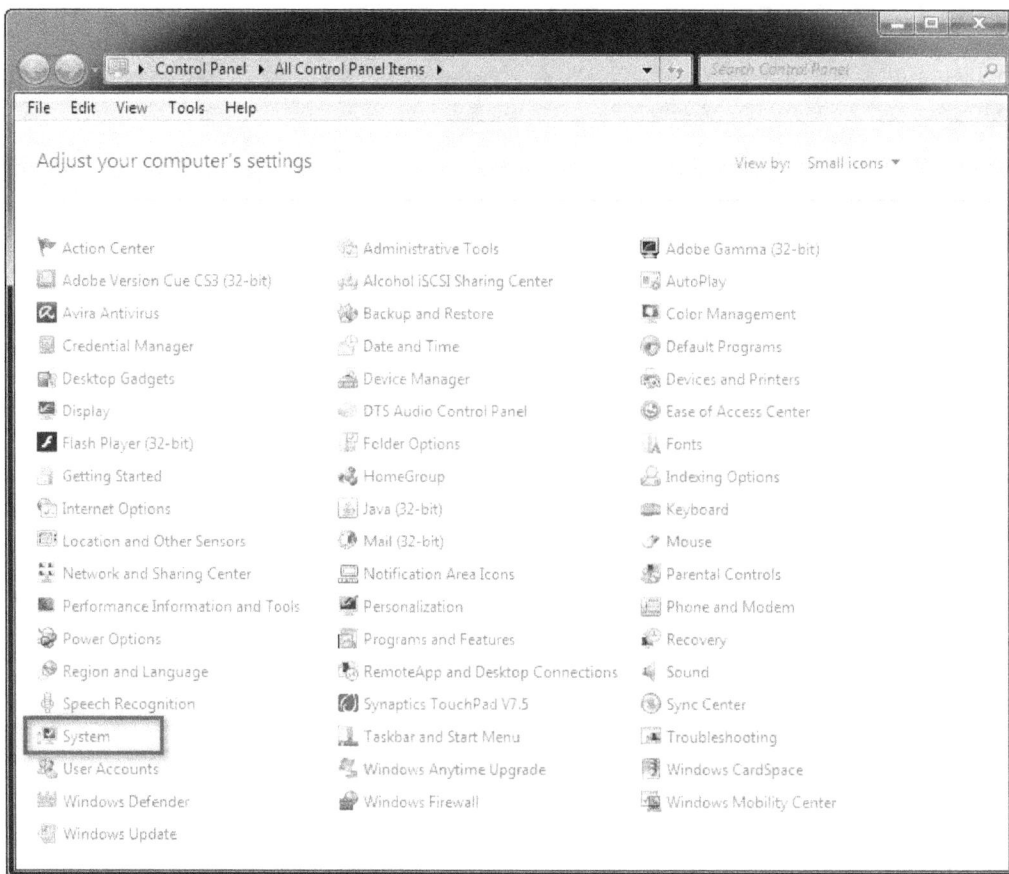

Windows 7 - Figure 33

Mark Versus Mr. Hacker.doc

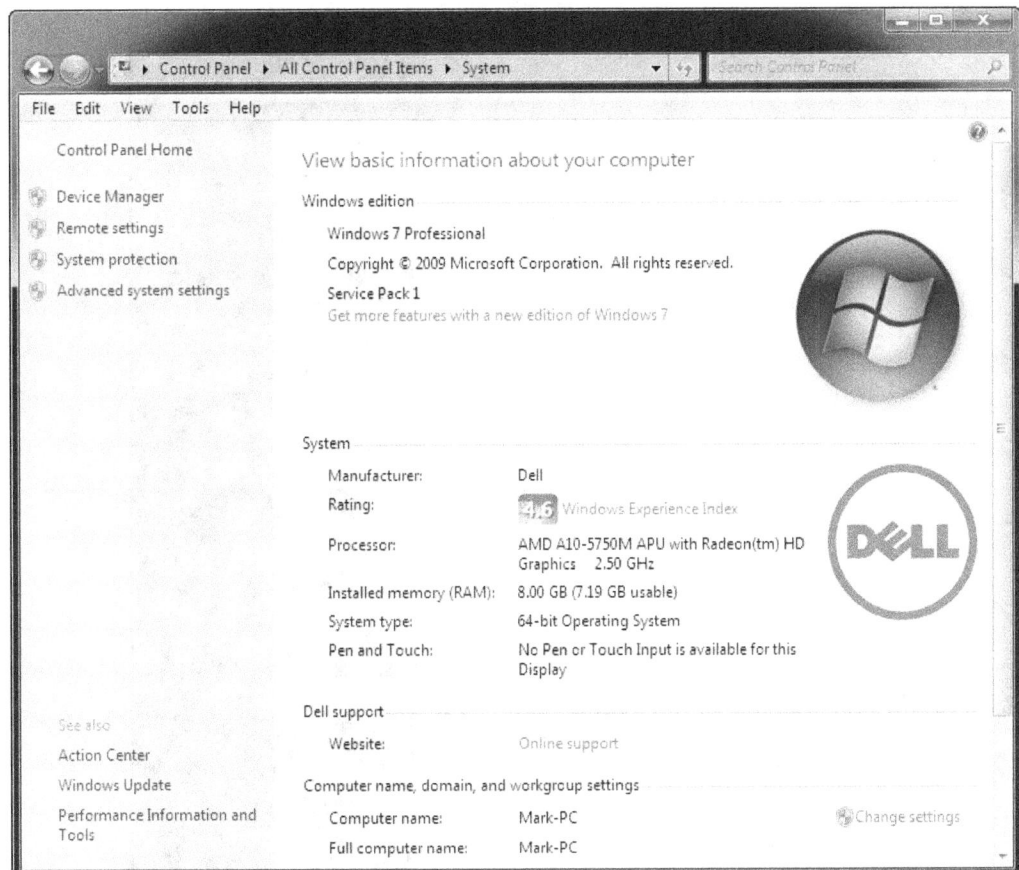

Windows 7 - Figure 34

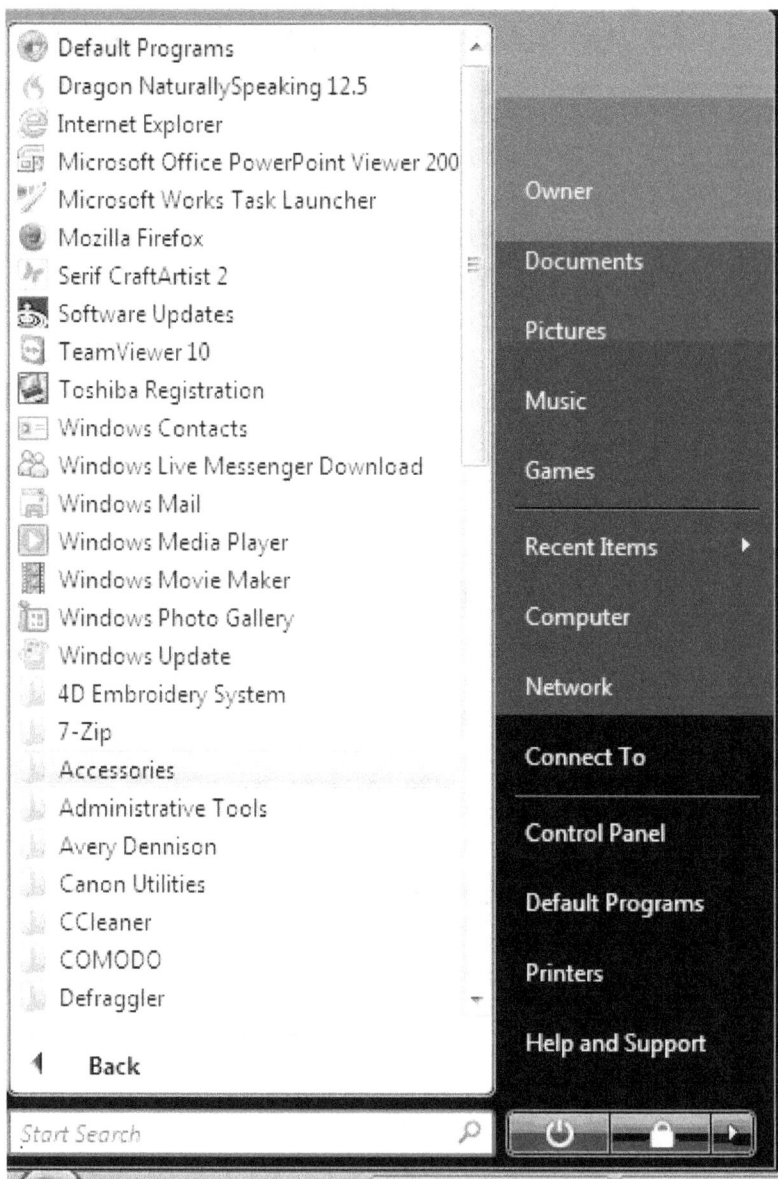

Windows 7 - Figure 35

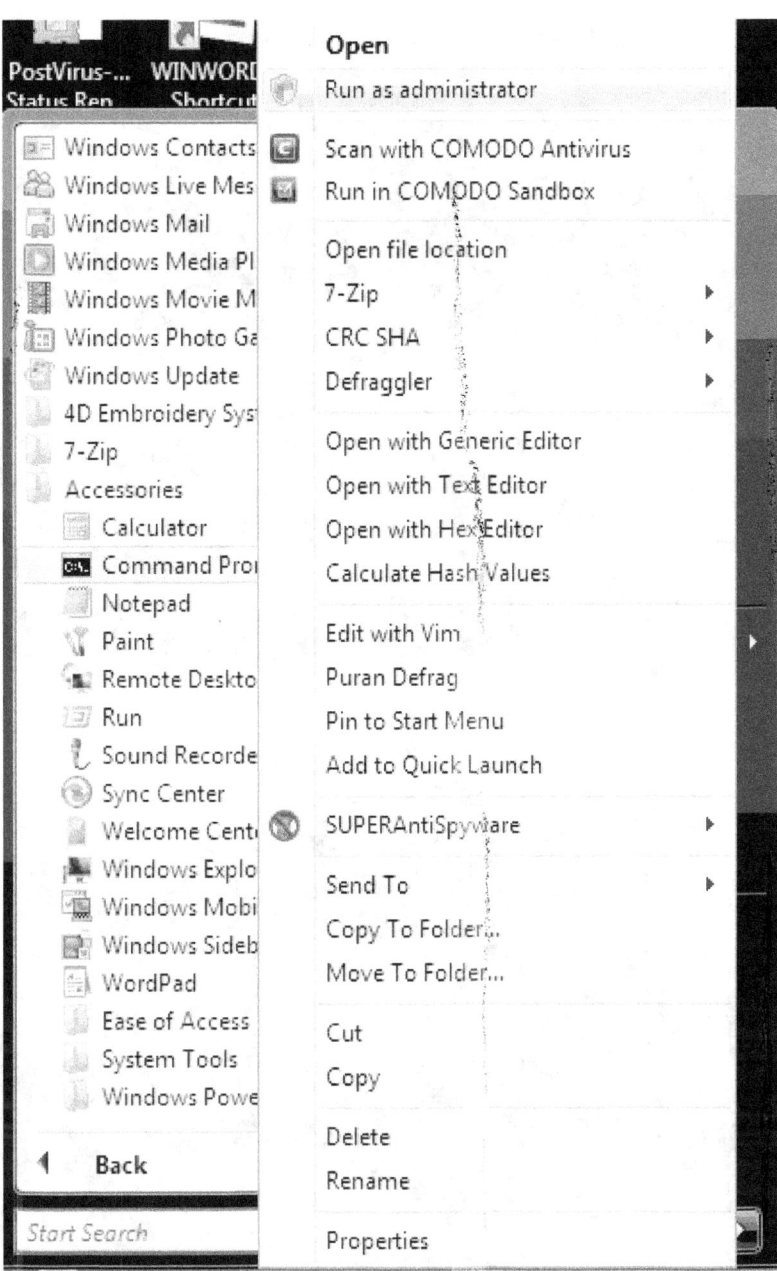

Windows 7 - Figure 36

The Command Prompt is the same on all versions of Windows.

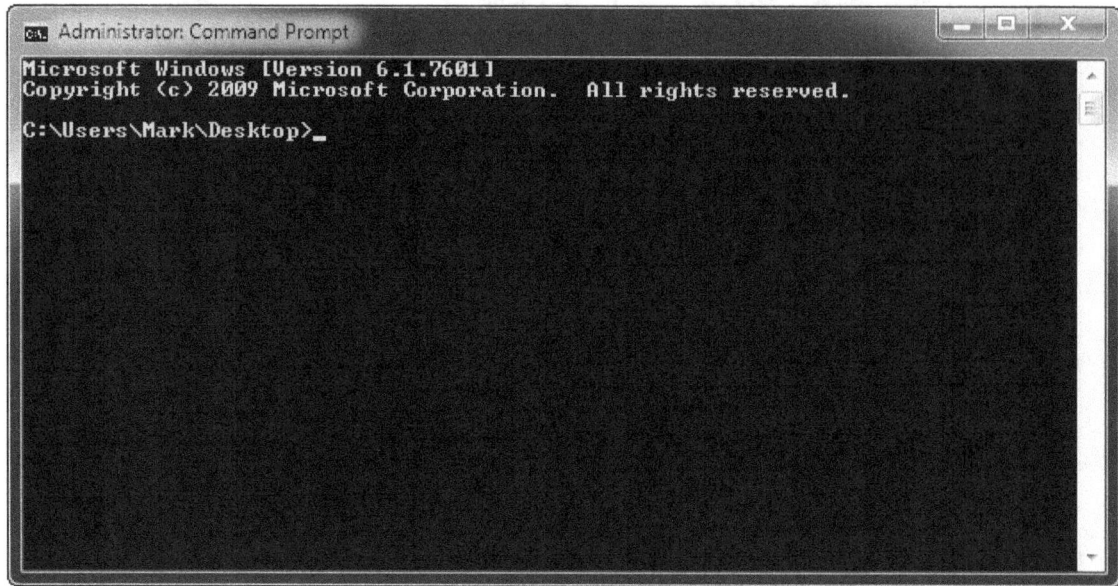

Windows 7 - Figure 37

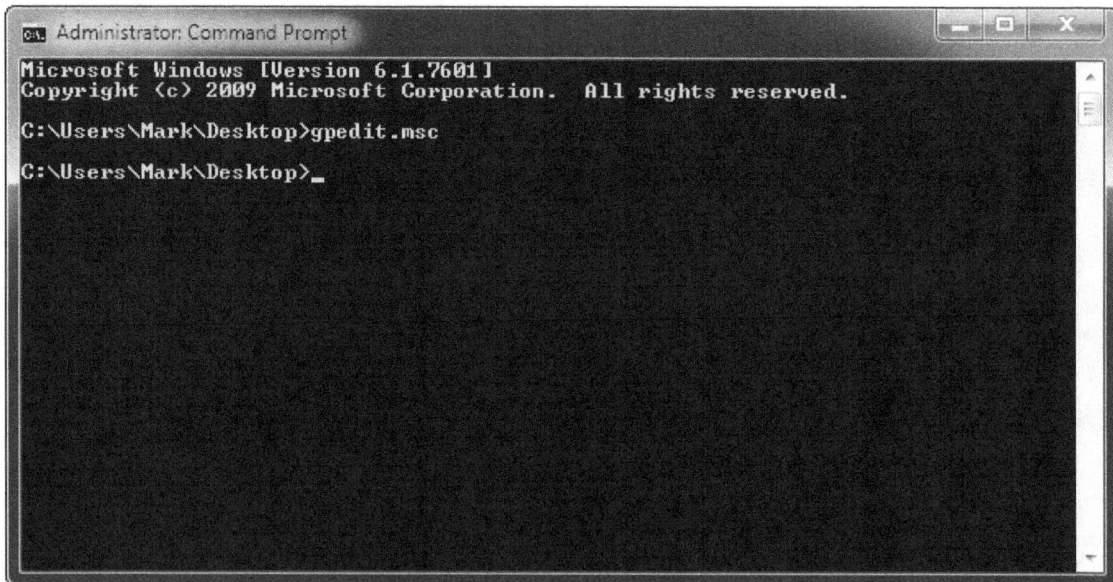

Windows 7 - Figure 38

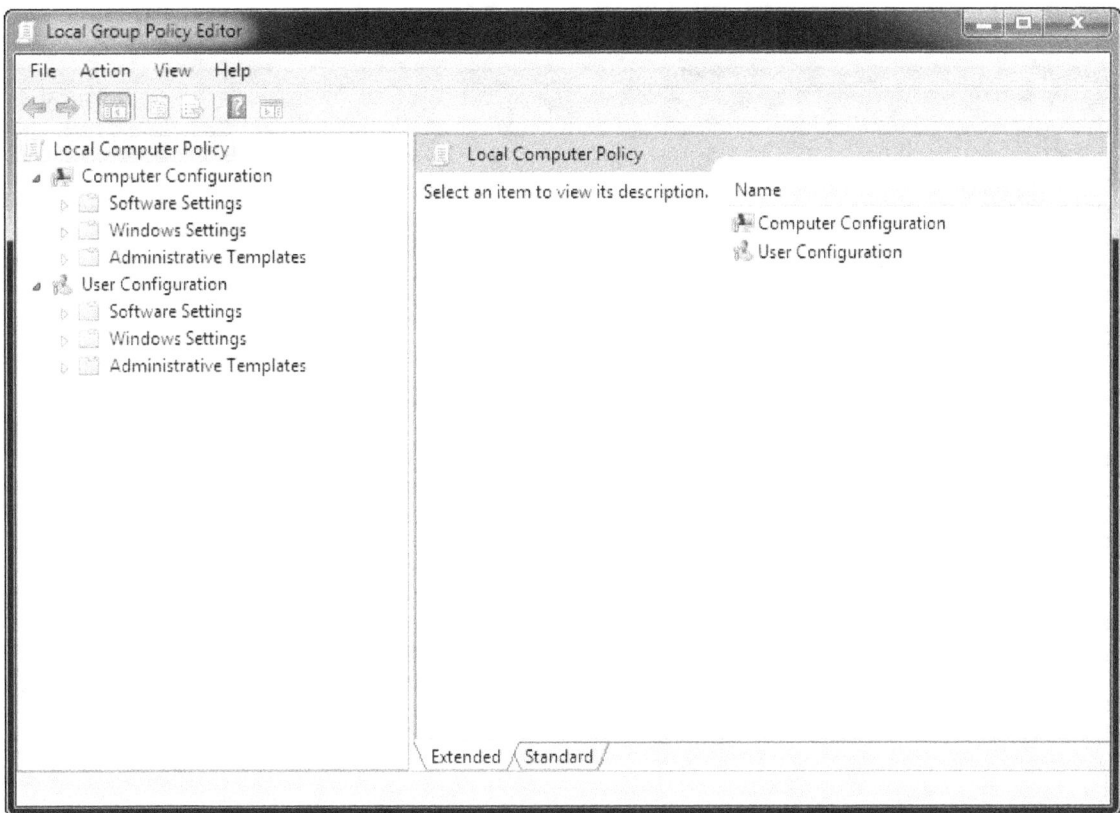

Windows 7 - Figure 39

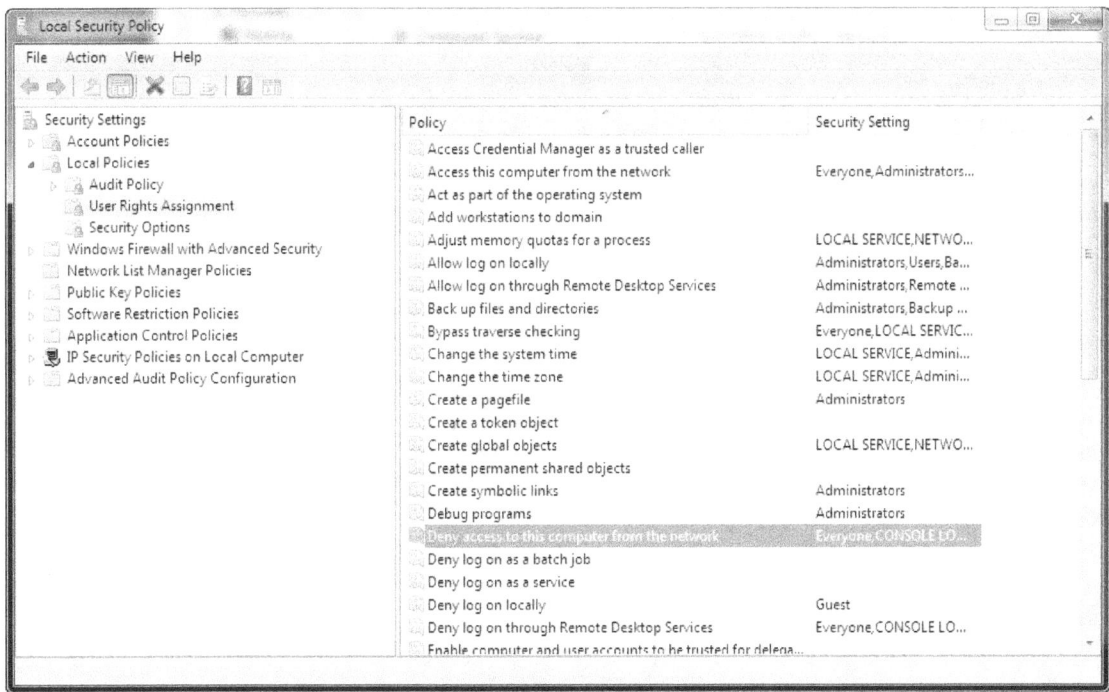

Windows 7 - Figure 40

Windows 7 - Figure 41

Windows 7 - Figure 42

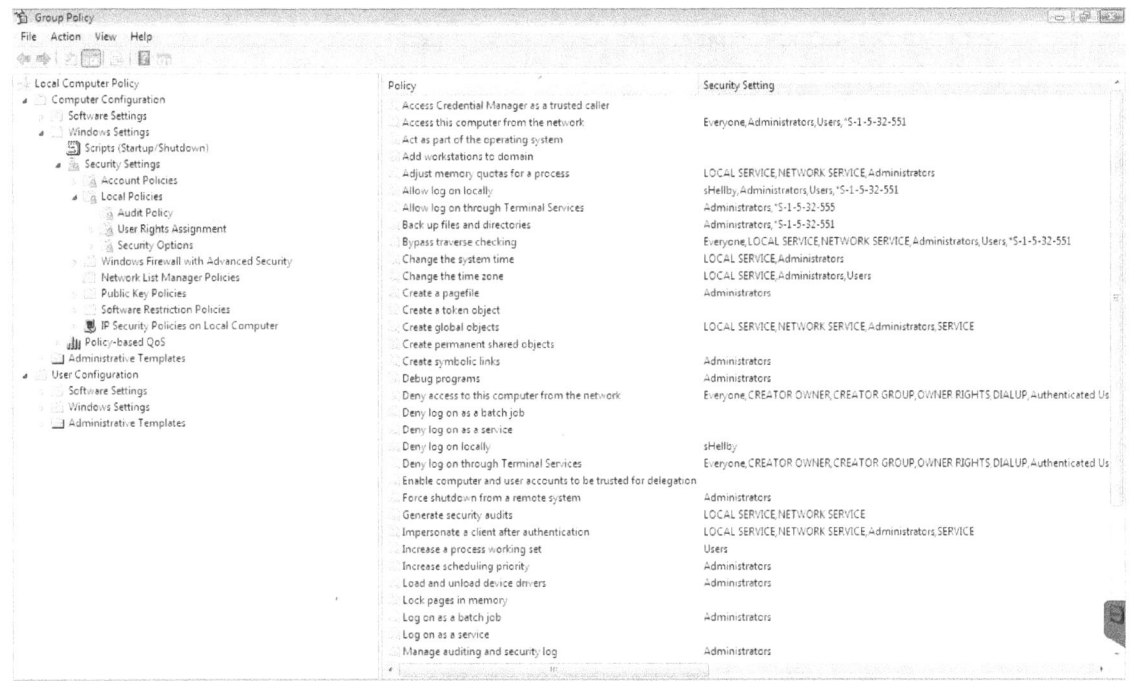

Windows 7 - Figure 43

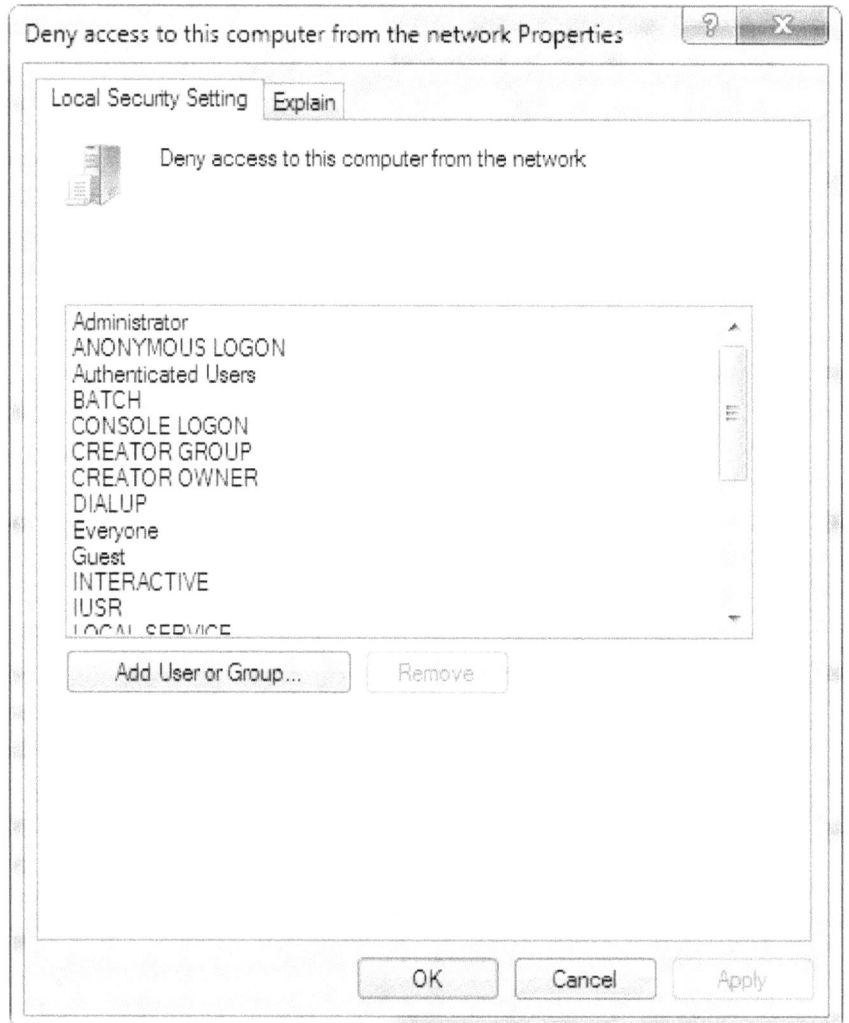
Windows 7 - Figure 44

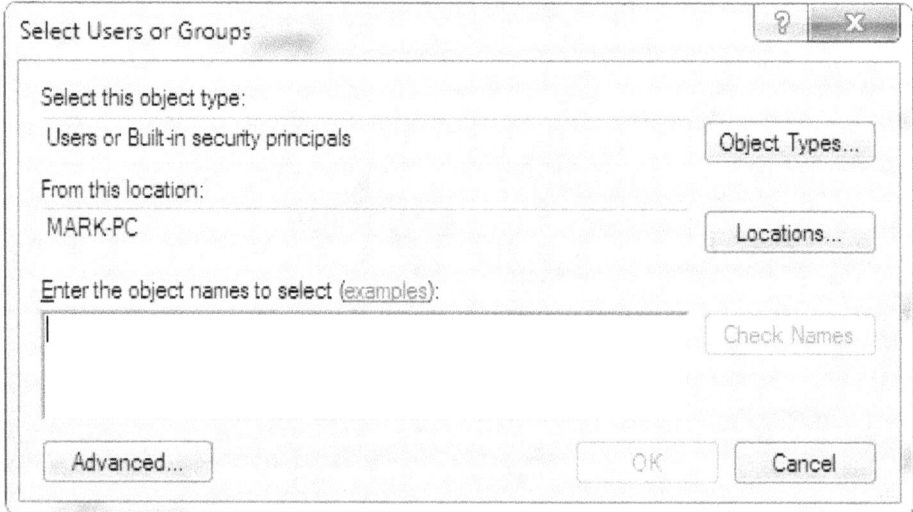
Windows 7 - Figure 45

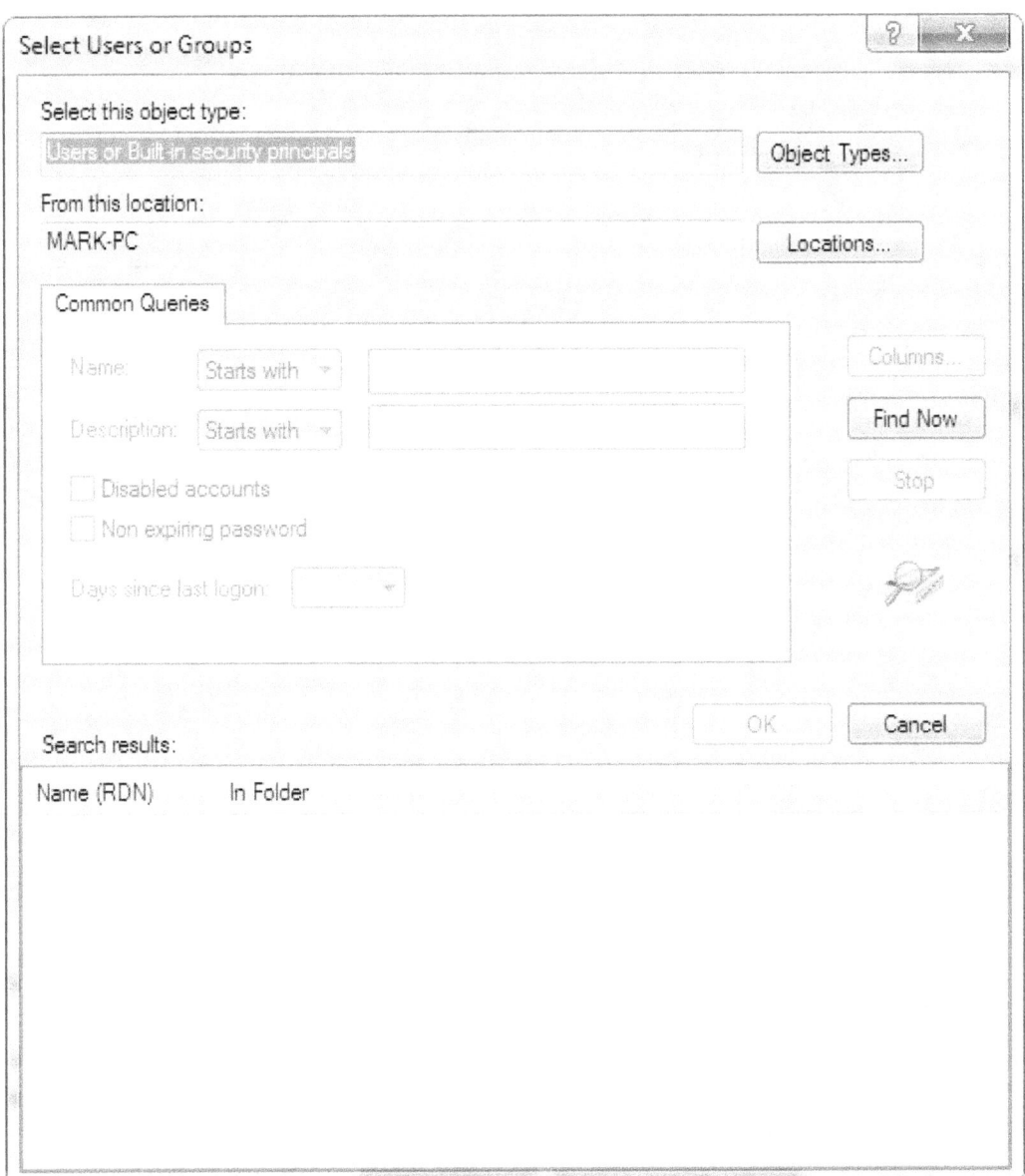

Windows 7 - Figure 46

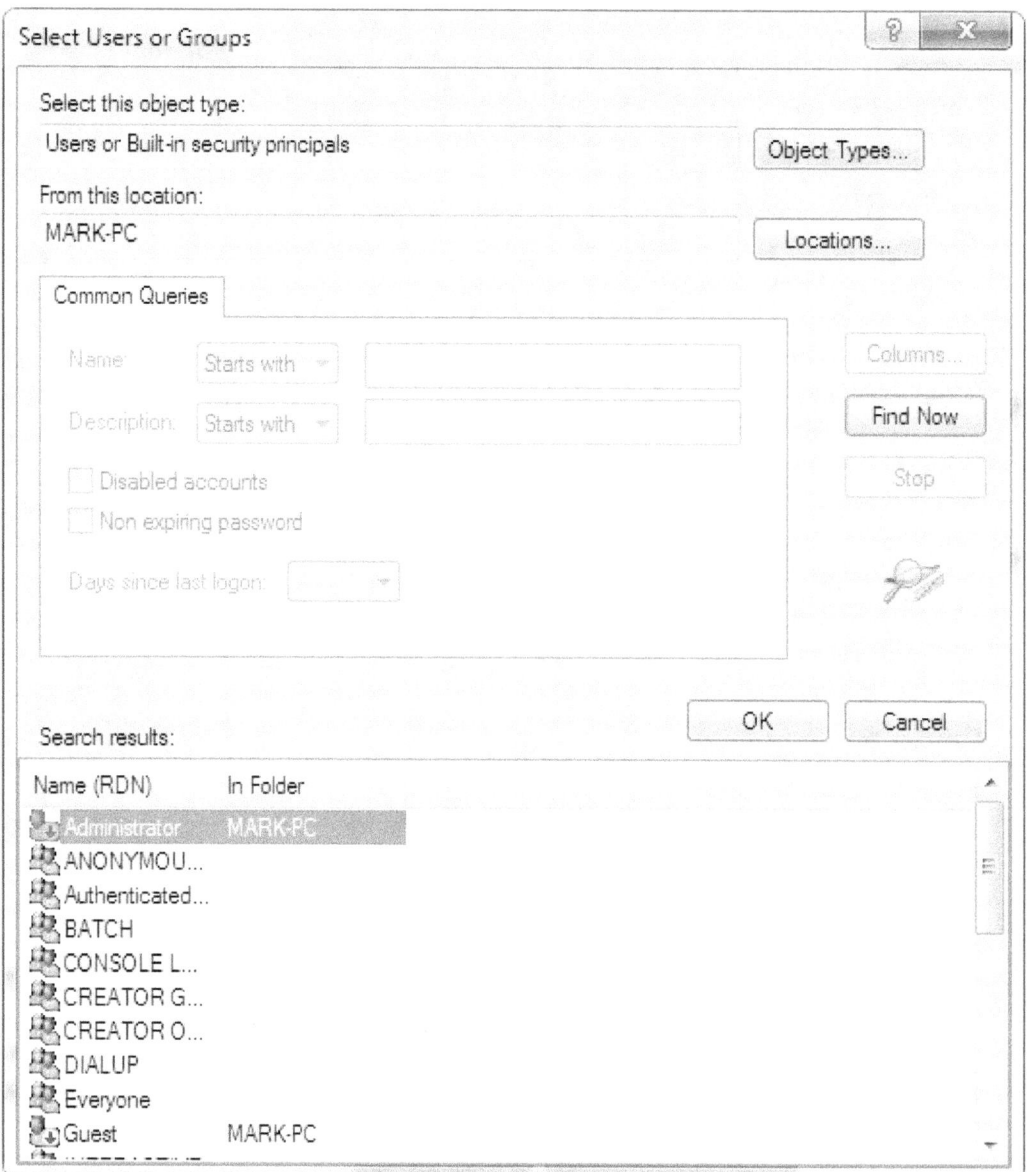

Windows 7 - Figure 47

Windows 7 - Figure 48

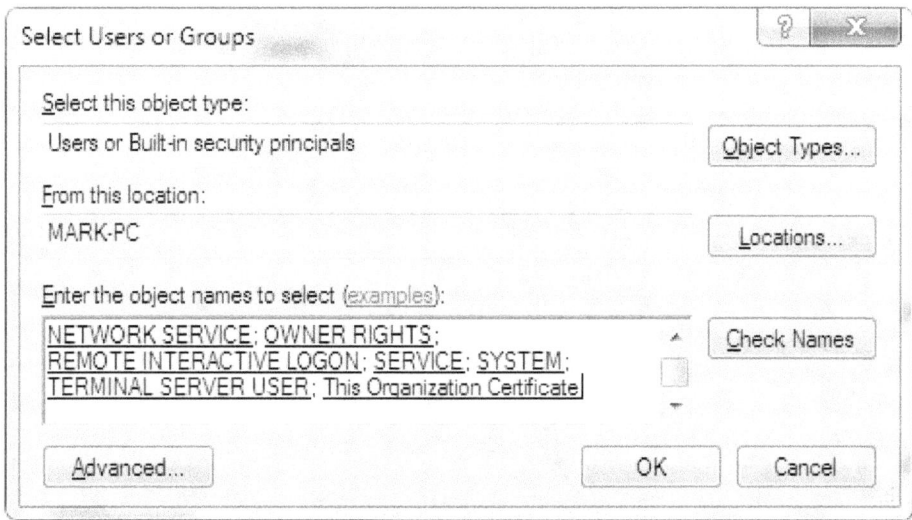

Windows 7 - Figure 49

Windows 7 - Figure 50

When you first look at the logs you might see this.
If so, just click on what you want to look at and
you should see what is in the next figure.

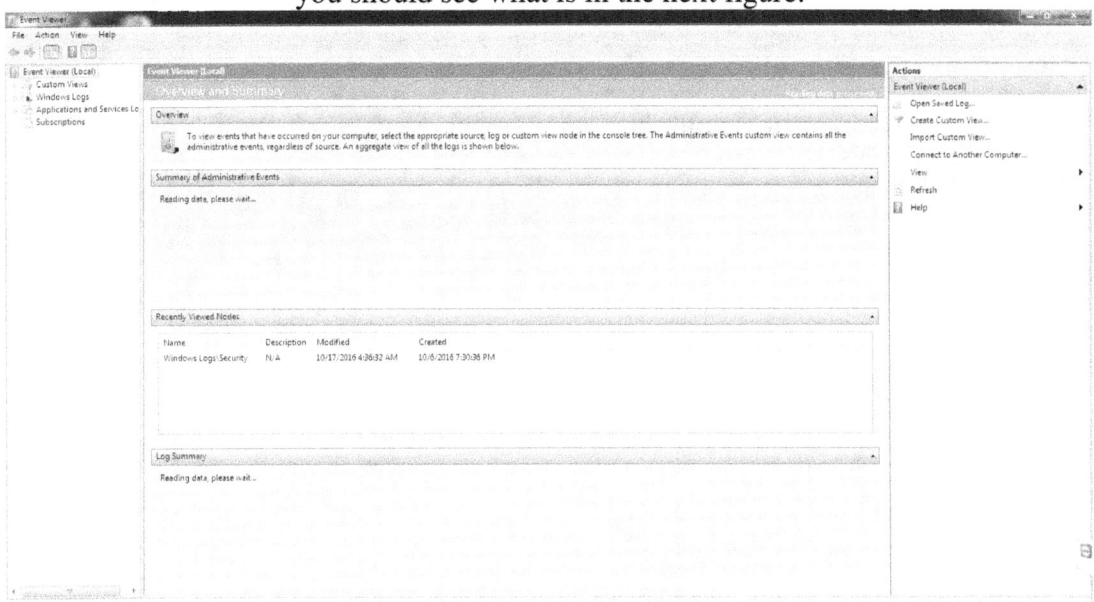

Windows 7 - Figure 51a

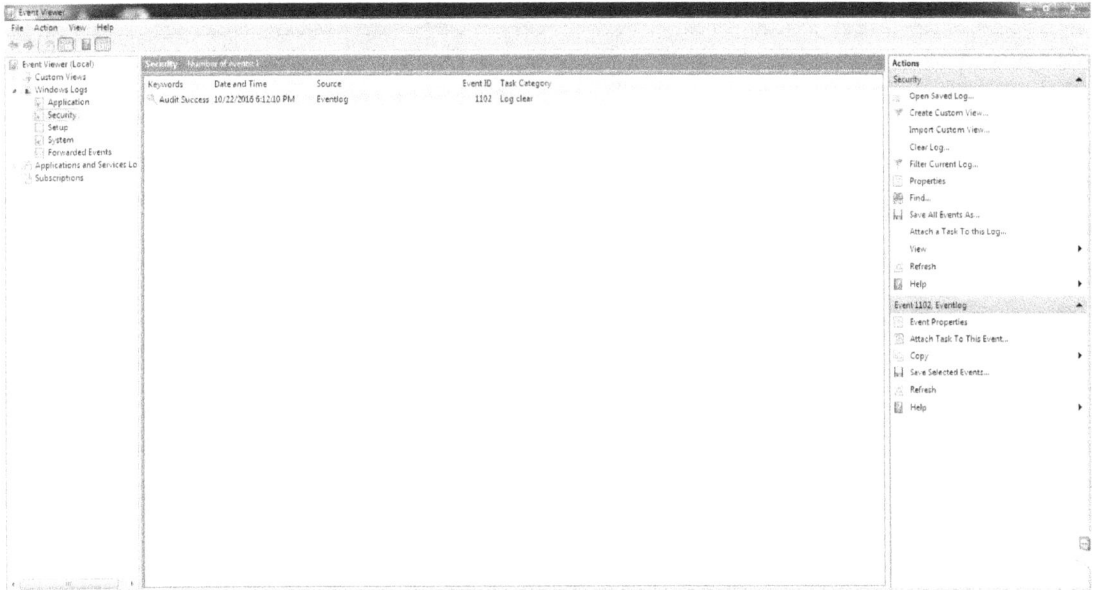

Windows 7 - Figure 51b

Mark Versus Mr. Hacker.doc

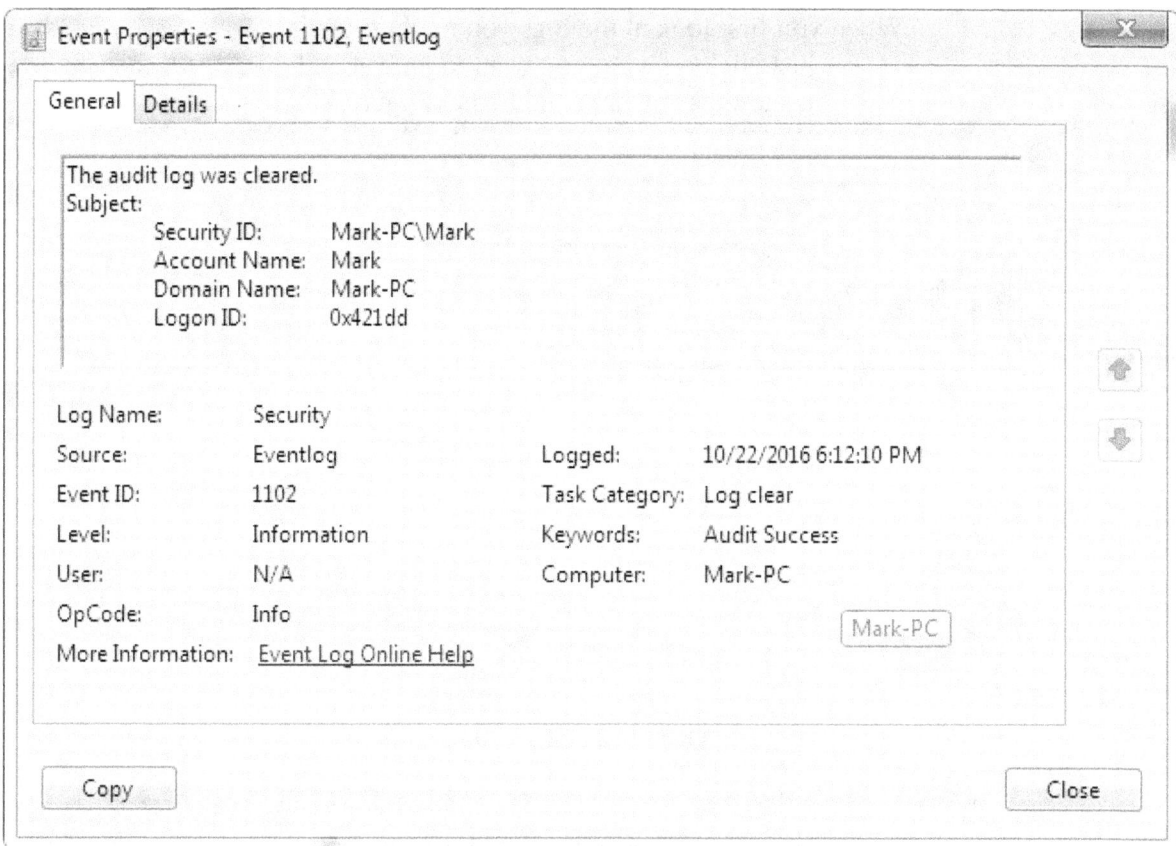

Windows 7 - Figure 52

Mark Versus Mr. Hacker.doc

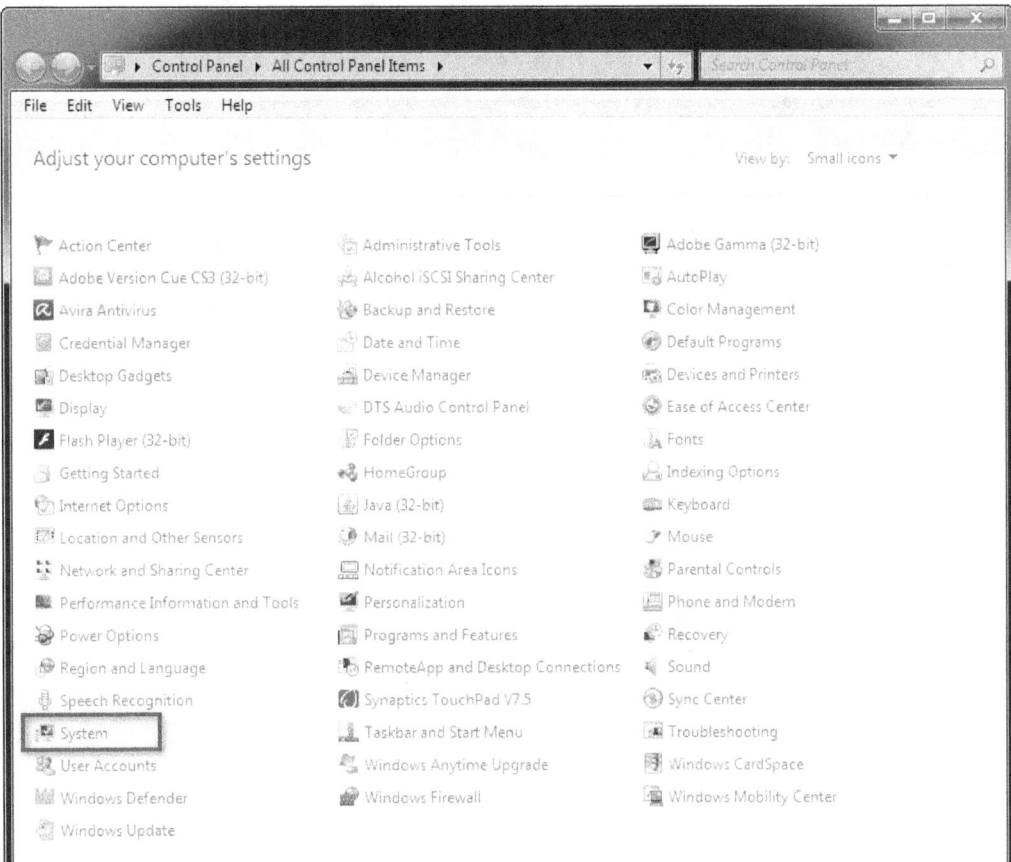

Windows 7 - Figure 53a

Mark Versus Mr. Hacker.doc

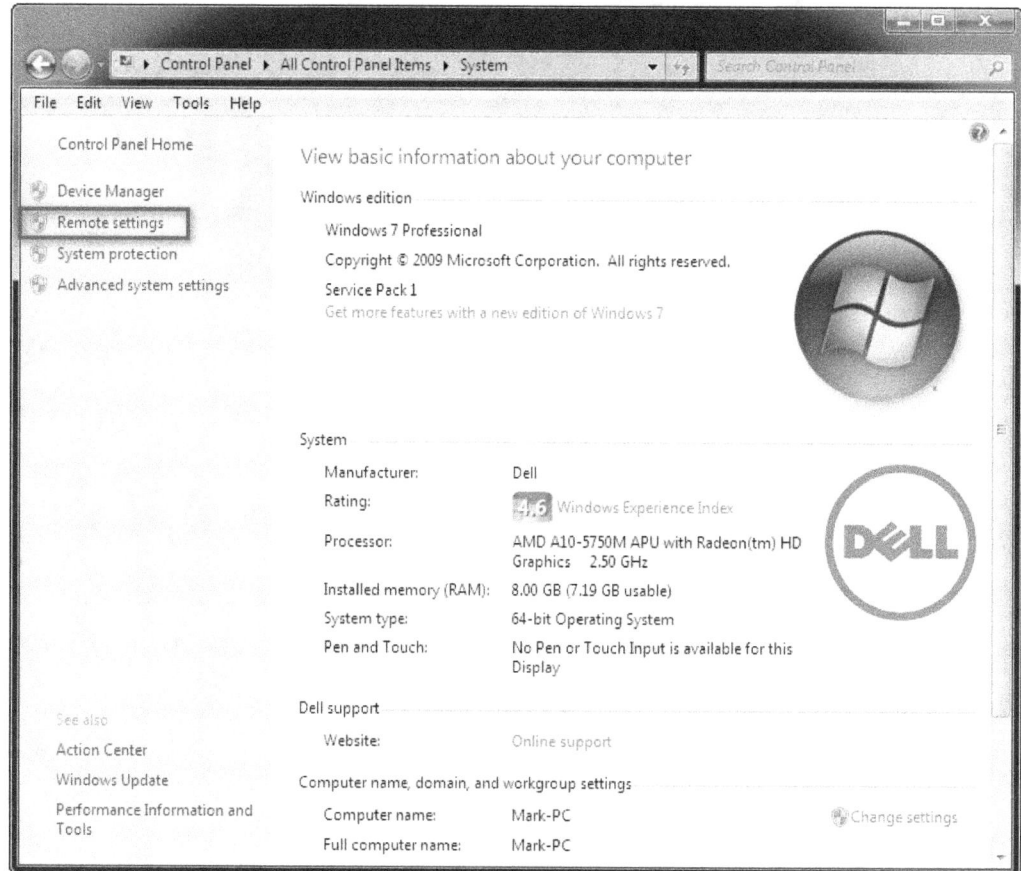

Windows 7 - Figure 53b

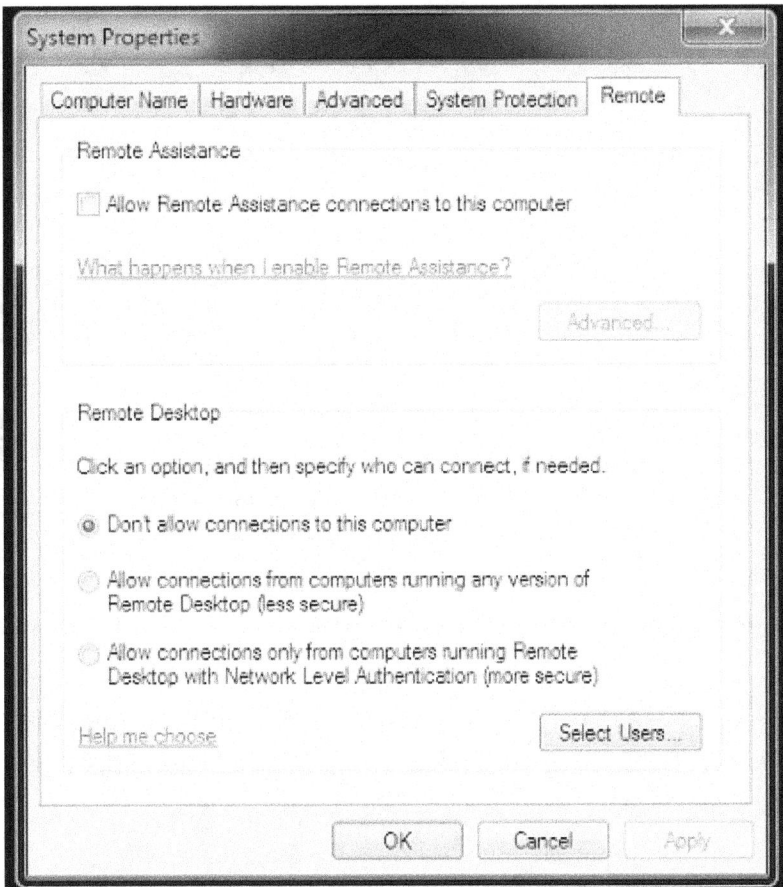
Windows 7 - Figure 54

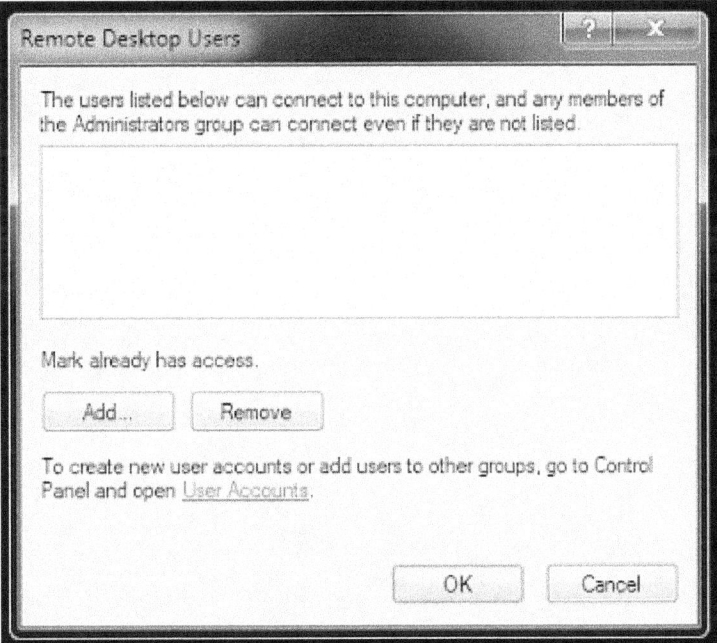
Windows 7 - Figure 55

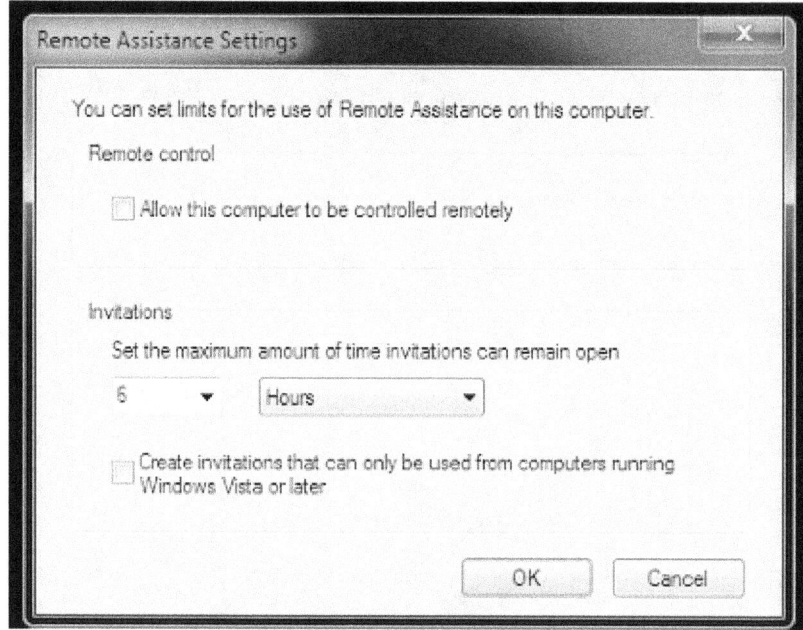
Windows 7 - Figure 56

All other figures deal with external programs to Windows so use the figures provided from #56 on to the end of the book.

Have fun!

Mark Versus Mr. Hacker.doc

Windows 8/8.1

Screen shots for Windows 8/8.1

Windows 8/8.1 Figures

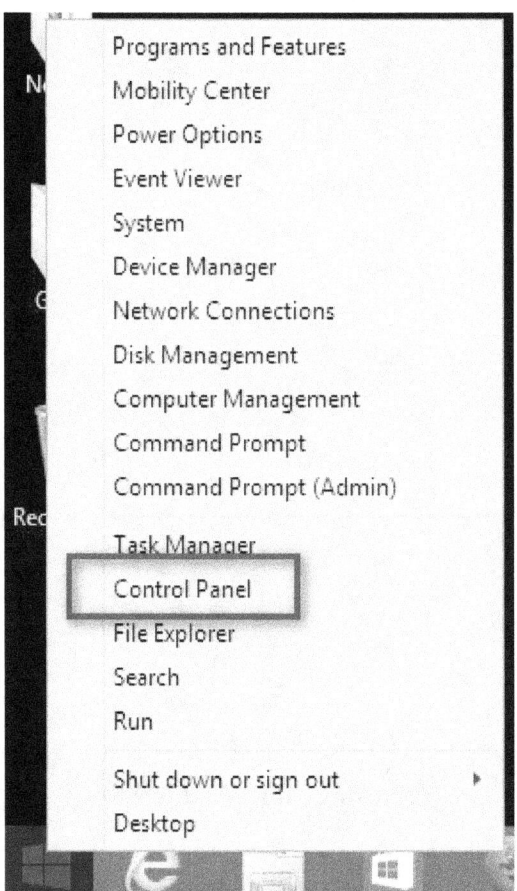

Windows 8/8.1 - Figure 1

Mark Versus Mr. Hacker.doc

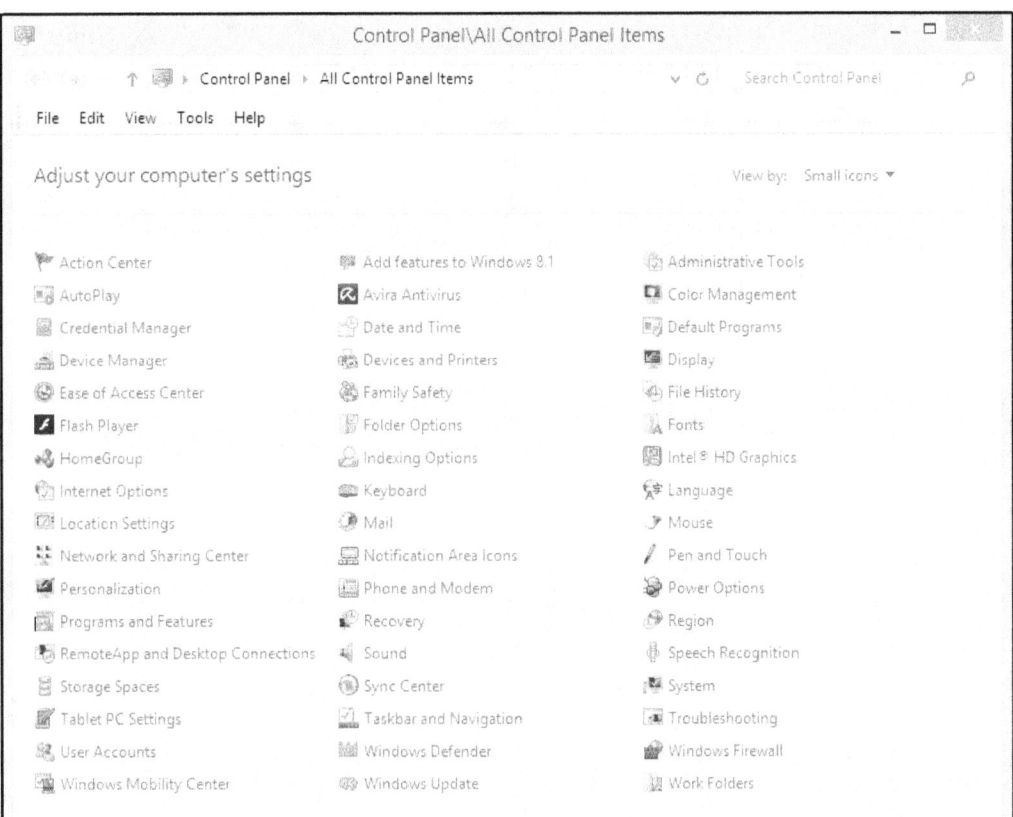

Windows 8/8.1 - Figure 2

Mark Versus Mr. Hacker.doc

Under Vista and the newer operating systems, instead of seeing an icon named "Display" – you instead click on the Personalization icon.

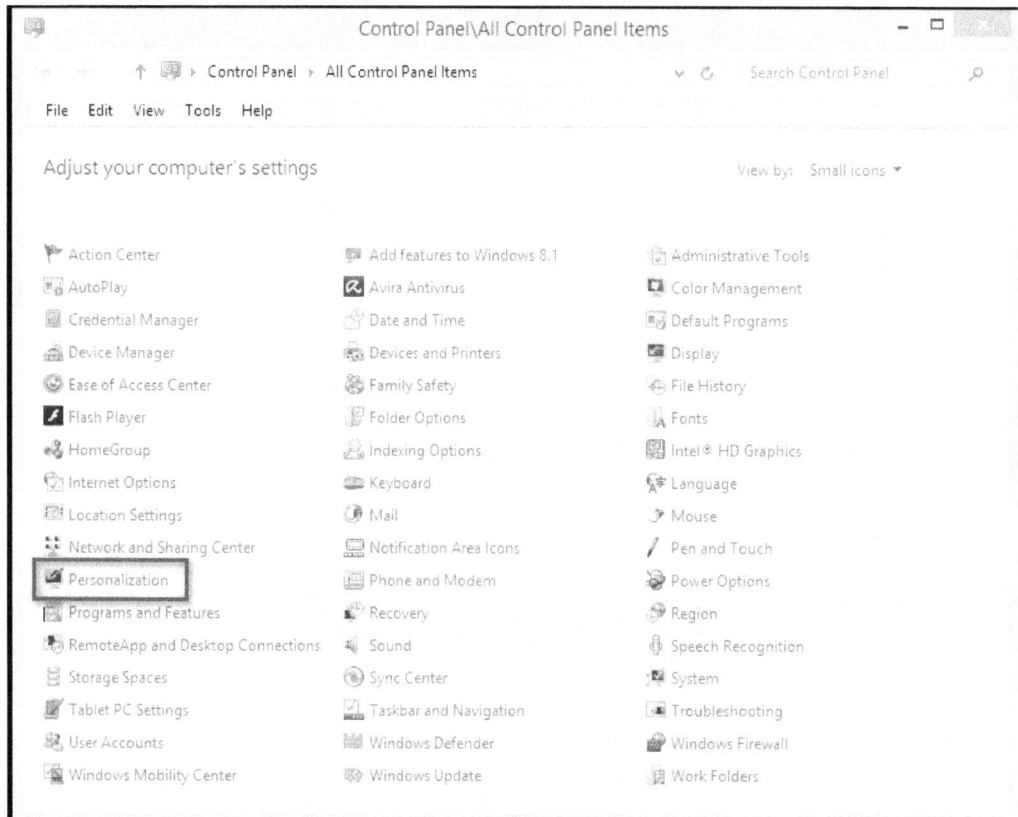

Windows 8/8.1 - Figure 3

Unlike Windows XP – under Windows 8/8.1 the Screen Saver option is a part of the Personalization dialog. So there isn't a figure 4 to be displayed here. Go to figure 5.

Page 185

Mark Versus Mr. Hacker.doc

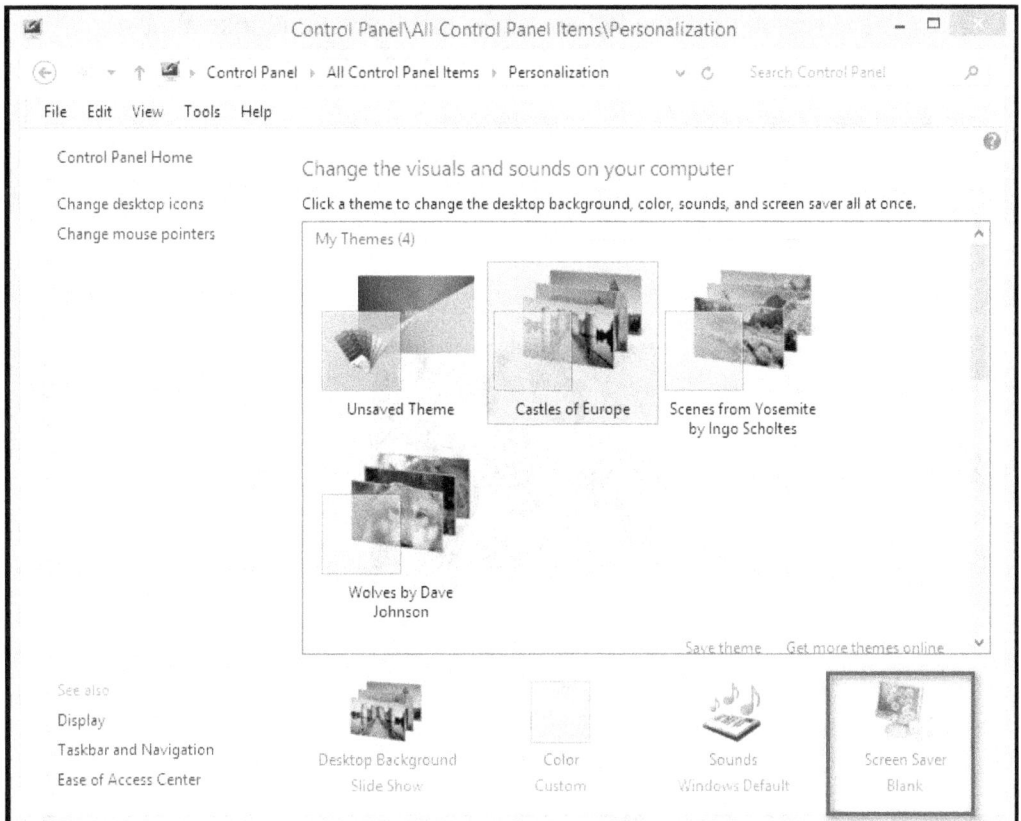

Windows 8/8.1 - Figure 4

And here you have the Screen Saver display which looks almost like the Windows XP Screen Saver dialog.

Windows 8/8.1 - Figure 5

Mark Versus Mr. Hacker.doc

In order to get to the Power Options, you have to go back to the Control Panel and select it from there.

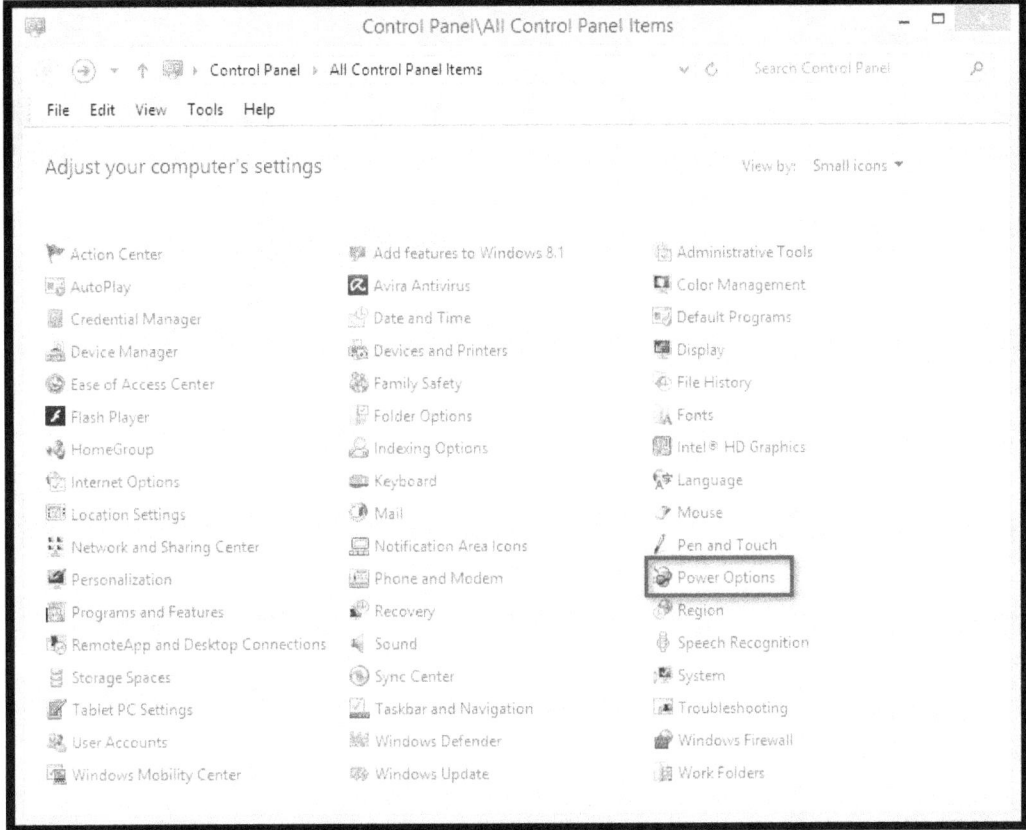

Windows 8/8.1 - Figure 6a

Note that under Vista, 7, 8/8.1, and 10 you first have to say
Which Power Plan you want to modify.

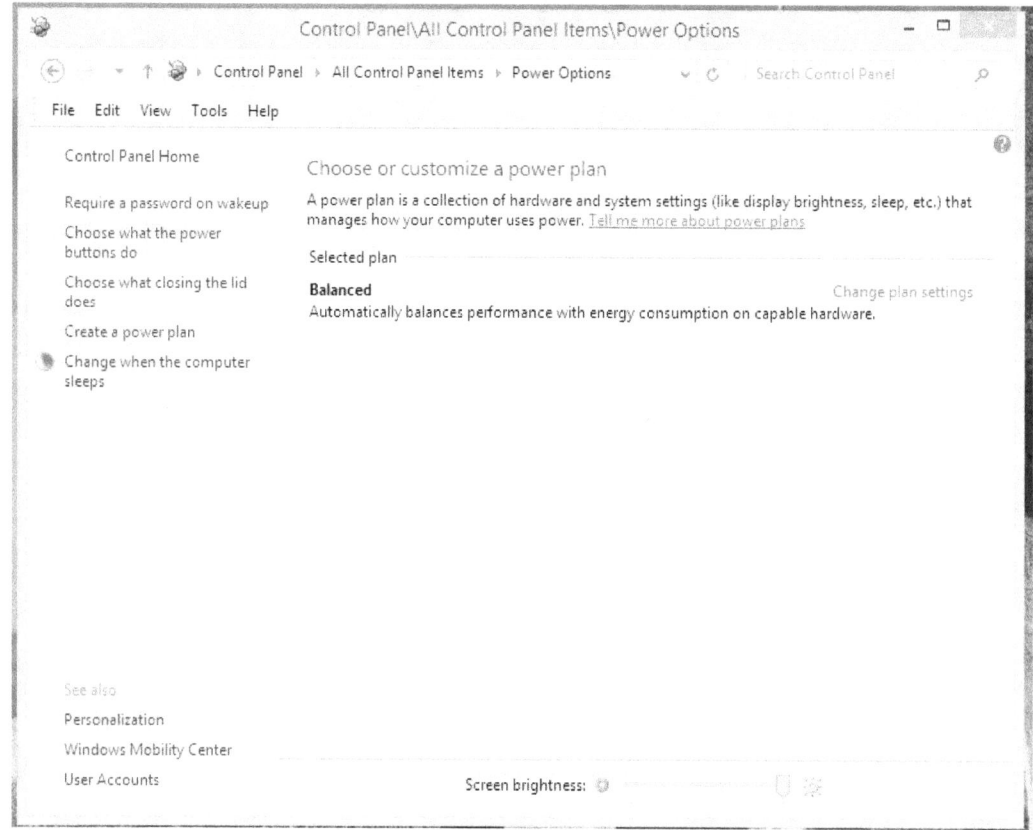

Windows 8/8.1 - Figure 6b

Once in the Power Plan area, change your time to turn off your display to be 30 minutes and to never shut down the computer when it is plugged in. Notice the "Change advanced power settings" link. We are going to use that next.

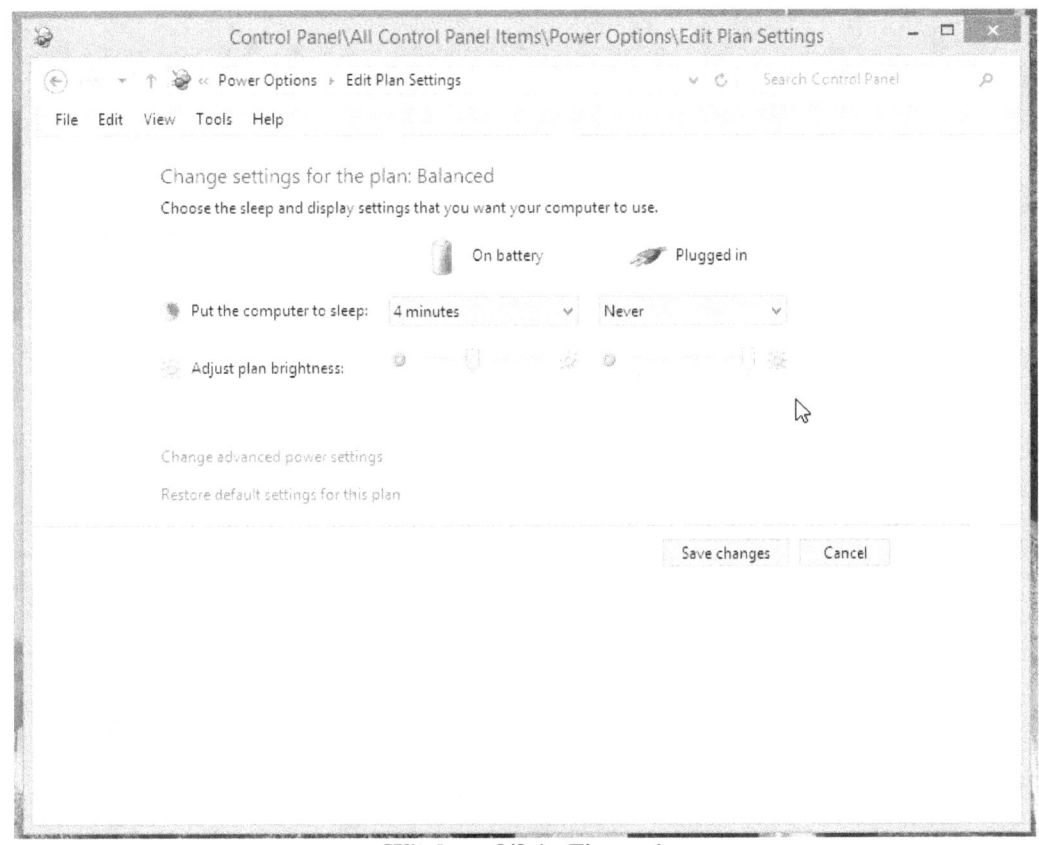

Windows 8/8.1 - Figure 6c

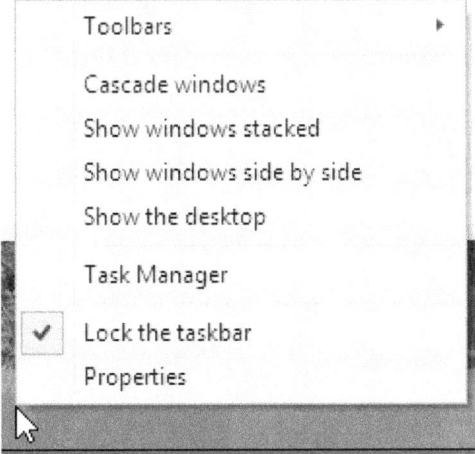

Windows 8/8.1 - Figure 17

Mark Versus Mr. Hacker.doc

Note under Windows 8/8.1 Microsoft changed what you first see.
No longer is there an "Applications" tab.
Note the "Fewer details" link in the bottom left corner.
Originally it read "More details" but if you click that link you will see what is shown here.

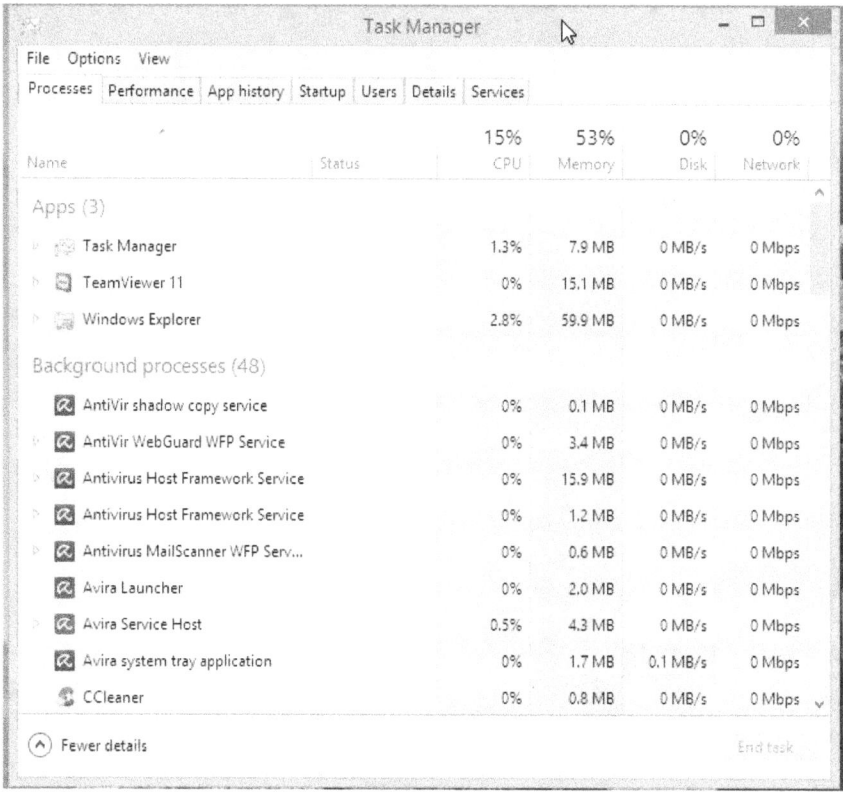

Windows 8/8.1 - Figure 18 - 9

Note that there is no way now to change the priority of a process. In order to change the priority of a program you have to download Microsoft's Process Explorer and use it to set the priority.

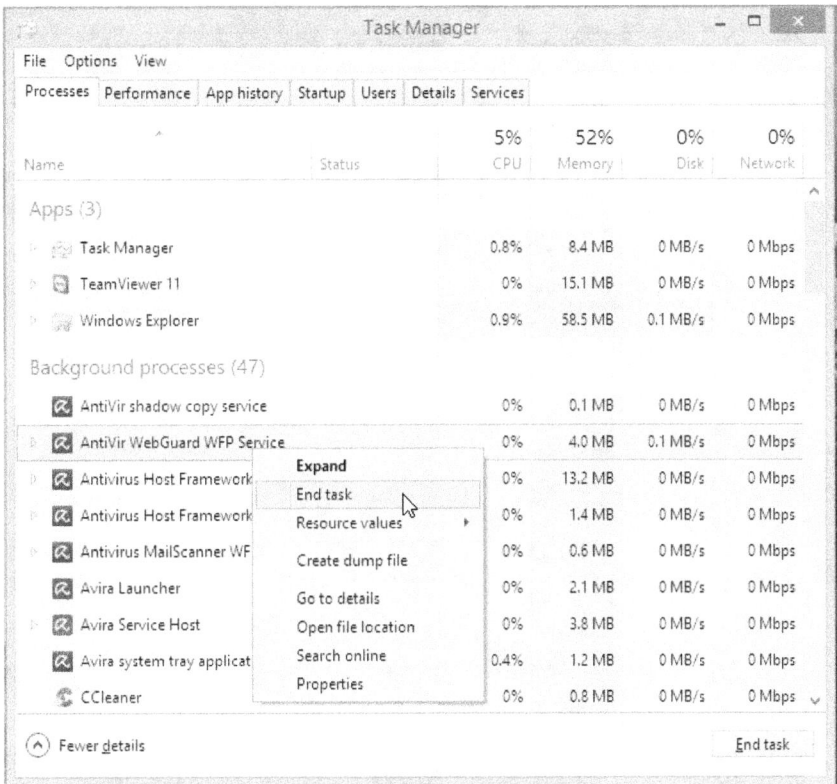

Windows 8/8.1 - Figure 10

Mark Versus Mr. Hacker.doc

Since TCPView looks the same on all platforms – here is the Windows XP version.

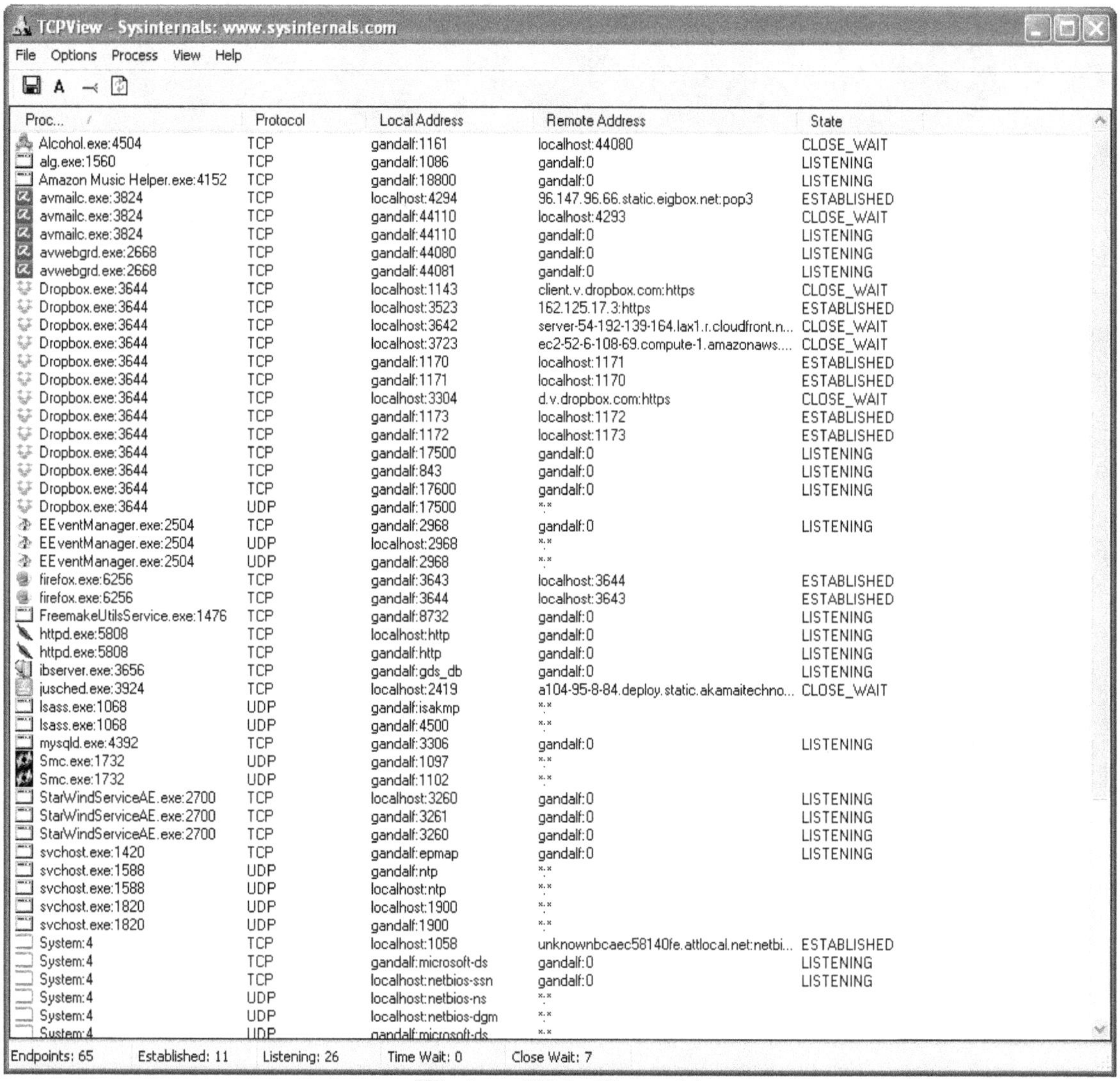

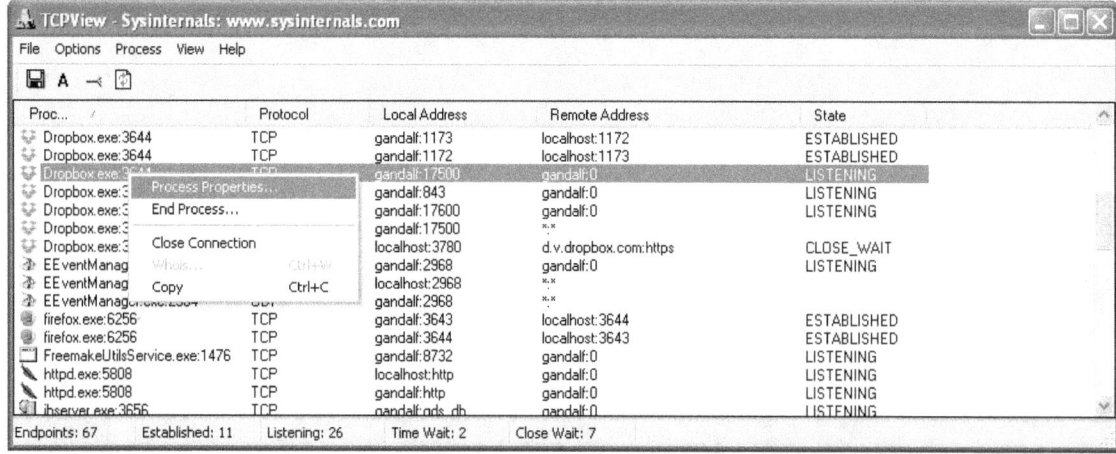

Windows 8/8.1 - Figure 11

Windows 8/8.1 - Figure 12

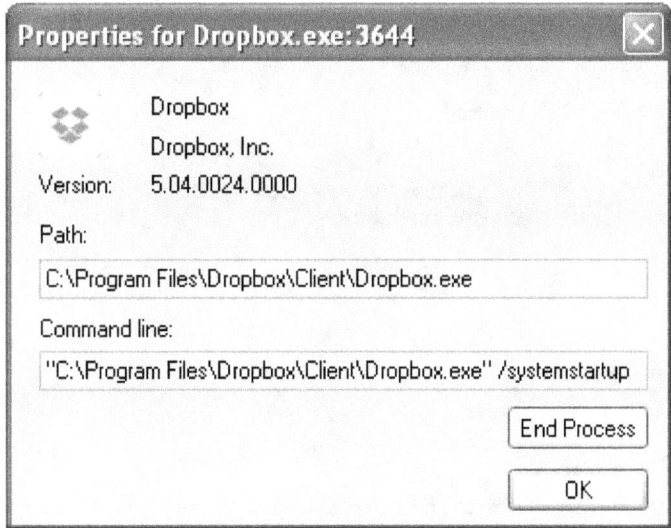
Windows 8/8.1 - Figure 13

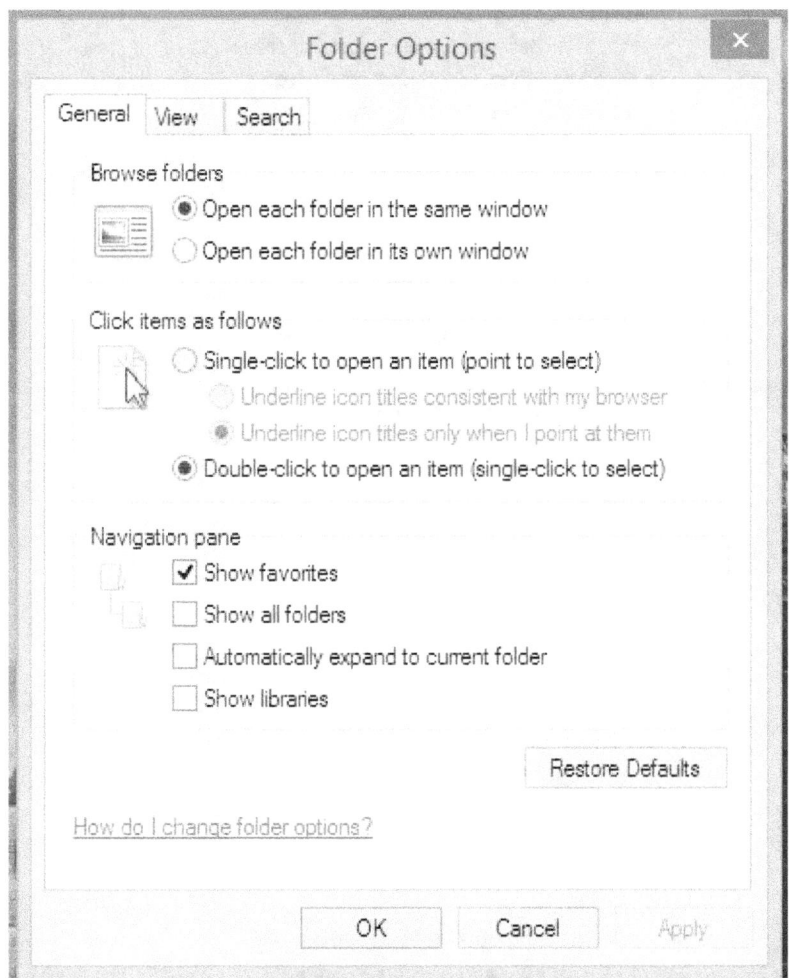
Windows 8/8.1 - Figure 14

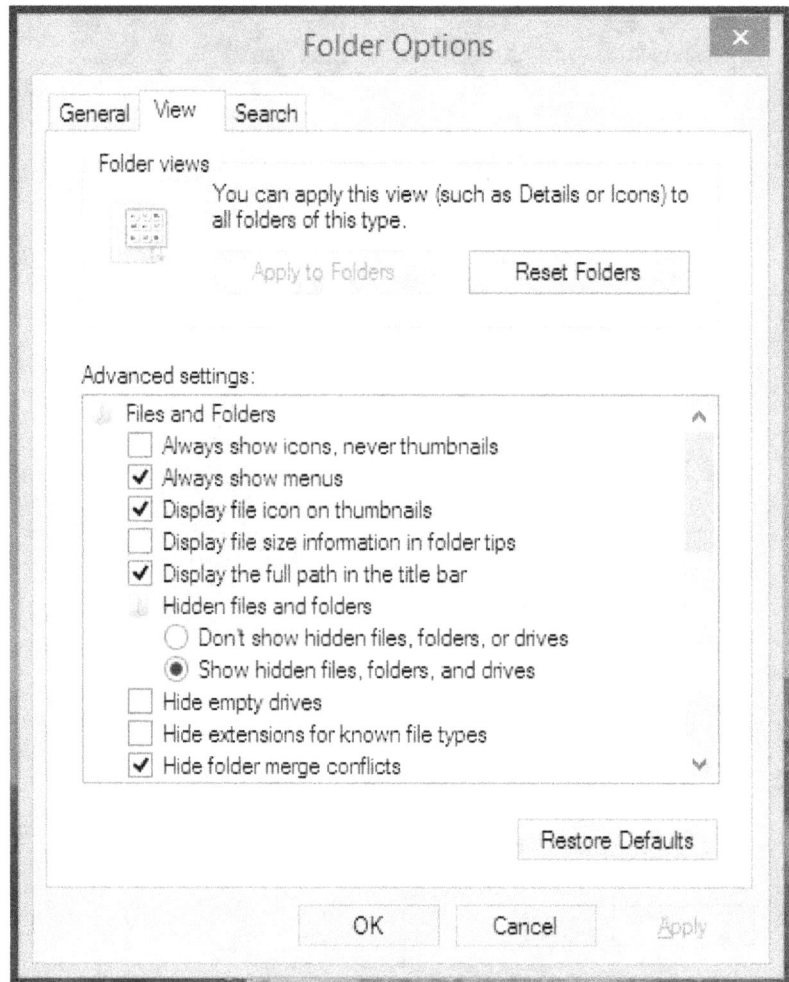

Windows 8/8.1 - Figure 15a

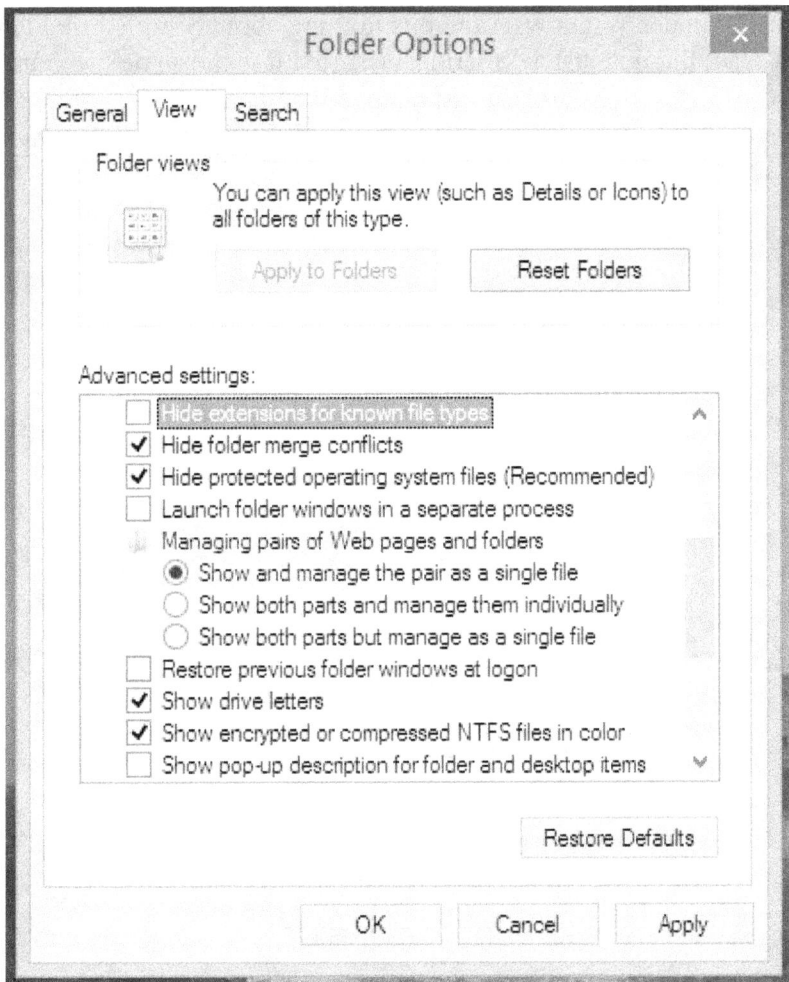

Windows 8/8.1 - Figure 15b

Mark Versus Mr. Hacker.doc

Notice that under Windows 7 there is nothing about Simple File Sharing.
Instead, there is just a "Sharing Wizard". It is the same program.
Microsoft just changed the name.

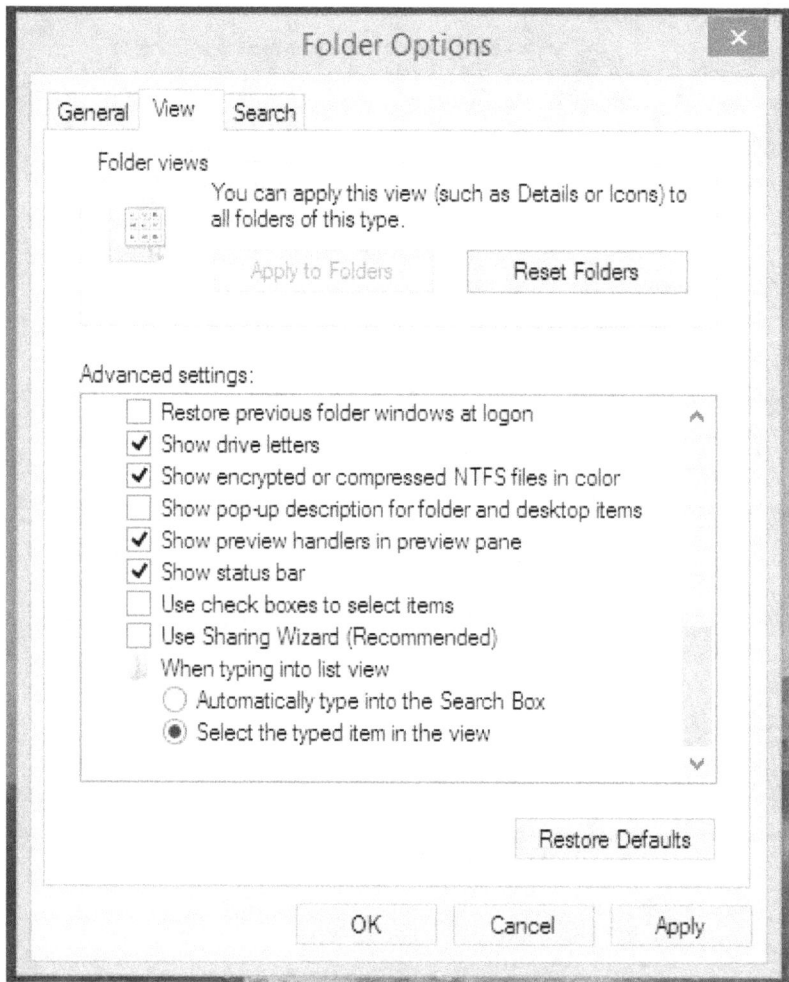

Windows 8/8.1 - Figure 16-17

Mark Versus Mr. Hacker.doc

In order to get the to System Restore area you first have to go to the control panel and then left click on the System icon.

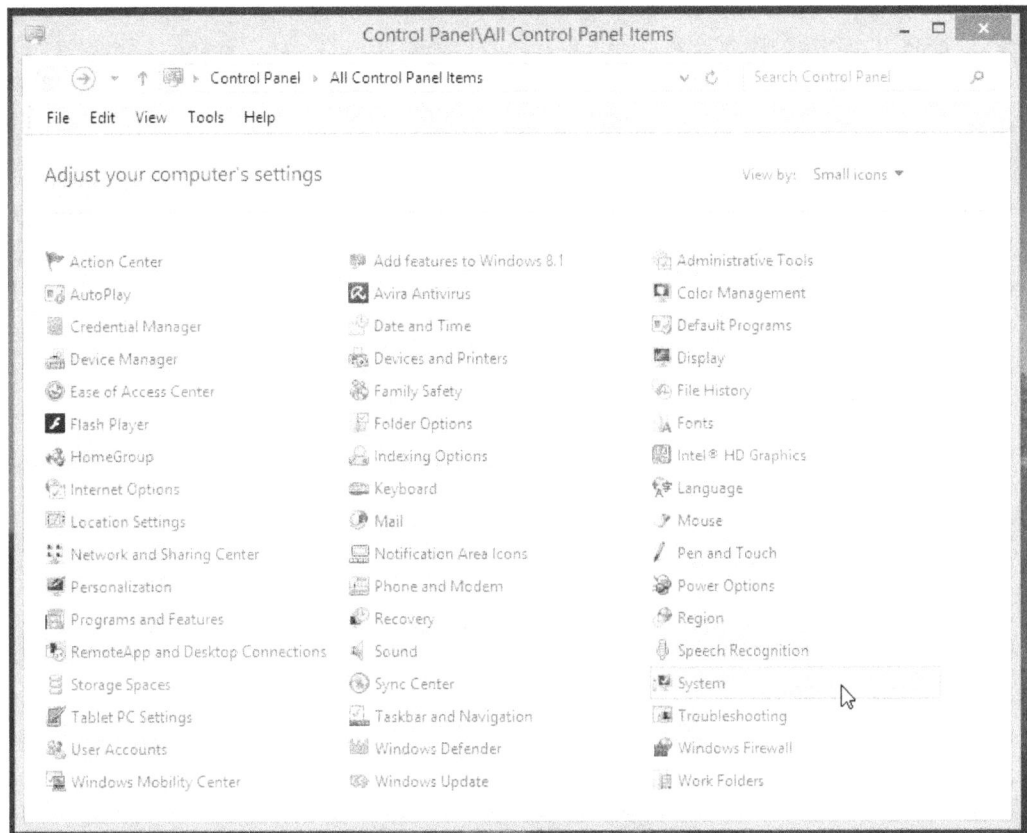

Windows 8/8.1 - Figure 18a

In the System dialog box, select the "Advanced system serttings".

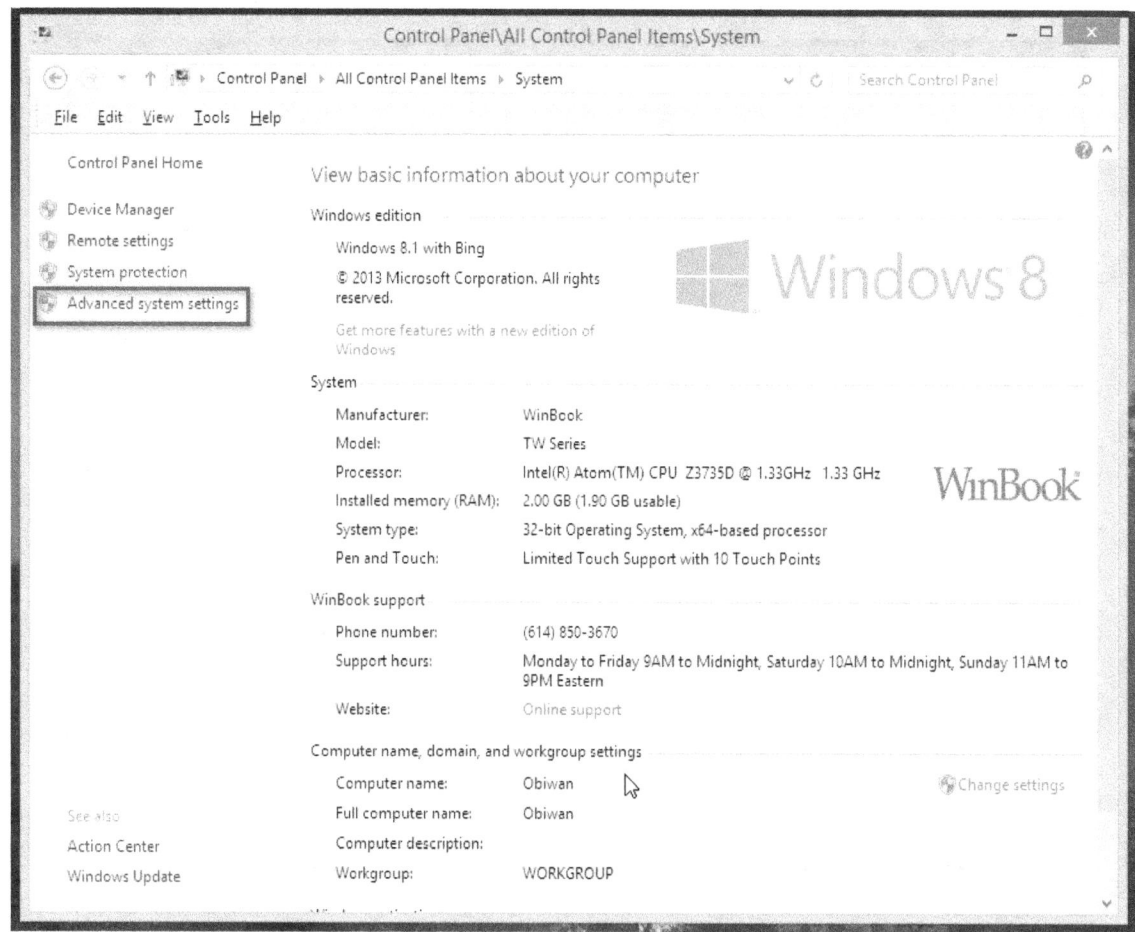

Windows 8/8.1 - Figure 18b

Mark Versus Mr. Hacker.doc

Here you can see that the System Restore is turned on for the Local Disk (or C: Drive). Use the Configure button to change this.

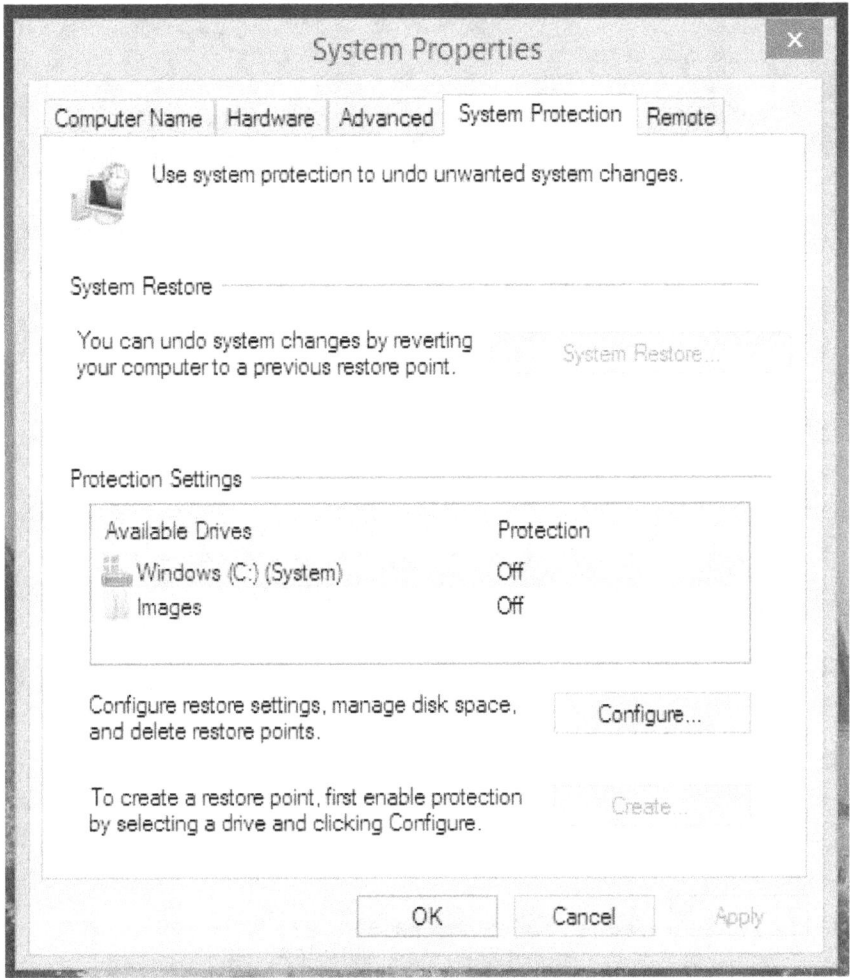

Windows 8/8.1 - Figure 18c

Here is what the dialog looks liked after you have pushed the Configuration button.

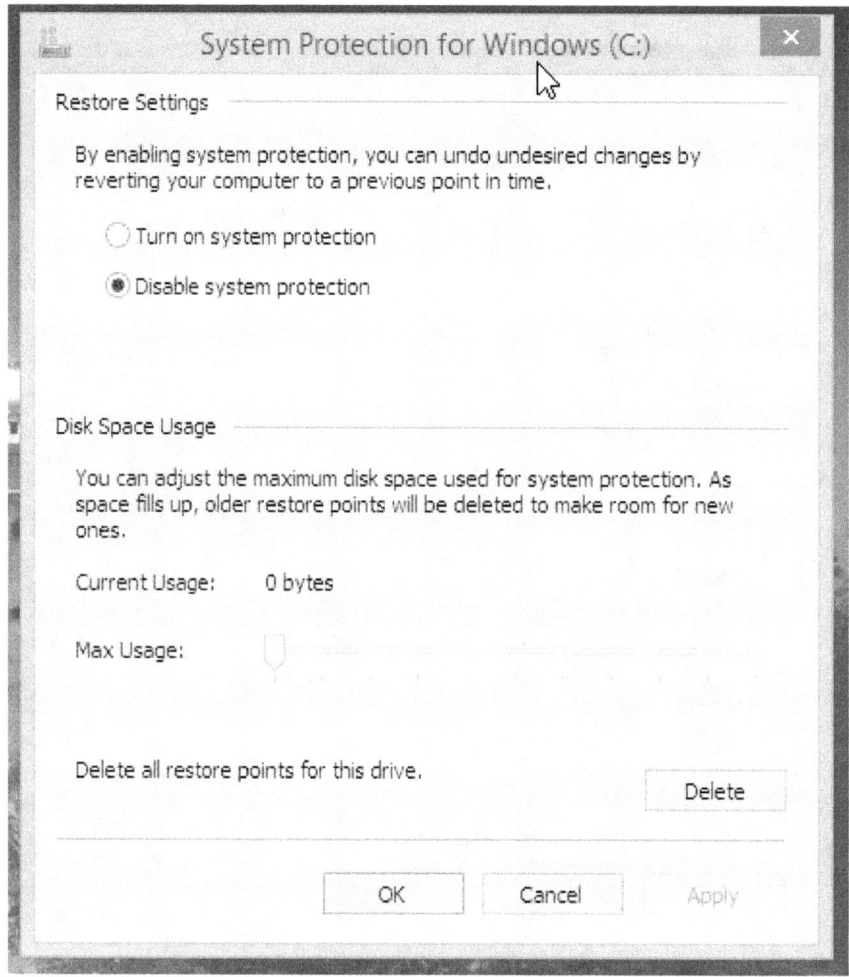

Windows 8/8.1 - Figure 18d

Under Windows 8/8.1 the command prompt is a part of the standard right-click on the Start button.

Windows 8/8.1 - Figure 19

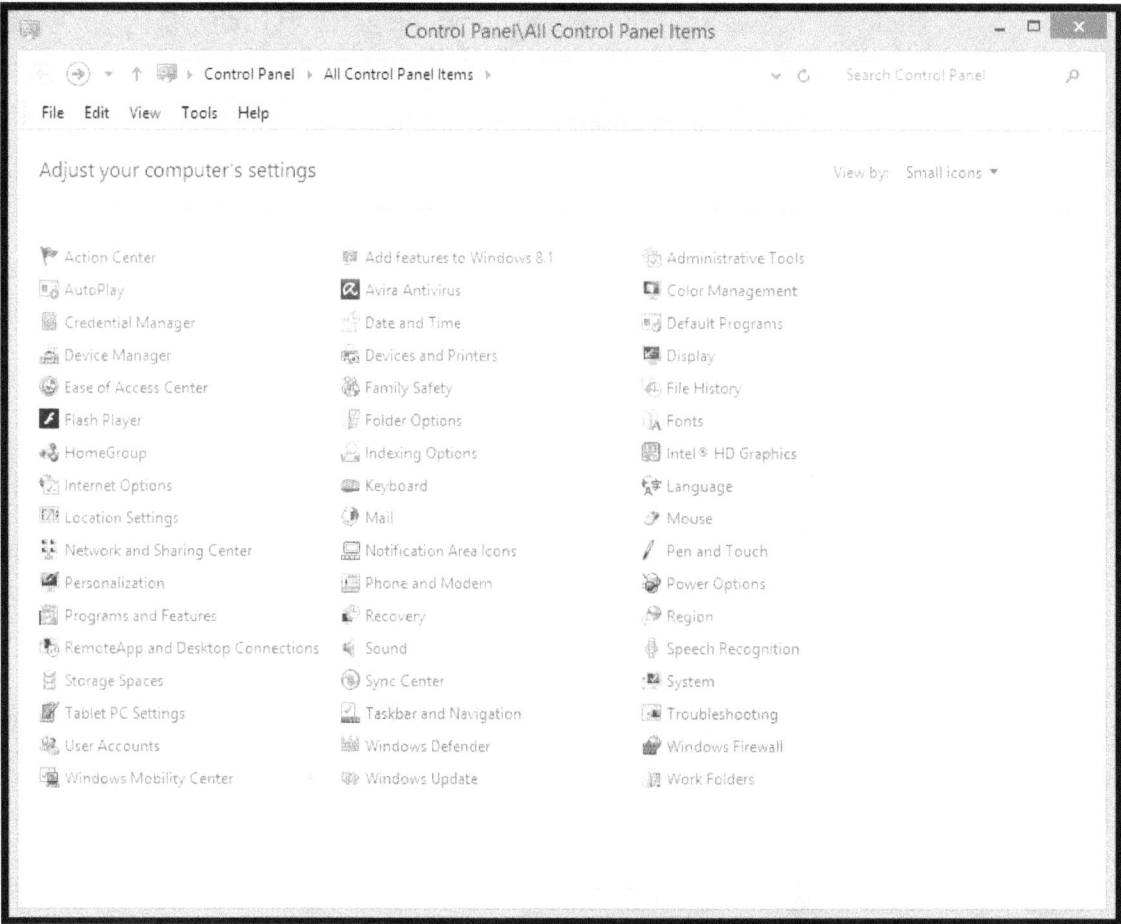

Windows 8/8.1 - Figure 20

Mark Versus Mr. Hacker.doc

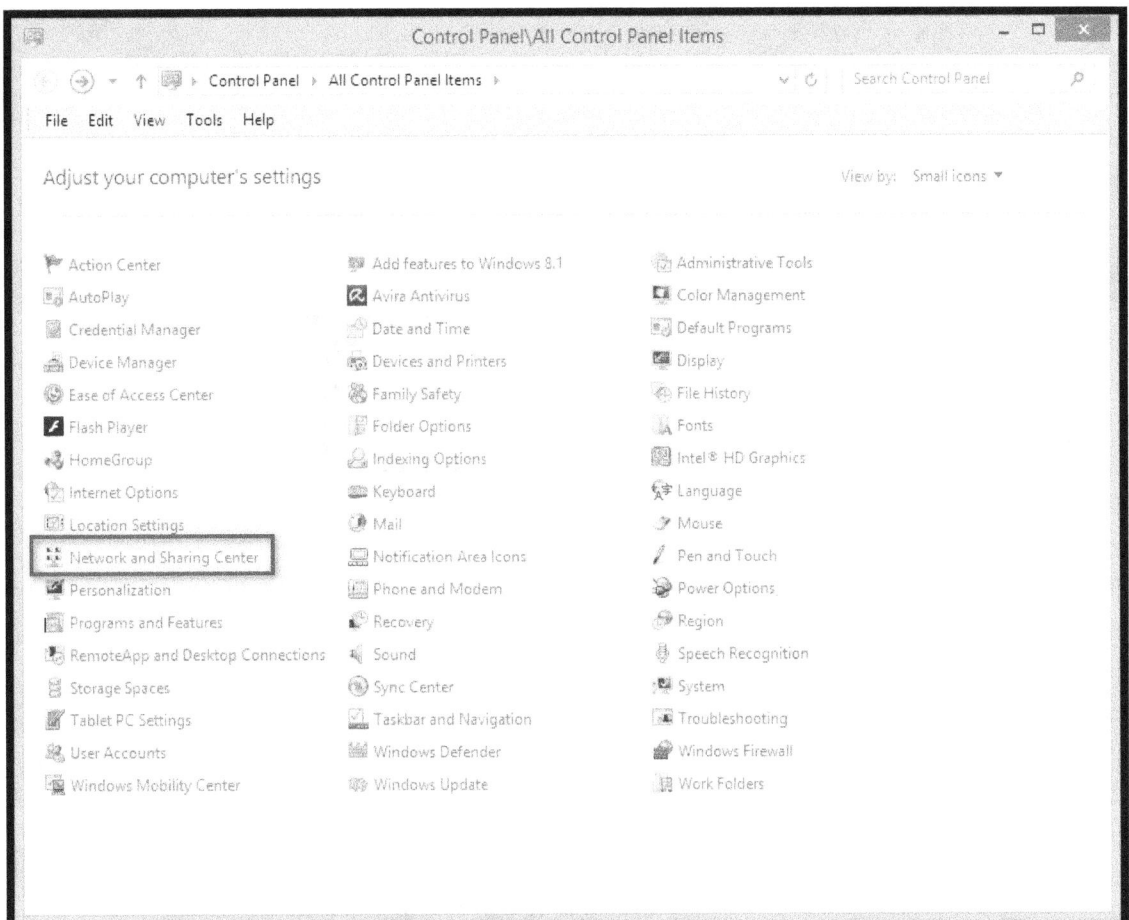

Windows 8/8.1 - Figure 21a

Mark Versus Mr. Hacker.doc

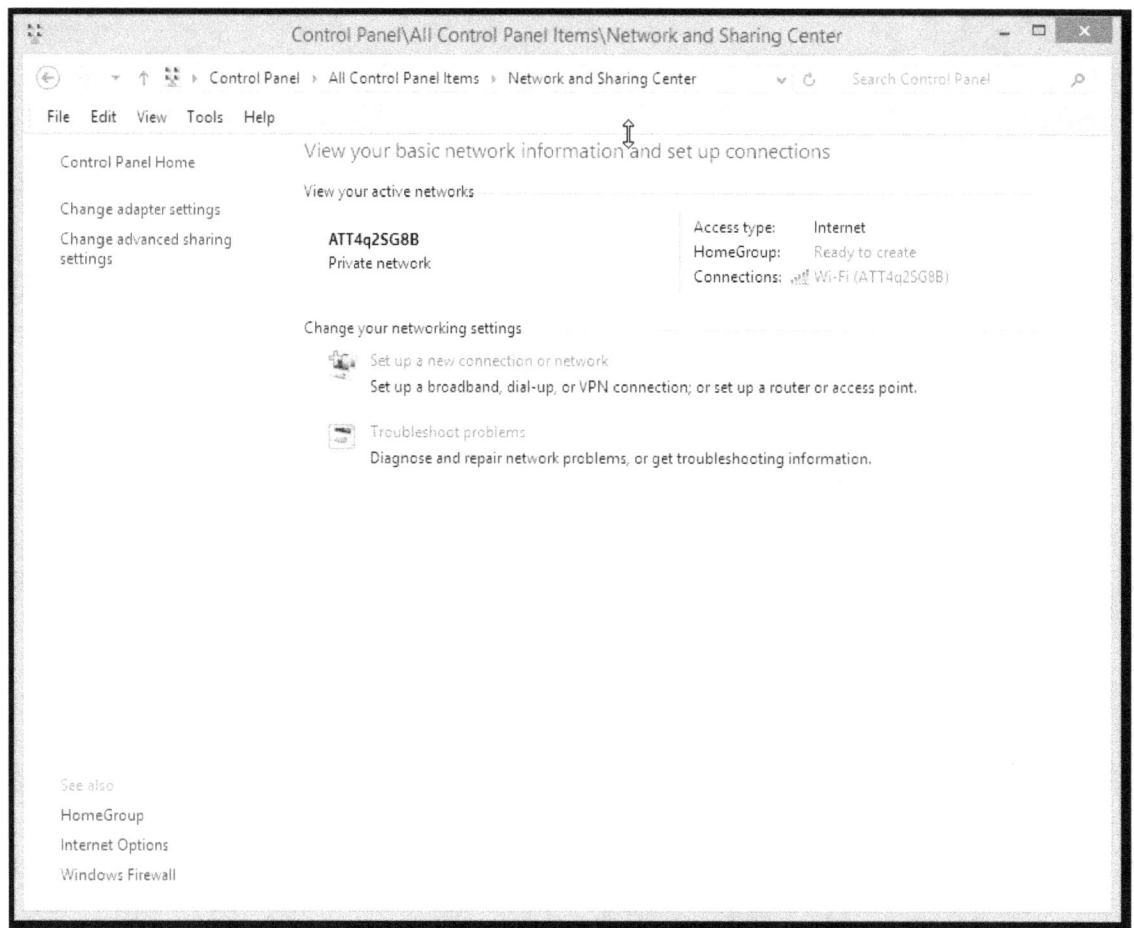

Windows 8/8.1 - Figure 21b

Mark Versus Mr. Hacker.doc

You can click on the "Change adapter settings" to get to the next step.

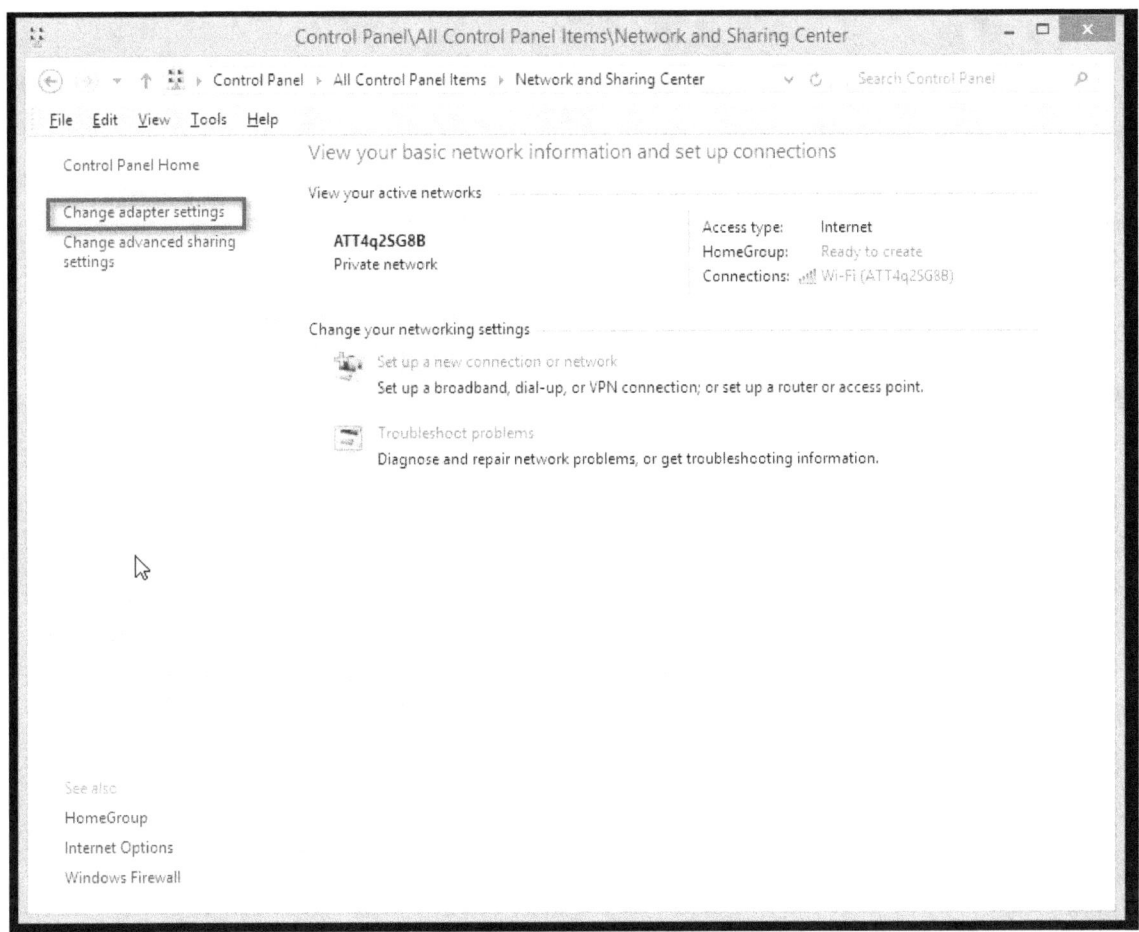

Windows 8/8.1 - Figure 21c

Mark Versus Mr. Hacker.doc

Or you can click on the connection itself.

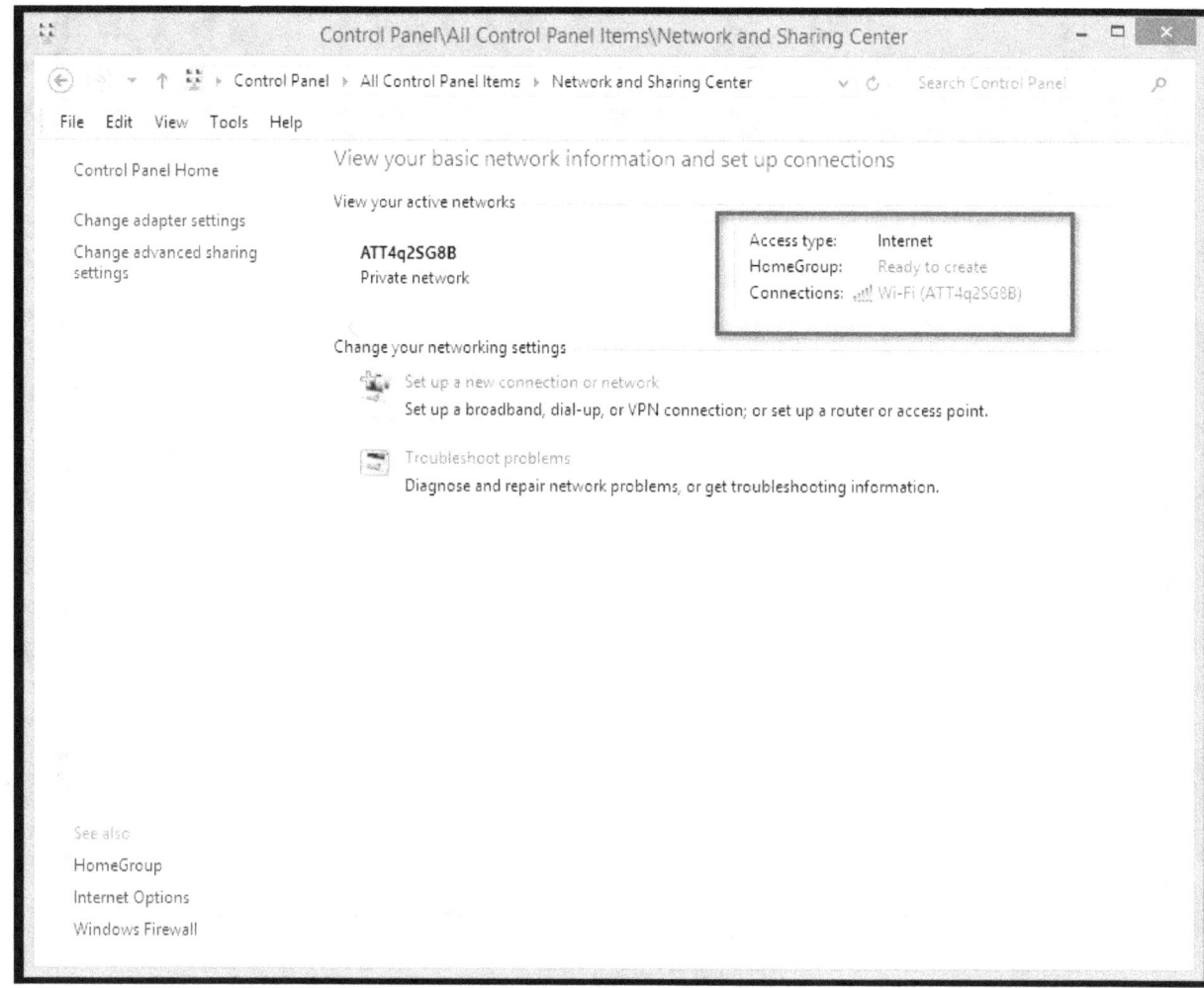

Windows 8/8.1 - Figure 21d

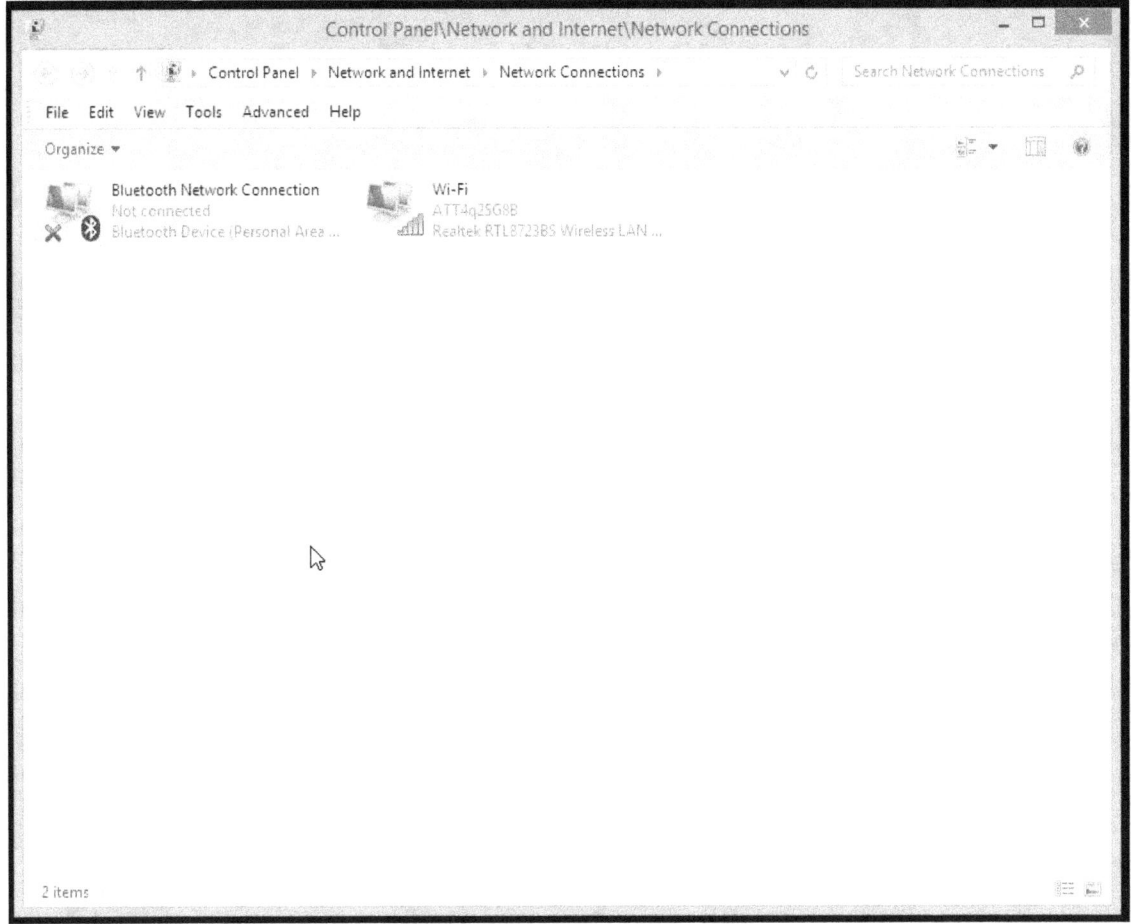

Windows 8/8.1 - Figure 21e

Mark Versus Mr. Hacker.doc

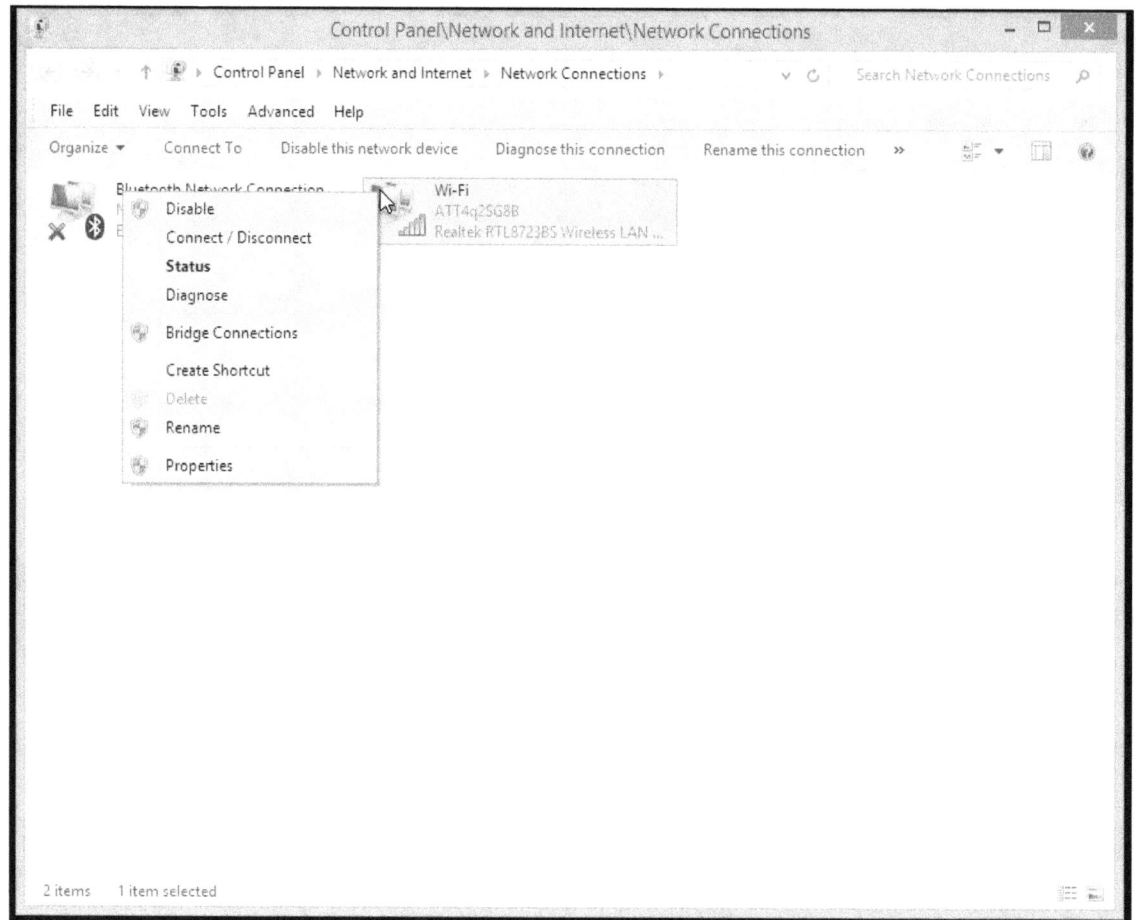

Windows 8/8.1 - Figure 22

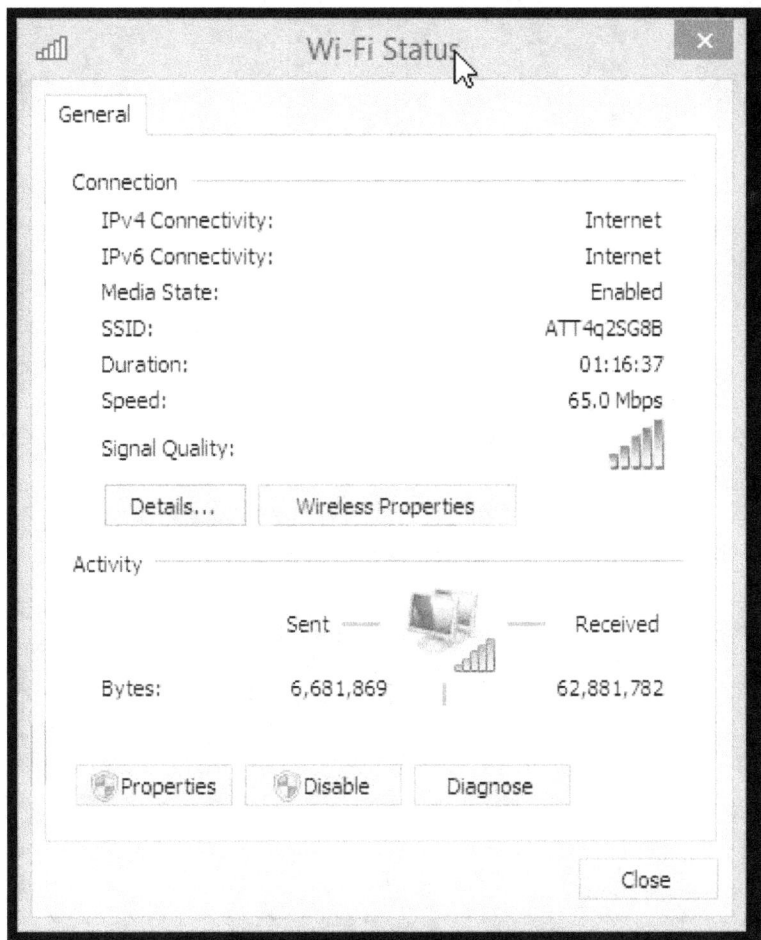
Windows 8/8.1 - Figure 23a

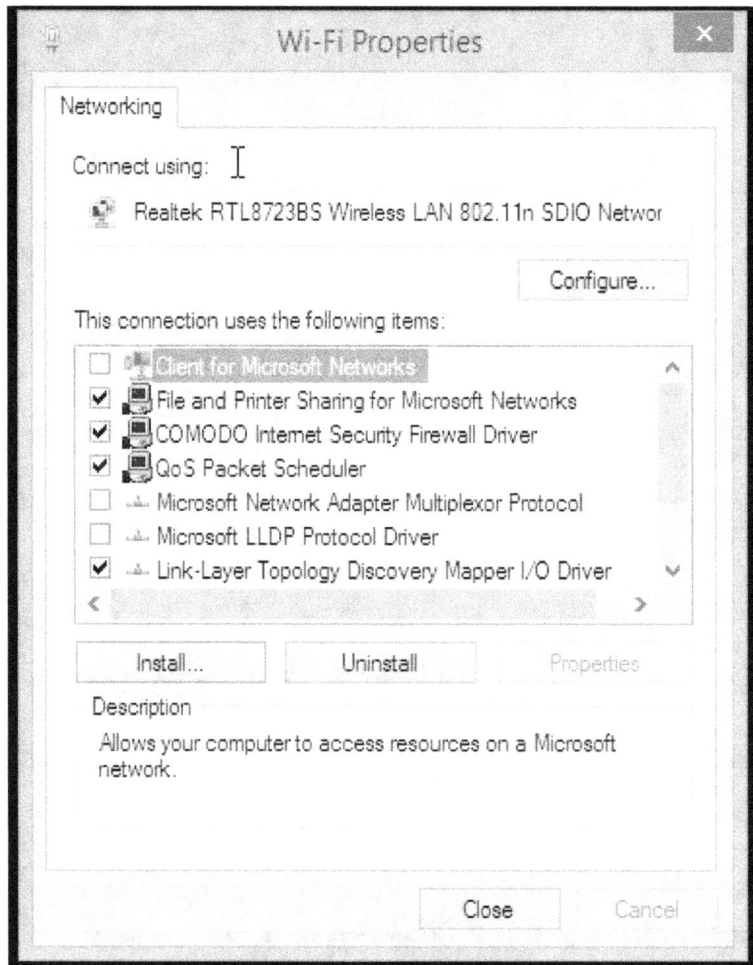

Windows 8/8.1 - Figure 23b

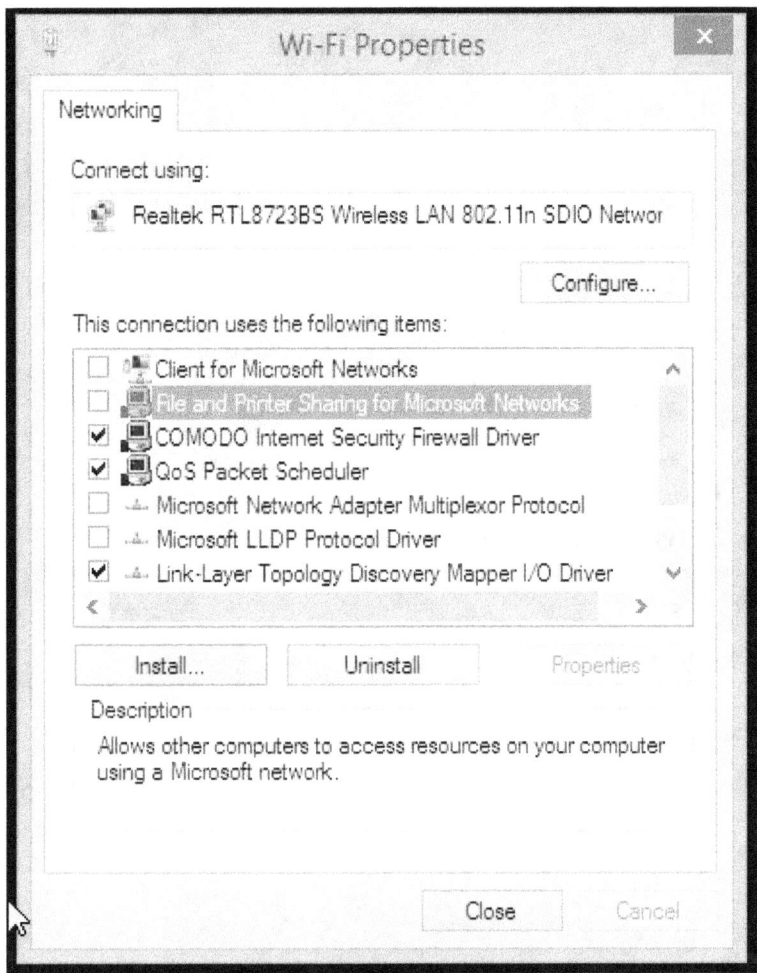

Windows 8/8.1 - Figure 24

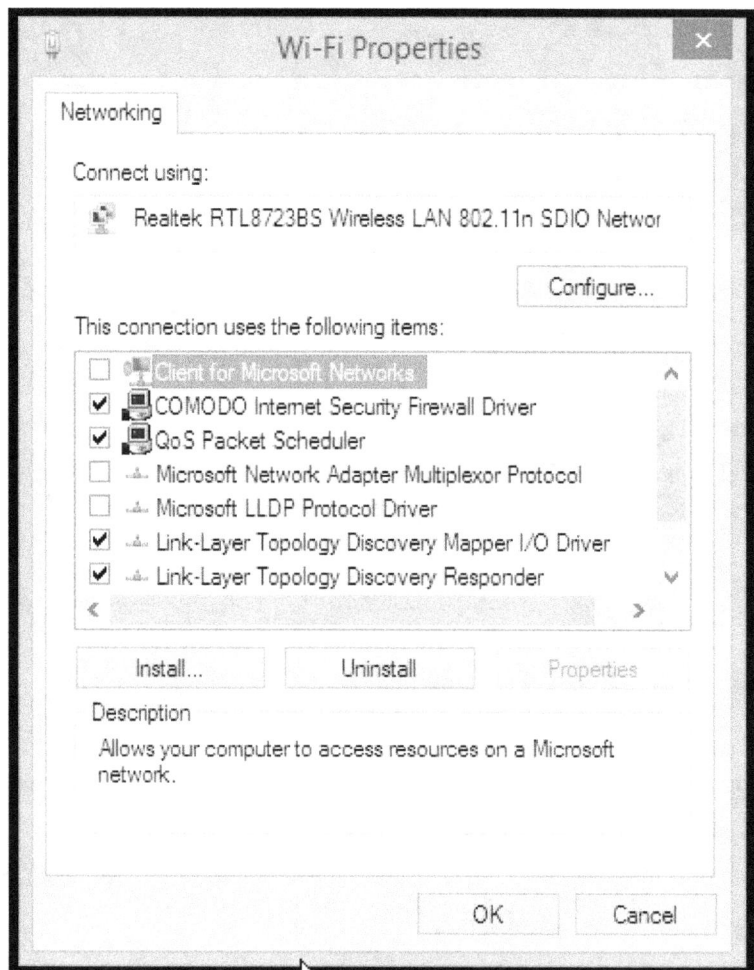

Windows 8/8.1 - Figure 25

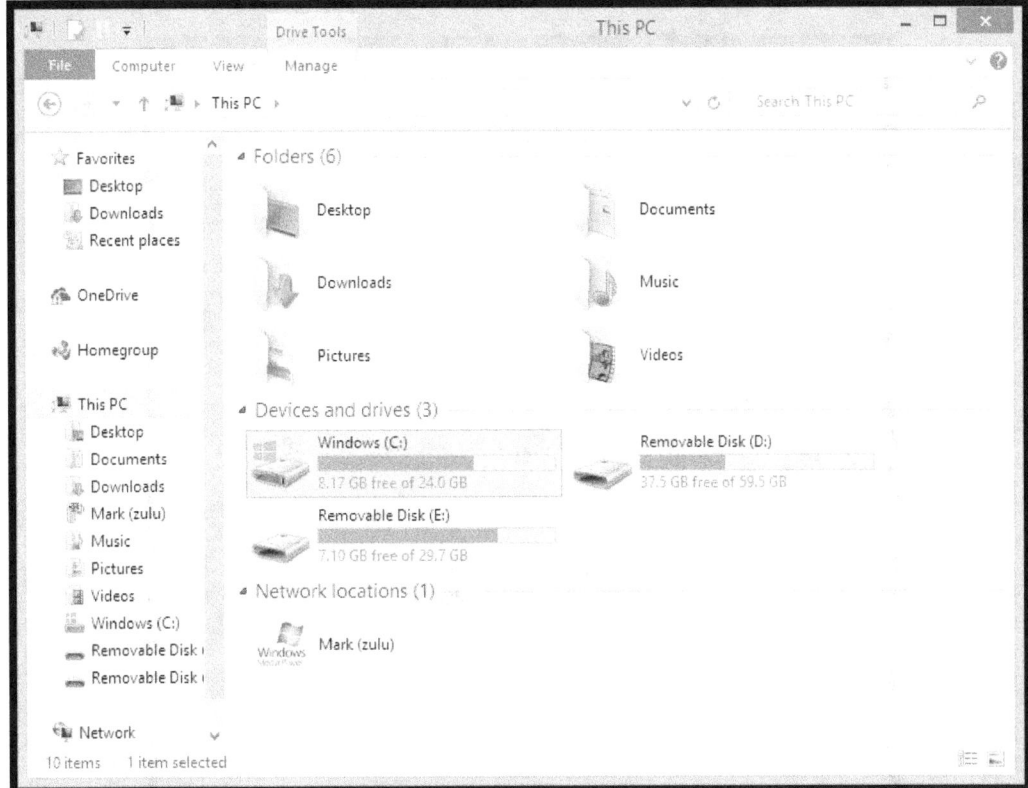
Windows 8/8.1 - Figure 26

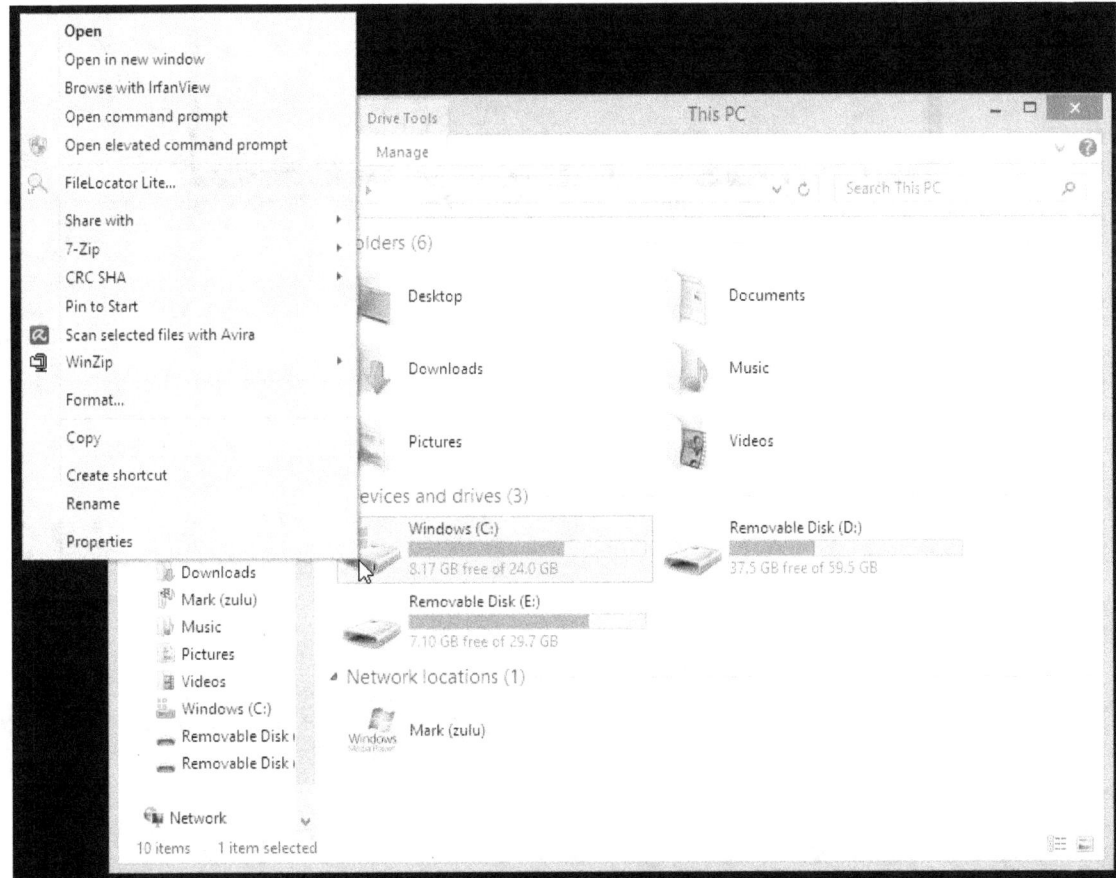
Windows 8/8.1 - Figure 27

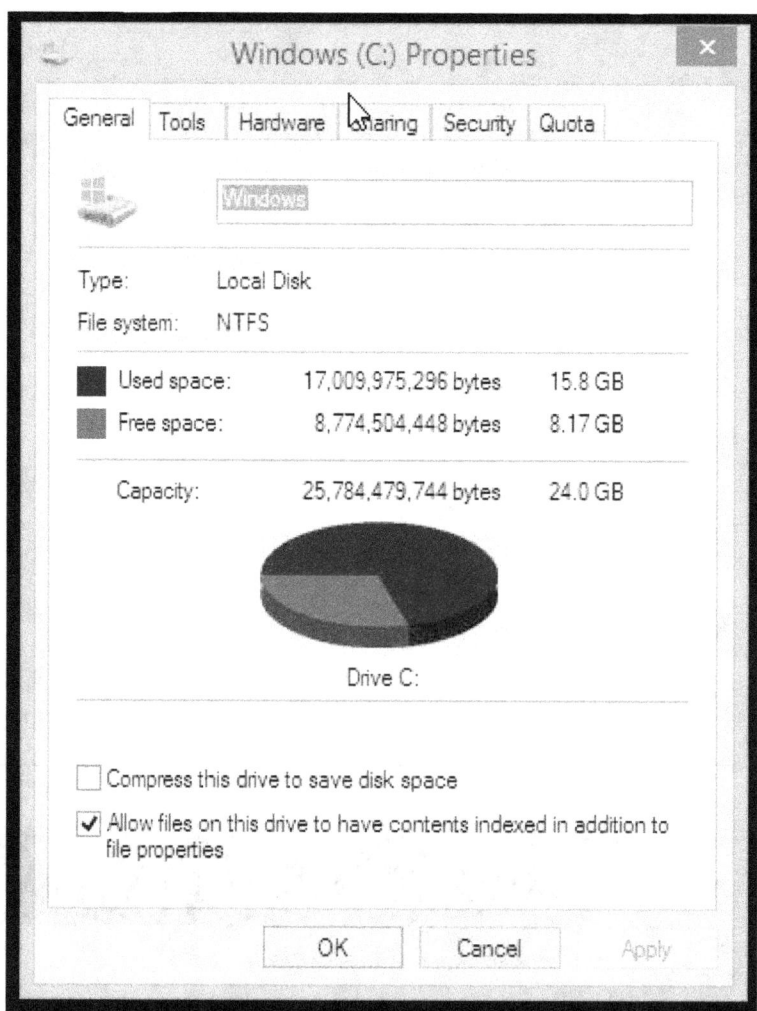

Windows 8/8.1 - Figure 28a

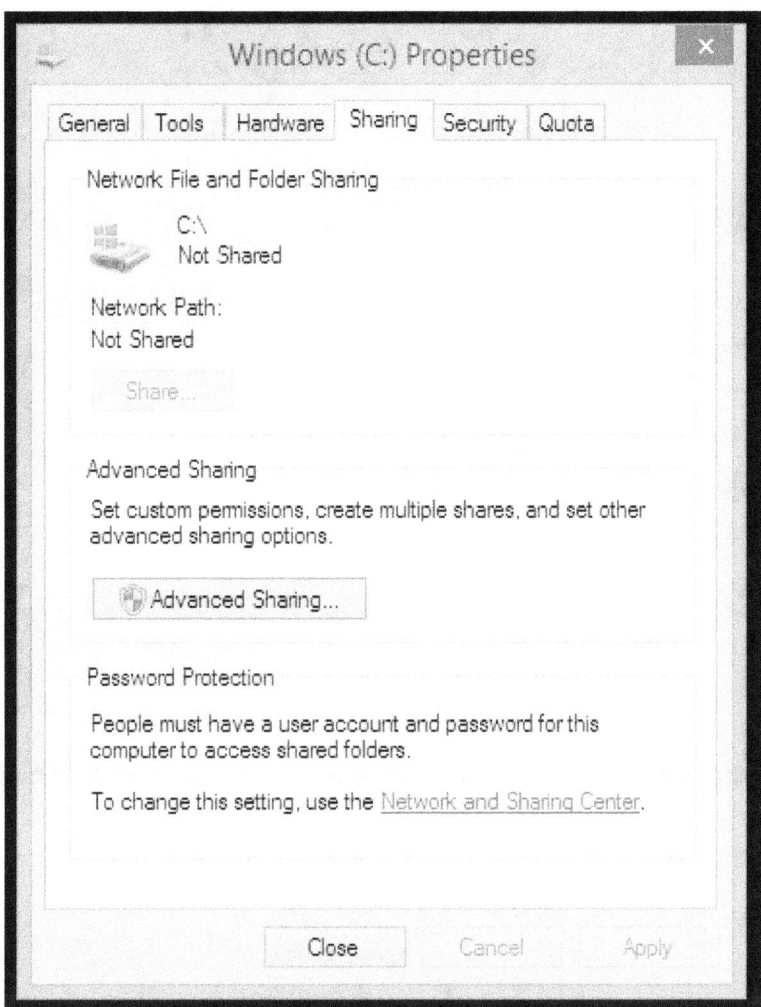

Windows 8/8.1 - Figure 28b

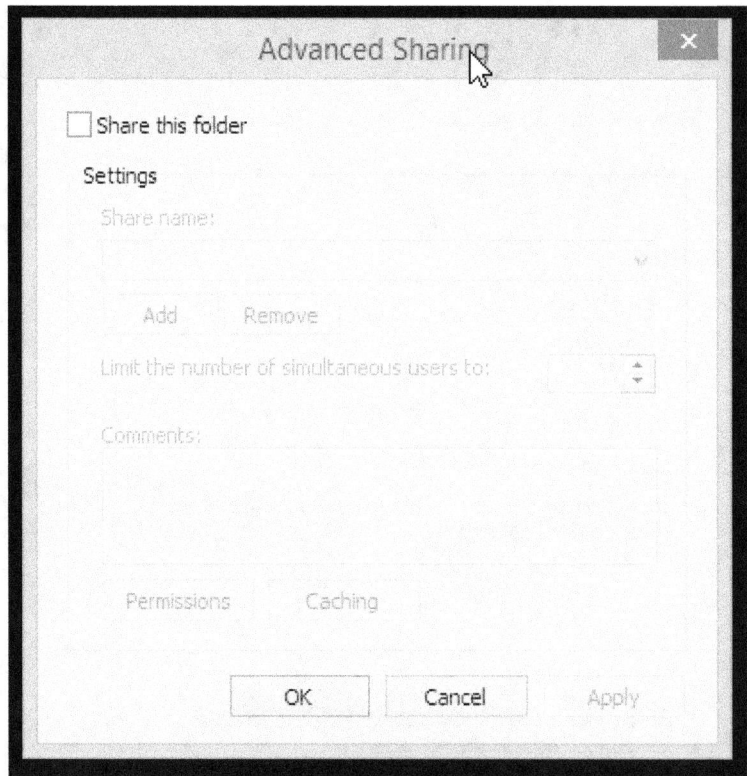

Windows 8/8.1 - Figure 28c

Under Windows 8/8.1 you just select "Command Prompt (Admin)".

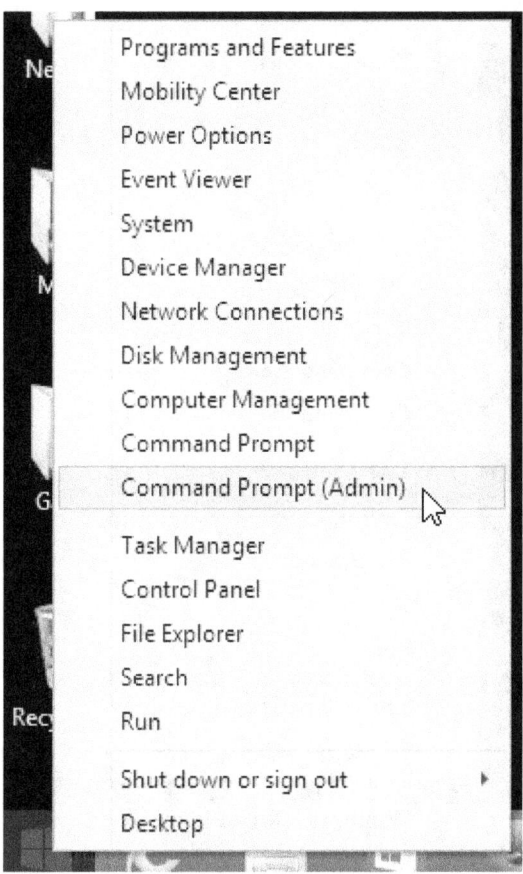
Windows 8/8.1 - Figure 29

Windows 8 – Figure 30 omitted because Windows 8 doesn't do that. It just runs as an administrator.

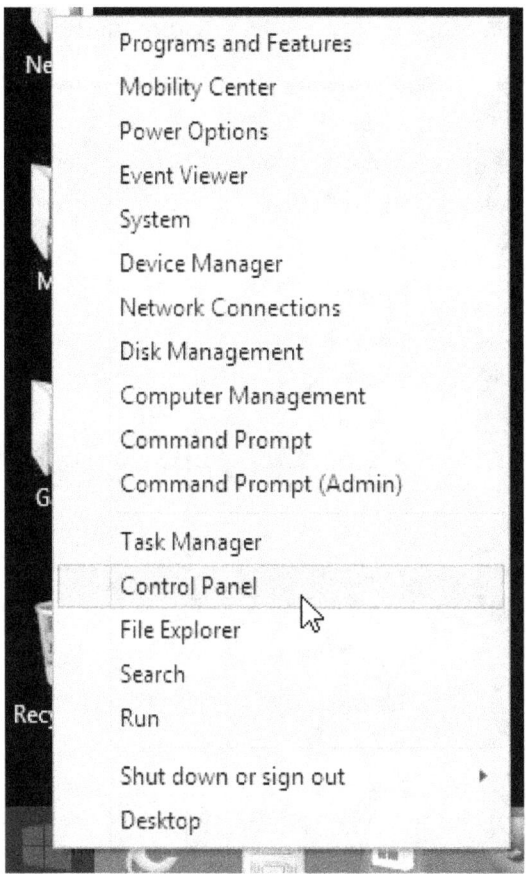
Windows 8/8.1 - Figure 31

Mark Versus Mr. Hacker.doc

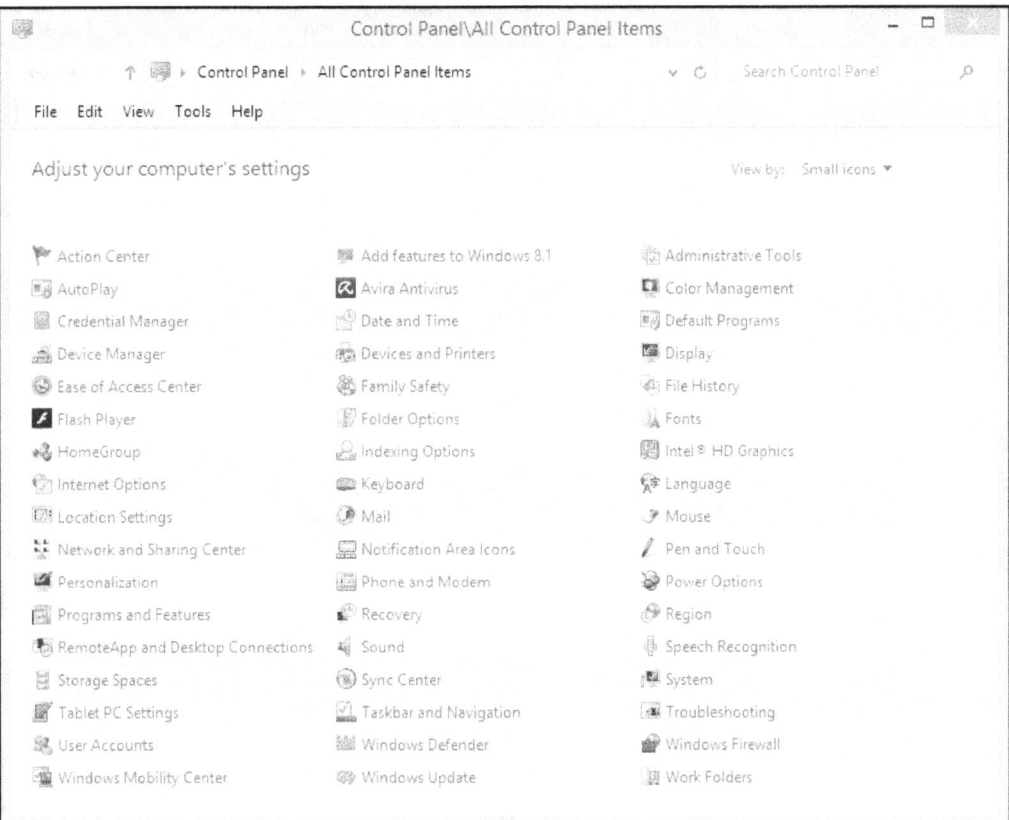

Windows 8/8.1 - Figure 32

Mark Versus Mr. Hacker.doc

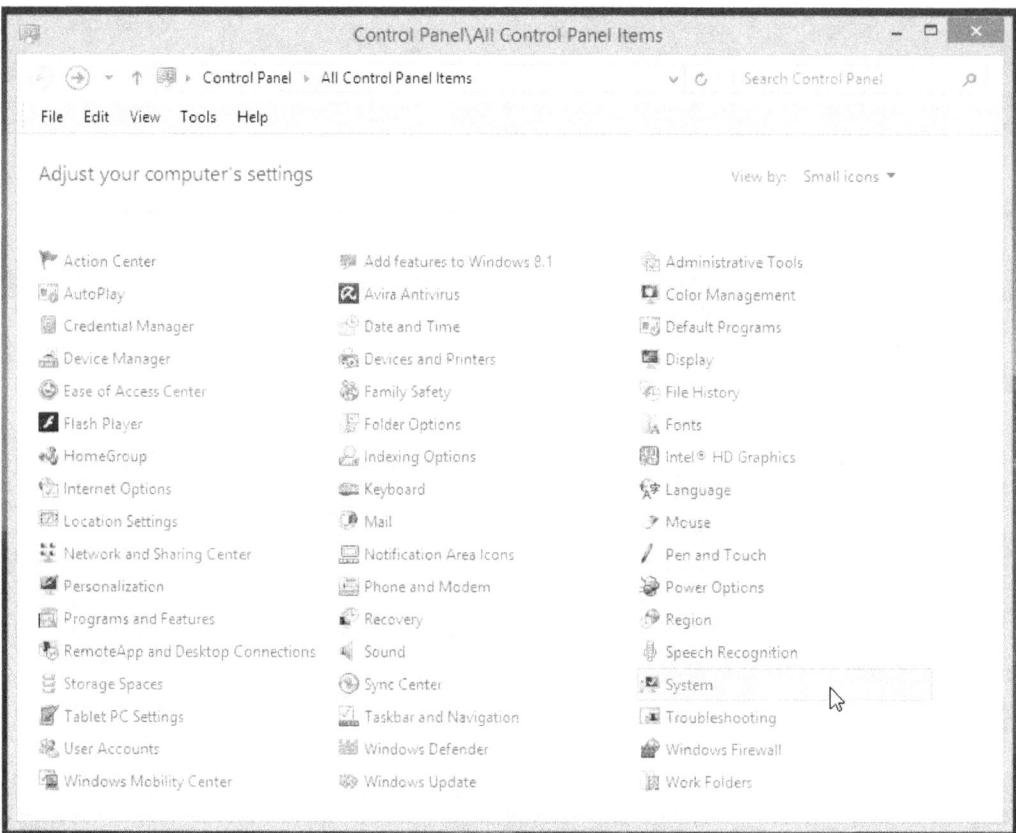

Windows 8/8.1 - Figure 33

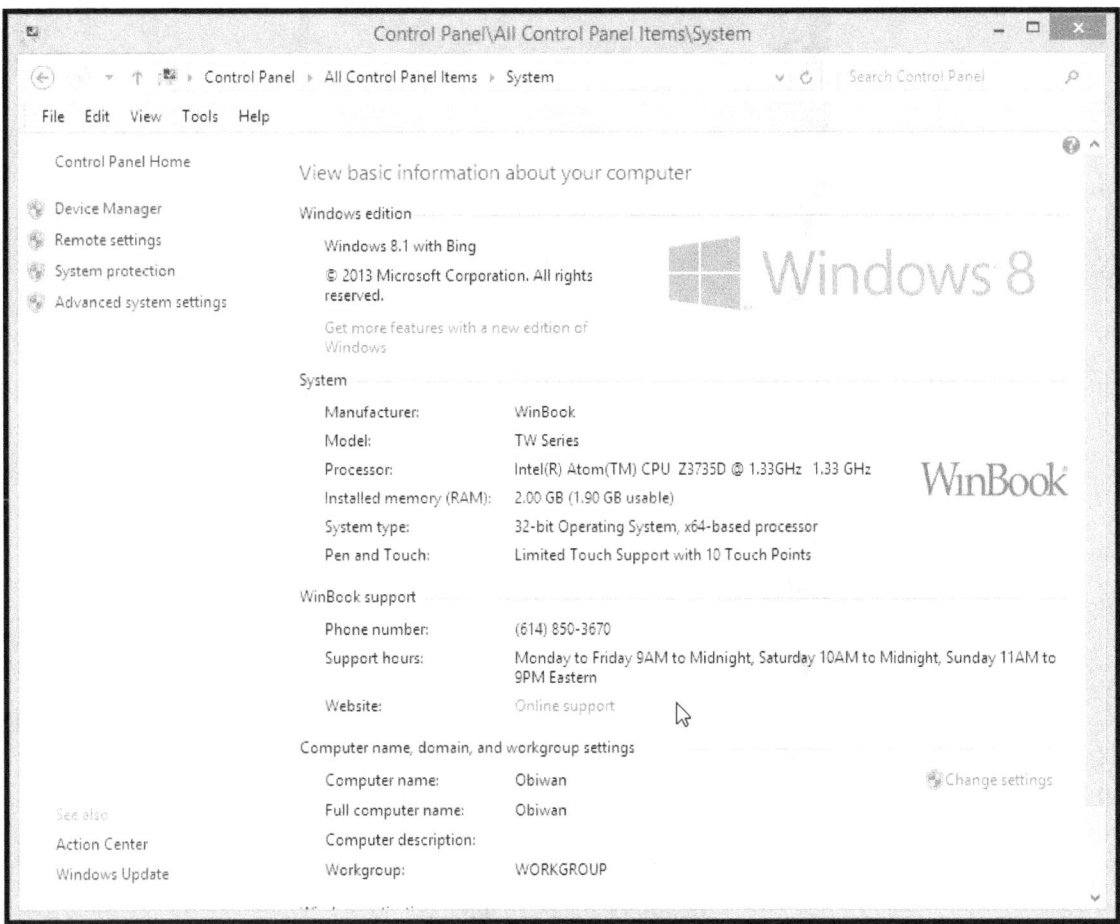

Windows 8/8.1 - Figure 34

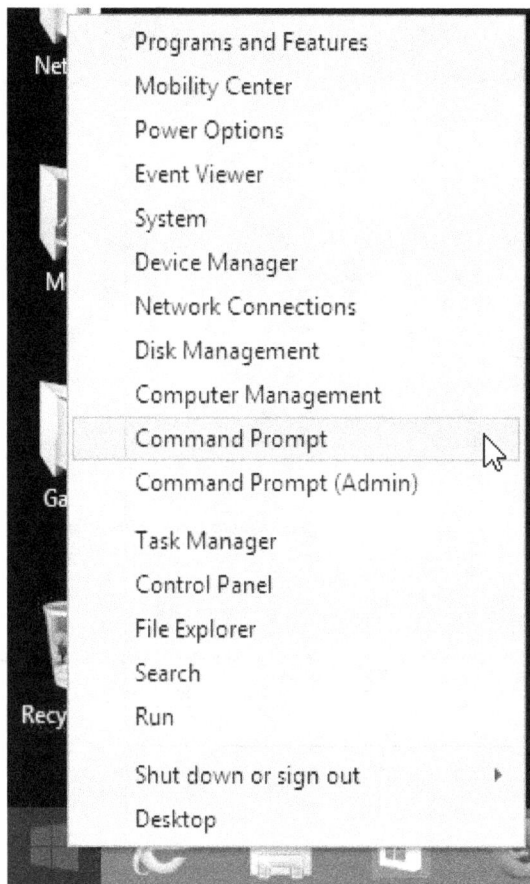

Windows 8/8.1 - Figure 35

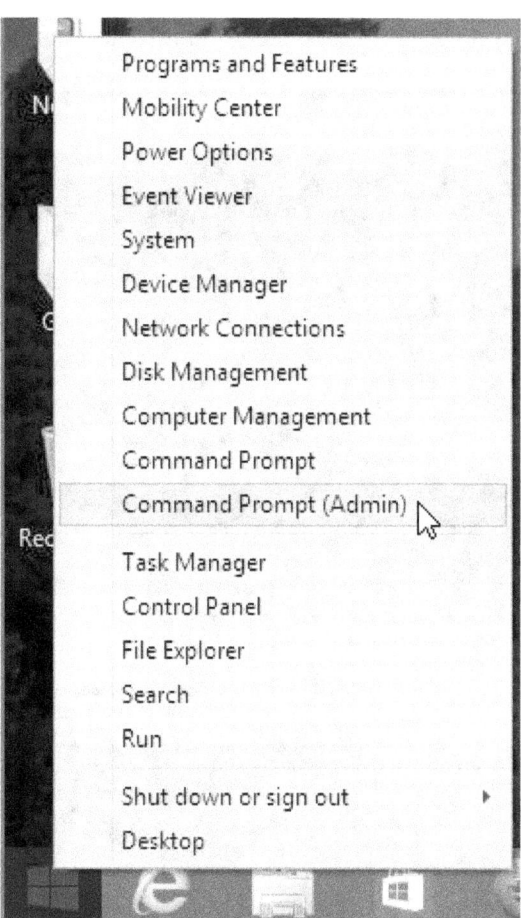

Windows 8/8.1 - Figure 36

The Command Prompt is the same on all versions of Windows.

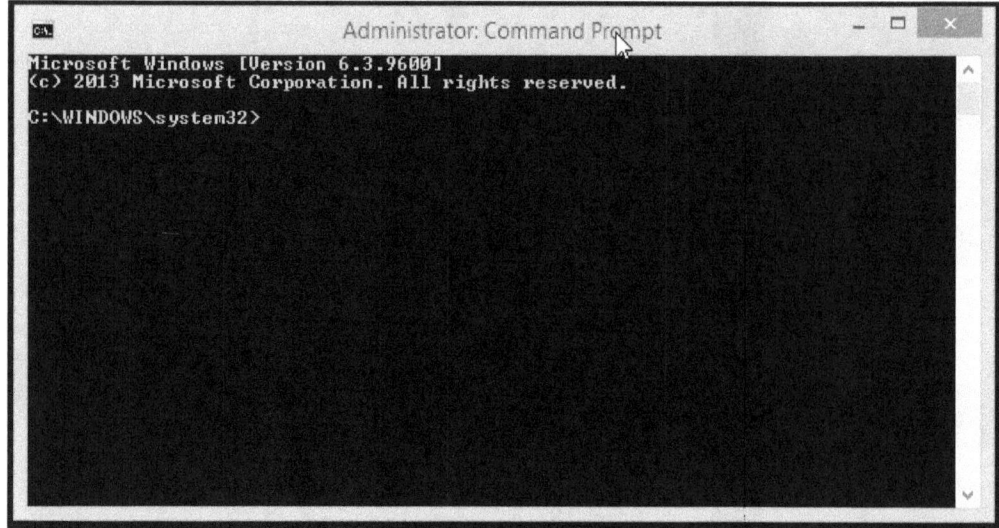

Windows 8/8.1 - Figure 37

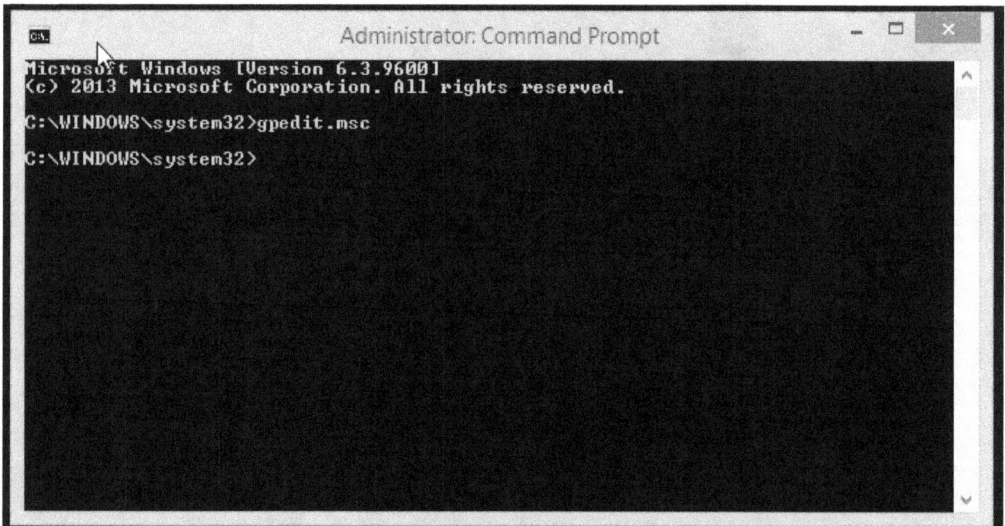

Windows 8/8.1 - Figure 38

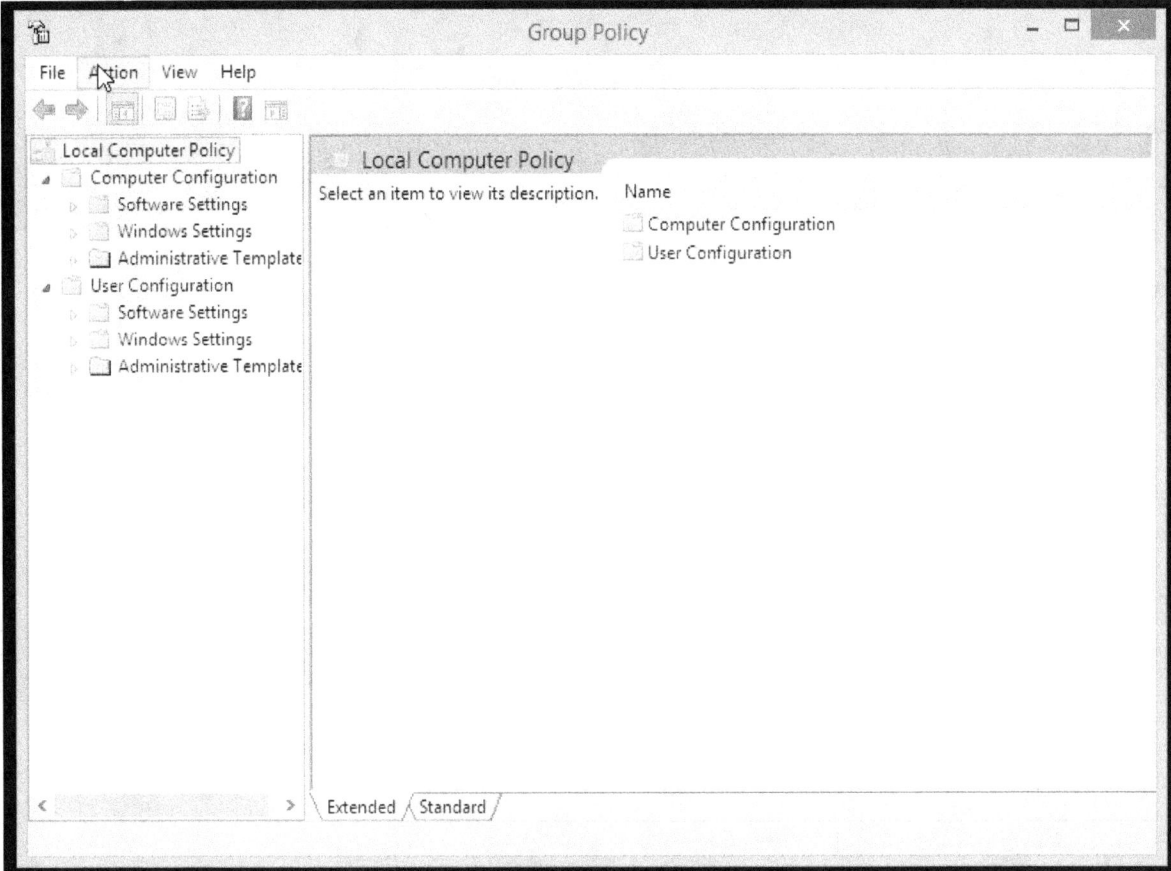

Windows 8/8.1 - Figure 39

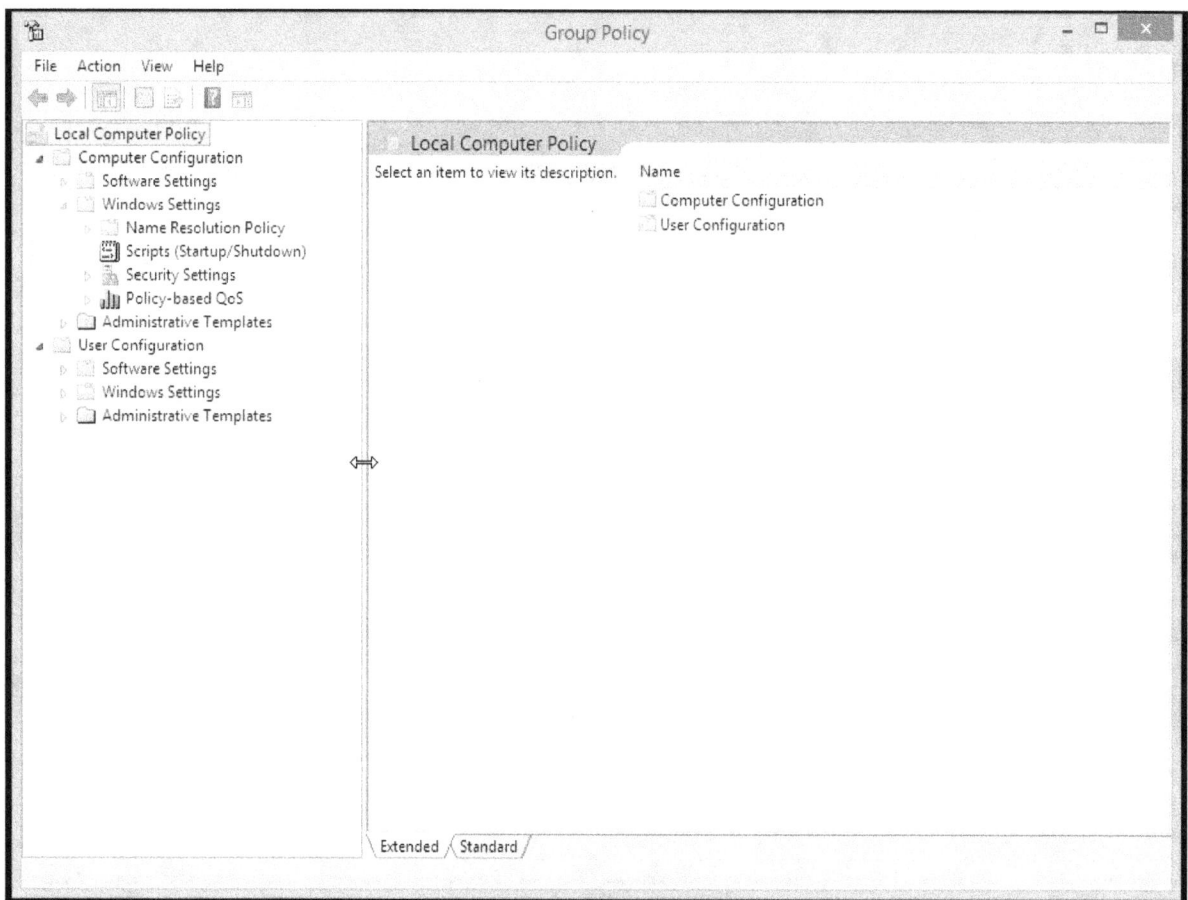

Windows 8/8.1 - Figure 40

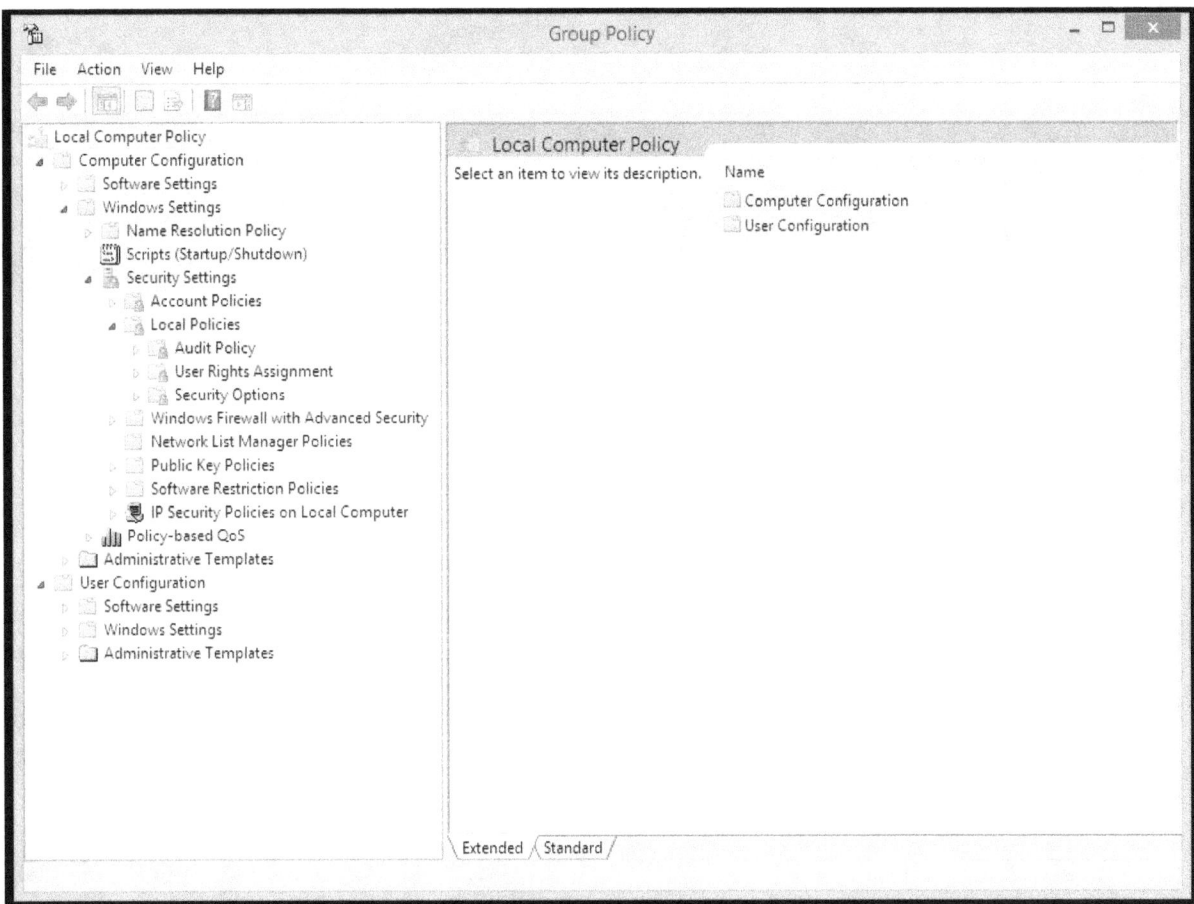

Windows 8/8.1 - Figure 41

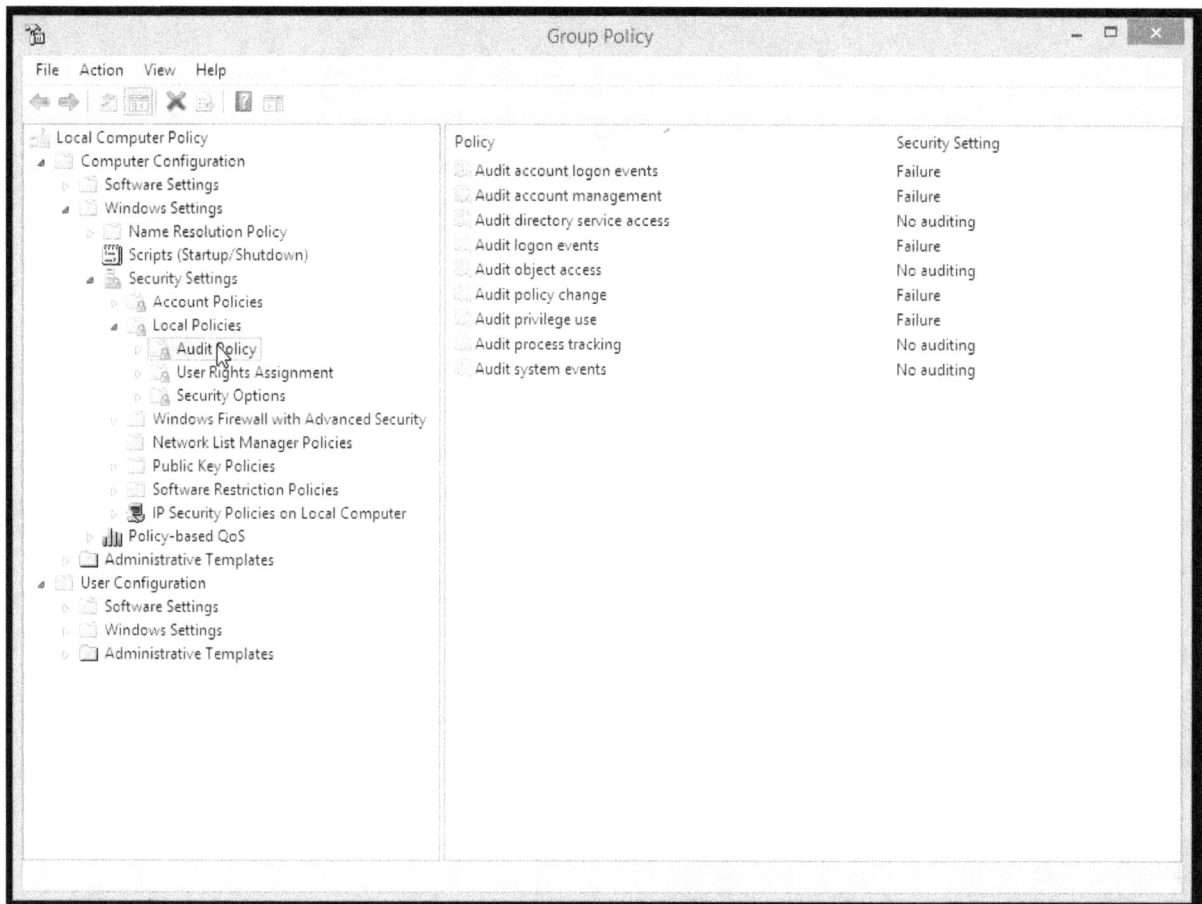

Windows 8/8.1 - Figure 42

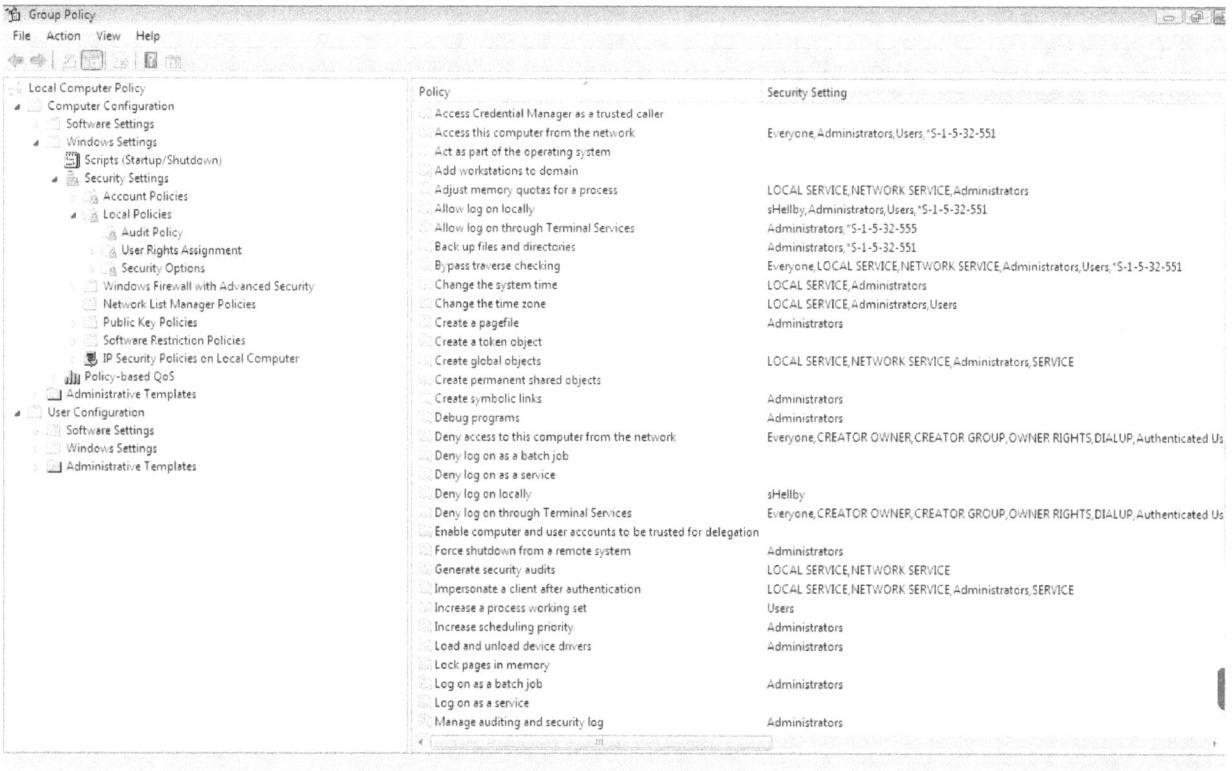

Windows 8/8.1 - Figure 43

Windows 8/8.1 - Figure 44

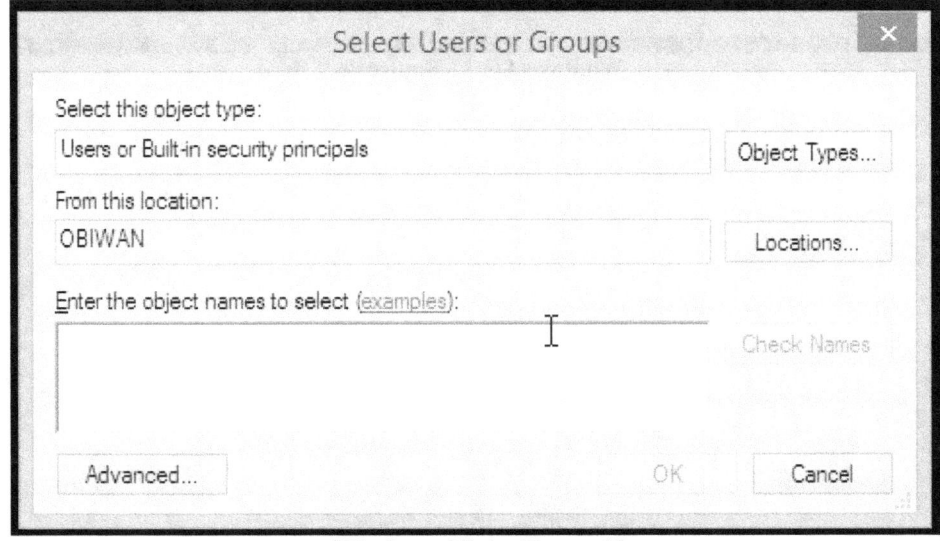

Windows 8/8.1 - Figure 45

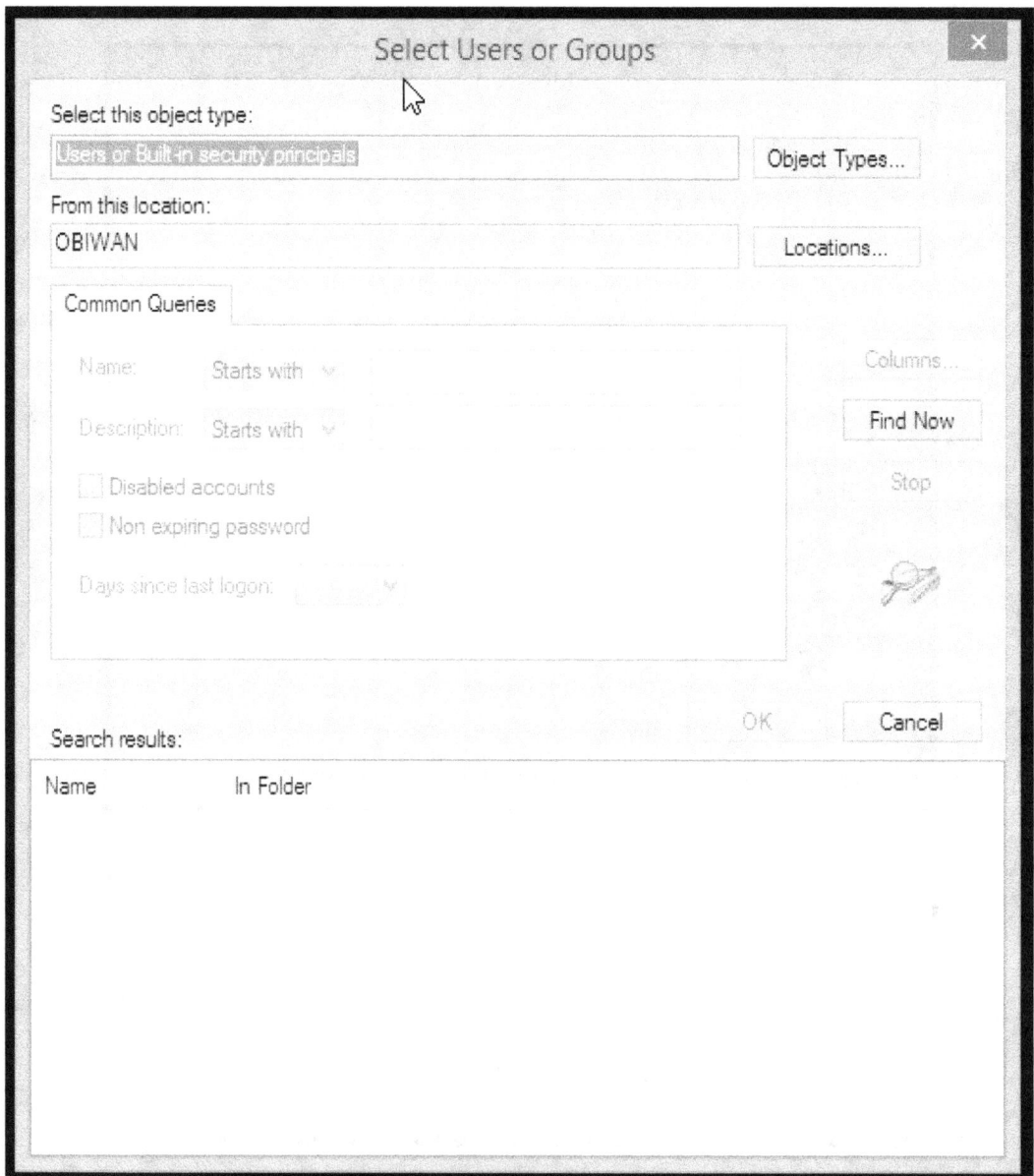

Windows 8/8.1 - Figure 46

Mark Versus Mr. Hacker.doc

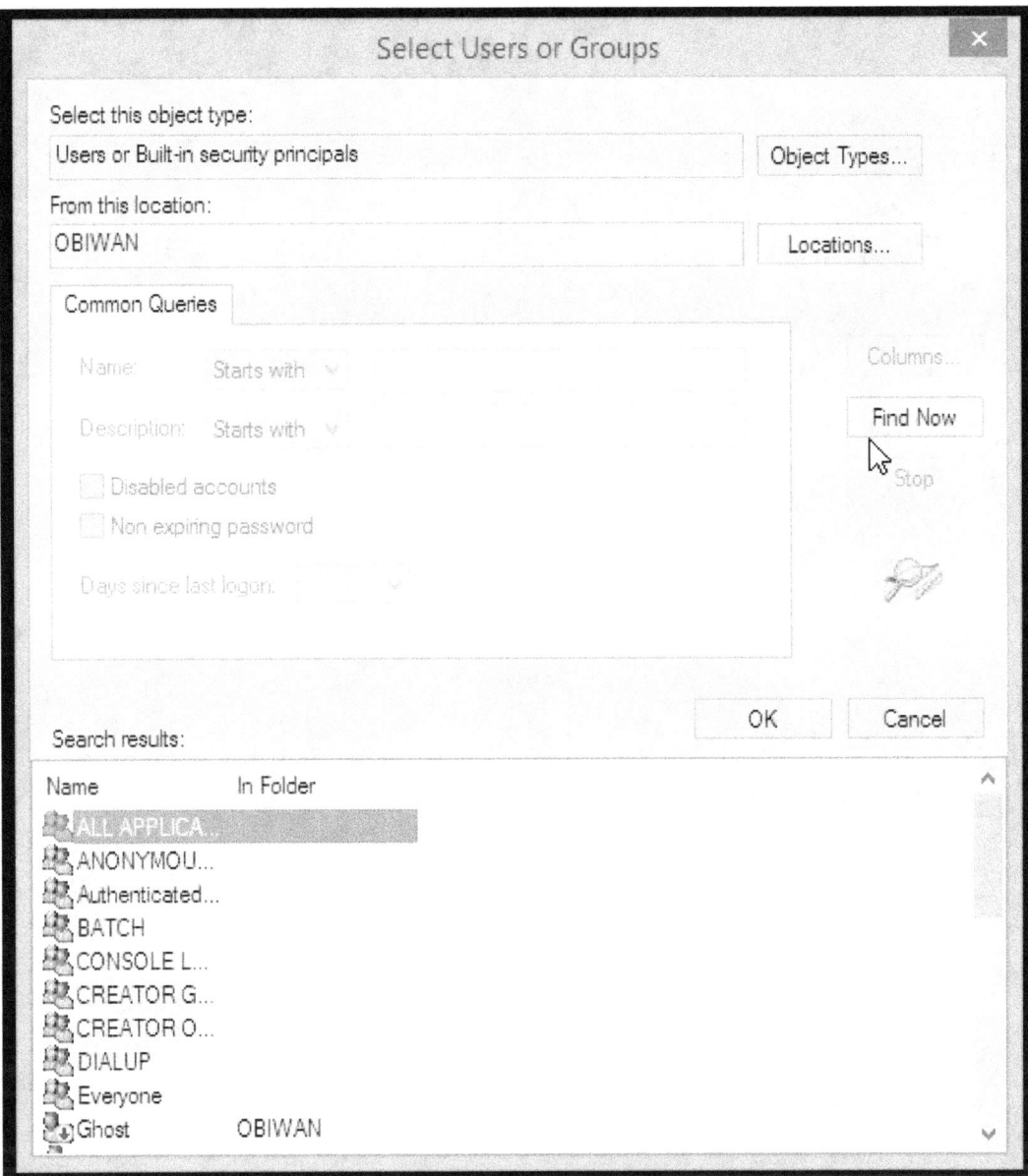

Windows 8/8.1 - Figure 47

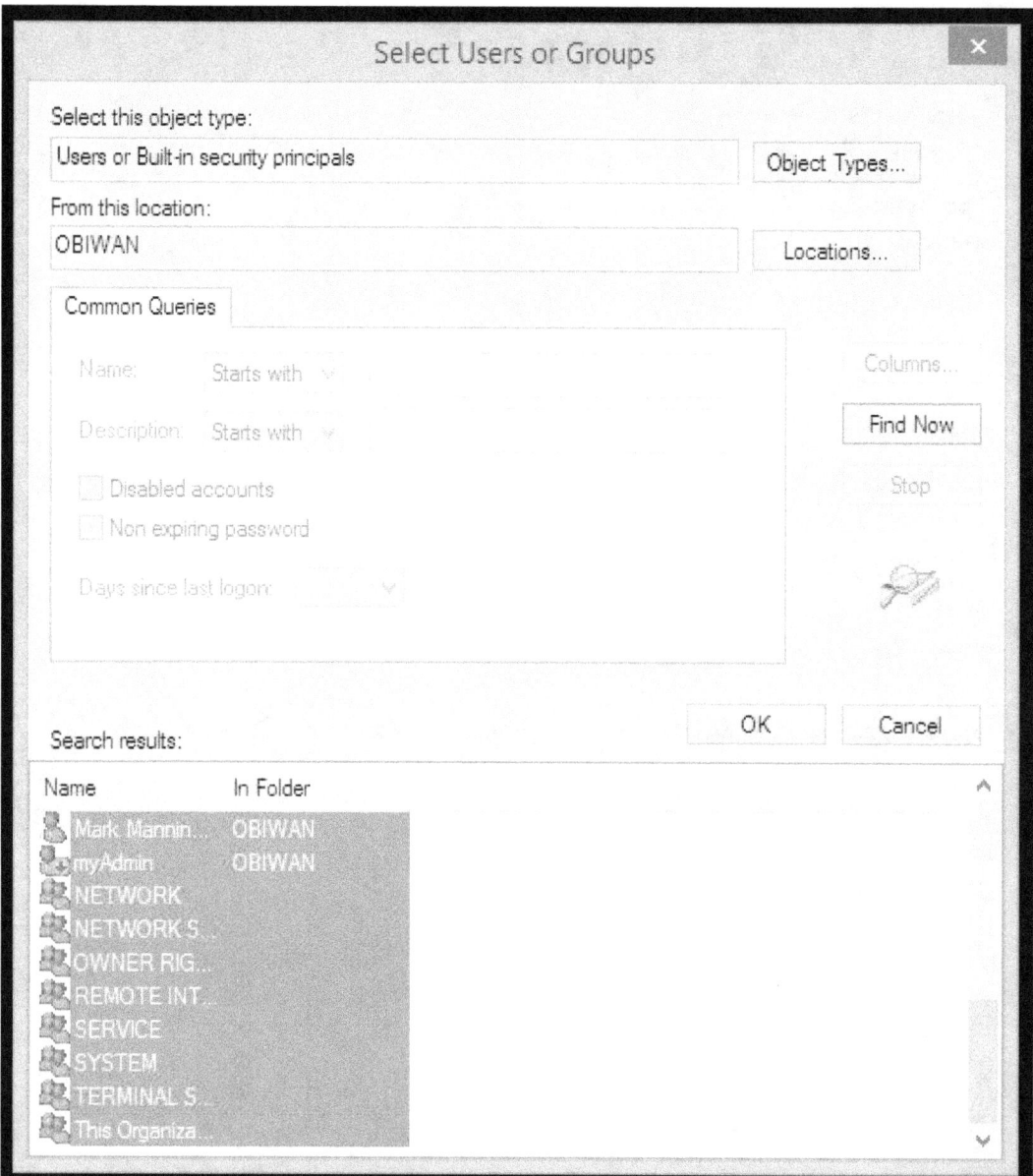

Windows 8/8.1 - Figure 48

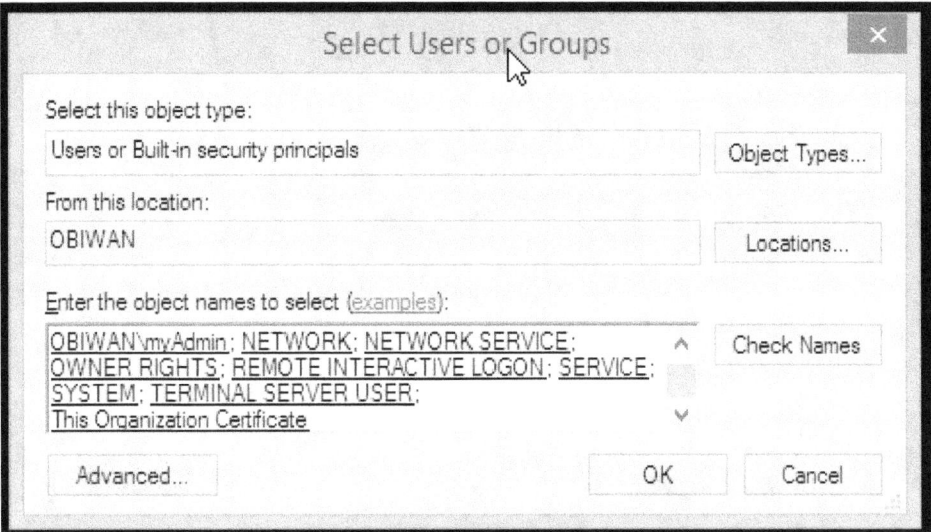

Windows 8/8.1 - Figure 49

Windows 8/8.1 - Figure 50

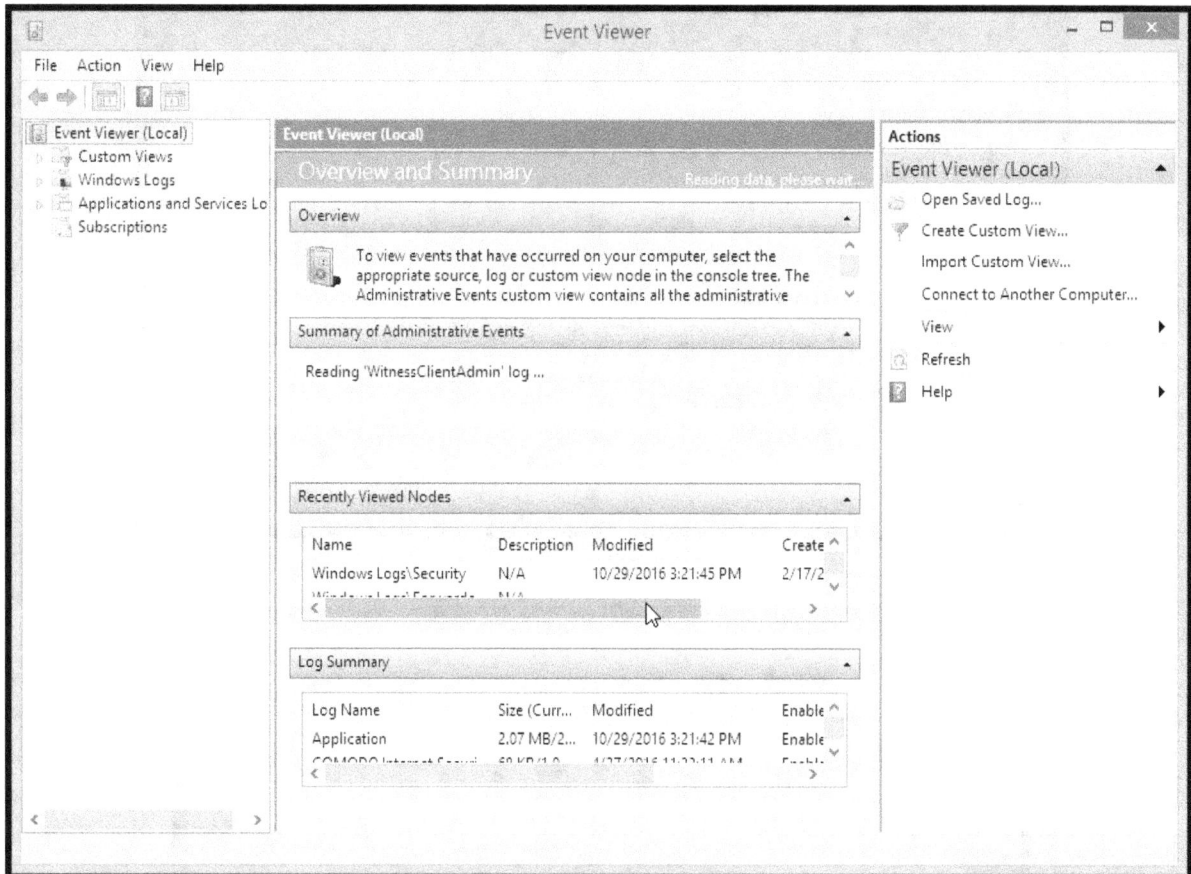

Windows 8/8.1 - Figure 51a

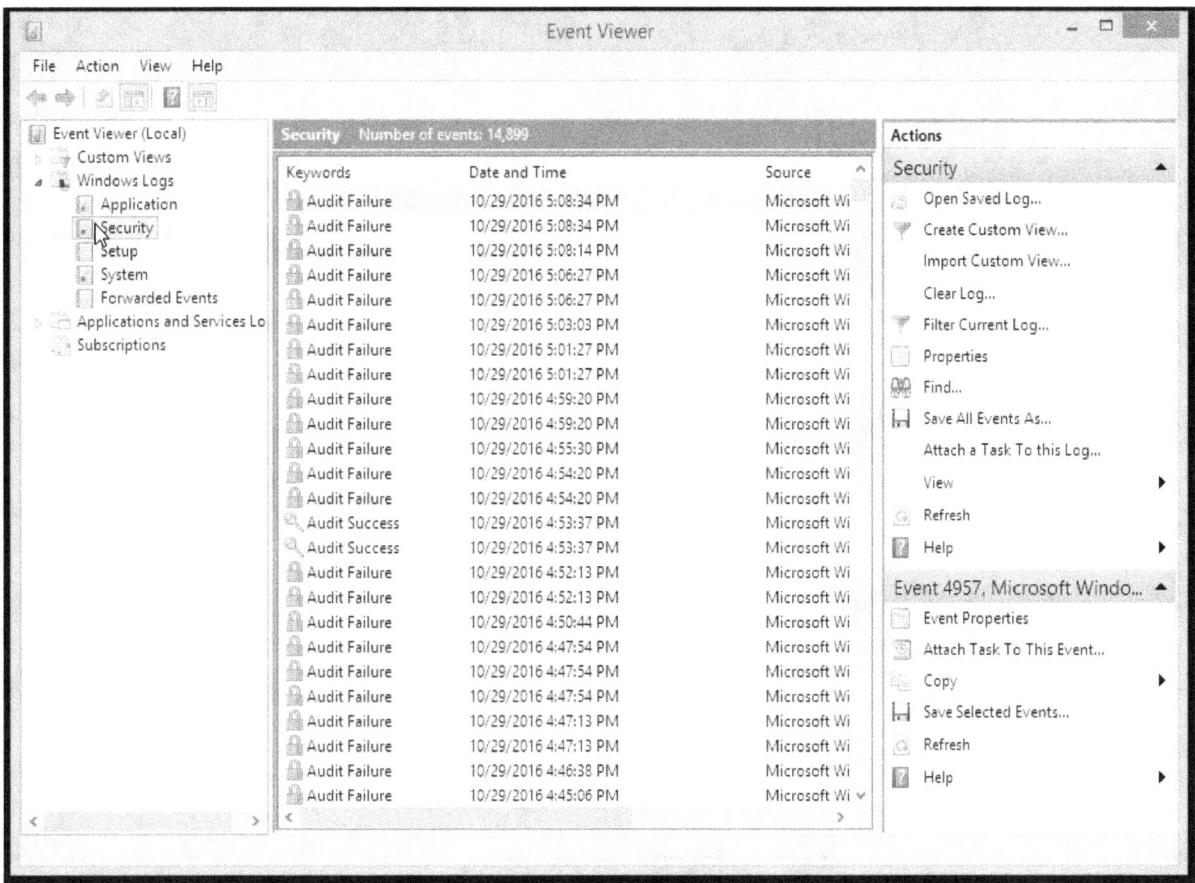

Windows 8/8.1 - Figure 51b

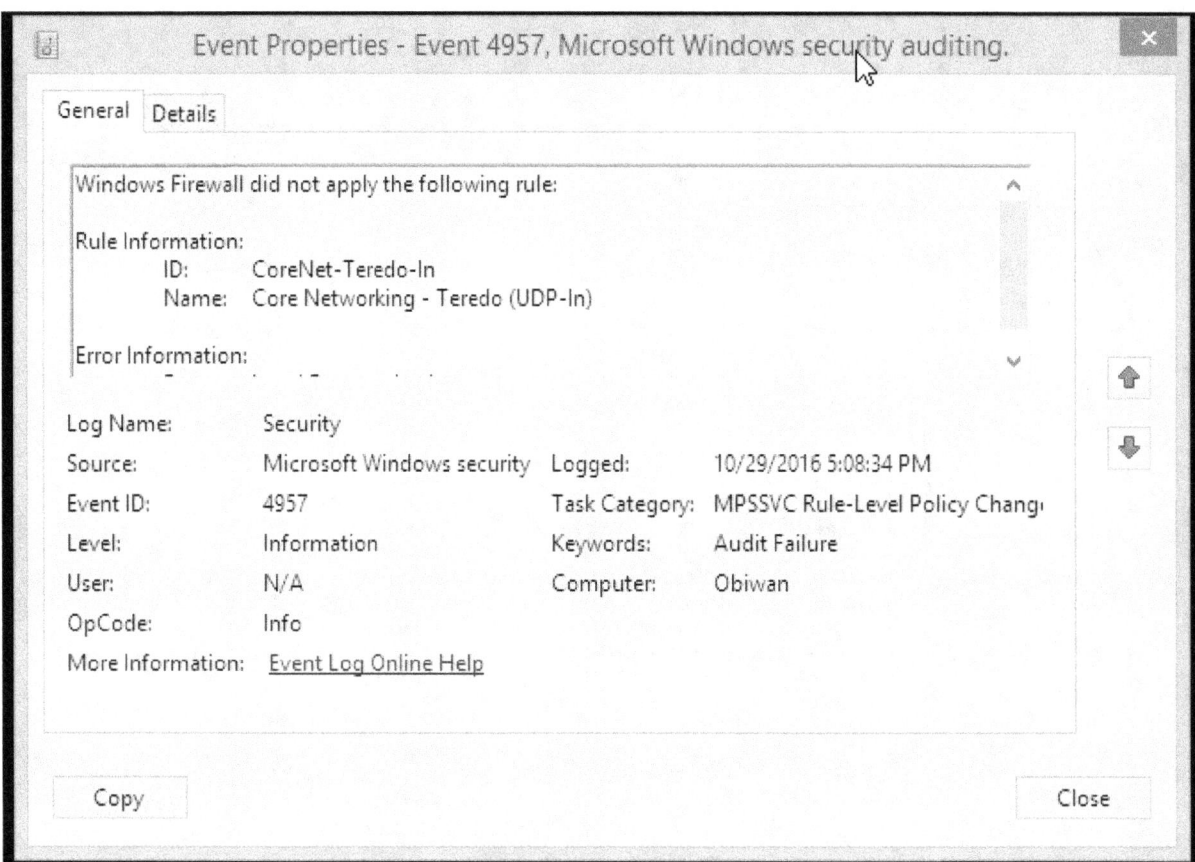

Windows 8/8.1 - Figure 52

Mark Versus Mr. Hacker.doc

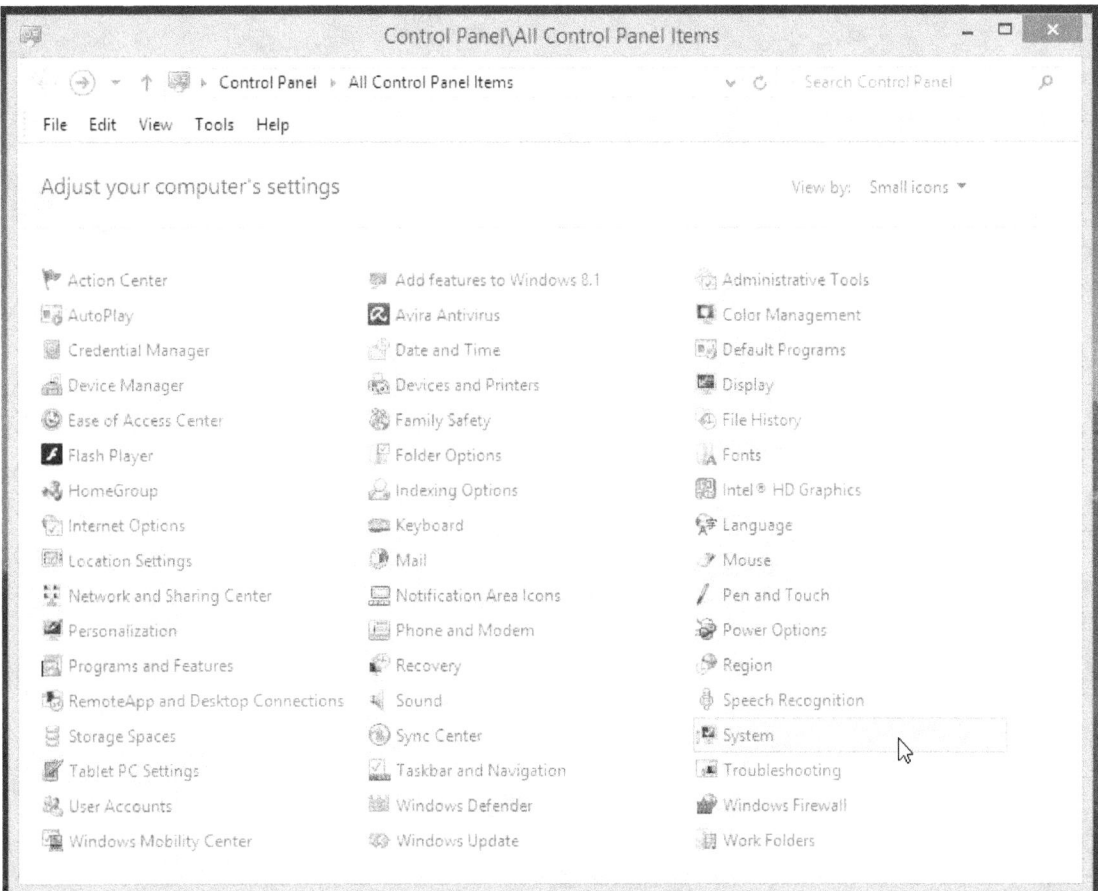

Windows 8/8.1 - Figure 53a

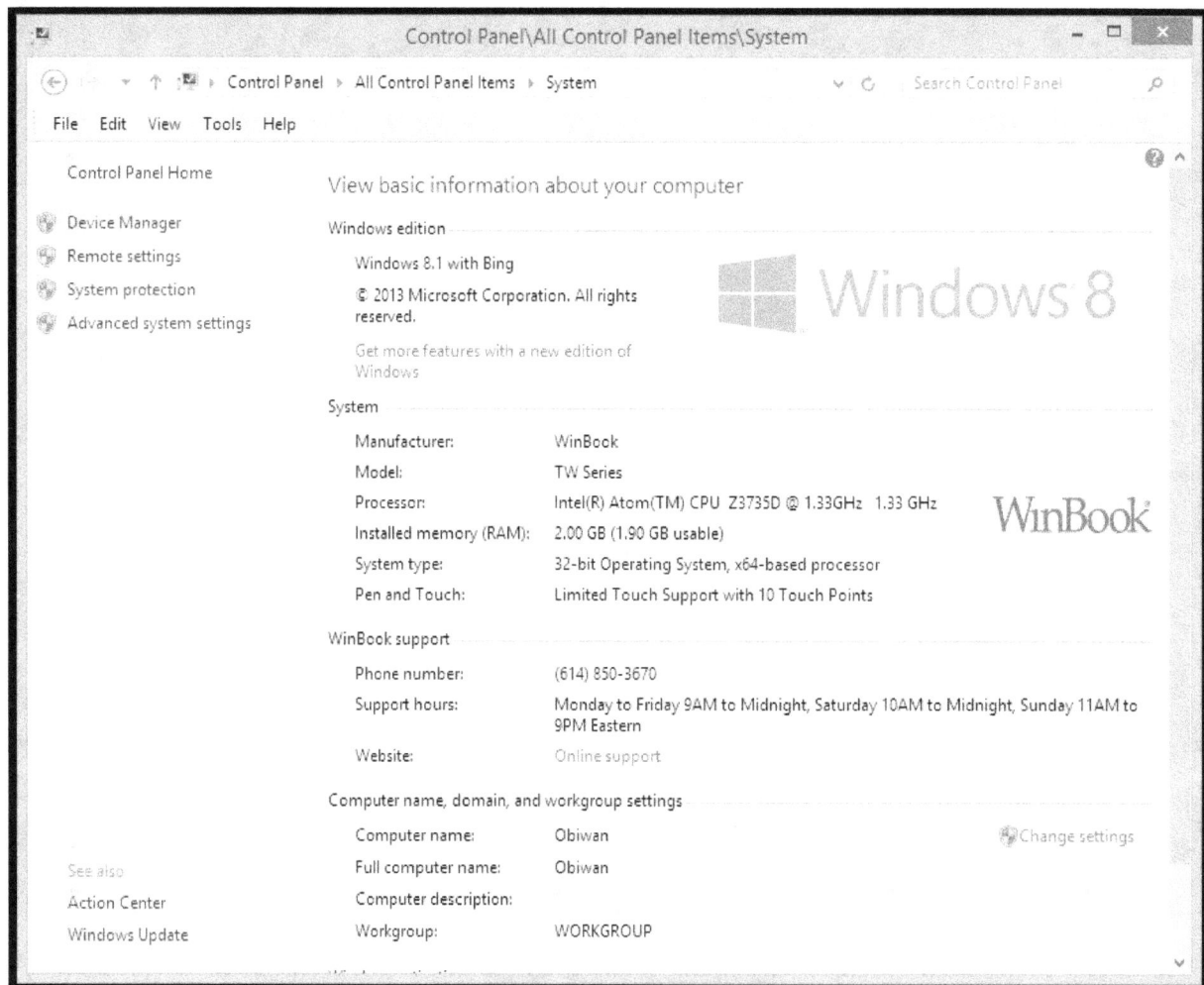

Windows 8/8.1 - Figure 53b

Mark Versus Mr. Hacker.doc

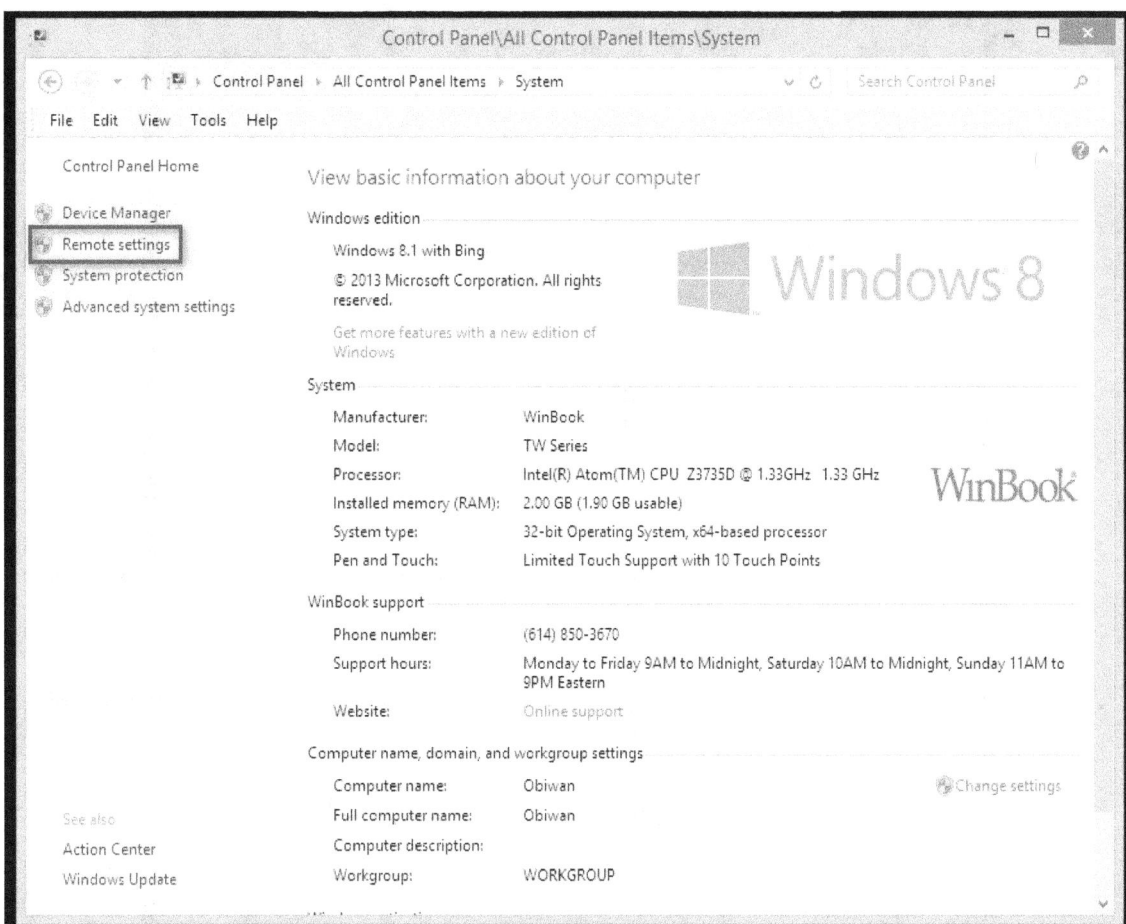

Windows 8/8.1 - Figure 54a

Mark Versus Mr. Hacker.doc

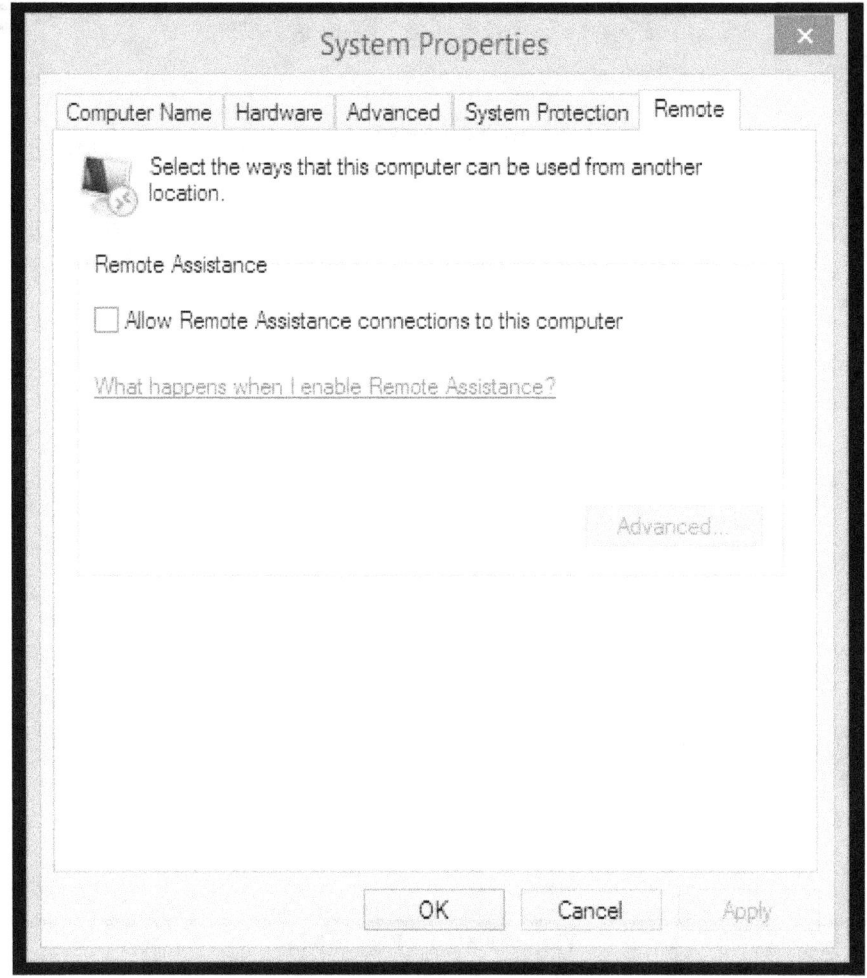

Windows 8/8.1 - Figure 54b

There is no Figure 55 for Windows 8/8.1.
Microsoft moved that dialog to another area.

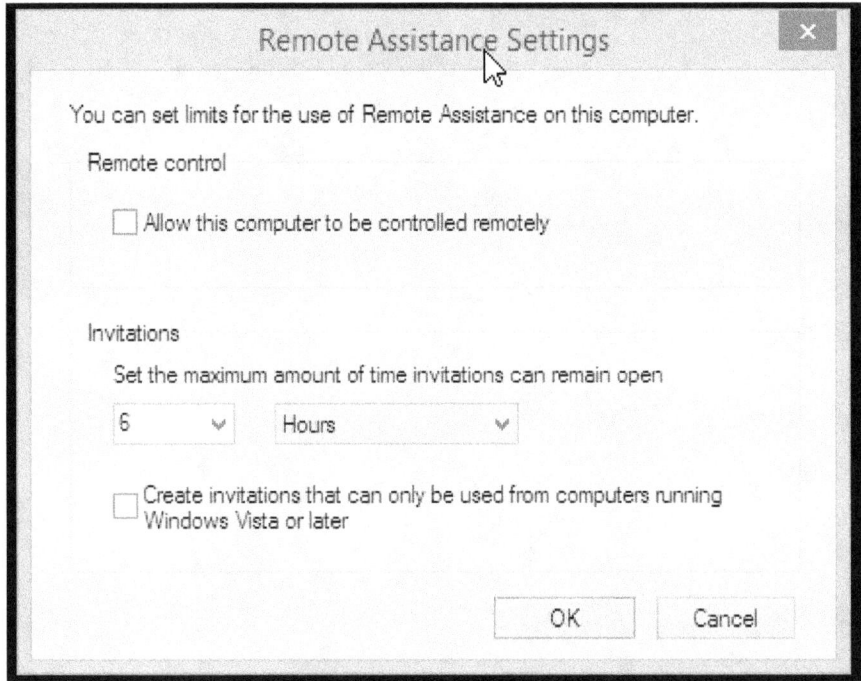
Windows 8/8.1 - Figure 56

All other figures deal with external programs to Windows so use the figures provided from #56 on to the end of the book.

Have fun!

Mark Versus Mr. Hacker.doc

Screen shots for Windows 10

Windows 10 Figures

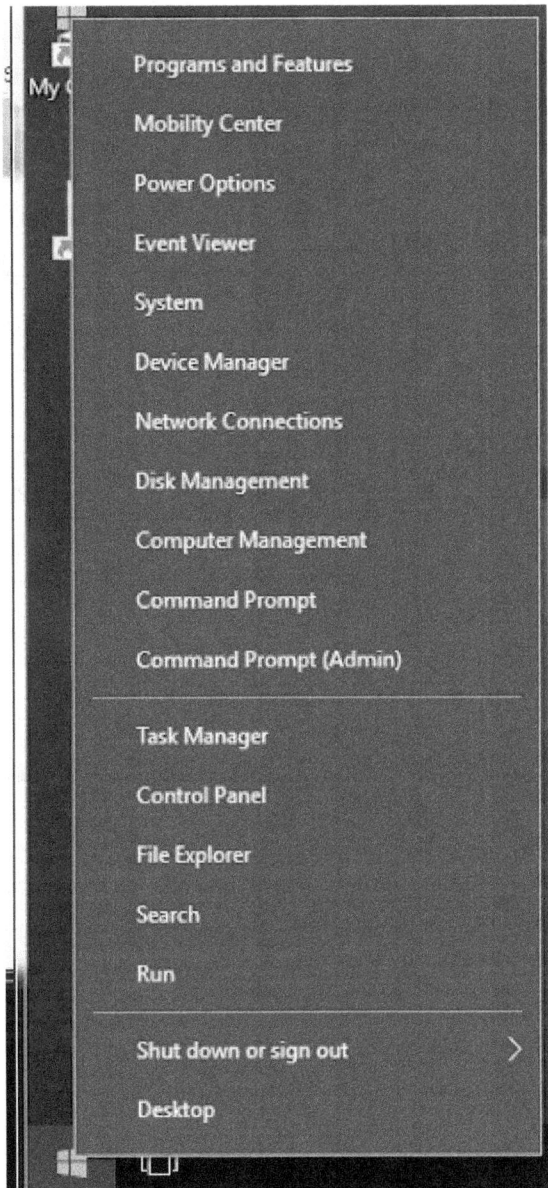

Windows 10 - Figure 1

Mark Versus Mr. Hacker.doc

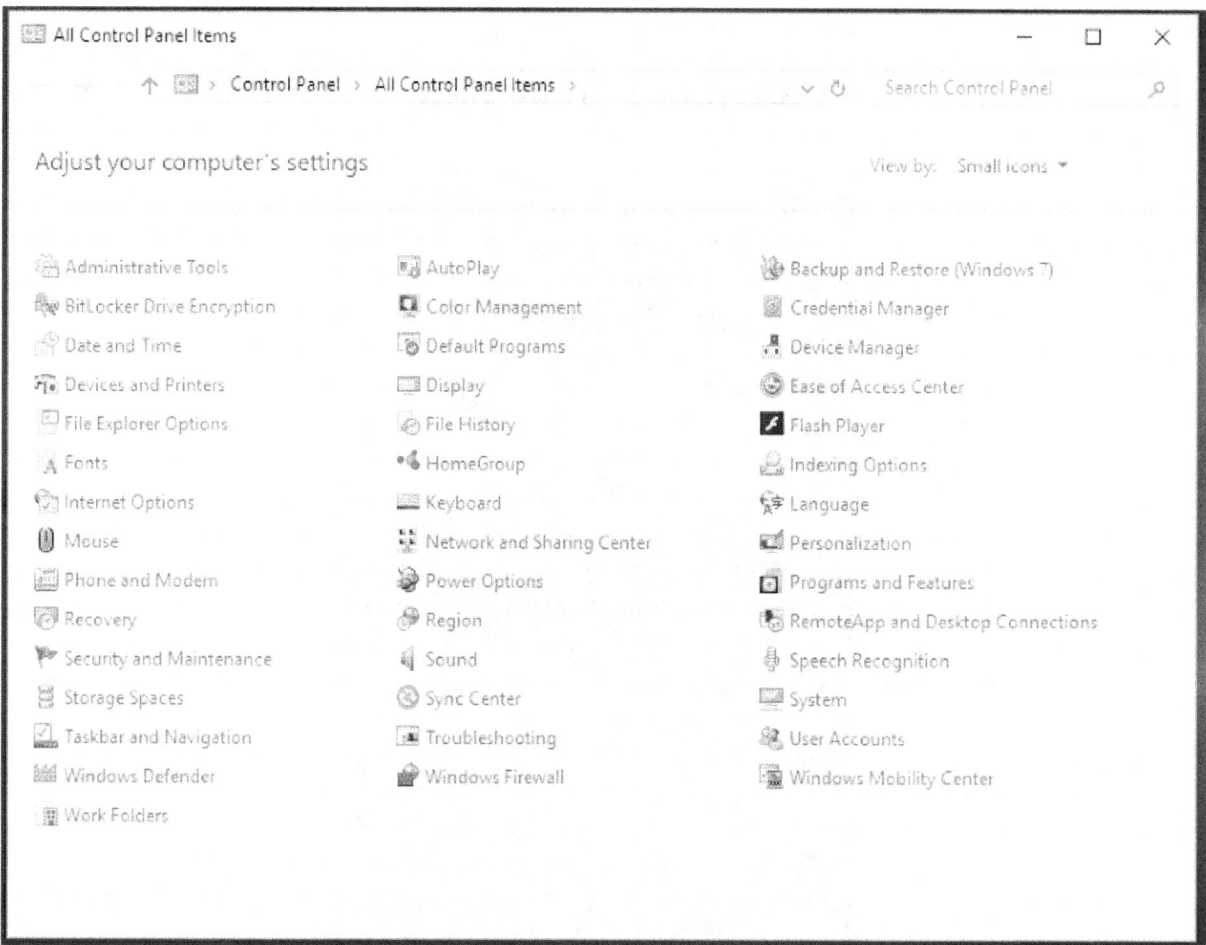

Windows 10 - Figure 2

Mark Versus Mr. Hacker.doc

Under Windows 10 you won't find a "Display" icon,
instead you click on the Personalization icon.

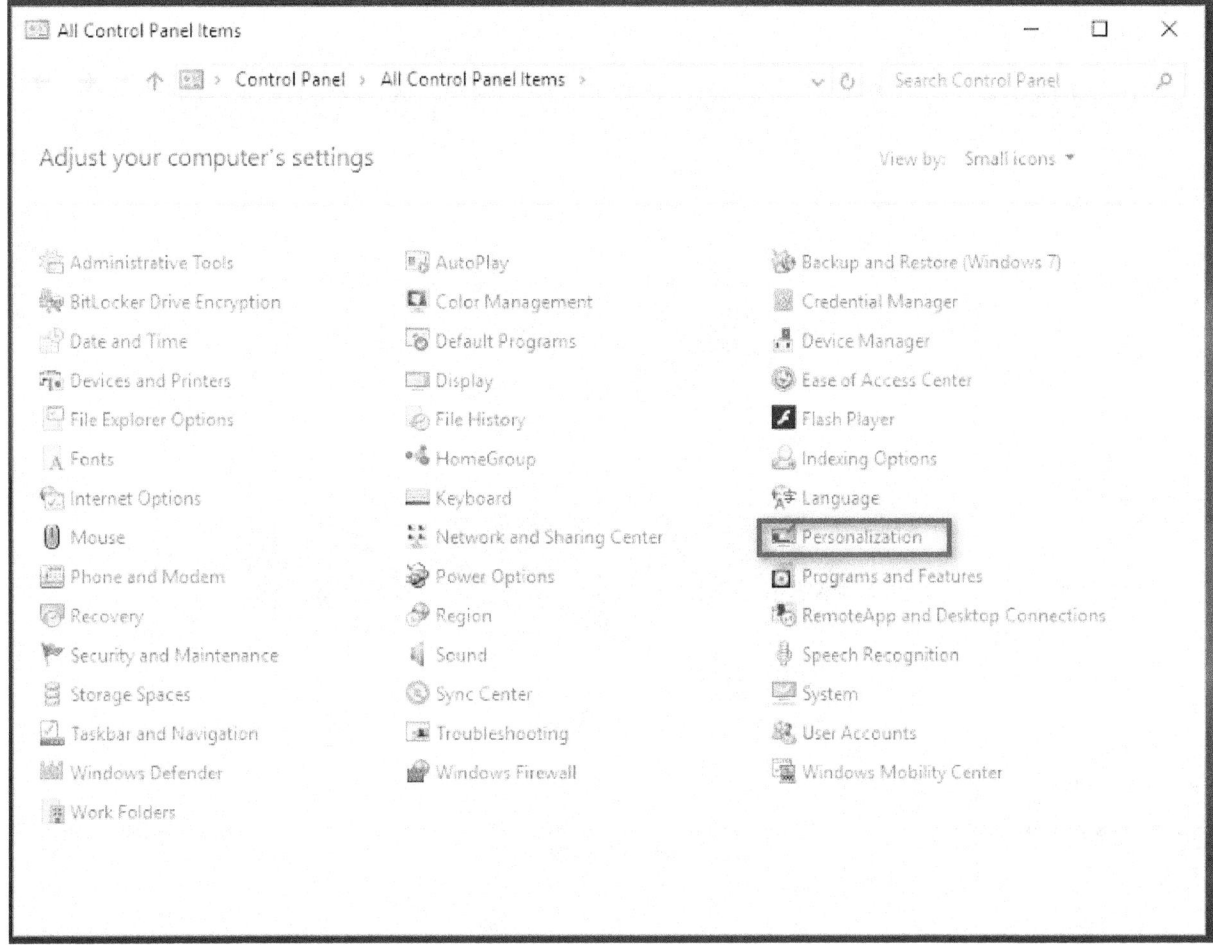

Windows 10 - Figure 3

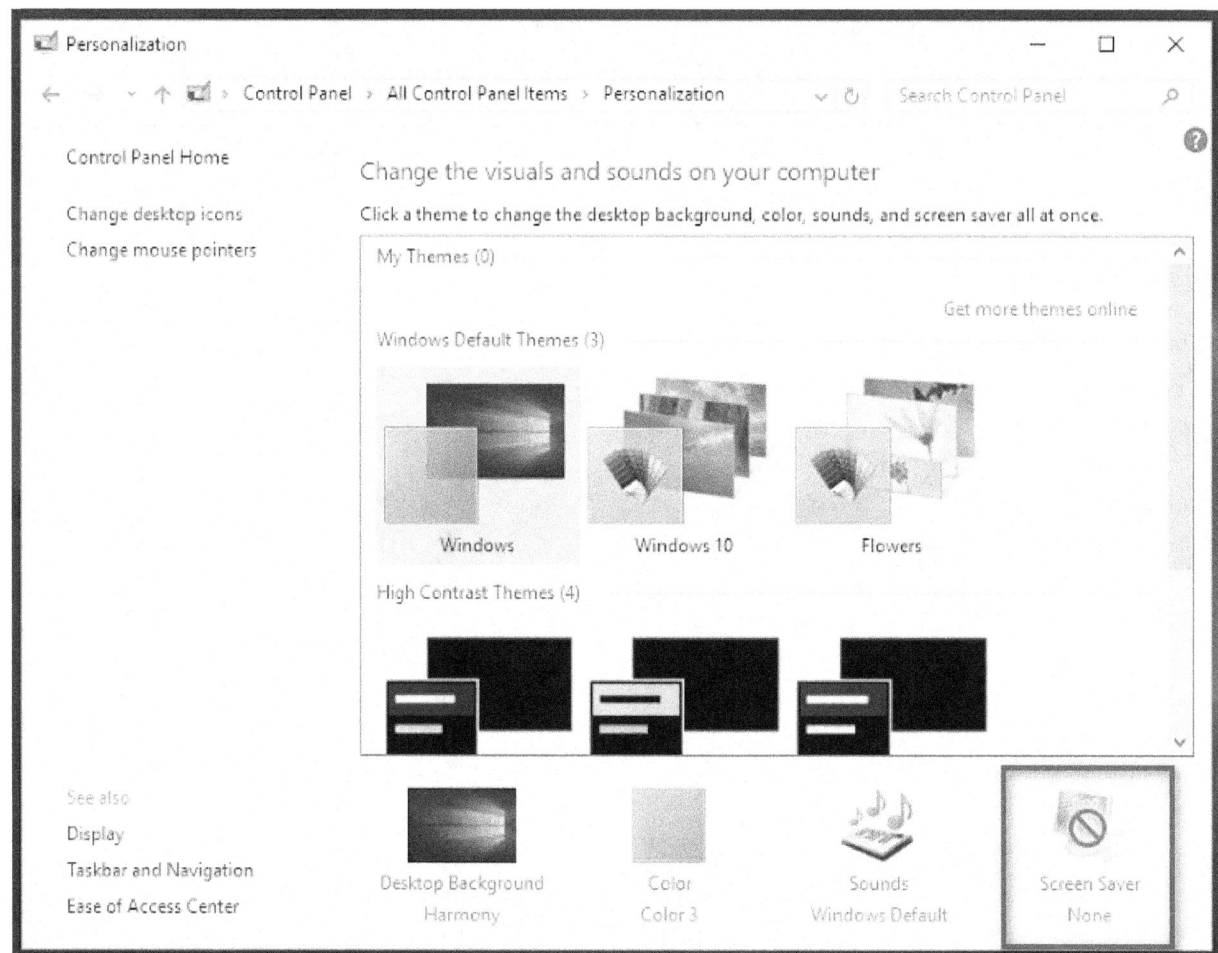

Windows 10 - Figure 4

And here you have the Screen Saver display which looks almost like the Windows XP Screen Saver dialog.

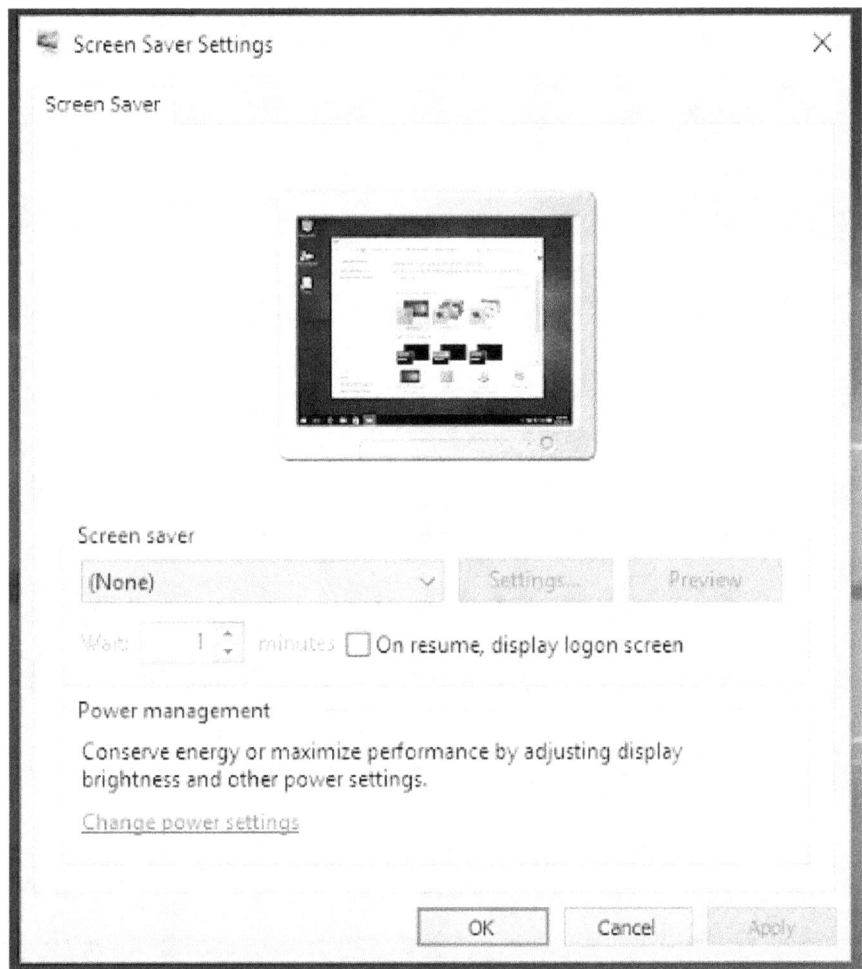

Windows 10 - Figure 5

Mark Versus Mr. Hacker.doc

In order to get to the Power Options, you have to go back to the Control Panel and select it from there.

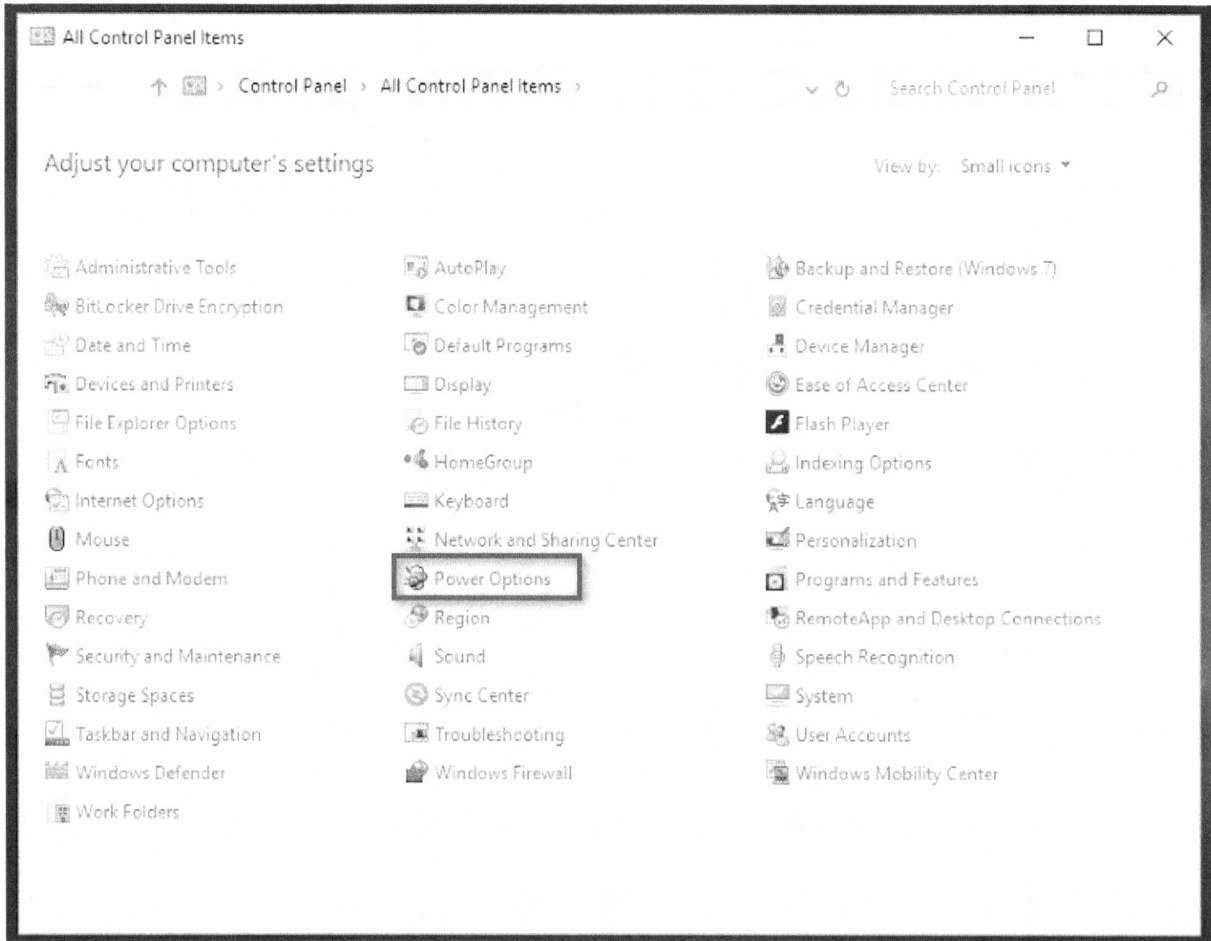

Windows 10 - Figure 6a

Note that under Vista, 7, 8/8.1, and 10 you first have to say
Which Power Plan you want to modify.

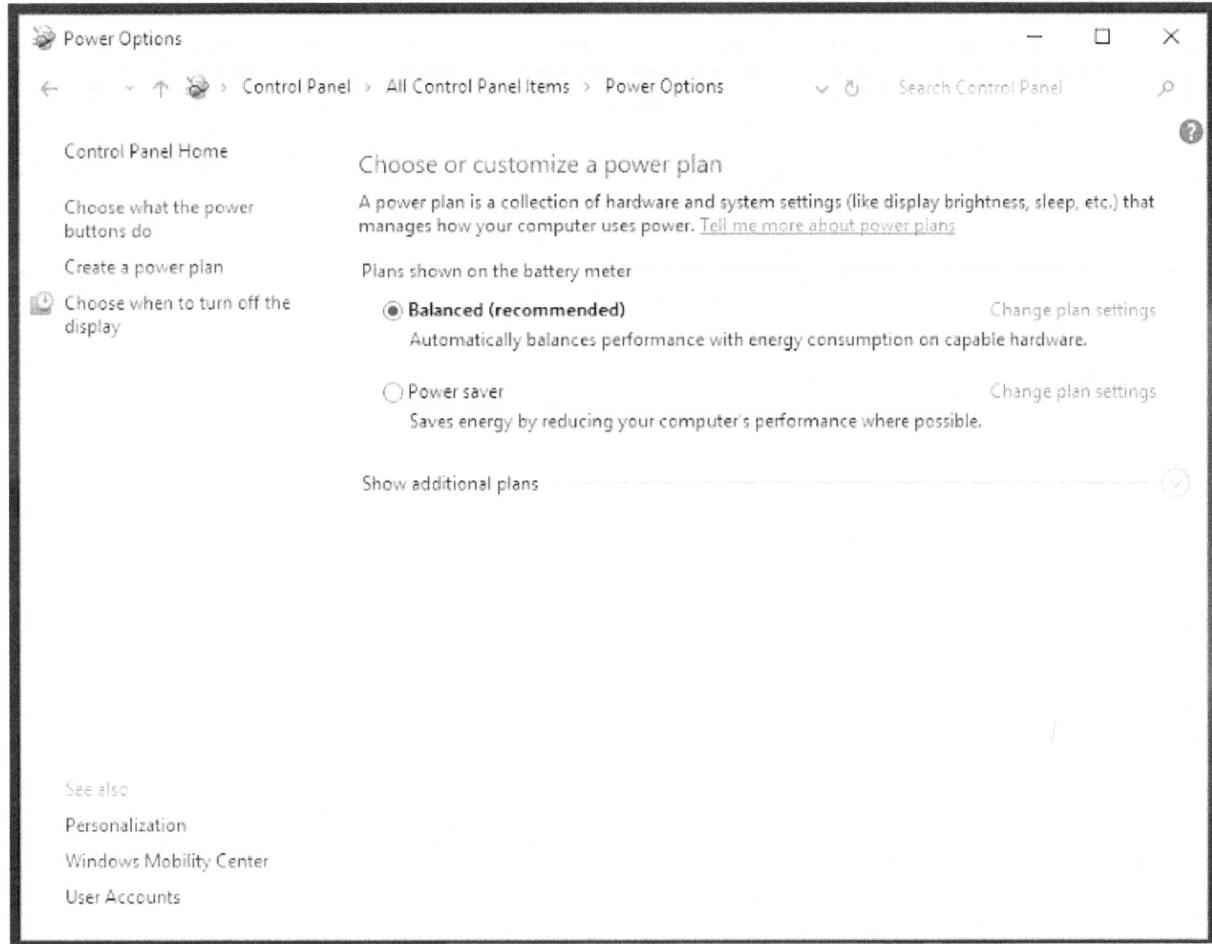

Windows 10 - Figure 6b

Once in the Power Plan area, change your time to turn off your display to be 30 minutes and to never shut down the computer when it is plugged in. Notice the "Change advanced power settings" link. We are going to use that next.

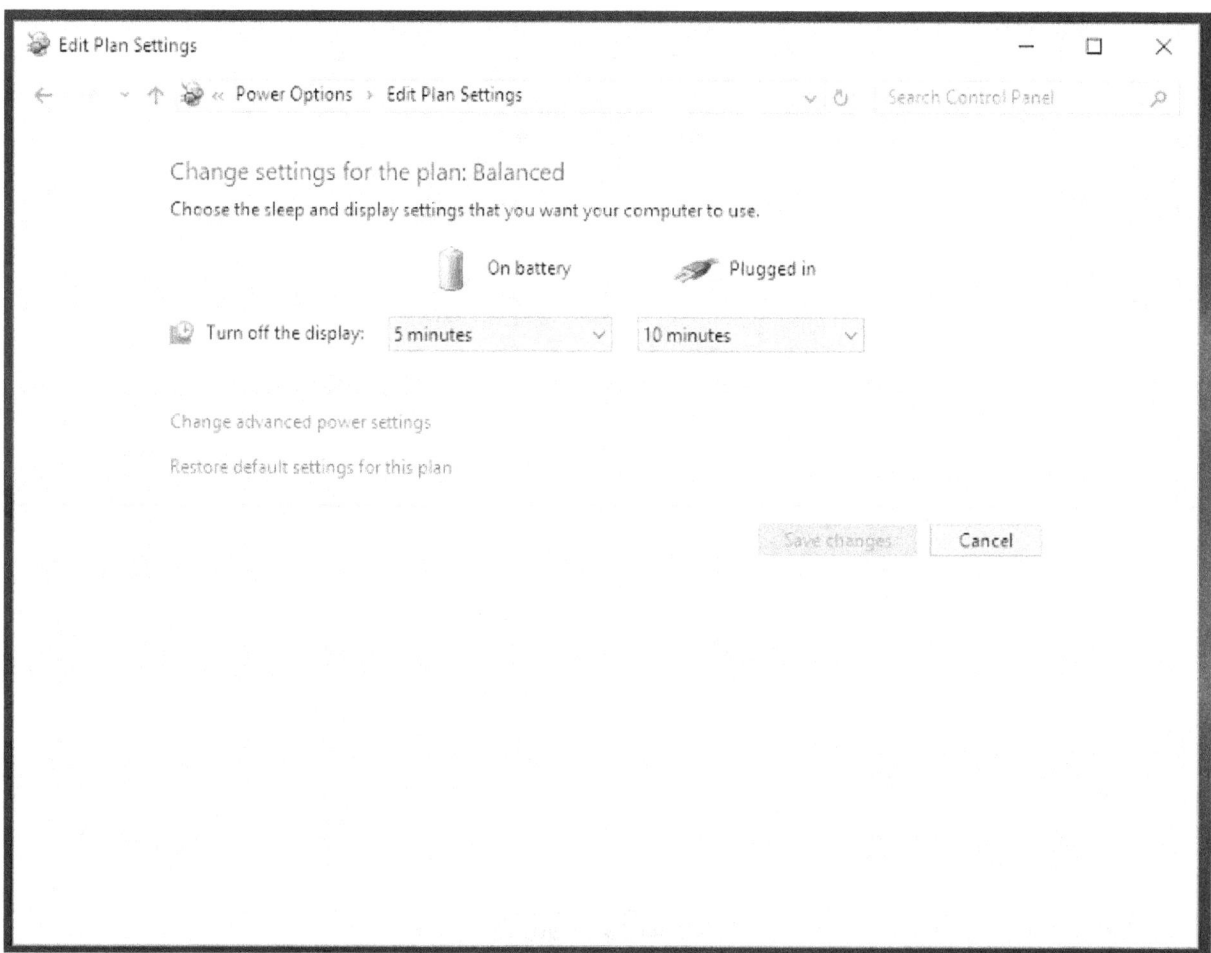

Windows 10 - Figure 6c

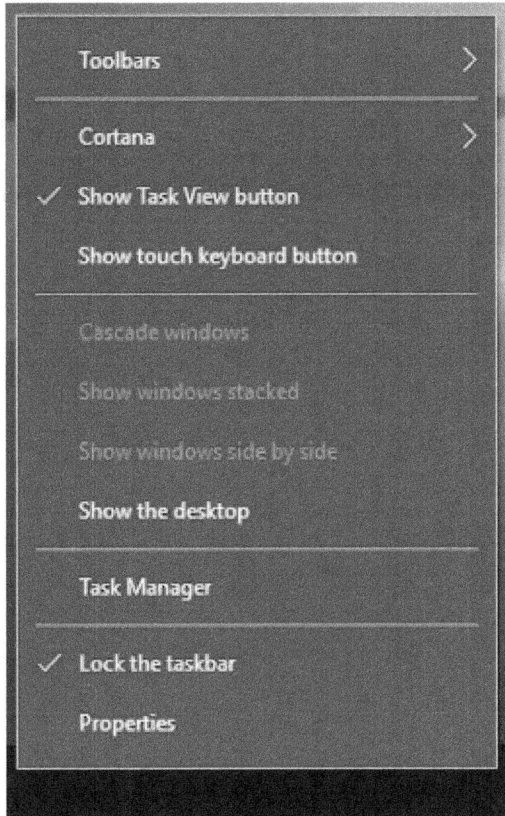

Windows 10 - Figure 7

Mark Versus Mr. Hacker.doc

Note under Windows 10 Microsoft changed what you first see.
No longer is there an "Applications" tab.
Note the "Fewer details" link in the bottom left corner.
Originally it read "More details" but if you click that link you will see what is shown here.

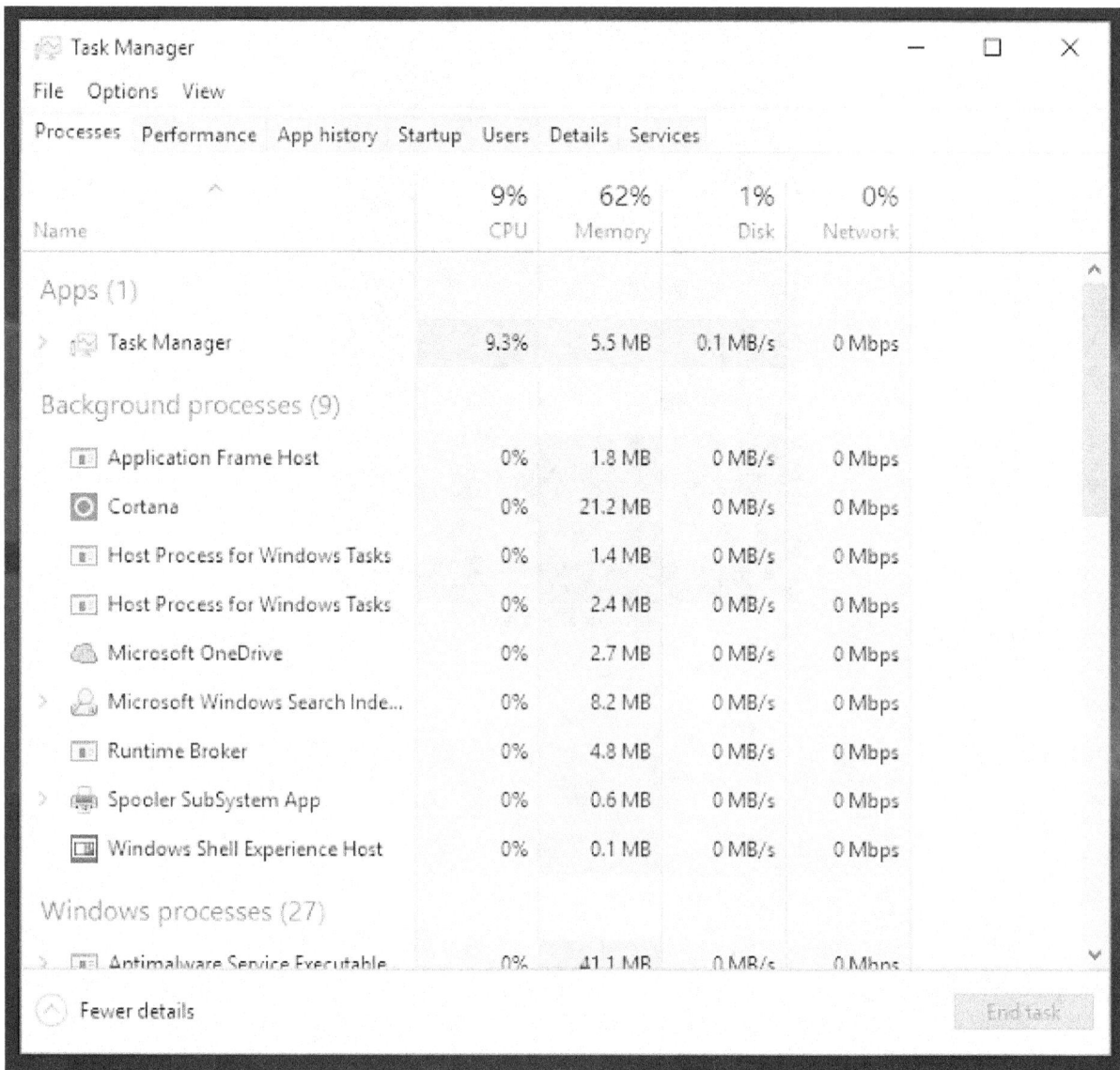

Windows 10 - Figure 8 - 9

Note that there is no way now to change the priority of a process.
In order to change the priority of a program you have to download
Microsoft's Process Explorer and use it to set the priority.

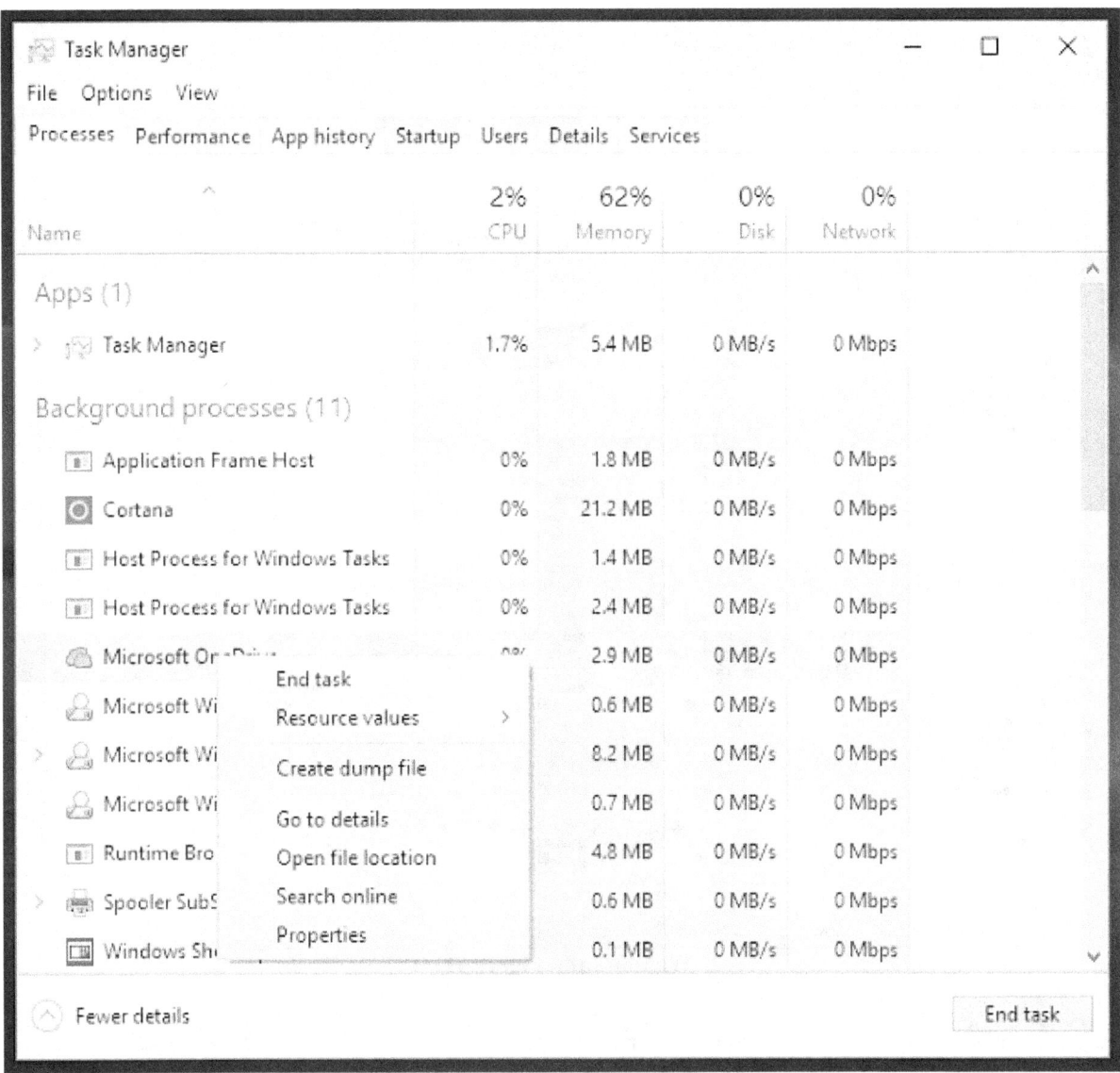

Windows 10 - Figure 10

Mark Versus Mr. Hacker.doc

Since TCPView looks the same on all platforms – here is the Windows XP version.

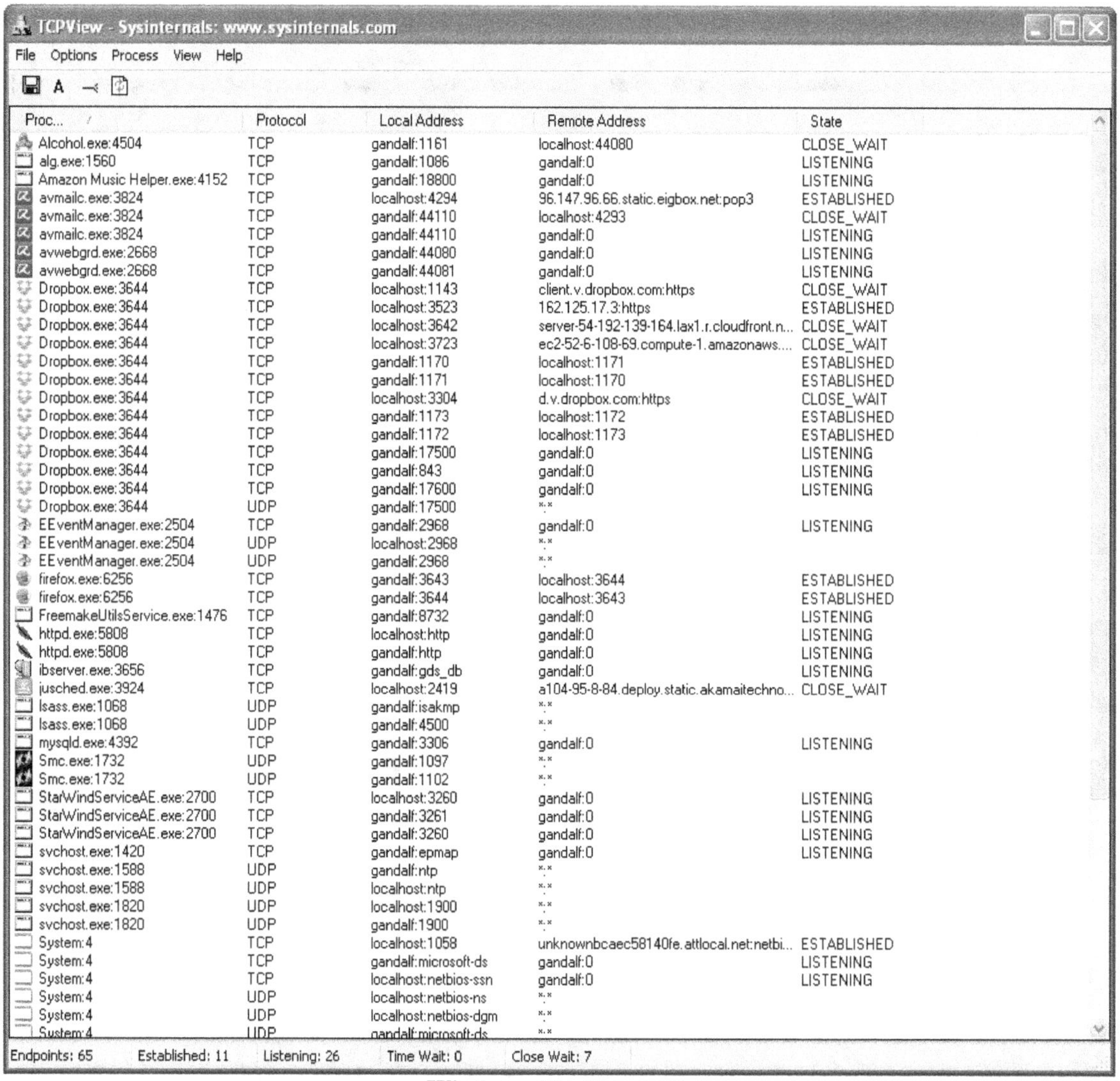

Windows 10 - Figure 11

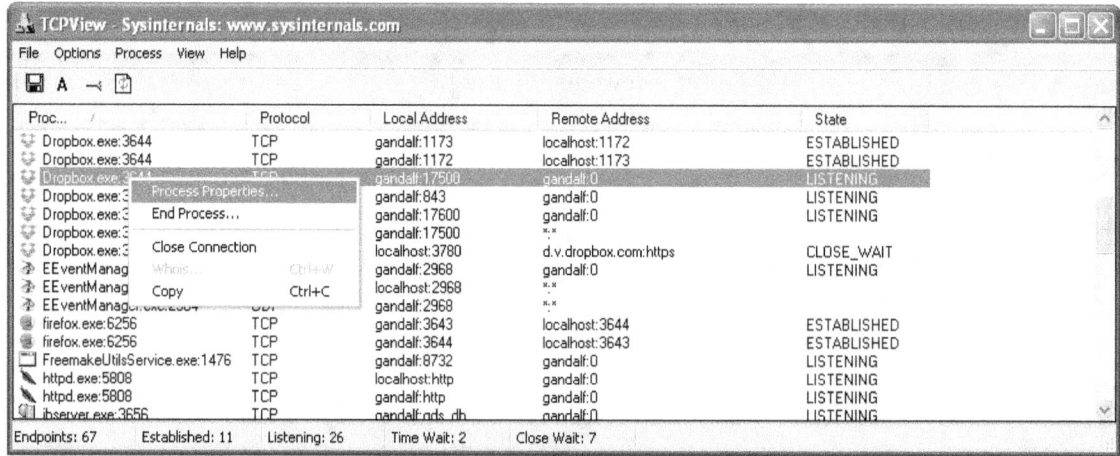

Windows 10 - Figure 12

Page 255

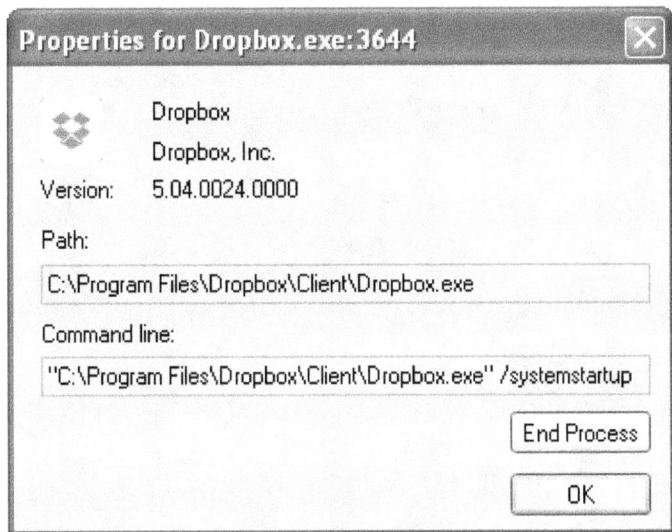
Windows 10 - Figure 13

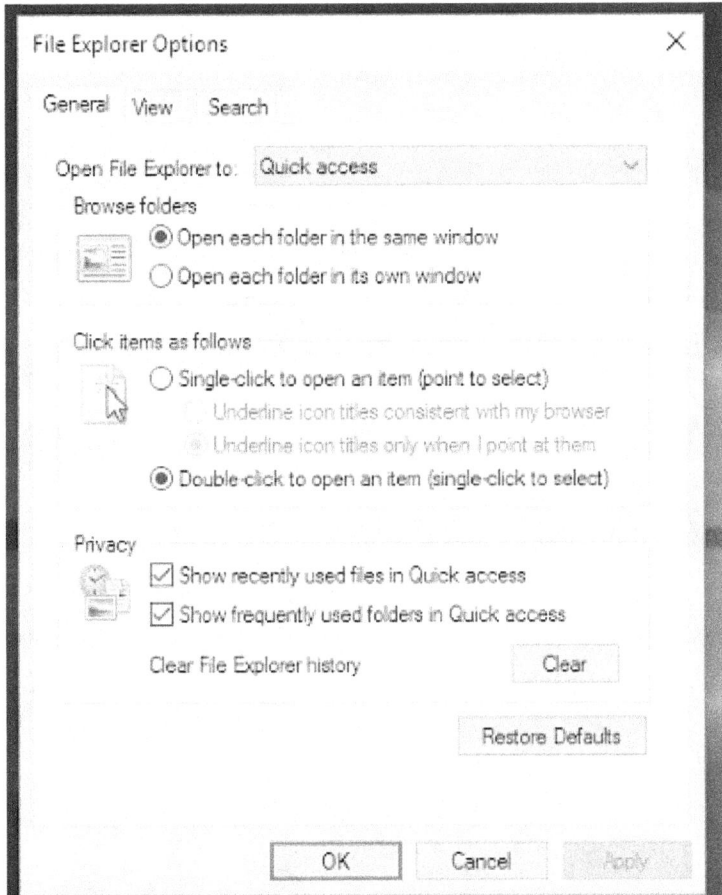
Windows 10 - Figure 14

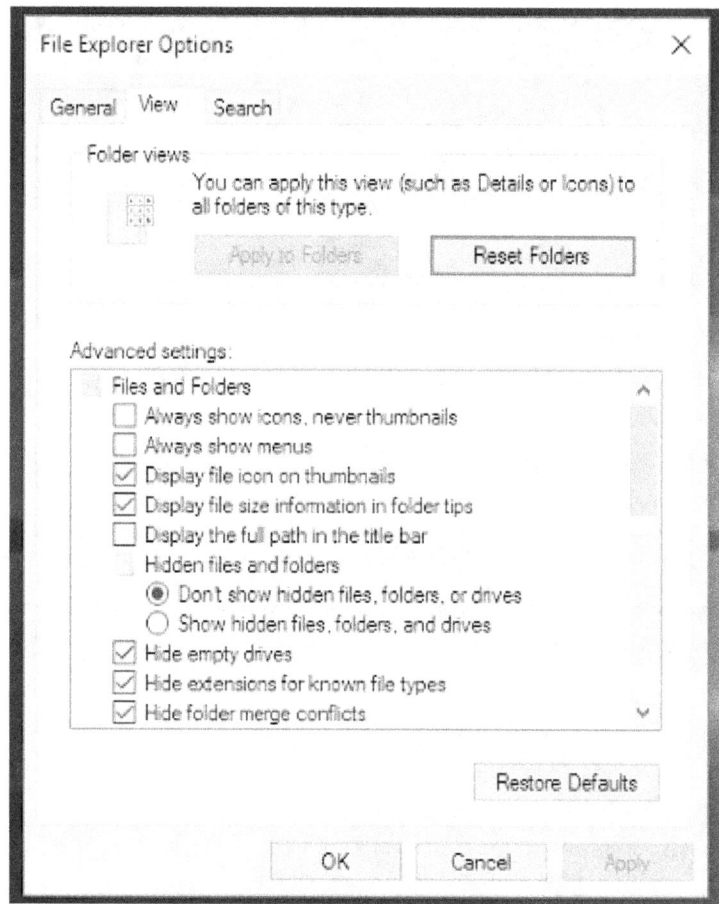

Windows 7 - Figure 15a

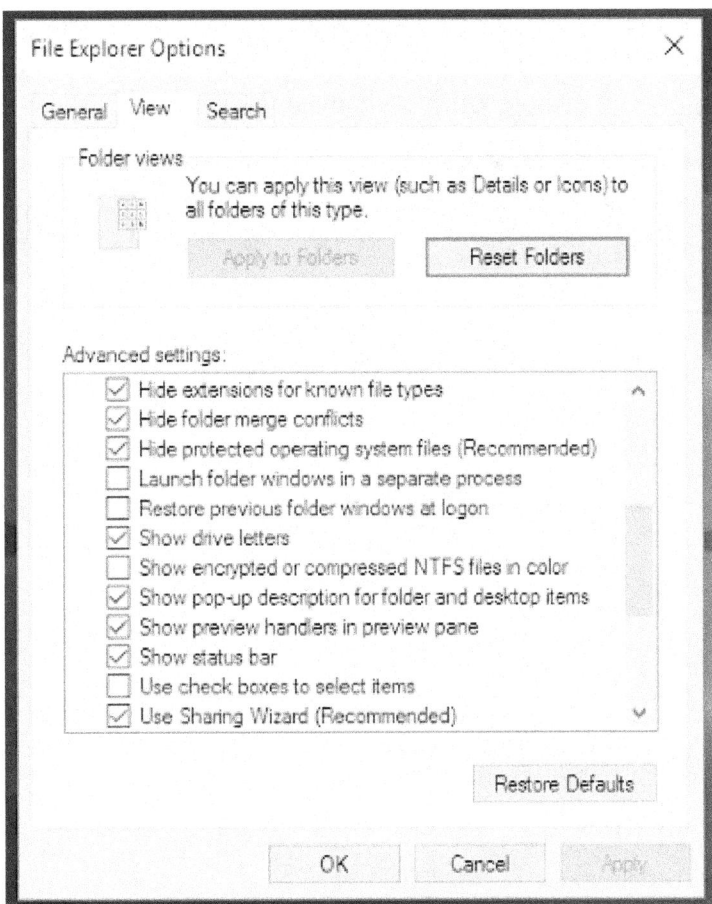

Windows 10 - Figure 15b

Notice that under Windows 7 there is nothing about Simple File Sharing.
Instead, there is just a "Sharing Wizard". It is the same program.
Microsoft just changed the name.

Windows 10 - Figure 16-17

Mark Versus Mr. Hacker.doc

In order to get the to System Restore area you first have to go to the control panel and then left click on the System icon.

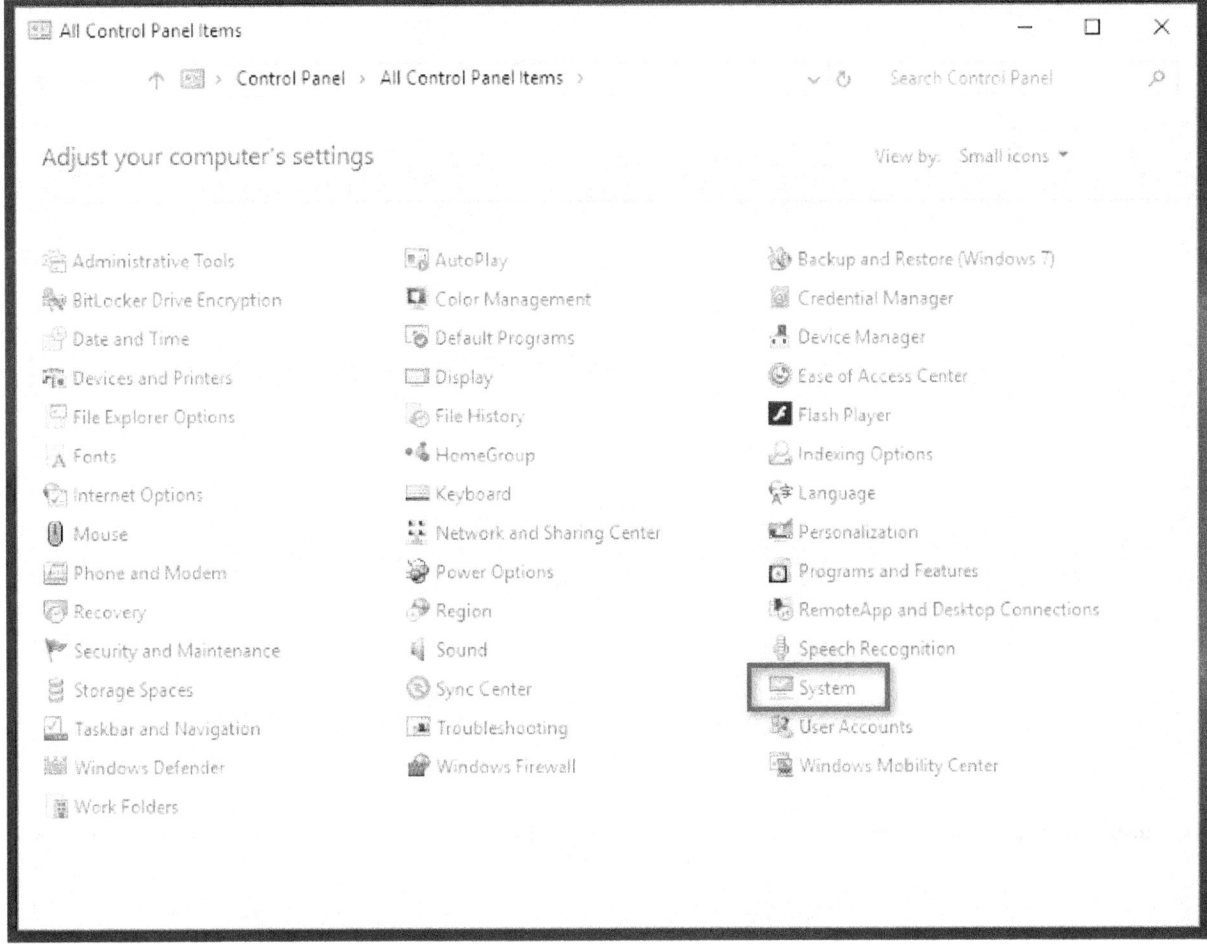

Windows 10 - Figure 18a

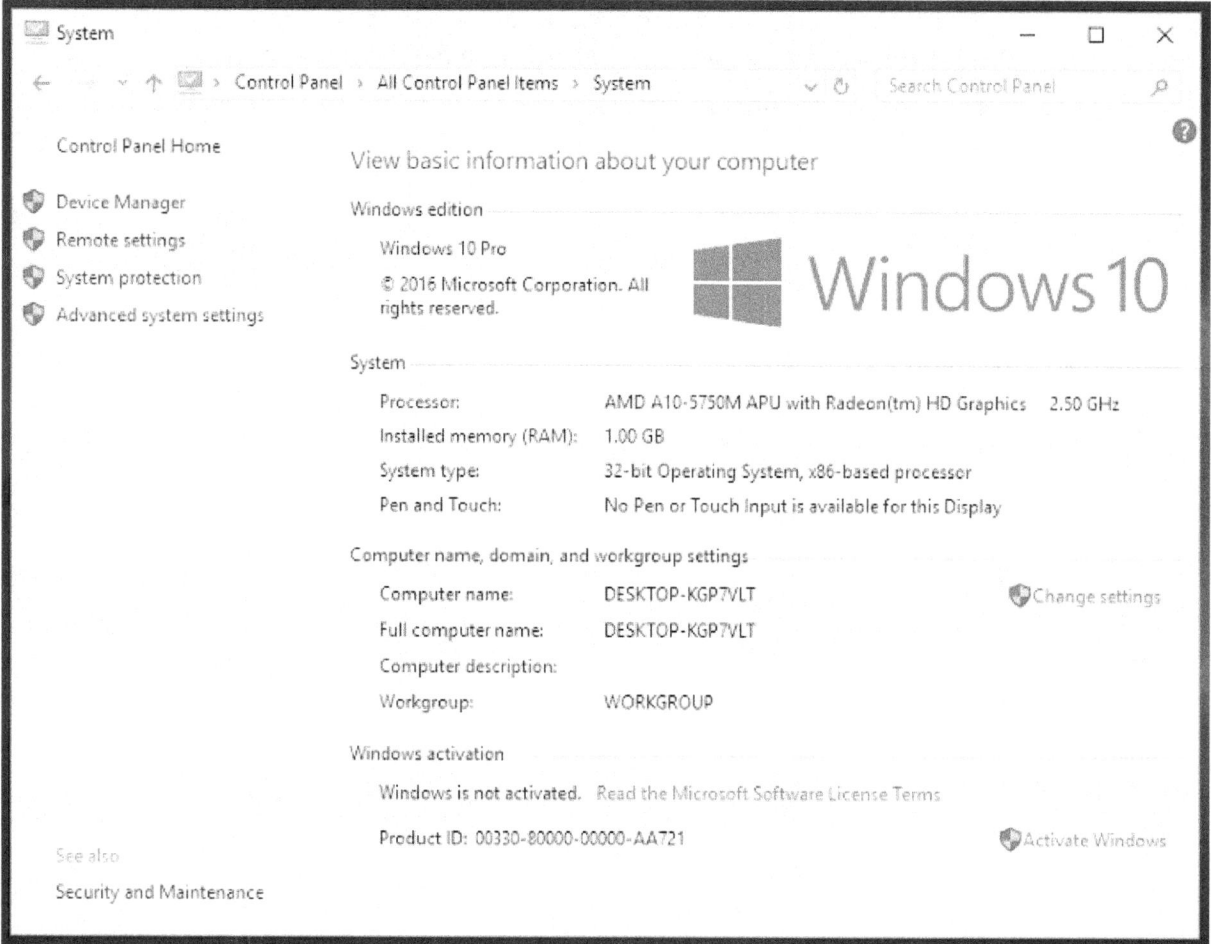

Windows 10 - Figure 18b

Mark Versus Mr. Hacker.doc

In the System dialog box, select the "Advanced system serttings".

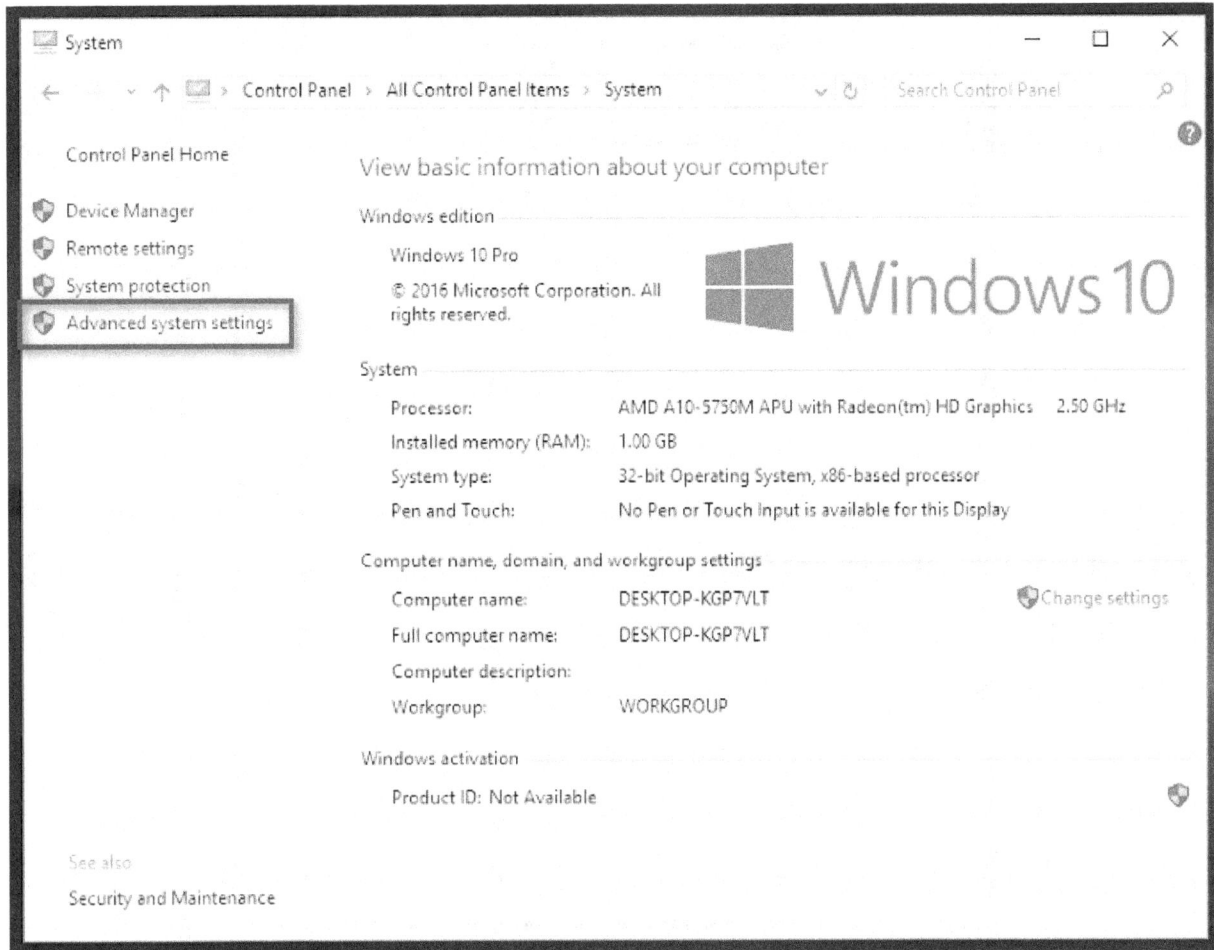

Windows 10 - Figure 18c

Here you can see that the System Restore is turned on for the Local Disk (or C: Drive). Use the Configure button to change this.

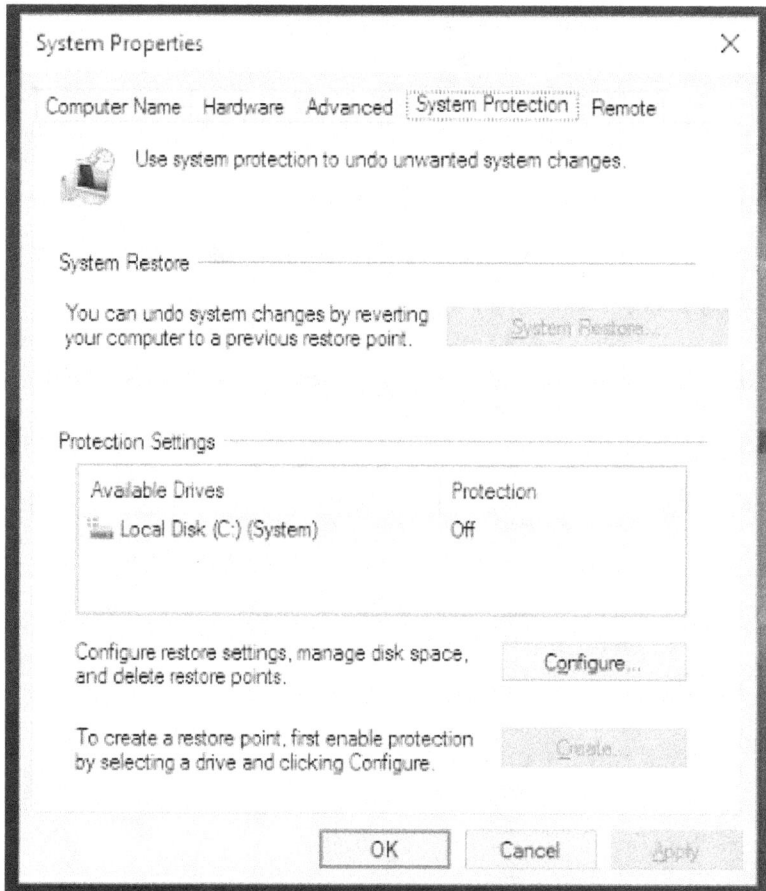

Windows 10 - Figure 18d

Here is what the dialog looks liked after you have pushed the Configuration button.

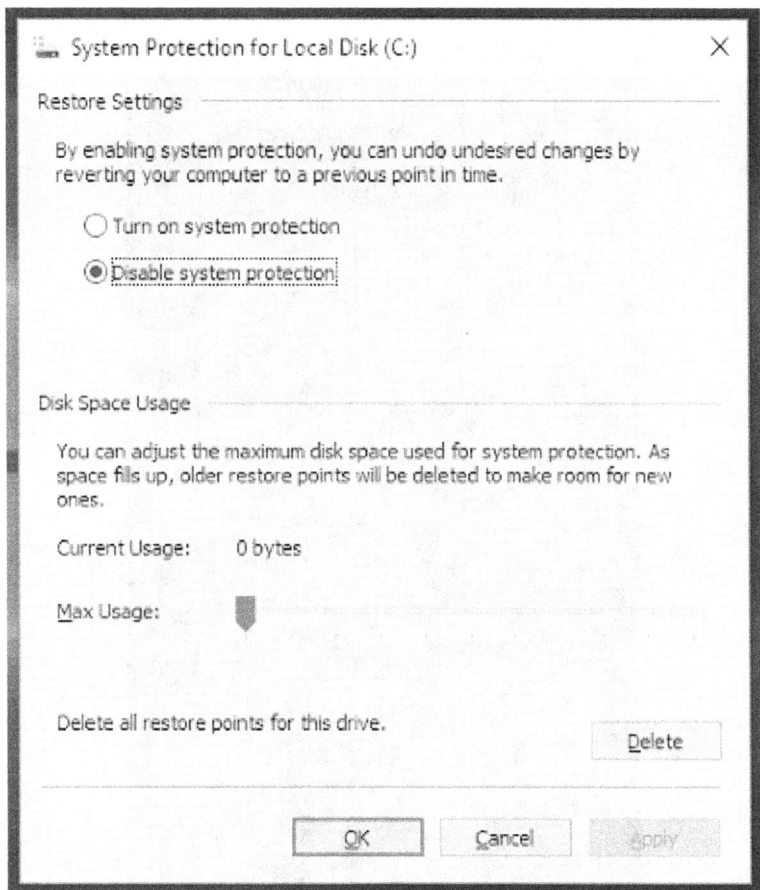

Windows 10 - Figure 18e

Under Windows 10 the command prompt is a part of the standard right-click on the Start button.

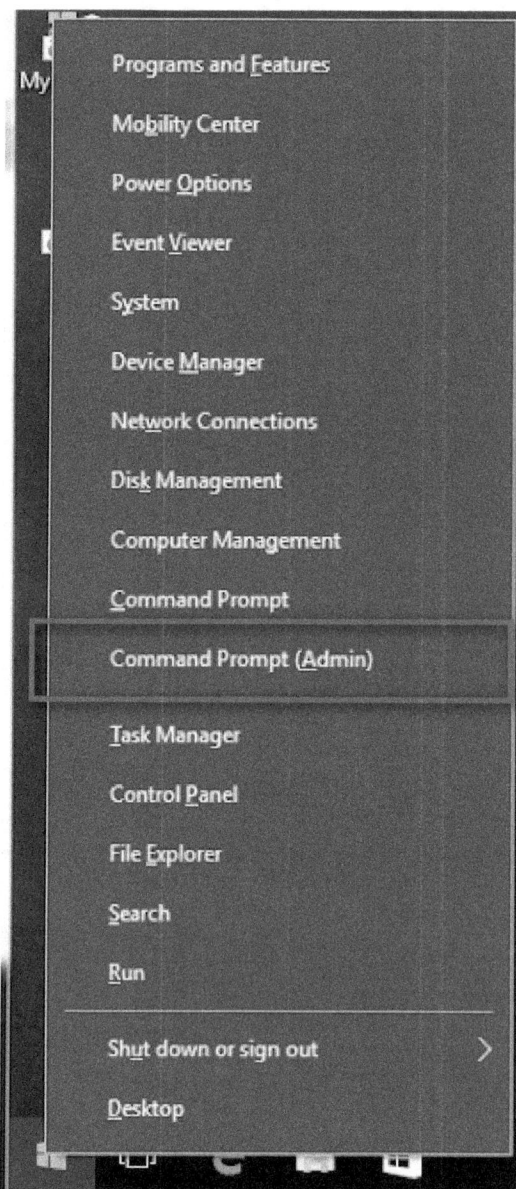

Windows 10 - Figure 19

Mark Versus Mr. Hacker.doc

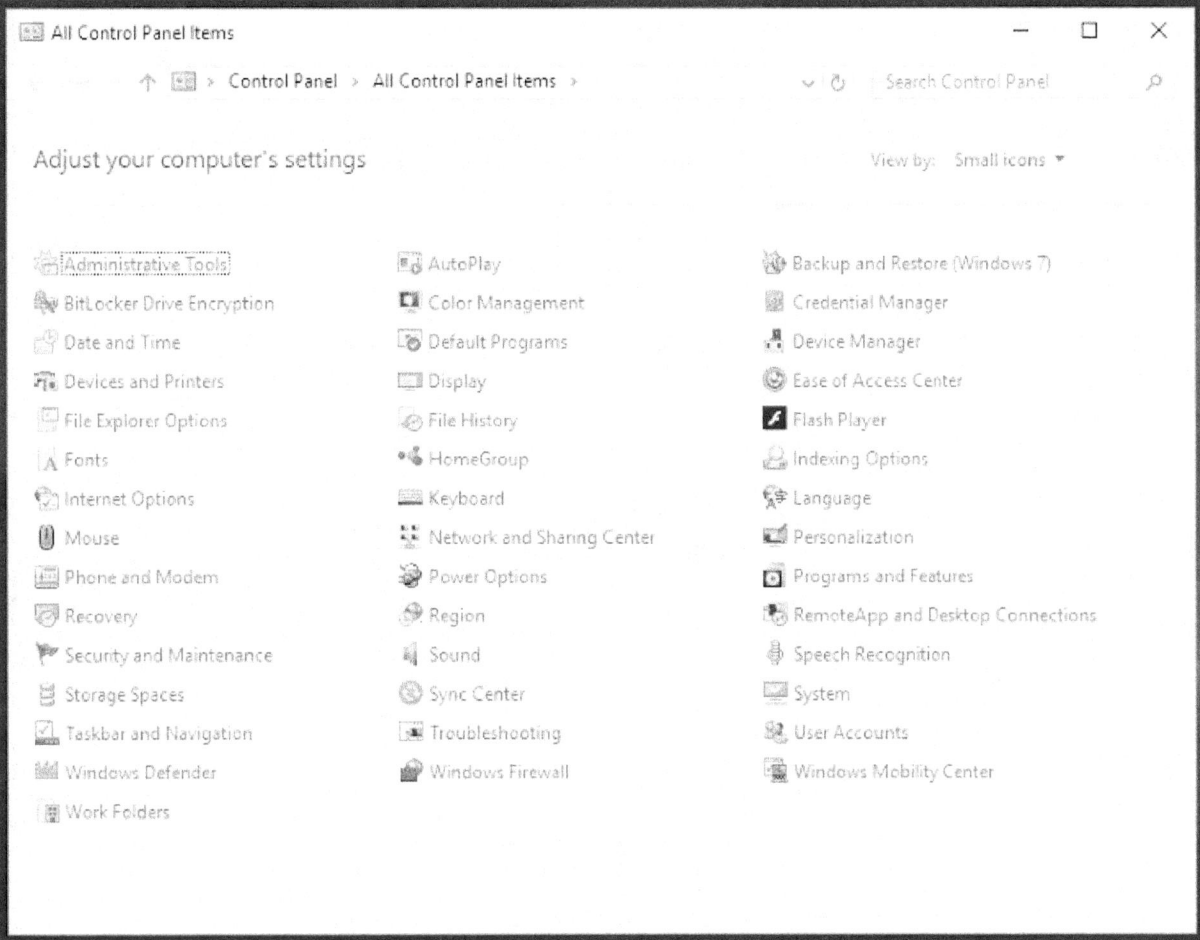

Windows 10 - Figure 20

Mark Versus Mr. Hacker.doc

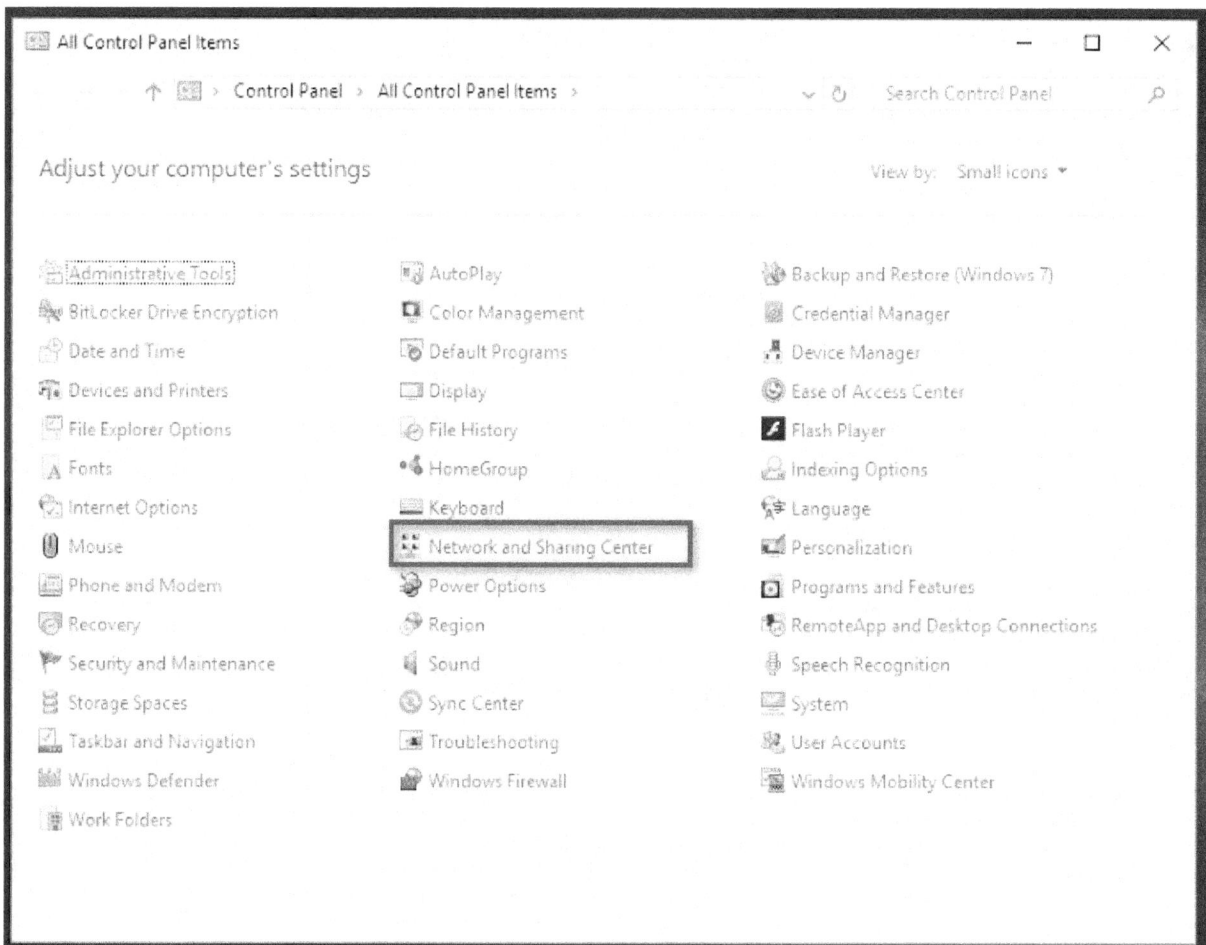

Windows 10 - Figure 21a

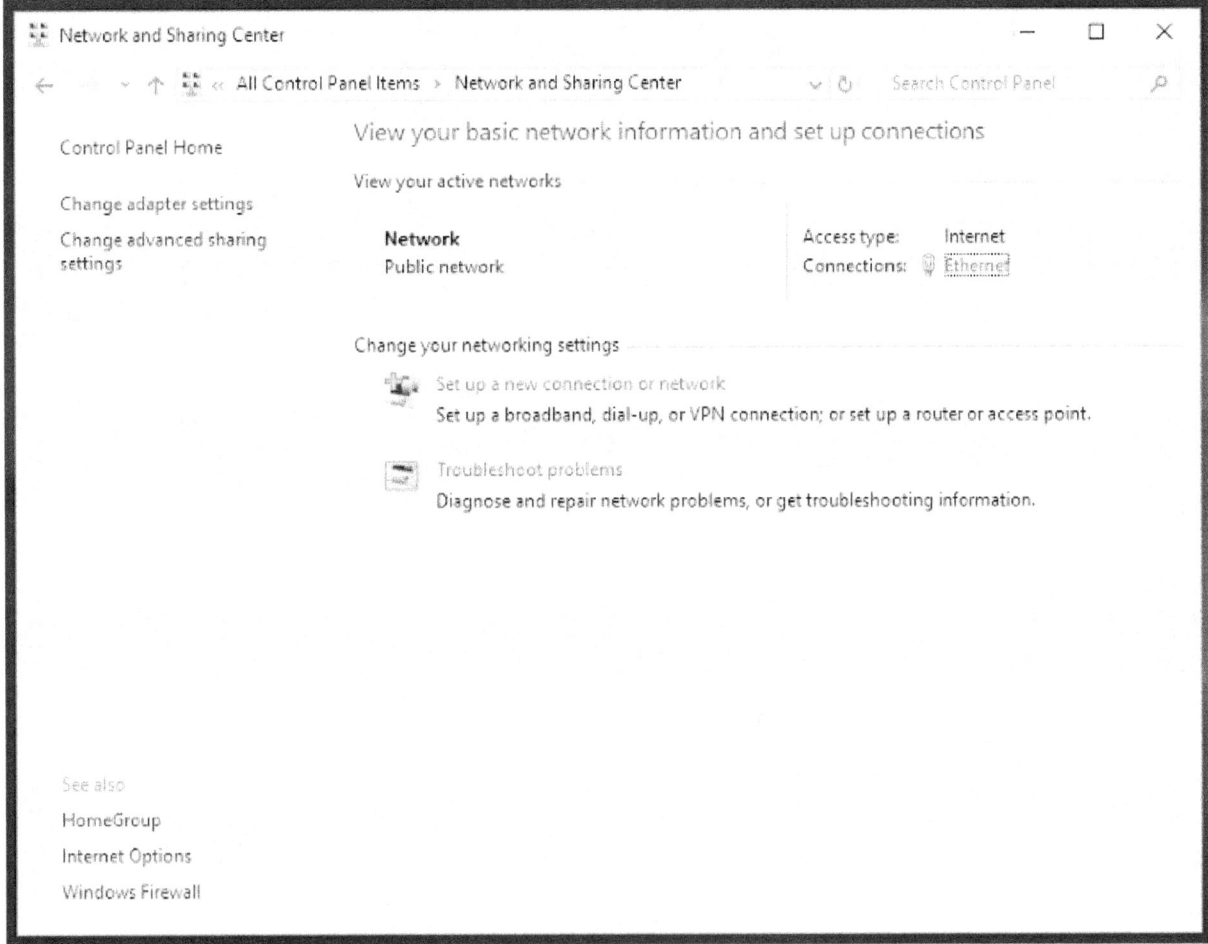

Windows 10 - Figure 21b

Mark Versus Mr. Hacker.doc

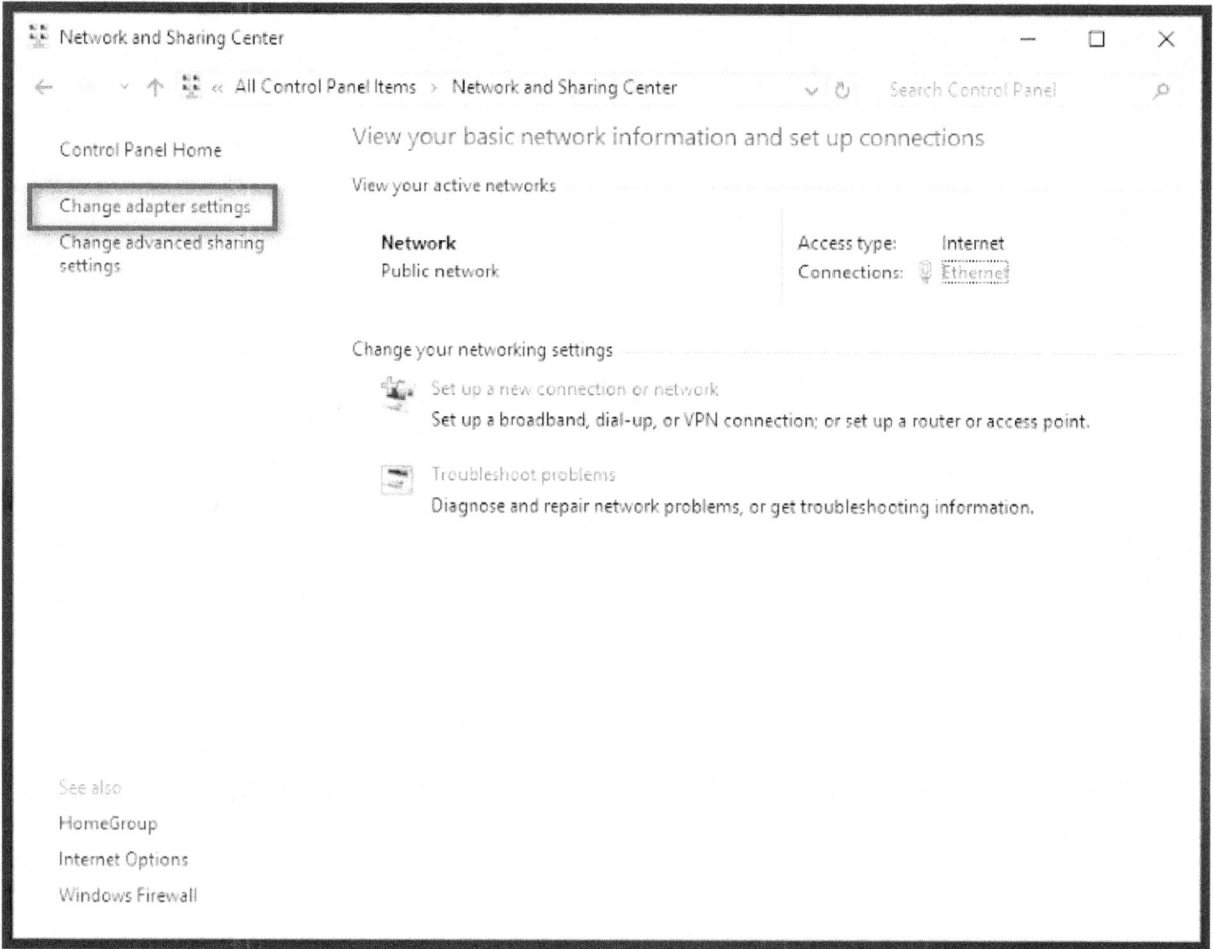

Windows 10 - Figure 21c

Mark Versus Mr. Hacker.doc

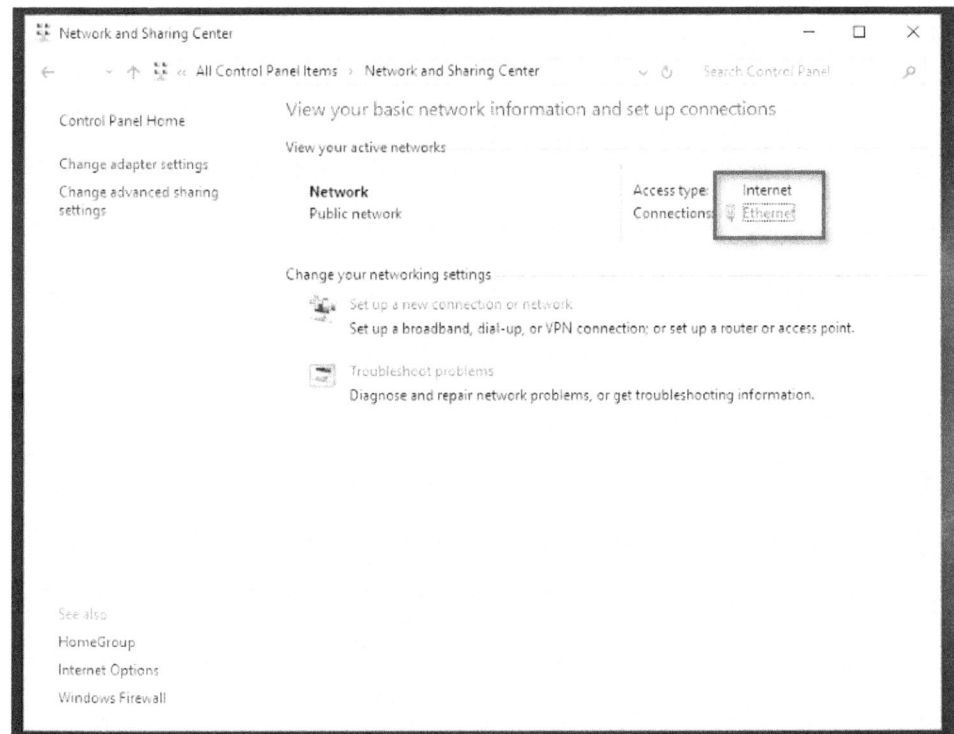

Windows 10 - Figure 21d

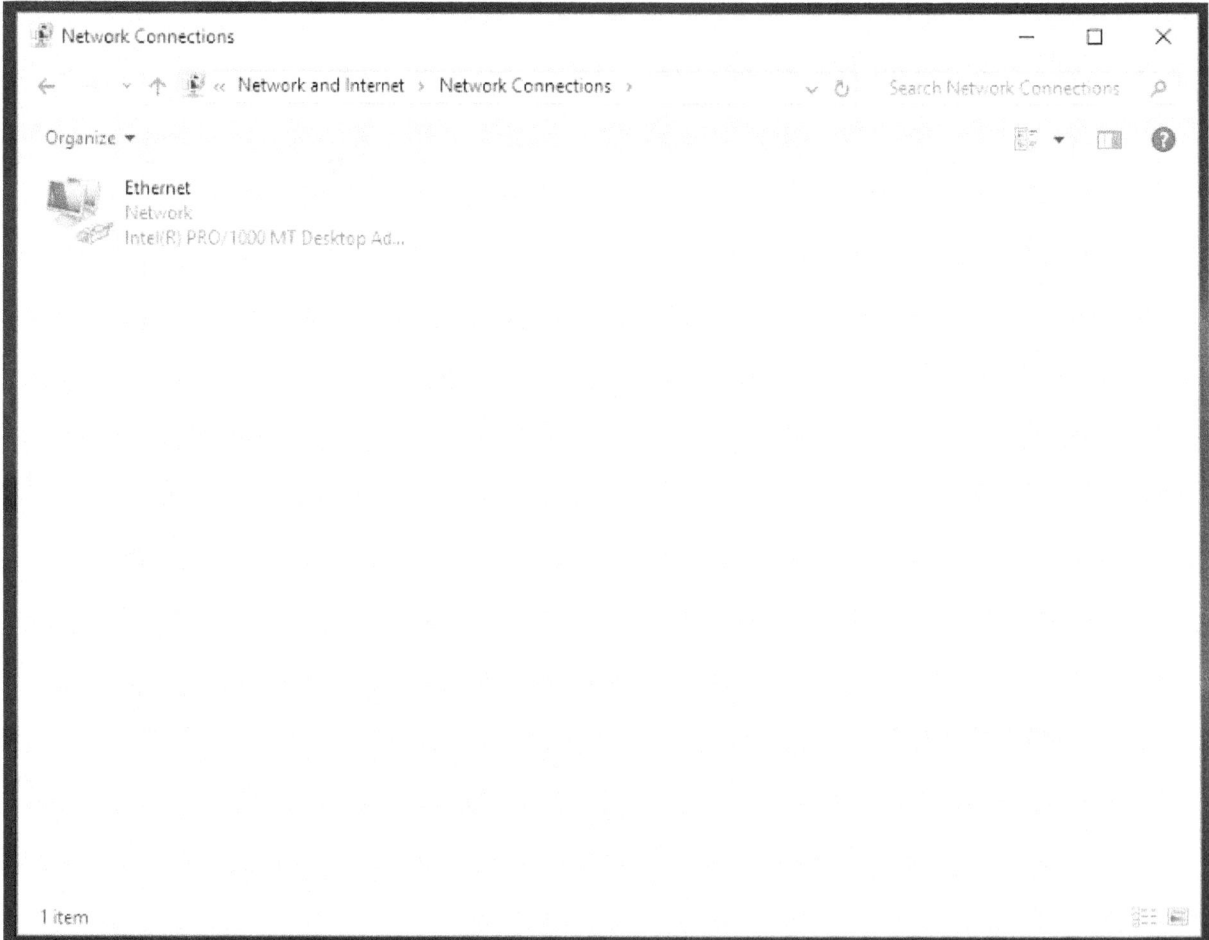

Windows 10 - Figure 21e

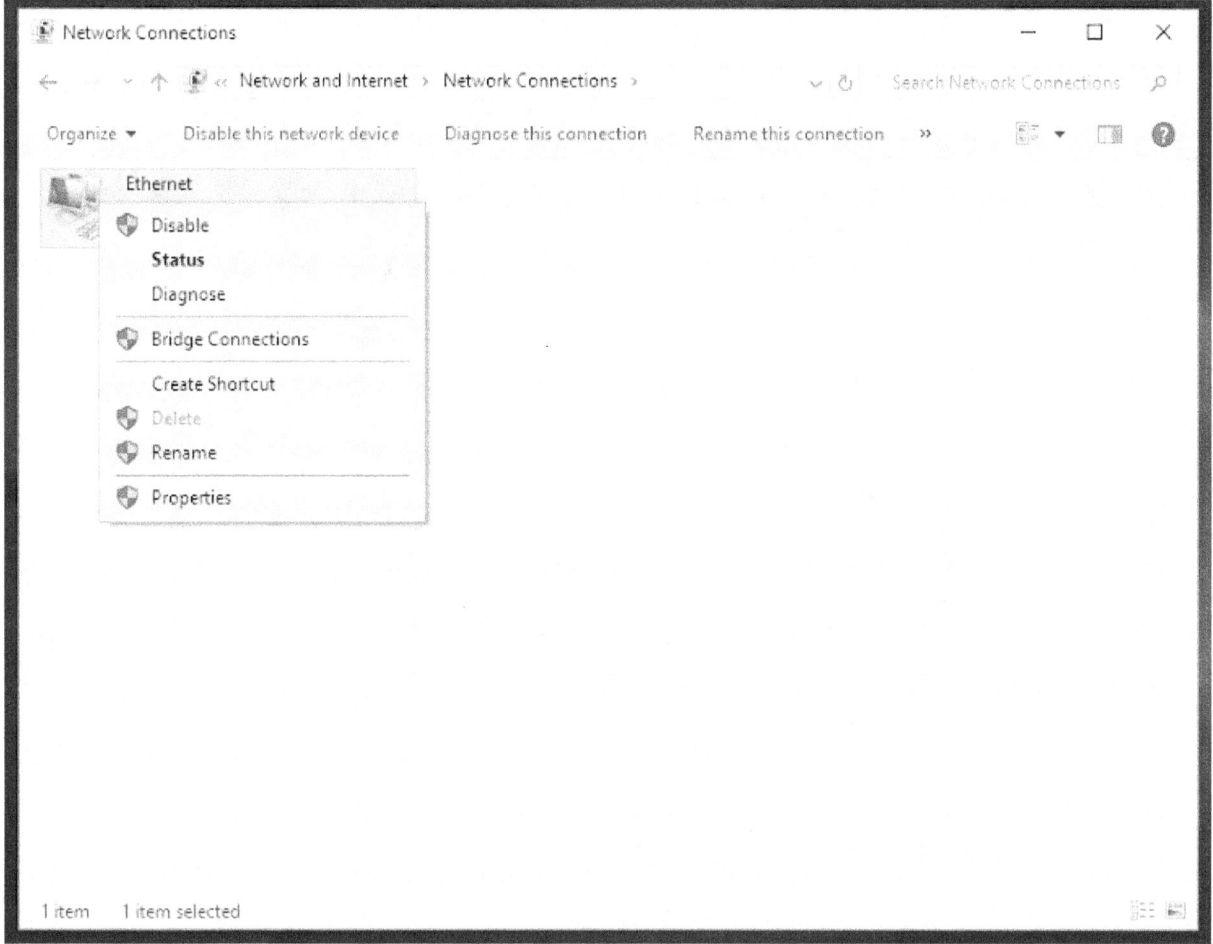

Windows 10 - Figure 22

Windows 10 - Figure 23a

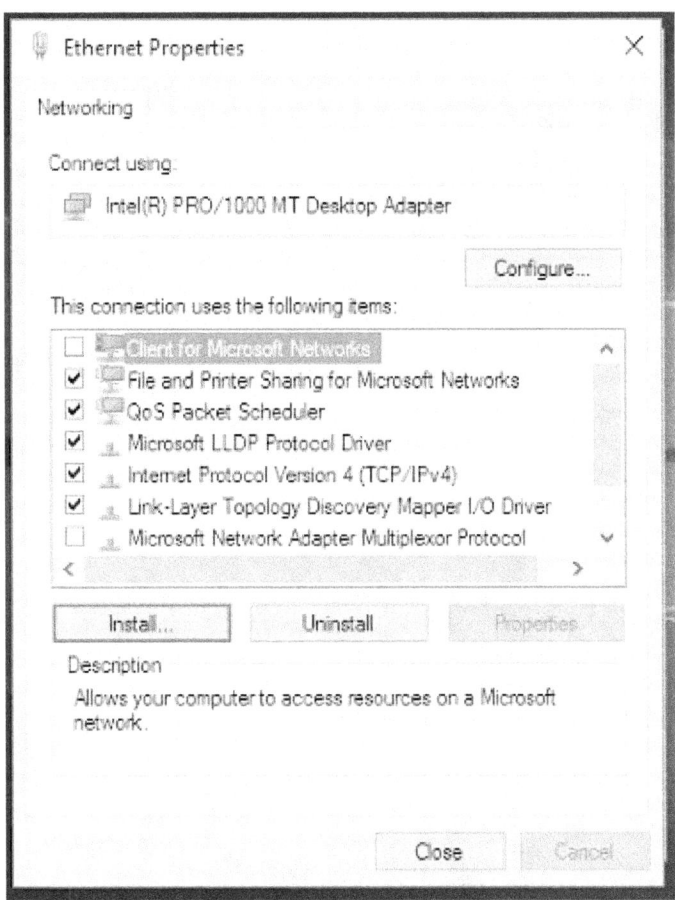

Windows 10 - Figure 23b

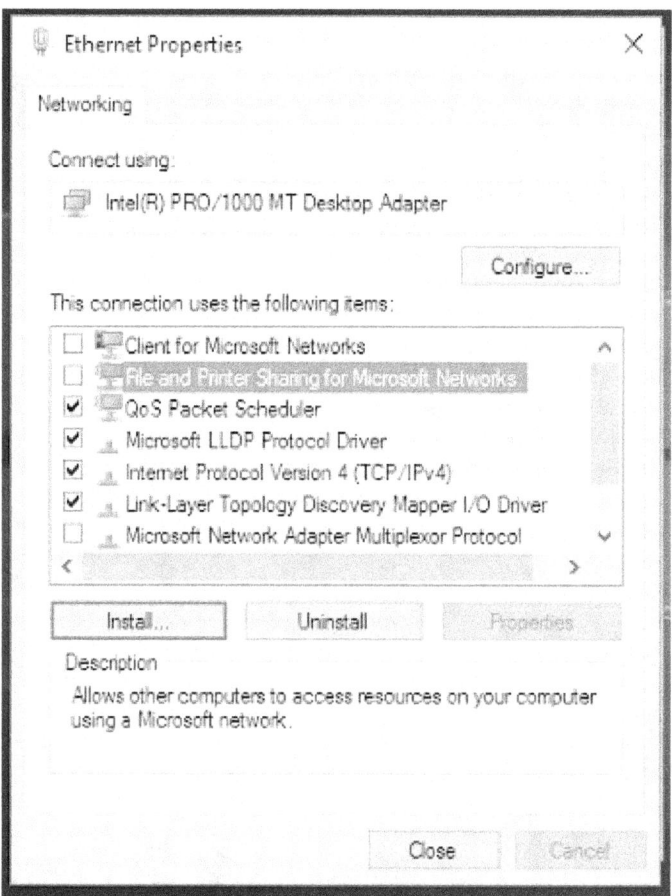

Windows 10 - Figure 23c

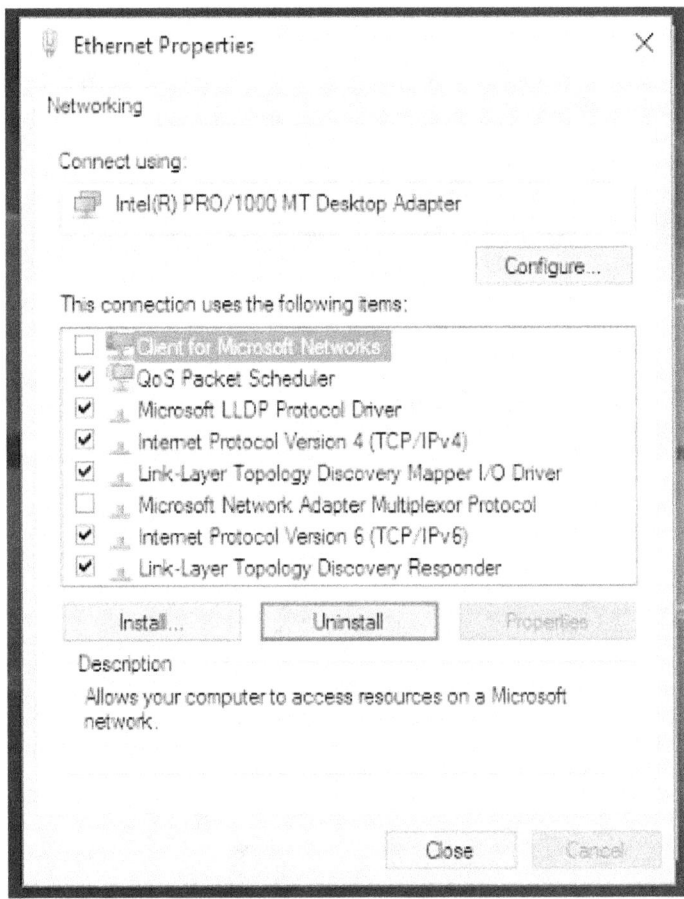
Windows 10 - Figure 24

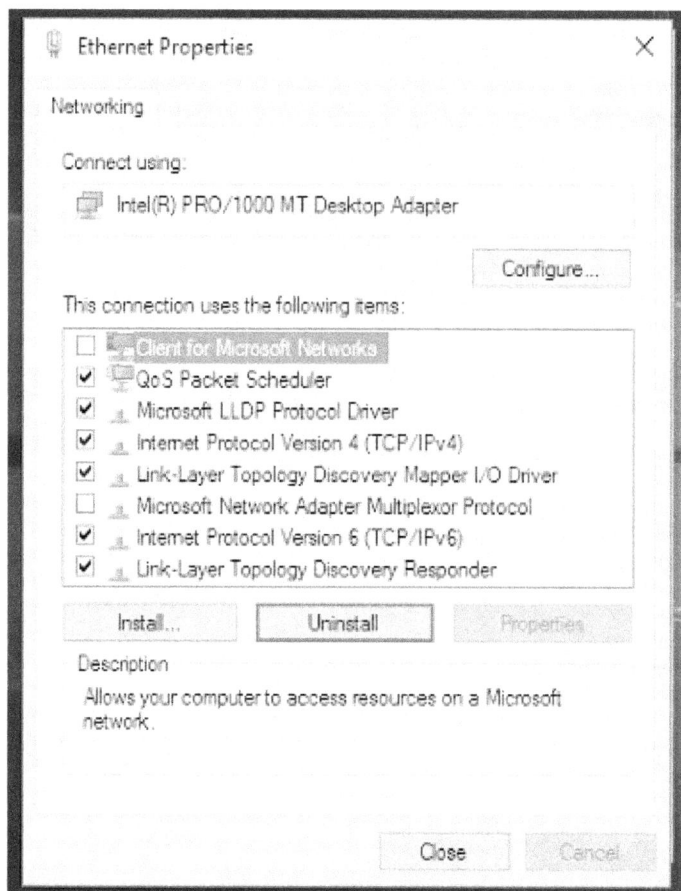
Windows 10 - Figure 25

Mark Versus Mr. Hacker.doc

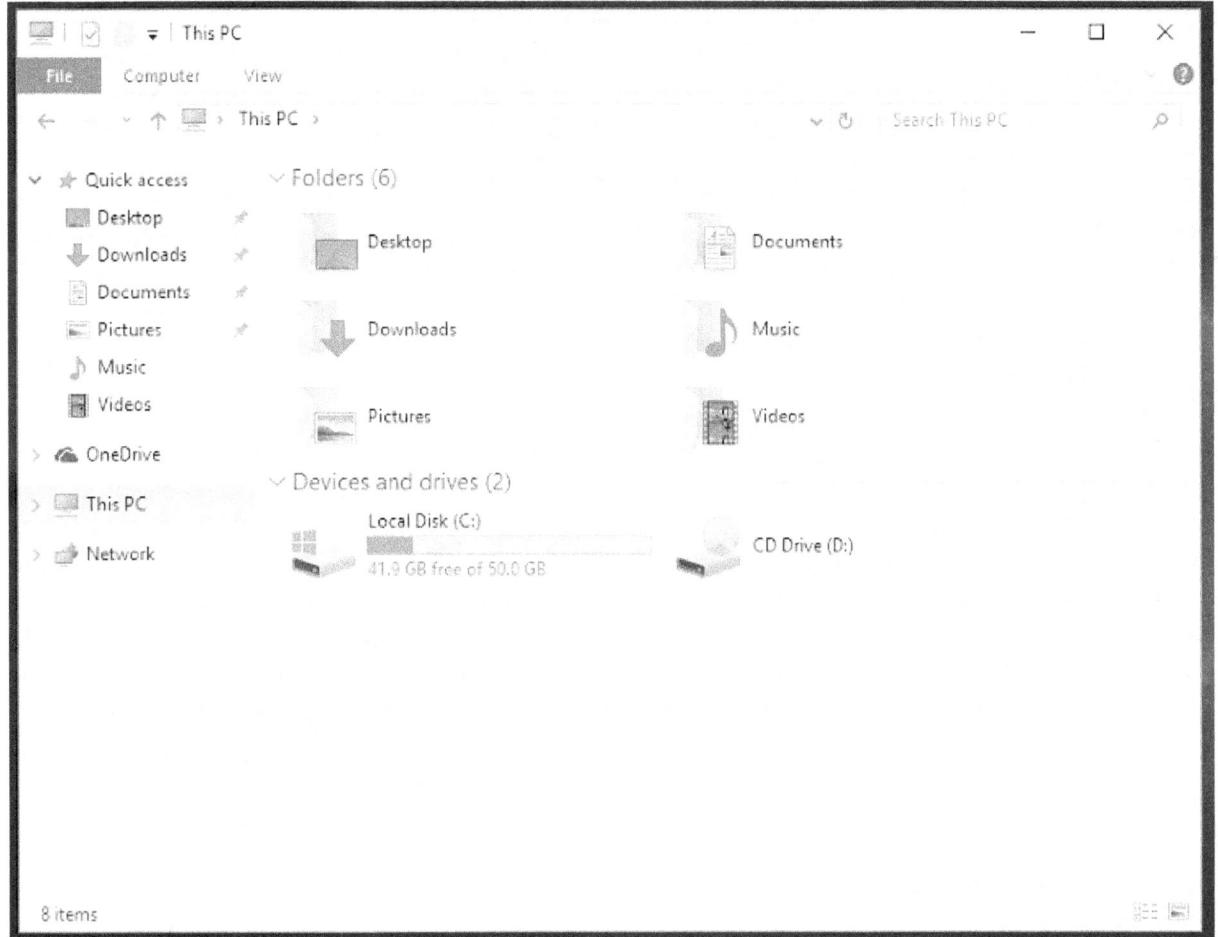

Windows 10 - Figure 26

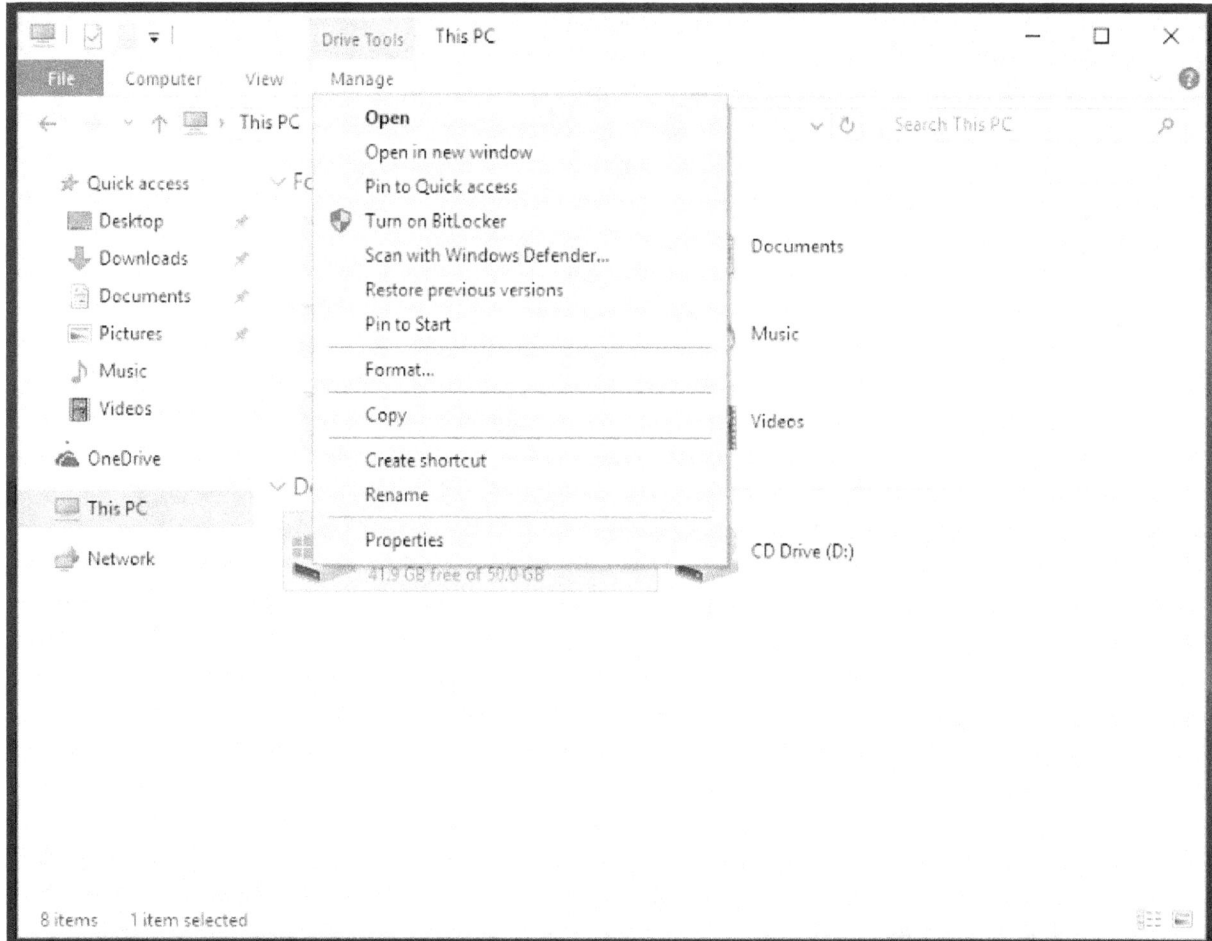

Windows 10 - Figure 27

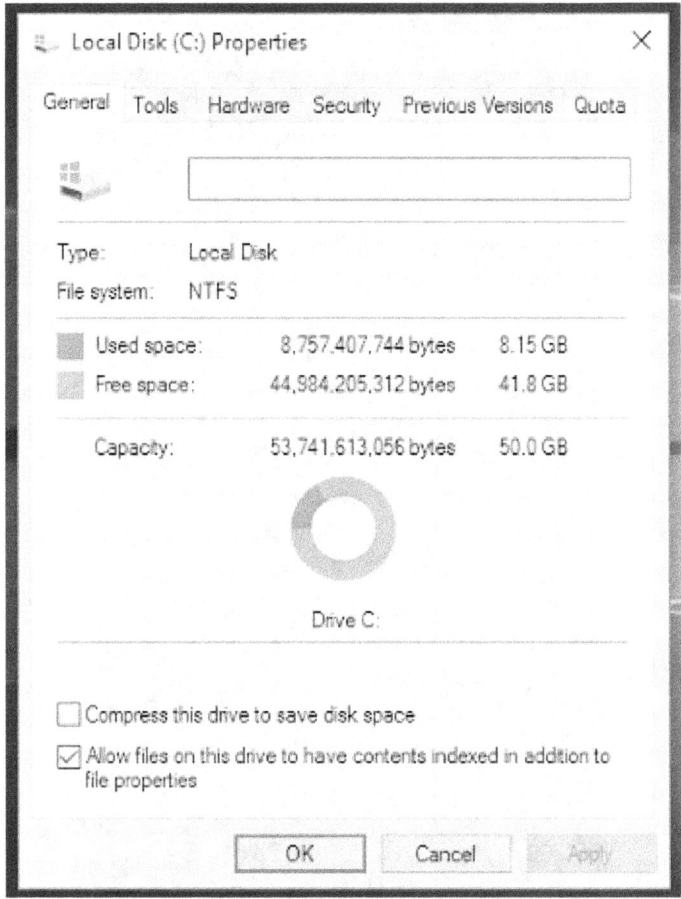
Windows 10 - Figure 28

Since sharing is not active – there is no sharing tab on the dialog.

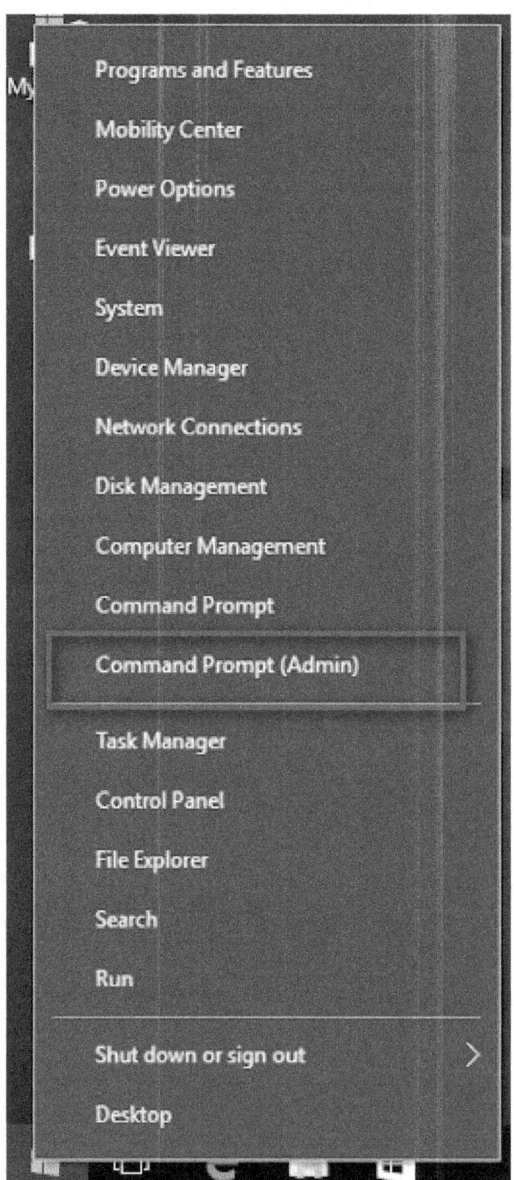
Windows 10 - Figure 29

Windows 10 – Figure 30 omitted because Windows 10 doesn't do that. It just runs as an administrator.

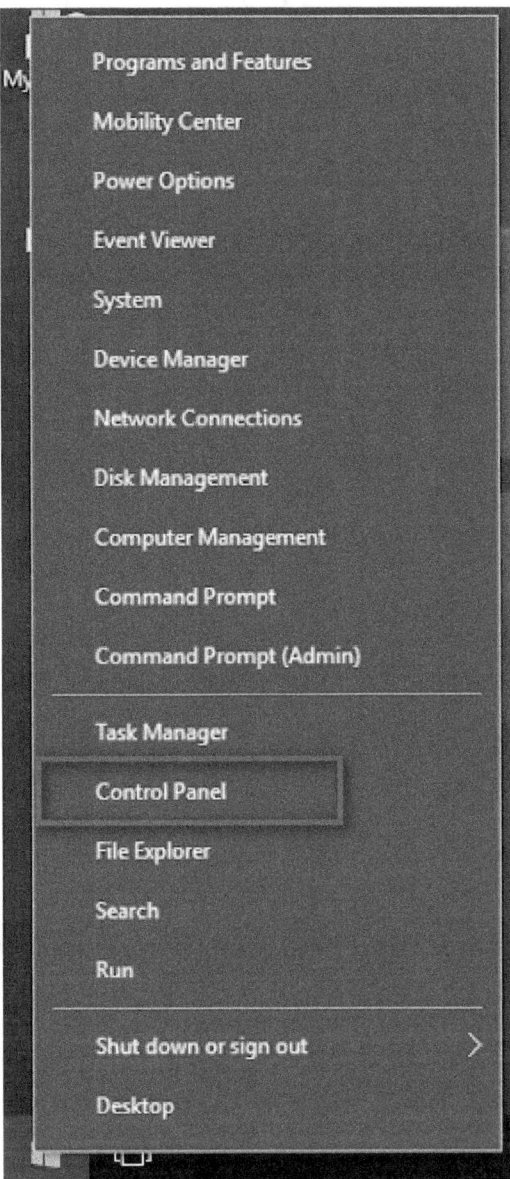

Windows 10 - Figure 31

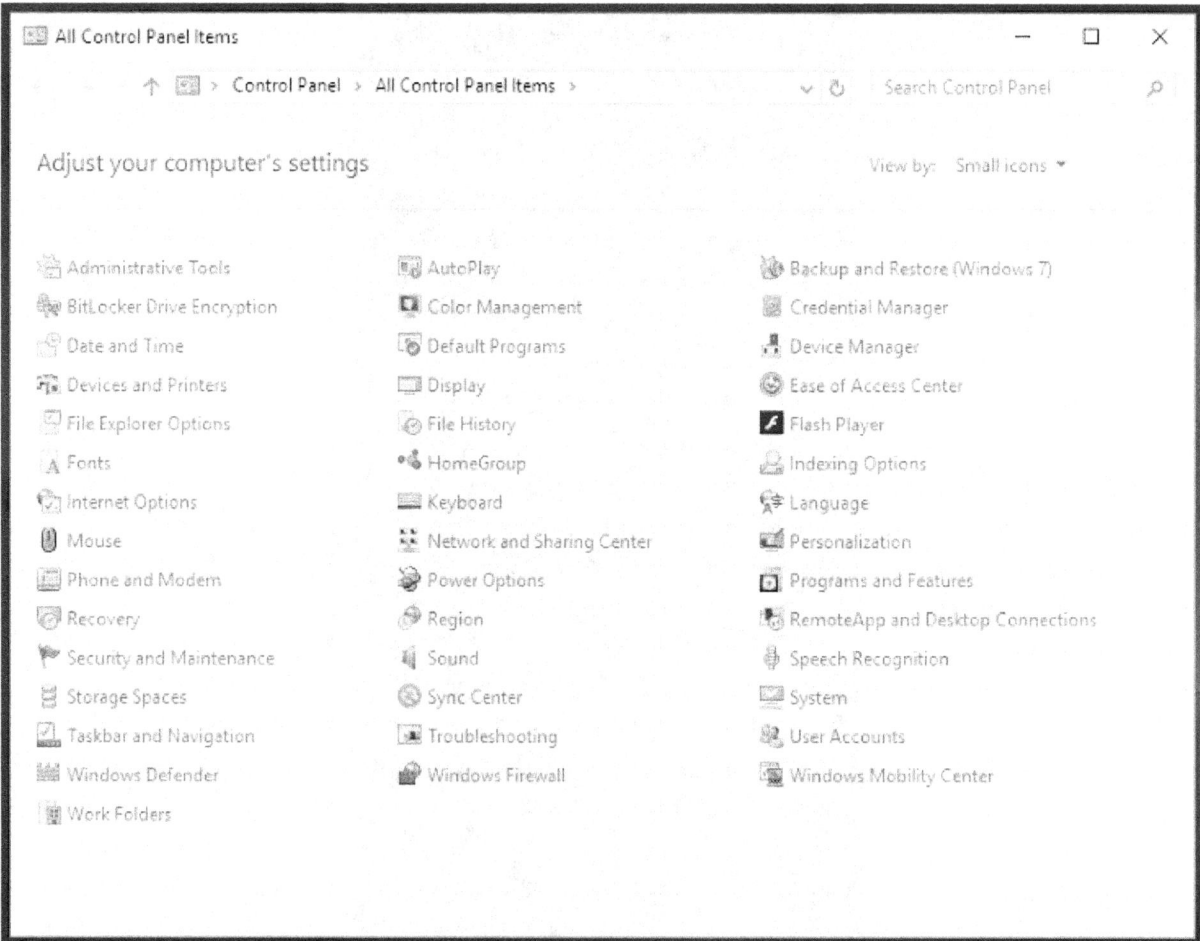

Windows 10 - Figure 32

Mark Versus Mr. Hacker.doc

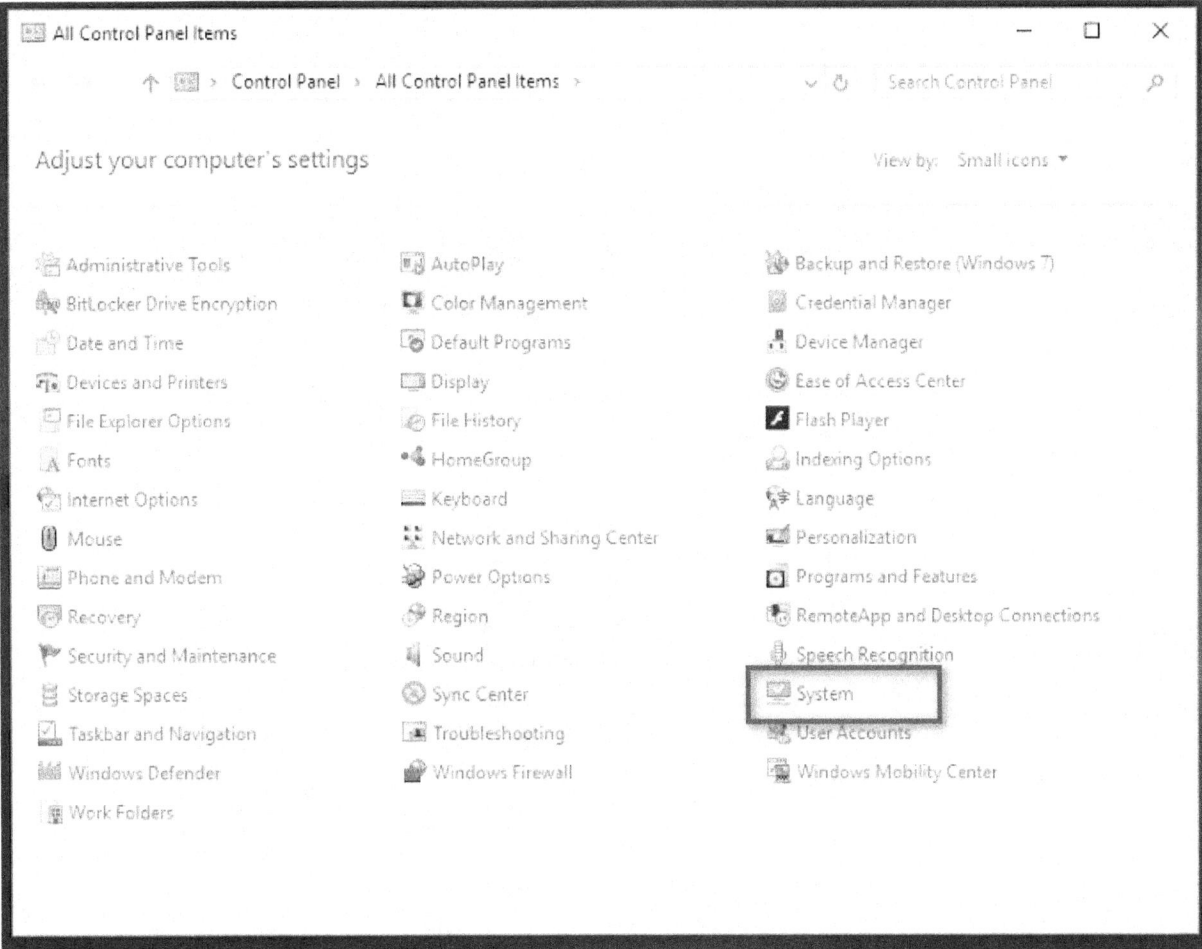

Windows 10 - Figure 33

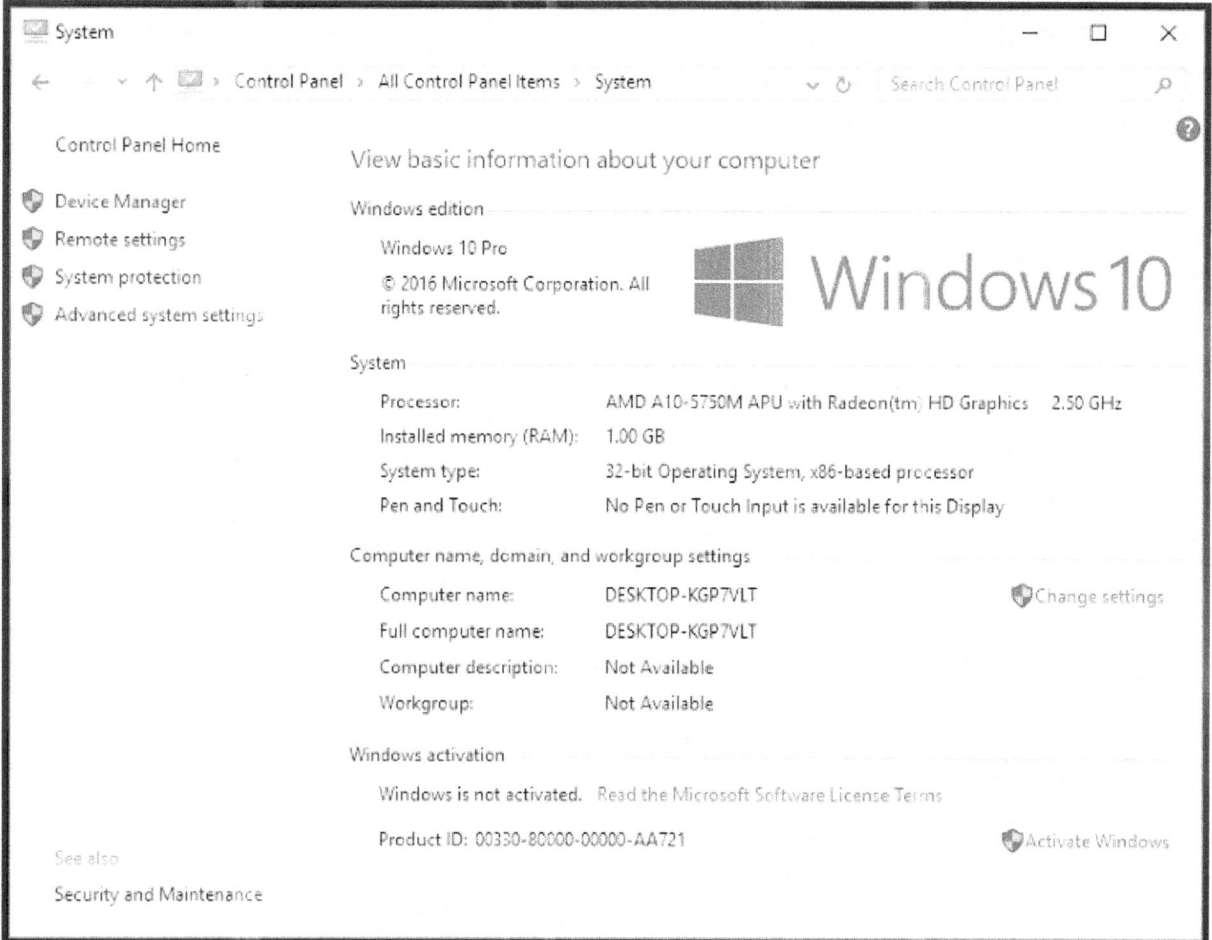

Windows 10 - Figure 34

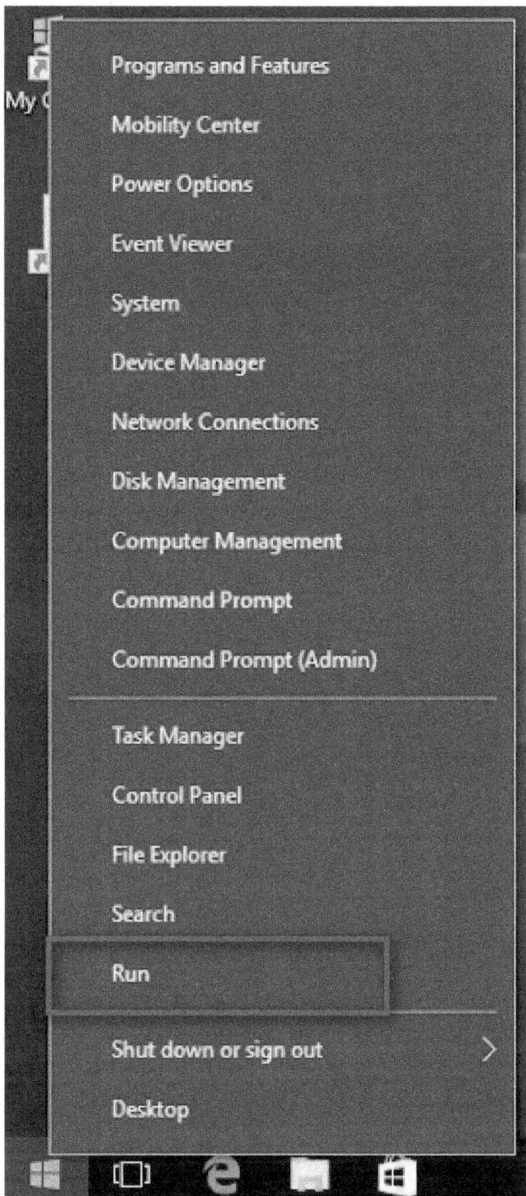
Windows 10 - Figure 35

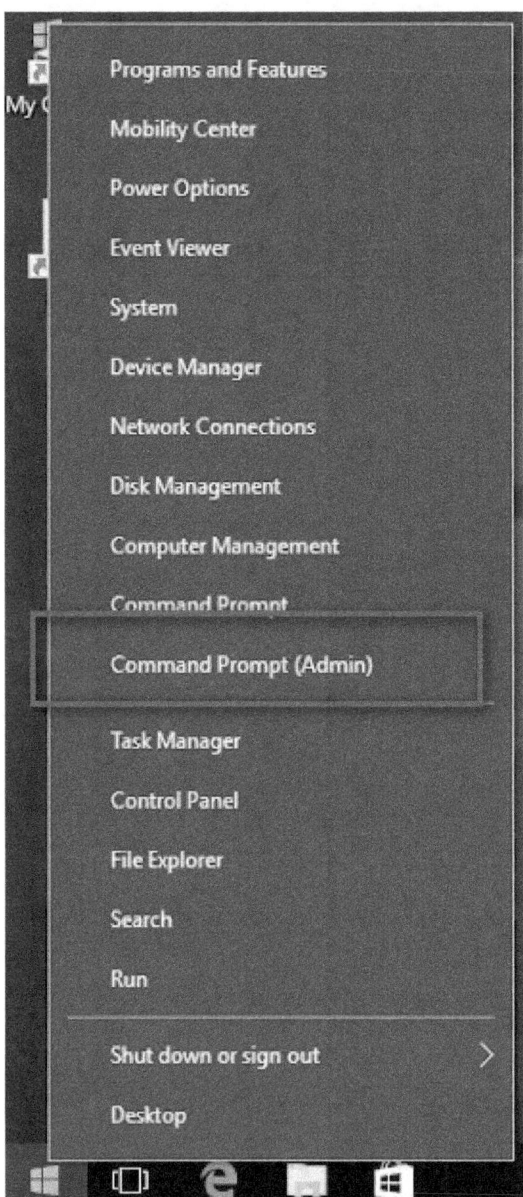

Windows 10 - Figure 36

The Command Prompt is the same on all versions of Windows.

Windows 10 - Figure 37

Windows 10 - Figure 38

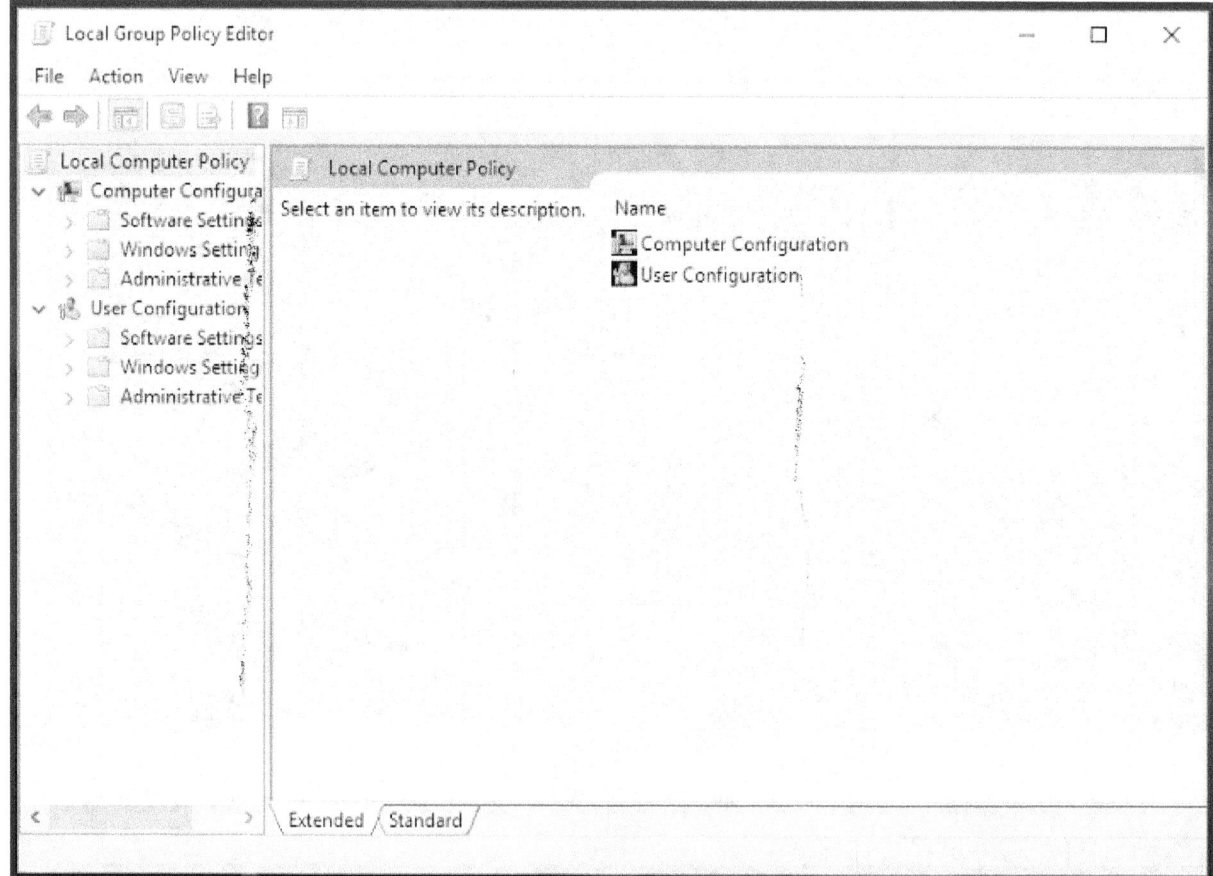

Windows 10 - Figure 39

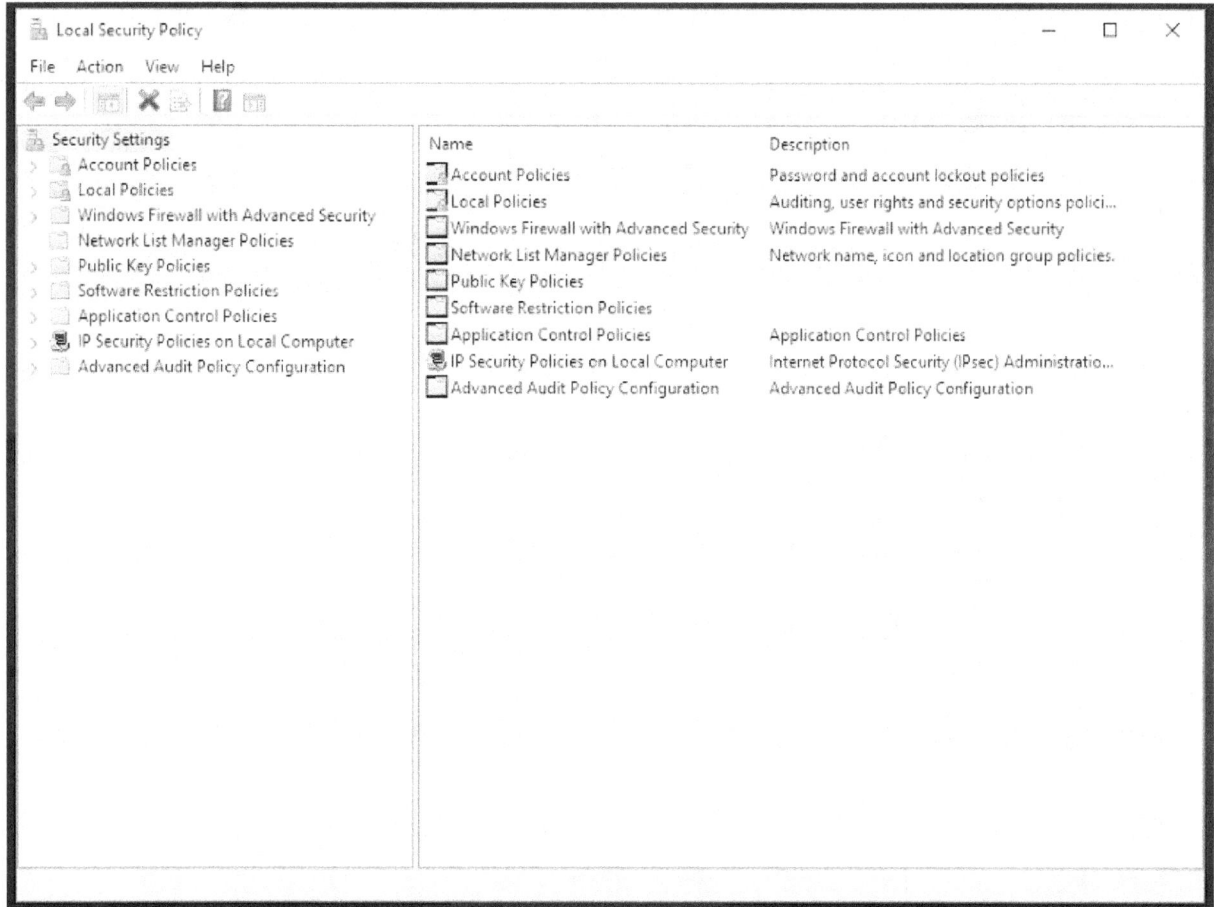

Windows 10 - Figure 40

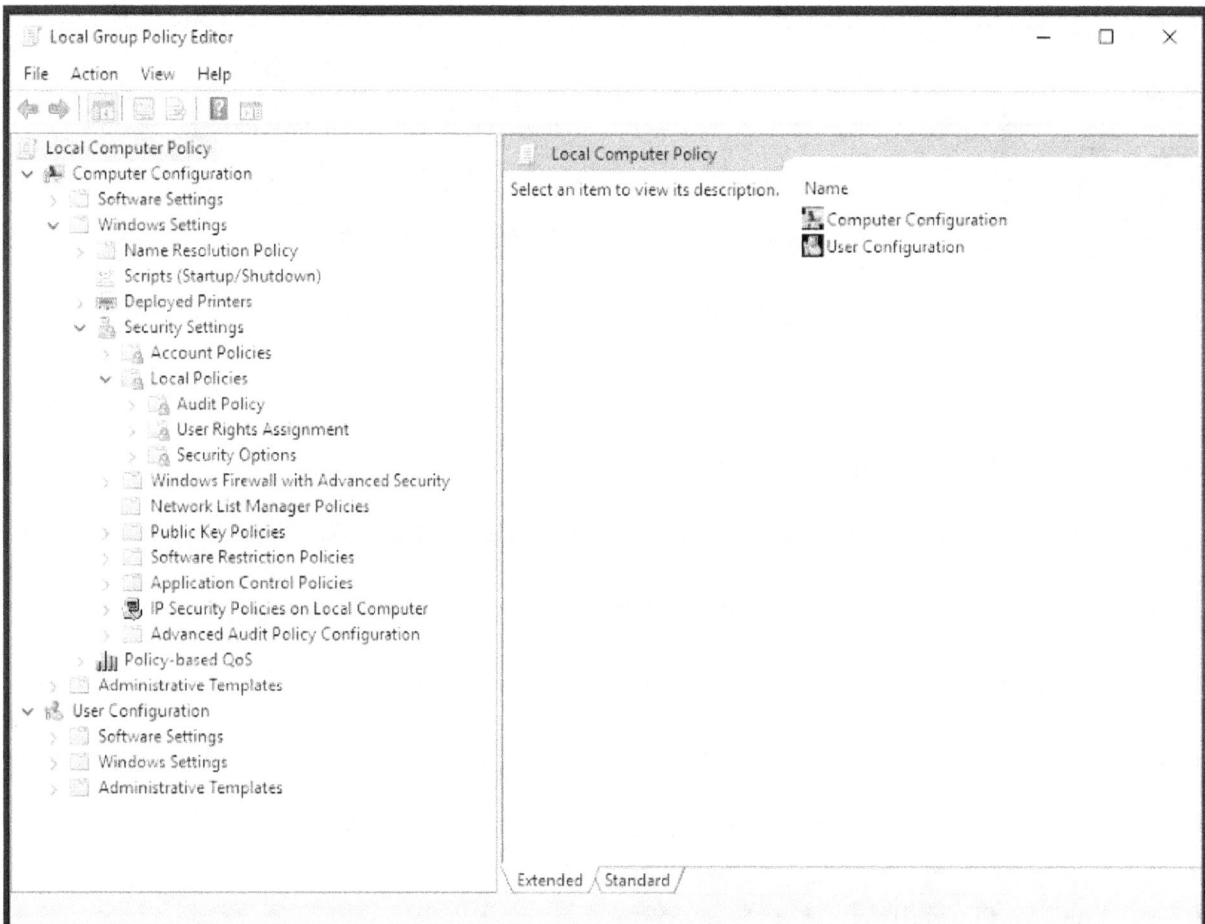

Windows 10 - Figure 41

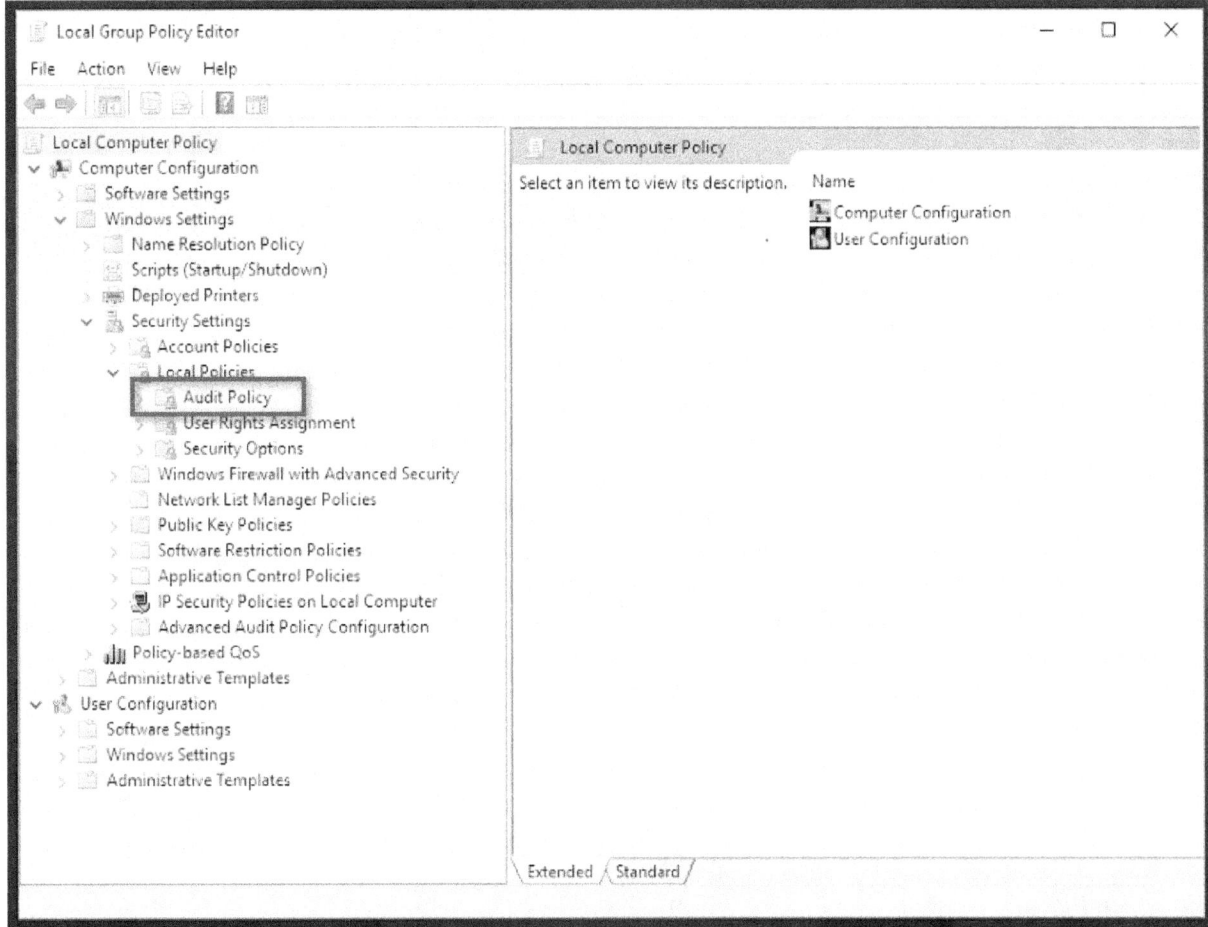

Windows 10 - Figure 42

Windows 10 - Figure 43

Windows 10 - Figure 44

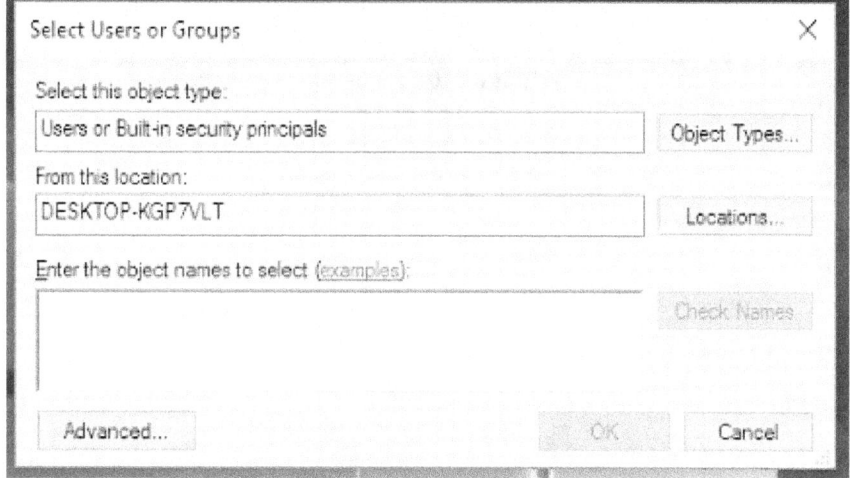
Windows 10 - Figure 45

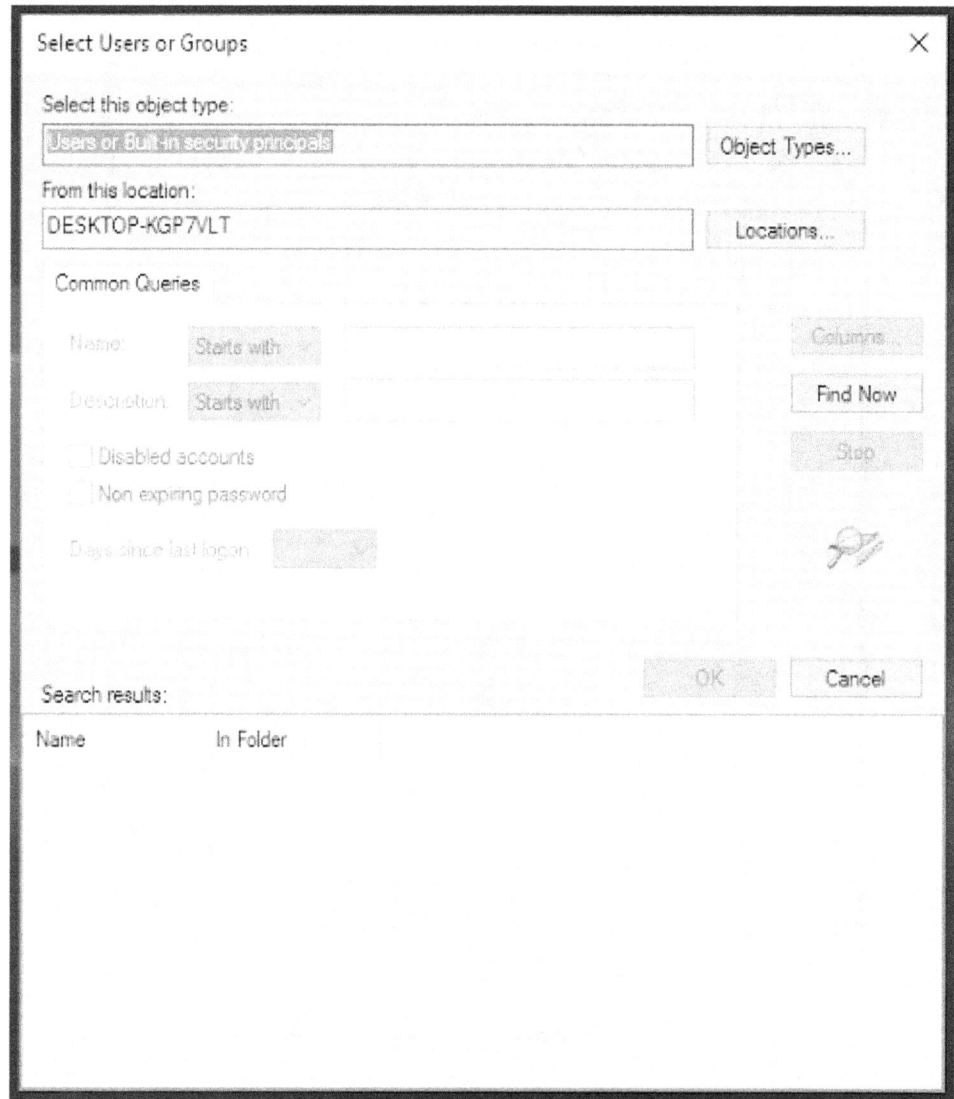

Windows 10 - Figure 46

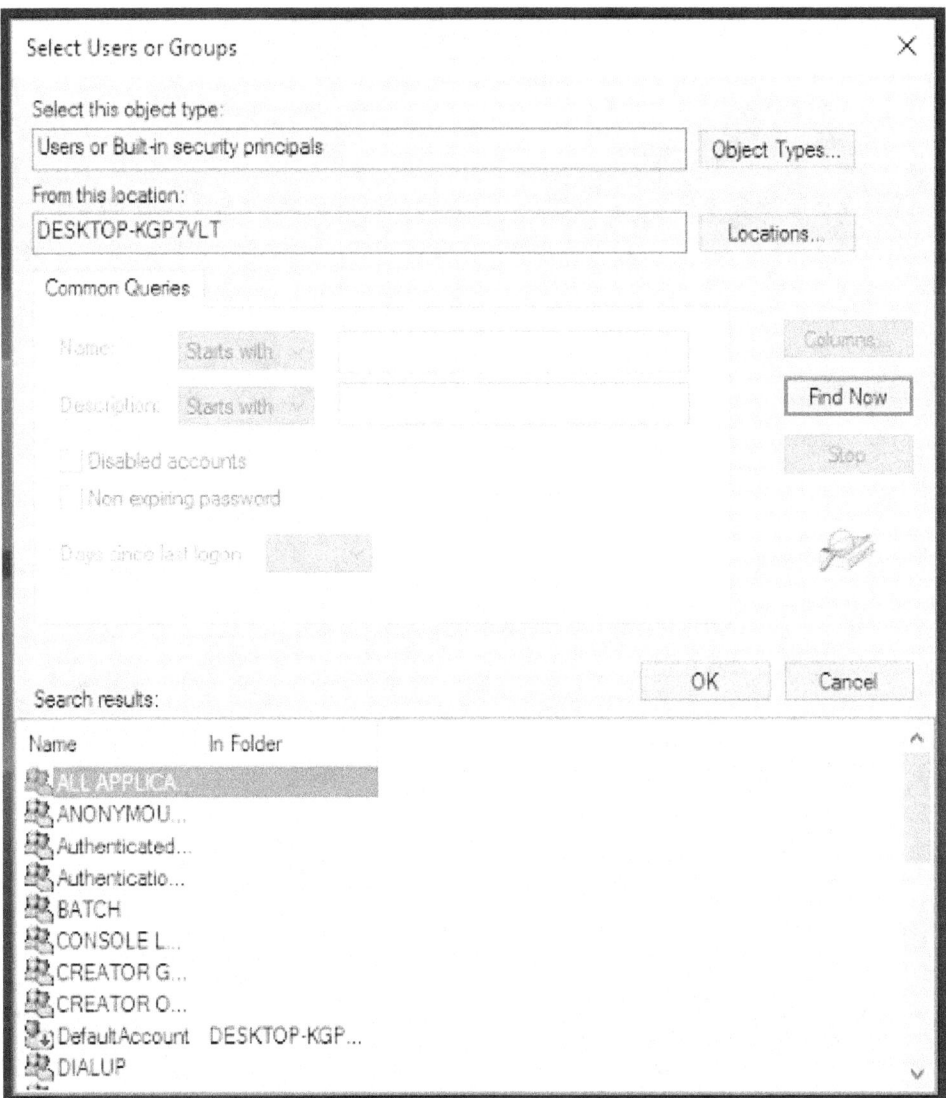

Windows 10 - Figure 47

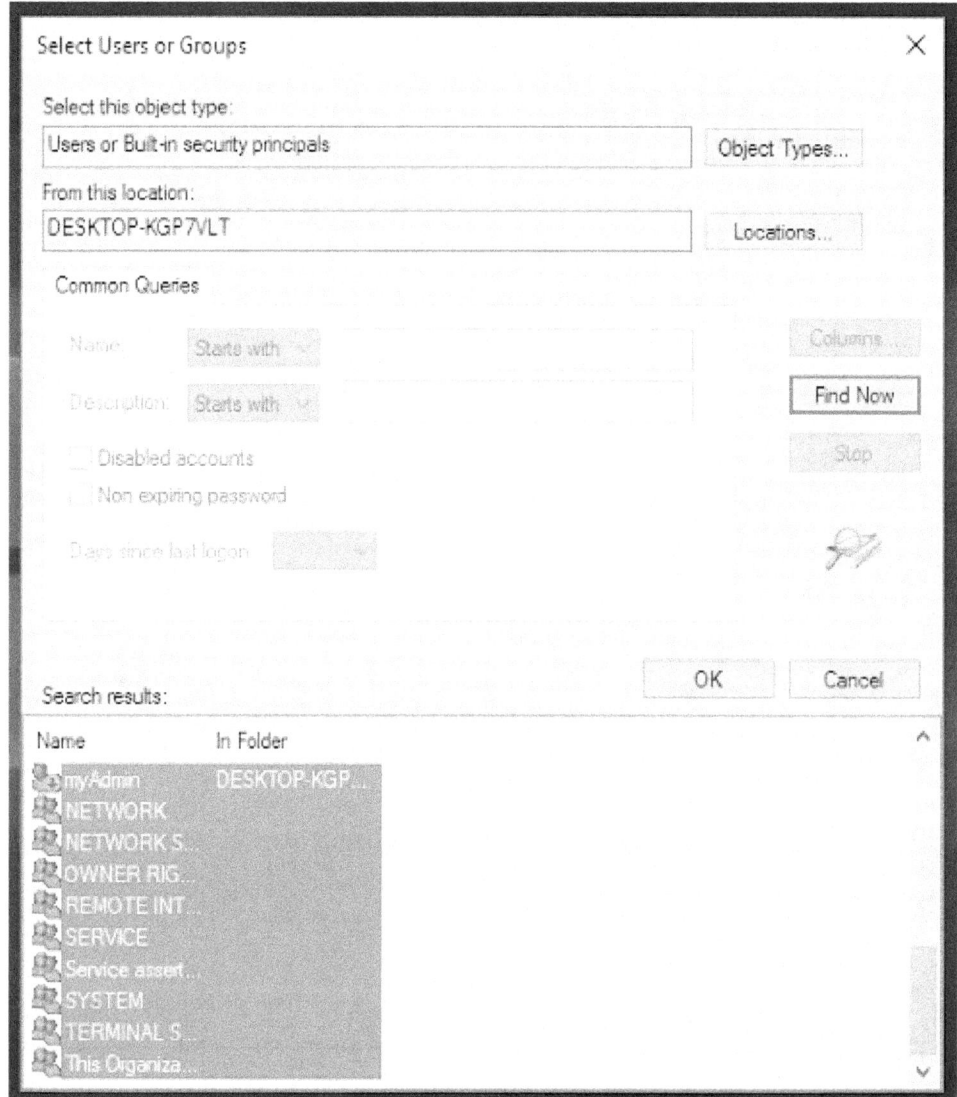

Windows 10 - Figure 48

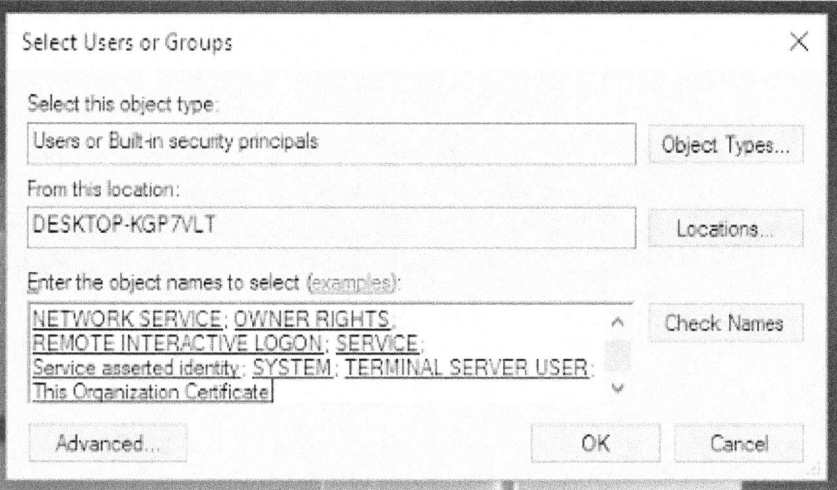
Windows 10 - Figure 49

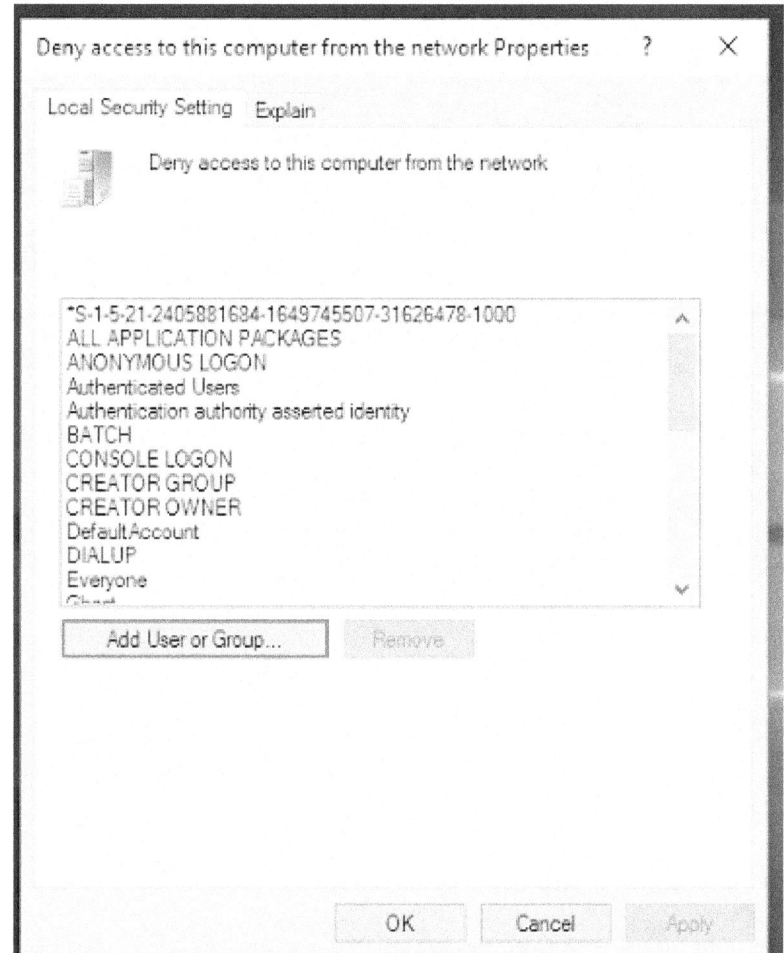
Windows 10 - Figure 50

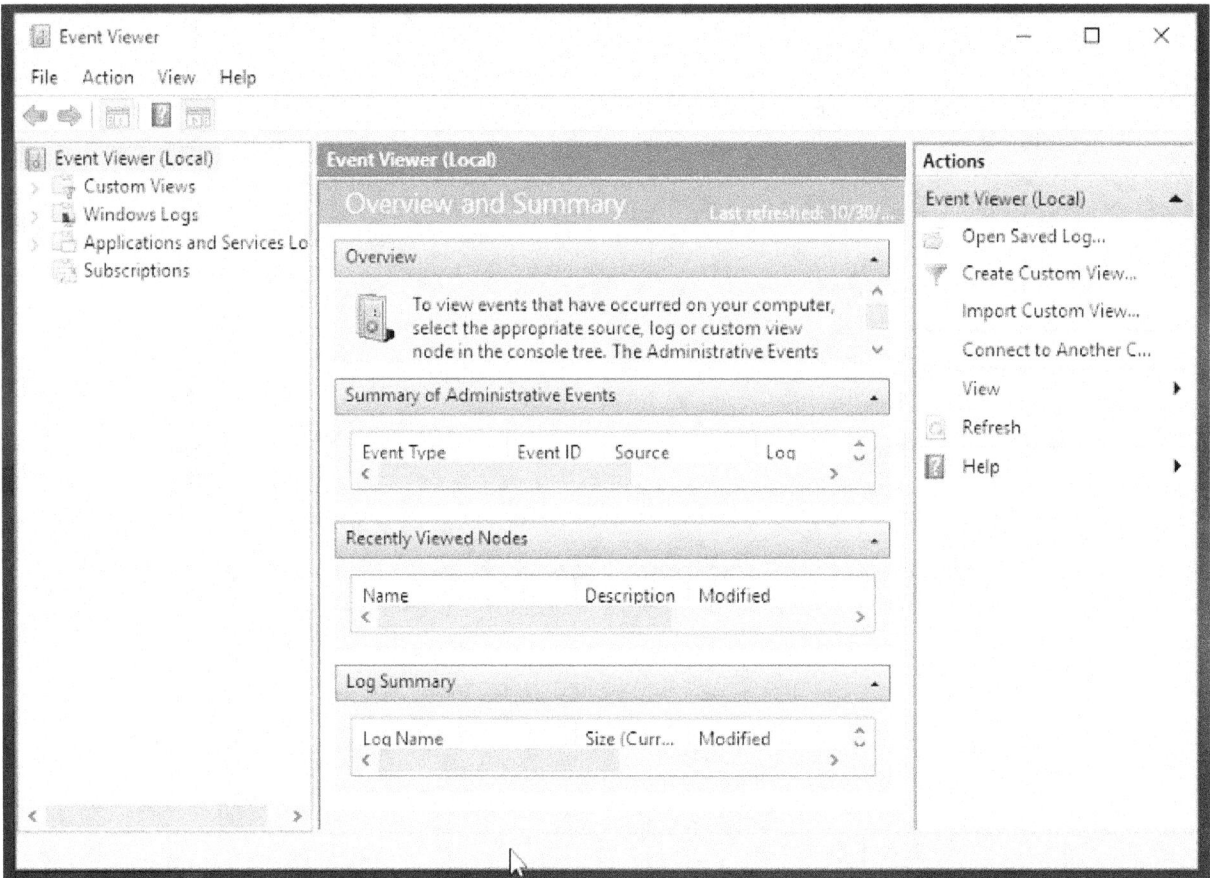

Windows 10 - Figure 51a

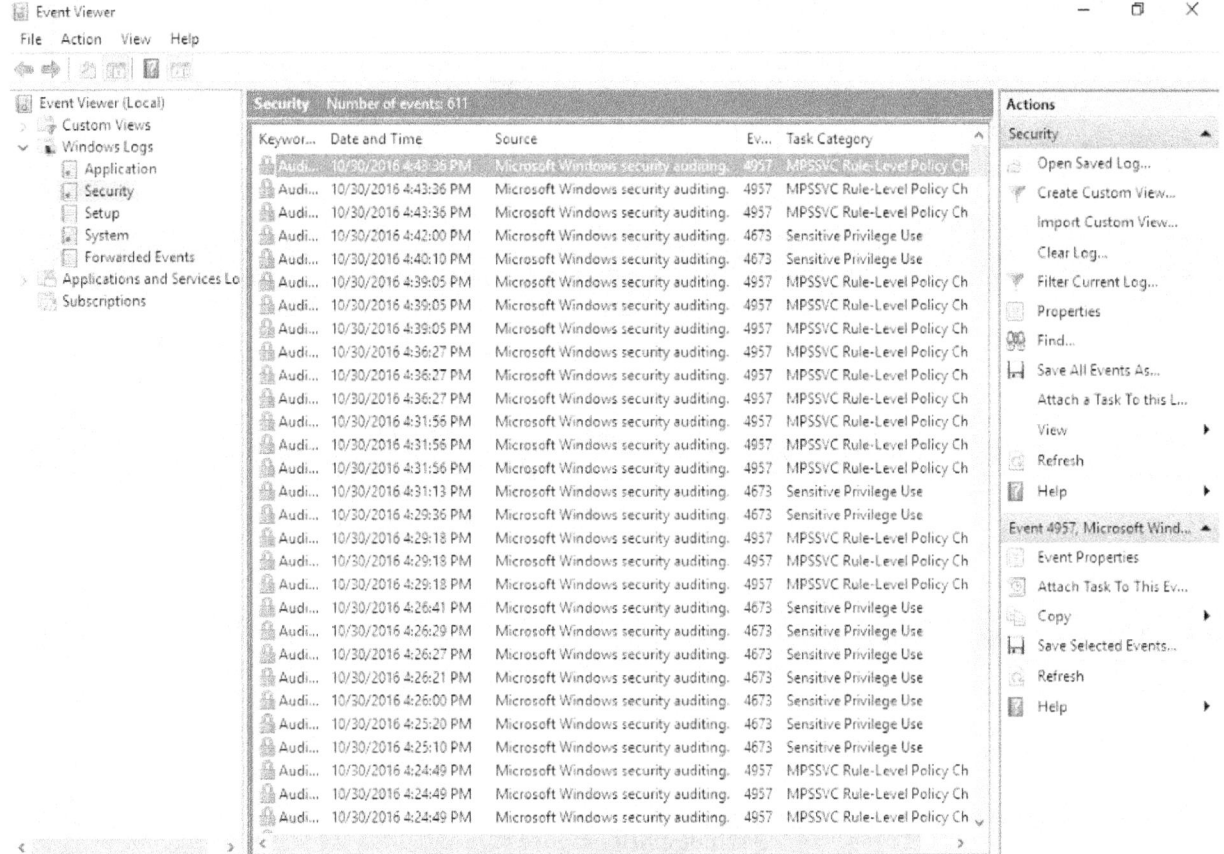

Windows 10 - Figure 51b

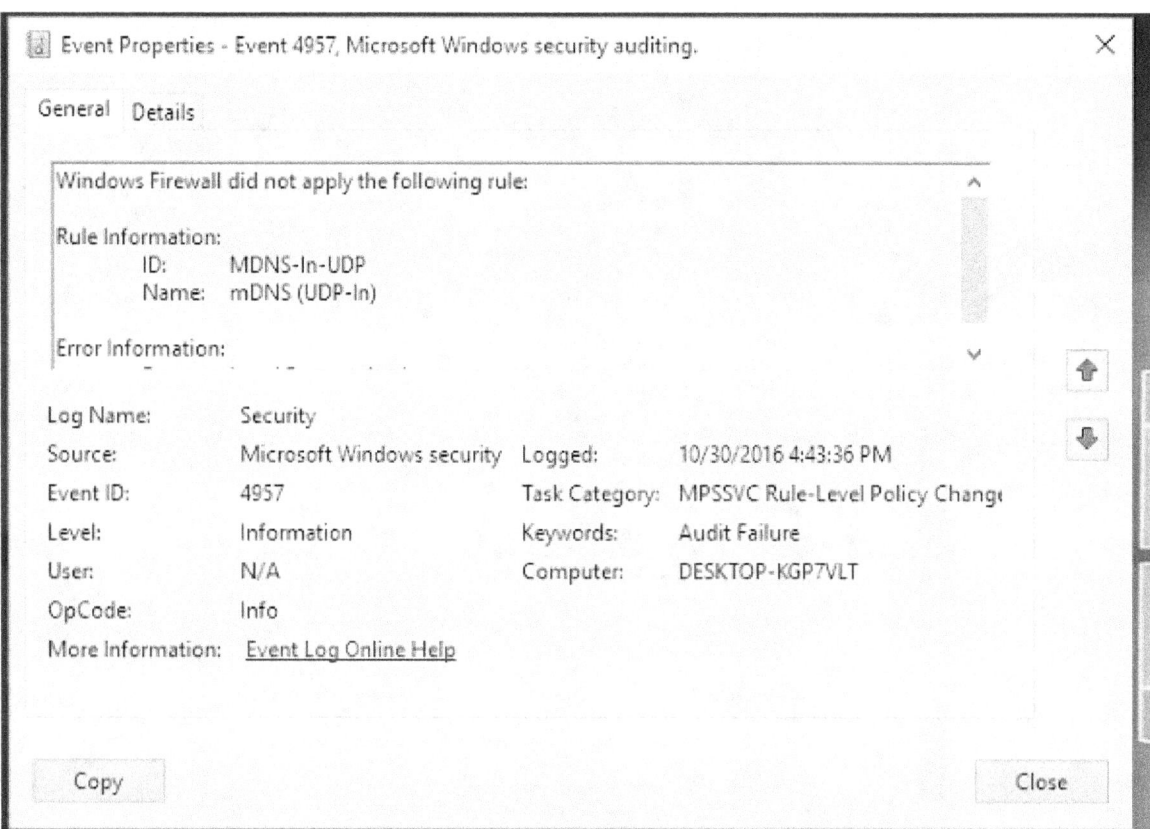

Windows 10 - Figure 52

Mark Versus Mr. Hacker.doc

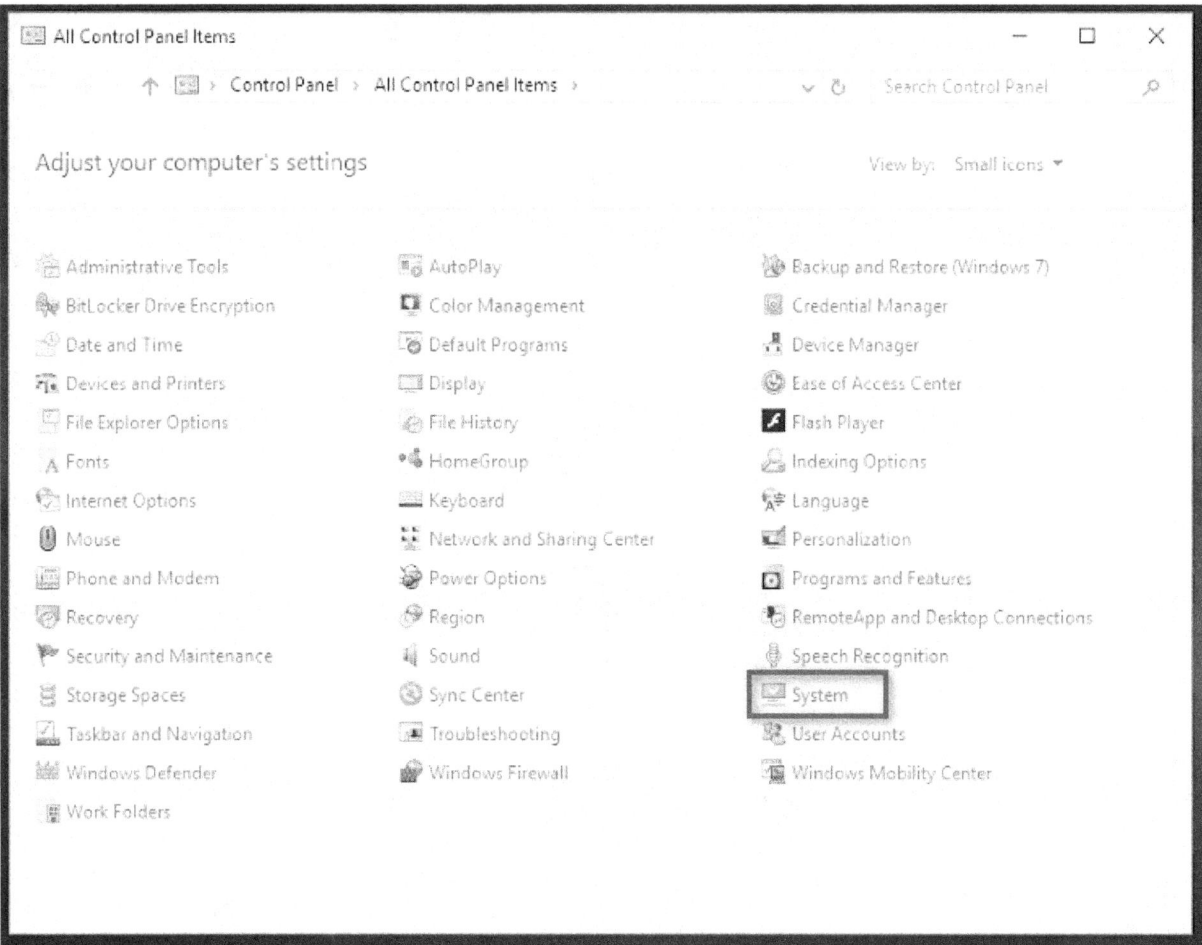

Windows 10 - Figure 53a

Mark Versus Mr. Hacker.doc

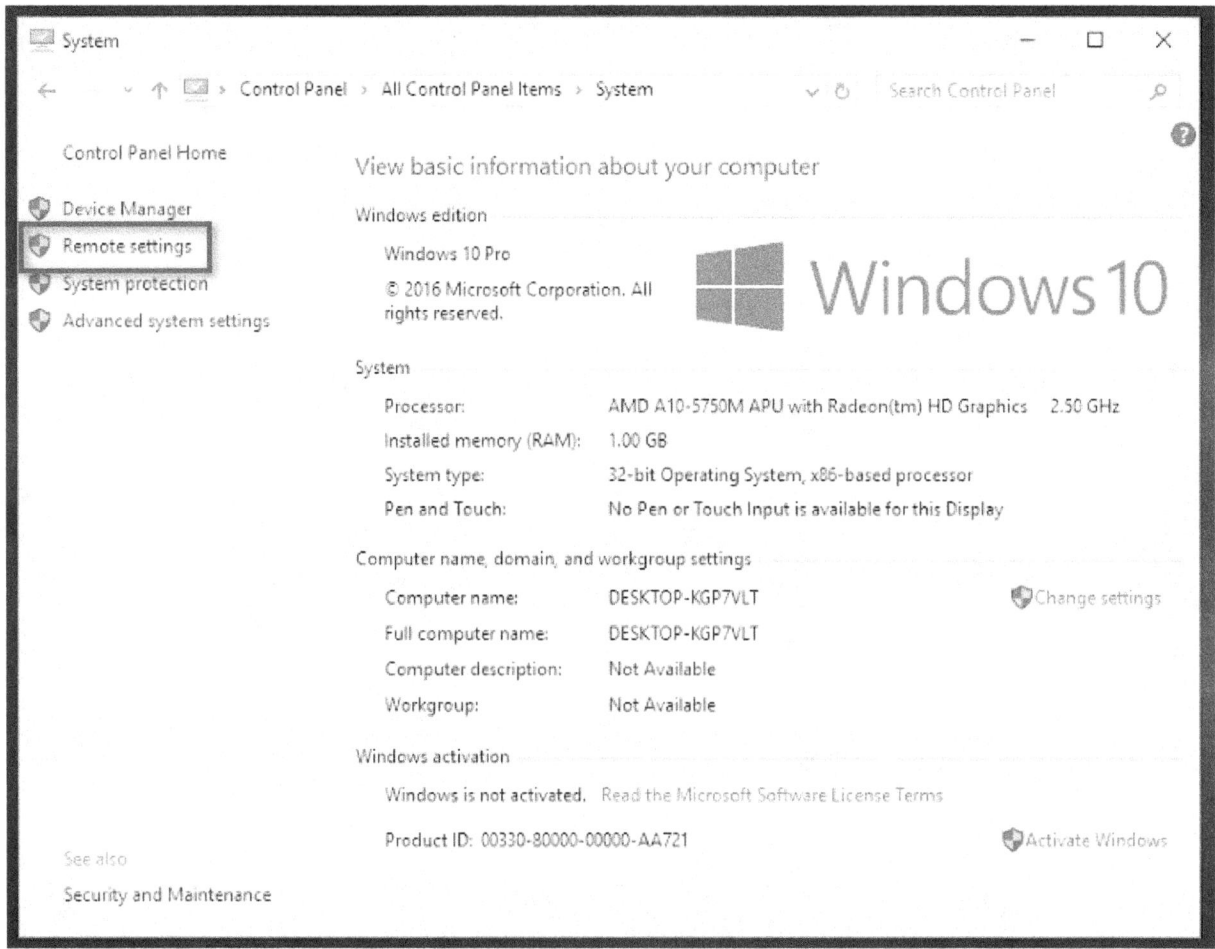

Windows 10 - Figure 53b

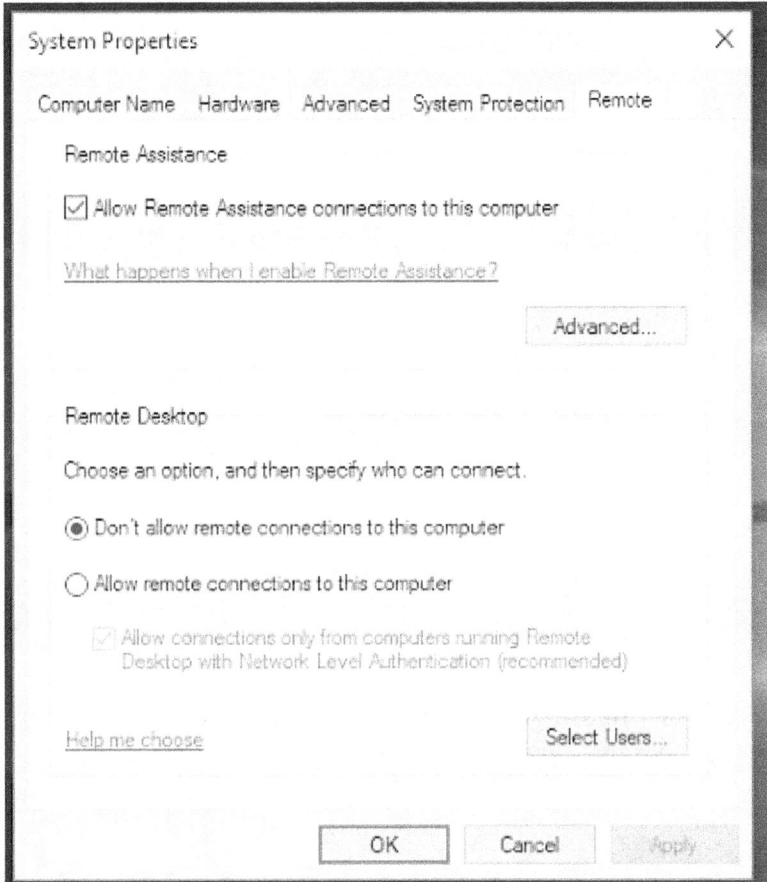
Windows 10 - Figure 54

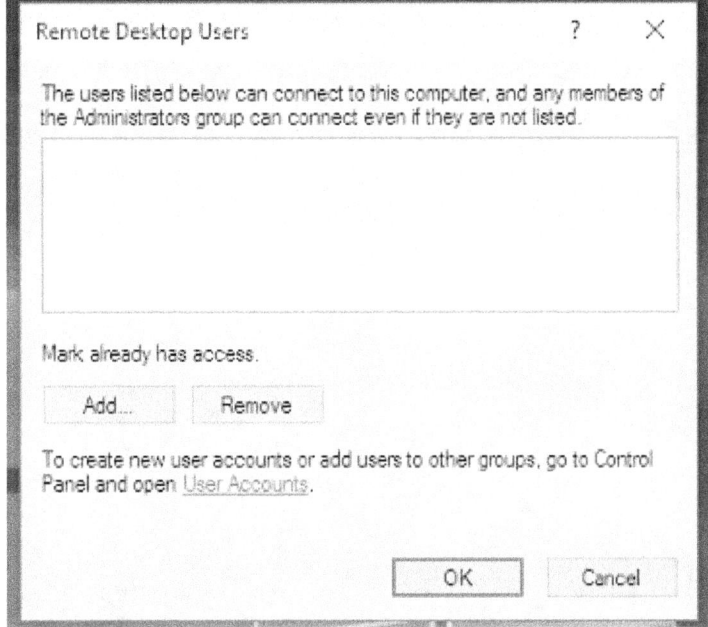
Windows 10 - Figure 55

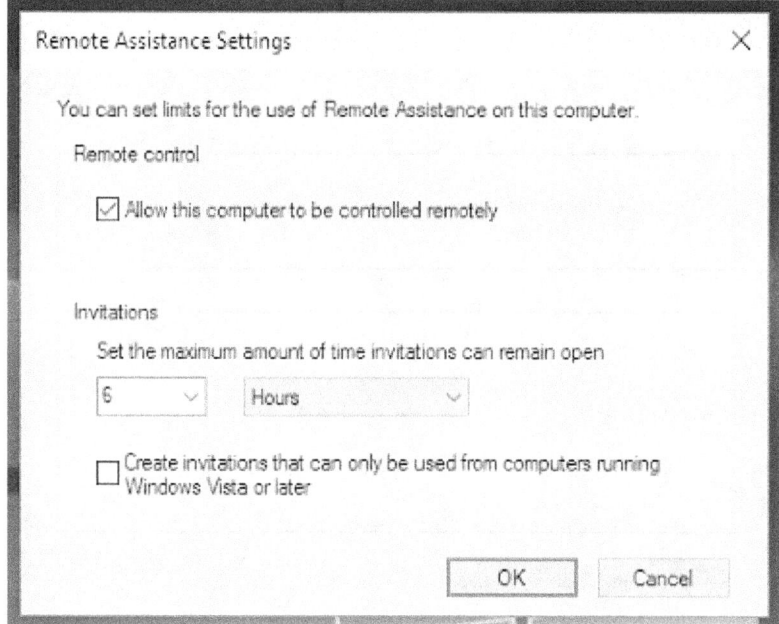
Windows 10 - Figure 56

All other figures deal with external programs to Windows so use the figures provided from #56 on to the end of the book.

Have fun!

www.ingramcontent.com/pod-product-compliance
Lightning Source LLC
Chambersburg PA
CBHW080905170526
45158CB00008B/1993